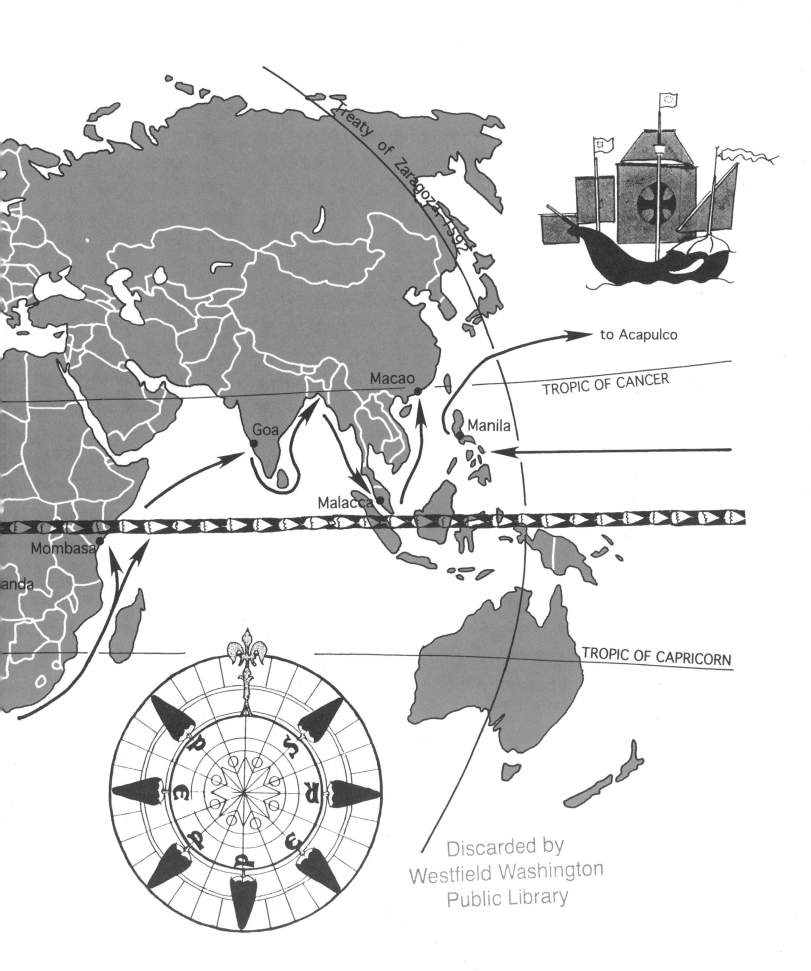

WE

D1061076

to Acapulco

TROPIC OF CANCER

Macao

Goa

Manila

Malacca

Mombasa

anda

TROPIC OF CAPRICORN

Treaty of Zaragoza, 1521

The Pepper Trail

History and Recipes from Around the World

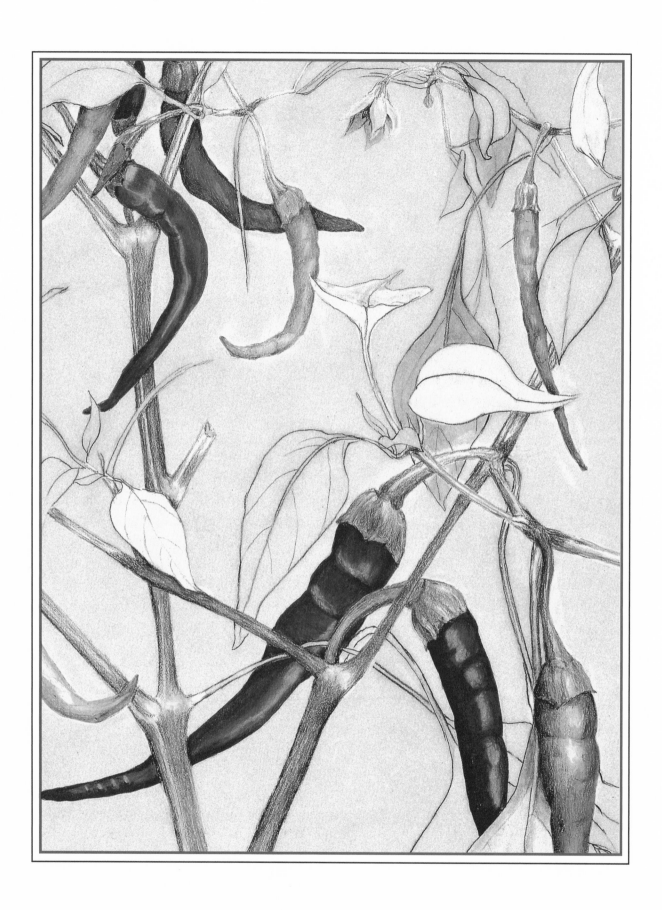

The Pepper Trail

History & Recipes
from Around the World

Written & Illustrated by

Jean Andrews

THE UNIVERSITY OF NORTH TEXAS PRESS
Denton, Texas

Permissions
University of North Texas Press
PO Box 311336
Denton TX 76203-1336
940-565-2142

Library of Congress Cataloging-in-Publication Data

Andrews, Jean.
The pepper trail:
history and recipes from around the world /
written and illustrated by Jean Andrews
p.   cm.
Includes bibliographical references (p.   ) and index.
ISBN 1-57441-070-9
1. Cookery (Hot peppers) 2. Hot peppers. I. Title.
TX803.P46A52 1999   99-222244 CIP
          641.6'384—dc20

Printed in Canada

Maps by cartographer John V. Cotter, Ph.D.
Design by Mary Ann Jacob

DEDICATION

To Isabella of Castile,

feminist Queen of Spain

whose intuition and support

of the Columbus quest

made the discovery of peppers possible;

a remarkable woman

who spent more time on the battlefield

than in the kitchen

Contents

Foreword

his is not your everyday cookbook. It is a cultural history of a food—with recipes—put together by an inquisitive scholar, gardener, cook, traveler, and artist who fell in love with peppers more than twenty years ago. During that time I attempted to learn what they are, where they came from, where they moved, and how they affected the cooking in the places they went. I thought others might be interested in what I discovered. It is written in two parts—the history, geography and background in the first and the cookery in the second, with a bibliography for those who want more. It bombards the reader with an awesome amount of data pieced together from various fragments of information into an overwhelming historical and geographical study of the pepper pod. It won't hurt my feelings if you just skip to the recipes, but you'll miss a hot story.

Peppers: The Domesticated Capsicums or *Peppers I*, my first book about the genus *Capsicum,* probably told the average reader more than one ever wanted to know about peppers. However, that book barely touched on the food aspect of peppers and had but twenty-four recipes. Since then I have not only revised and updated that book but I have also traveled the pepper trail, from Bolivia to the Far East, Tibet to Timbuktu and back, tracking the pungent pod. It is my intent in this book to take up where the first book left off and again tell you more than you might want to know, but this time about how and why the American capsicums moved from their prehistoric Bolivian

place of origin and traveled around the world affecting the foodways of both hemispheres, and also, how you, patient reader, can hone your *Capsicum* cooking skills. To me, it is a fascinating story. Bear with me as I share some of my findings. Not all of the fascinating happenings (both appealing and appalling) on my pepper travels are here—maybe that's another book!

As I delved deeper into the directions taken by the *Capsicum* peppers after Christopher Columbus discovered them, it appeared to me that as peppers followed the ancient trade routes they had a great effect on the cuisines of the lands along the way. Once capsicums reached the Old World they fell into the hands of spice merchants. I began to wonder why the spice trade went one way and not another five hundred years ago? how it went and what it went in? who carried it? why some people responded to the introduction of peppers and others didn't? why cuisines have certain characteristics and not others? and on and on. These questions took me not only to libraries, where I found much about the spice trade but only a little about the early movements of peppers. They also took me to many countries along the pepper trail including much of Africa, the Middle East, Central Asia, and Monsoon Asia—India, Nepal, Bhutan, Tibet, Sri Lanka, Thailand, Indonesia—plus Xinjiang, Sichuan and Hunan in China as well as Latin America. Our swift little pod had done a significant part of its travel within the first fifty years after Columbus brought it back to Spain, which makes for a very long-ago story in times very, very different than those we now live in. The more I looked into this saga, the more I became convinced that the presumptive pepper trail by which Columbus took the American plant to Spain and whence they progressed to Europe was not the only pathway followed into Europe and the Middle East. So I set out to learn what I could about our peripatetic pod.

At the onset I learned that the historical background for studying *Capsicum* cookery is complex. In most peppery food areas throughout the world, political and economic systems that consisted of either a small local privileged upper class or conquering Europeans, attempted to dominate the daily lives and actions of the native masses. This form of class system deeply affected the cuisine, creating a division in the quantities and varieties of food consumed by different sections in the same populace, forming—by force, in the case of slavery—the food patterns of large populations. Within most of these cultural groups, religion added its food taboos. These factors combined to produce cuisines unlike our typical Americanized-European cookery.

I also discovered that in spite of the necessity for every human of whatever race on earth to eat regularly, little has been written concerning the foodways of various culture groups in relation to their total cultural history. There are excellent food books like *Food in Chinese Culture* edited by K. C. Chang, but thumbing through book after book on history and culture of a particular group, one finds chapters on such topics as: racial composition, political organization, economic life, family, philosophy, religion, science, art, literature, recreation and amusement, and secret societies, but little or nothing on foodways. Are they just taken for granted, or is it because the day-in day-out preparation and serving of family meals has always been "woman's work" and therefore considered less important? The manner in which food is selected, prepared and served is always the result of the culture in which it occurs, as indeed are the accessories and rituals that accompany the rudimentary activity of eating. Actually, I can say with a sigh of relief that I can see a growing interest in the study of foodways as a means for understanding culture. Although food is eaten as a response to hunger, it is much more than filling one's stomach to satisfy nutritional requirements; it is also a premeditated selection and consumption process providing emotional fulfillment. The way in which food is altered reveals the function of food in society and the values that society supports.

In this volume I have tried to give my readers some background for the cuisines that embrace peppers but it is preposterous to attempt to describe the foodways or food culture of many groups of people in one chapter. Each paragraph begs for elaboration, qualification, and more research to round out the story.

Special thanks go to the scholars who read and approved the first three chapters. Expressly Terry Jordan, ethnogeographer and author of *The American Backwoods Frontier* plus too many others to list, who advised on Chapter 1; Professors Alfred Crosby, author of *Ecological Imperialism* and *The Columbian Exchange*; Robert King, linguist and expert on things Indian; L. Tuffly Ellis, historian and former director of the Texas State Historical Association; Elizabeth Fernea, author and Middle East specialist; Charles Heiser, botanist and *Capsicum* authority who wrote *Seeds to Civilization* and *Of Plants and Man*; Billie L. Turner and Guy L. Nesom, taxonomists; Ernest N. Kaulbach, medievalist who helped with translations; Tom Mabry, plant chemist; William Doolittle, geographer, and geographer/cartographer John Cotter who drew the maps. Special thanks go to Carol Kilgore for her editing. On the few occasions when the vast libraries at the University of Texas at Austin did not contain the material I needed, the interlibrary loan staff at the Texas State Library acquired it for me. Without their diligence in digging out obscure references I could not have put this book together. To all the originators of the recipes included here, most of whom I have come to know personally, my heartfelt appreciation. Last but not least, my right arm and both of my legs for library research—UT-Austin nutrition student, Tera Laird—who did not know when she agreed to be my helper how many trips she was going to make to libraries to fetch and tote the books you will find in this bibliography, plus others which had to be reviewed.

I offer no apologies for any Texas bias readers of this book may discern—I am a fifth-generation Texan and proud of it! Enjoy!

PART I

The Pepper

How Our Food Got Hot

Which Way Did They Go?

hat is it? Spice, herb, condiment, vegetable, garnish, medicine, decoration, icon, or landscape feature? It's all of the above. It's SUPERPOD! *Capsicum* pepper has become, after salt, the most frequently used seasoning agent and condiment in the world and an important fresh vegetable throughout the temperate zones. *Capsicum* cookery is found not only in Mexico, the American Southwest, the Caribbean, and most points south, but also in the Far East, Africa, the Balkans, the Mediterranean, even Korea! Capsicums certainly must have what it takes to have earned such veneration as a culinary ingredient in so many varied cuisines.

In my book *Peppers: The Domesticated Capsicums*, I explored the domesticated capsicums of the western hemisphere[1] but I did not discuss the cuisines that favor them. Since the publication of that book, I have traveled the ancient spice routes through the peppery places of the world. I have poked through markets, visited kitchens, and searched out home gardens and commercial fields where I examined capsicums and collected seeds and recipes, which I brought home to cultivate and test. From all of this I have concluded that only two of the four or five *Capsicum* species that were domesticated from their wild state in the western hemisphere came to play a significant role in the cui-

sines of the eastern hemisphere. How did these American capsicums get there in the first place? What happened to cause the diffusion of domesticated capsicums out of the New World, their place of origin? Where and how did they move after Columbus carried them to Iberia in 1493? Where and why were certain ones adopted and not others? I will try to answer those questions and more, as well as to show how the Portuguese were more responsible for the distribution of capsicums and other New World foods to the eastern hemisphere than were the Spaniards who first discovered them in the western hemisphere. The five characters in this play are the *Capsicum* cousins— *annuum*, *frutescens*, *chinense*, *baccatum*, and *pubescens*. In the world's theaters, the lead is played by *C. annuum*, while *C. chinense* has the supporting role. The first three have interchangeable parts; in fact, the characters of those three are so hard to distinguish that the character played by *C. frutescens* may be eliminated. Although their roles are more limited, the last two are easily recognized, rugged individualists.

We all know what happened in 1492, but did you know that Christopher Columbus also discovered capsicums? Prior to his first voyage to the West Indies, tropical capsicums were unknown to any inhabitant of the Old World (in spite of some undocumented claims to the contrary) or to those in the lands north of present day Mexico.[2] The first Old World pictures with

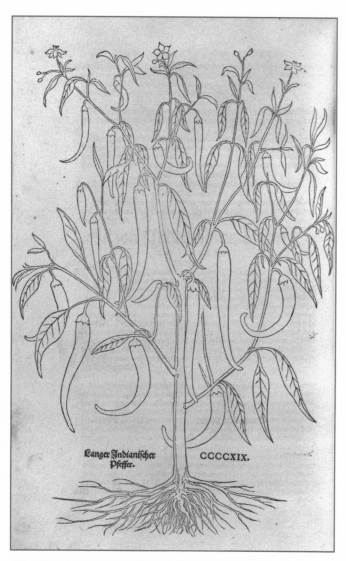

The Capsicum *which blazed the pepper trail. Fuchs,* De historia stirpium *(From the Rare Books and Manuscripts Library, Harry Ransom Humanities Research Center, University of Texas at Austin.)*

descriptions of capsicums were published in a German herbal[3] written by the physician Leonhart Fuchs[4] in 1542. For that reason we must assume that the major post-Columbian distribution of capsicums took place between 1492 and 1542, although Fuchs's herbal may have been in preparation as early as 1532. All of those pictured appear to be *C. annuum* var. *annuum,* the annual pepper. The questions are: How did they get to Fuchs in Europe that early? Why are they the Mesoamerican[5] species and not those which scholars have demonstrated to be indigenous to South America and the West Indies at the time of the discovery of the Americas (*C. chinense* and *C. frutescens*)? Even if a wild Mesoamerican *C. annuum* was the only one of its kind

found in the West Indian islands visited by Columbus during his first three voyages or by others who followed him to the West Indies or went to Brazil, there would not have been sufficient time for a wild plant to have been domesticated and developed into the several types of fruits shown by Fuchs in 1542, only fifty years after "the discovery" of *Capsicum* peppers by the Spaniards. Those fifty years between 1492 and 1542 become our critical time frame.

Our information on Renaissance foodways prior to the discovery of the Americas (hereinafter called simply "the discovery") is restricted by ambiguous or deficient evidence. We must depend on authorities who wrote long after the fact, and we are at the mercy of the vagaries of translation. I will present my case based on circumstantial evidence and wide study. However, a few concepts are commonly agreed upon. One point of agreement is that European meals in the late fifteenth and early sixteenth centuries, our critical time frame, were pretty dreadful. In fact, many have claimed they stank.[6] Disguising the odor of spoilage was the traditional reason for using spices during that period, but was not the *only* reason for their use. More likely, it was the need to enhance or modify the unpalatable flavor of brined or pickled foods with spices that inadvertently started explorers on the spice-driven quest which led to our colorful *Capsicum.*

Because of the paucity of primary sources, much must be left to conjecture in any attempt to place peppers in a setting of time and place. The various scenarios I am about to suggest for the movements of peppers between 1492 and 1542 are based on what is known of world trade and affairs during that period, and what is known of the movements of the more economically important New World plants such as maize, beans and tobacco during the early part of the sixteenth century. At that time the movement of men and cargo between the New World and the Old World was controlled by Spain and Portugal, long before the rise of sea power among the other Europeans challenged their domination.

Writing about African peppers, botanist W. Hardy Eshbaugh (1983:846), without giving reasons, mentions the possibility of *Capsicum annuum*[7] growing in the West Indies at the time of the discovery, when other scholarly studies indicate that at that time it grew only in Mesoamerica, the place where it was domesticated[8] (Heiser, 1976:206; McLeod et al., 1983:563; Pickersgill, 1984:113; Andrews, 1995:17). If that was the case, the Spaniards could not have introduced the Mexican chilli pepper to the West Indies directly from Mexico, as Mexico was not discovered by the Spaniards until 1517, and the conquistador Hernán Cortés did not invade Mexico until 1519. Notwithstanding that the Mexican *C. annuum* var. *annuum* may have been available to Spanish explorers before the discovery and conquest (1521) of Mexico, the Nahuatl word "chilli" was not, and chilli is the name by which capsicums became known in India and the Far East.[9] Given the state of communication at that time, this Mexico-Fuchs time frame (1521–1542), now but twenty-one years, was too narrow, but it helped convince me that the Spaniards had acquired the Mexican domesticates somewhere within the Spanish Main (map 3, page 11) before Cortés captured Moctezuma,[10] but where and how did they get there? The search was on!

The result of research by some of the foremost *Capsicum* scholars, such as Charles Heiser, Paul Smith, Barbara Pickersgill, W. Hardy Eshbaugh, and M. J. McLeod,[11] was a distribution map (map 1), published before the first edition of my *Peppers: The Domesticated Capsicums* in 1984, which gave rise to my later questions and search. Taking that map at face value, we should be able to place a specific explorer in a specific region, thereby allowing us to speculate on which *Capsicum* species he would probably have encountered. My problem with that illustration grew from the absence of *Capsicum annuum* from the West Indies. The map seemed to be based on an assumption that no pre-Columbian diffusion by trade and/or migration had spread the Mesoamerican *C. annuum* to the West Indies as migration had carried the *C. chinense* from South America to those islands. Yet Columbus had found it in Hispaniola.

Given the slow transportation and communication systems at the end the fifteenth and beginning of the sixteenth centuries, in order for New World *Capsicum annuum* to have been as widely distributed in the Old World as it became within such a short time after the discovery, Columbus had to have found domesticated *C. annuum* var. *annuum* within the Spanish Main, either on the mainland where the map depicts, or from the islands before 1519–1521, and he did. On the

basis of descriptions by chroniclers of those expeditions—Martyr, Ferdinand Columbus, Chanca—I think he found it in both places. I have envisioned three possible scenarios that might account for *C. annuum* having been found on his first voyage. At the risk of being tedious for some readers, I will present them, because that finger-shaped red pepper which went around the world changing the food habits of millions is so significant, we should try to determine how it came to be in the Greater Antilles where Columbus found it.

My first scenario involves happenings thousands of years ago. Published archaeological reports prove that *Capsicum annuum* was being cultivated as early as 7000 to 5000 B.C. by peoples in Mexico, including the Tamaulipas culture in the southwestern part of the state of Tamaulipas, Mexico (Mangelsdorf, et al., 1964:430).[12] Later studies demonstrate that migrations by several groups of non-agricultural Paleo-Indians from the Central American coast of Mesoamerica to the Greater Antilles of the West Indies by way of the Mid-Caribbean Island chain occurred after 5000 B.C. and before 2500 B.C. (Rouse, 1966:235; Cruxent and Rouse, 1969:50–52; Watts, 1987:44–48; Wilson, 1990:17; map page 6). In fact, within that period, during certain seasonal conditions of winds and currents, the movement of rafts equipped with mat sails from Cape Gracias a Dios, Nicaragua, to Jamaica and Hispaniola (*Española* in Spanish) may have been quite easy, even for novice sailors who were big game hunters from mainland Mesoamerica following sea mammals—manatee and seals. Those late Paleo-Indian rafters could easily have brought the indigenous Mesoamerican red peppers, either wild or domesticated, with them, because *C. annuum* was known to be a regular item in their diet since 7,000 B.C. Tools of the same type used by Mesoamerican big game hunters of the Central American region during that period have been found in Hispaniola. This theory presumes that the first migration was accidental but that occasional others probably came afterwards. It has been pointed out that "the assembly of a viable breeding population on a remote island through pure chance is quite unlikely. The first Americans need not have been restricted to overland routes for their movements" (Cruxent & Rouse, 1969:51–52). Both the West Indians and the Mesoamericans had the technical capabilities to travel

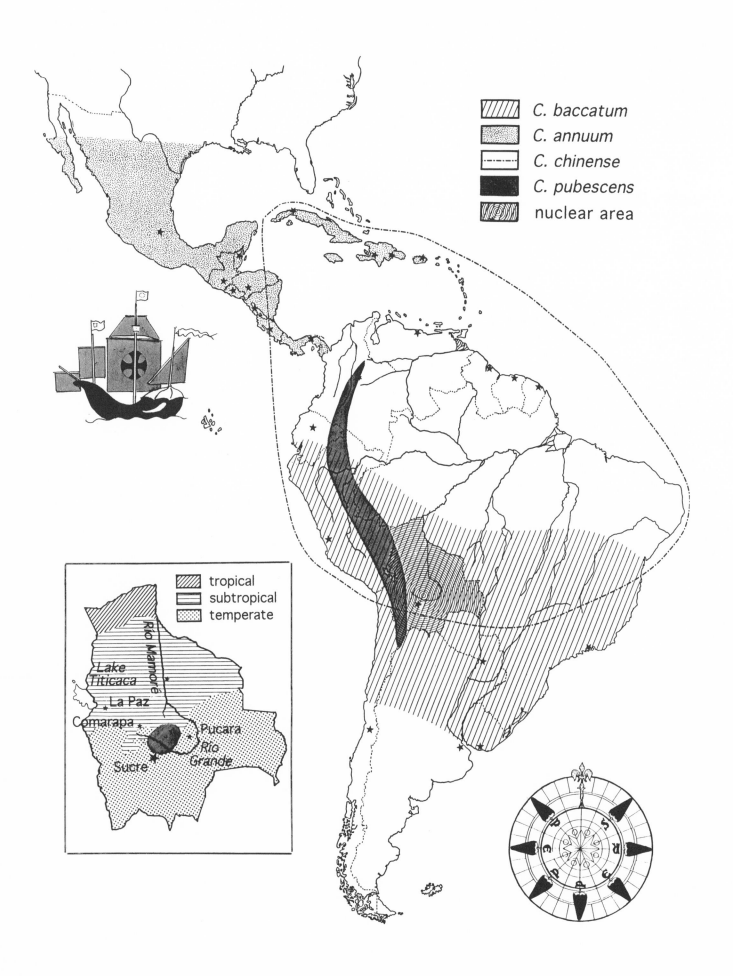

C. baccatum
C. annuum
C. chinense
C. pubescens
nuclear area

tropical
subtropical
temperate

Río Mamoré
Lake Titicaca
La Paz
Comarapa
Sucre
Pucara
Río Grande

between the two areas (Rouse, 1966:235). At any rate, there were hunters and gatherers inhabiting the Greater Antilles when the agriculturists arrived from South America about the time of Christ, and I contend that *C. annuum* was also there. The new migrant farmers from South America would have had sufficient time to domesticate the pungent Mesoamerican spice even if that had not already been done before it was brought from the mainland.

During this same Paleo era, which antedated the arrival of agriculturists, land birds could have performed their historical function of *Capsicum* seed dispersal, as they had when they carried the wild precursors of *Capsicum annuum* var. *annuum* from its place of origin in South America north to Mesoamerica before prehistoric man made his way to that region. Although gulls and terns eat fruit to some extent, especially in Northern Europe, sea and shore birds are not the likely carriers (Ridley, 1930:495).

In the meanwhile, yet another group of early inhabitants, Mezo-Indians from the mainland, followed those first big-game hunters to Hispaniola, or they may simply have been descendants of those Paleo-Indians who evolved in the Greater Antilles. Those first two groups would have had plenty of time—three thousand undisturbed years—to have consciously or unconsciously selected bigger and bigger peppers from those that came from Mesoamerica with their ancestors, even though they were not farmers.

Later, between 250 A.D. to 1000 A.D., Neo-Indians who were migrant agriculturalists and potters—Ara-

Map 1
(Distribution at Time of European Discovery)

This is the map which triggered my question leading to this study. On the original map, demonstrating the distribution of the five domesticated Capsicum *at the time of the European discovery of the New World,* Capsicum annuum *was not shown as being in the West Indian islands where Columbus first landed. Nonetheless, in light of Martyr's descriptions of peppers Columbus collected on his first voyage and the illustrations in Fuchs's herbal only fifty years later, we know it was there. That omission has been corrected on this map and the text presents several scenarios outlining possible routes from its Mesoamerican place of domestication to Hispaniola where Columbus found it growing. (After Heiser 1976a; McLeod et al. 1982)*

waks from South America—traveled north along the Lesser Antilles to Hispaniola, where they overran those more primitive nonagricultural inhabitants, causing the remainder to retreat to remote regions before the discovery. Hispaniola then became pre-eminent in West Indian cultural development. These South American farmers, who brought with them the Amazonian *Capsicum chinense,* could have undertaken the cultivation and domestication of the wild and/or domesticated Mesoamerican pepper transported from Central America by the Paleo-Indians so long before—they had time enough before Columbus arrived. At any rate, *C. annuum*, along with Mesoamerican species of corn, beans and squash, were all in Hispaniola when Columbus arrived (Martyr, 1904; Oviedo, 1959:15; Fuchs, 1543), although they may not have been there for a long time because few West Indian natives knew how to utilize maize for making bread.

However, my second plot has the already domesticated *Capsicum annuum* following established pre-Columbian trade routes running from Mesoamerica up and down the Central American corridor, across northern South America, and north through the Antilles. Casting doubt on this scenario is the fact that scholars tell us that although the movement of Mesoamerican domesticates to South America was in process at the time of the discovery, it was interrupted by that occurrence before reaching Venezuela and the Lesser Antilles (Sauer, 1966:5). The pre-Columbian peoples of South America and the West Indies, as far north as the Tropic of Cancer, practiced vegetative or root agriculture—cuttings, tubers, roots—while those of Mesoamerica and northward into the area of the United States supplanted that mode of agriculture with seed planting (Sauer, 1969:40, 62). Somehow the two modes had begun to mix in the Greater Antilles prior to the European arrival, indicating the arrival of domesticated seed from Mesoamerica, but seeds were still less important than roots (Sauer, 1966:6). Seed crops filtered throughout the agricultural parts of South America as less-utilized consorts of root crops, but it was rare for maize to become a staple crop in early South America. Mesoamerican seed plants have not been reported as being in the Lesser Antilles until after the arrival of Europeans.

More extensive archaeological studies in Cuba may bolster the status of my third proposal, which is that

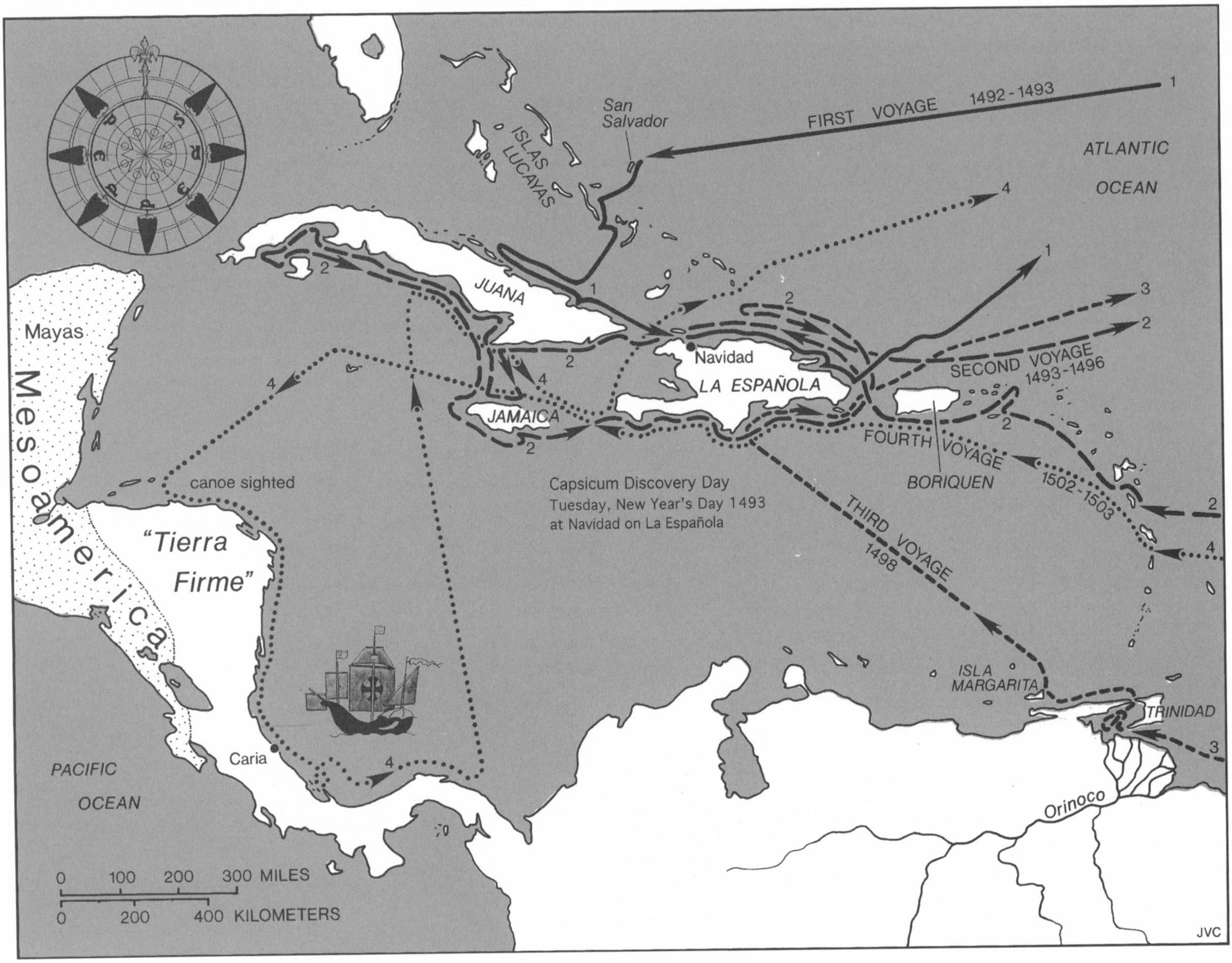
FIRST VOYAGE 1492-1493
San Salvador
ISLAS LUCAYAS
ATLANTIC OCEAN
JUANA
Navidad
LA ESPAÑOLA
SECOND VOYAGE 1493-1496
JAMAICA
FOURTH VOYAGE 1502-1503
BORIQUEN
Mayas
Mesoamerica
canoe sighted
Capsicum Discovery Day
Tuesday, New Year's Day 1493
at Navidad on La Española
THIRD VOYAGE 1498
"Tierra Firme"
ISLA MARGARITA
TRINIDAD
Caria
PACIFIC OCEAN
Orinoco
0 100 200 300 MILES
0 200 400 KILOMETERS
JVC

Map 2 (The Four Voyages of Columbus)

The Voyages of Christopher Columbus: 1492–1503

the seed for capsicums, corn, beans, and squash came overseas from Mayan seed farmers not too long before the discovery. The Yucatán Channel is less than 120 miles wide between that peninsula and the island of Cuba. Was it possible for occasional Mayan seafarers to cross that sea in their great canoes in five or six days? I think so, and there is evidence that once in a while they did (Sauer, 1966:212; Rouse, 1966:236). Also, regular seasonal migrations of land birds across that channel are evident. The fact that many land birds consume pepper seed (page 7) is not only well documented but readily observed. Pre-Columbian contact, with its resulting diffusion, is not to be discounted.

Enough speculation. Let's look at where and how Columbus acquired that finger-shaped[13] pepper (*Capsicum annuum* var. *annuum*) that set the Old World on fire. In a letter to the King and Queen and their treasurer after his first voyage (1492–1493), Columbus did not mention peppers by name, but he did speak of the natives eating meat with very hot spices (Andrews, 1984:2; C. Columbus, 1493). Among the entries in the log[14] of that first voyage is one for November 4, 1492, from Cuba, in which we are told that Columbus brought samples of black pepper and cinnamon to show the natives what he was looking for. Several weeks later, on November 21, Martin Alonzo Pinzón, the defiant captain of the caravel *Pinta,* left the group and sailed from Cuba in search of gold. Then, on Christmas day, the two remaining ships reached the coast of Hispaniola, where the ill-fated *Santa Maria* ran aground and was lost. Lack of space on the *Niña* for the shipwrecked crew necessitated leaving thirty-nine volunteers on the island.[15] A fortress was built from the timbers of the wrecked ship and was named *Navidad* (Christmas). Near that site, on New Year's Day 1493, Columbus recorded a momentous culinary circumstance in his journal—"the pepper which the local Indians used as spice is more abundant and more valuable than either black or melegueta pepper [grains of paradise—a fiery African native of the ginger family]" (map 2, page 8).[16] He left a recommendation that those who were to remain on Hispaniola collect as much of it as possible (Morison, 1963:142). Two weeks later, near Samana Bay at the other end of the island, Columbus continued to record what they were seeing. Besides cotton and other things, there was much *ají,* the native pepper. He found it to be much stronger than black pepper, and the people wouldn't eat without it. He estimated that one could load fifty caravels a year with it in Hispaniola (Ibid:154). Mark your calendars! January first is *Capsicum* discovery day.

The account of the first voyage by the royal historian Peter Martyr is of great importance, because not only does he write of maize[17] found growing in the islands in 1492, but he also describes the pungent spice used by the natives. In that description is found this relevant remark: "When it [pepper] is used there is no need of Caucasian pepper. The **sweet pepper** [my bolding] is called *boniato,* and the hot pepper is called caníbal, for they are sharp and strong as cannibals (Andrews, 1984:4; Anghiera 1904:225–26). "Sweet pepper" is a key piece to our puzzle. As yet, *C. chinense* has no known sweet varieties other than the one I call *rocotillo,* from Perú, which has a mild pungency. Those

varieties growing in the West Indies are renowned for their pungency. It is improbable, therefore, that the reference is to a pepper of that species, but refers instead to a Mesoamerican *C. annuum* var. *annuum,* which already had sweet varieties at that time.

On the second journey (1493–1496), Diego Chanca, physician to the voyage, wrote that the aborigines ate a vegetable called *agí* (or *ají*) to give a sharp taste to fish and bird dishes (Chanca, 1494). Columbus also logged peppers on his second voyage (Morison, 1963:216). In a letter to the sovereigns written during that trip, Columbus listed peppers as one of the things he brought to them (Ibid:281); however, the third voyage (1498–1500) was so plagued with problems for Columbus that neither he nor his chroniclers mentioned foods. Fortunately for my tale, he took his illegitimate fourteen-year-old son Ferdinand with him on his fourth voyage (1502–1504).[18]

The first continental landing on the coast of Honduras, where the adventurers encountered people of the high Mesoamerican culture very unlike those of the Caribbean islands, was made on that voyage. Soon after that, the Europeans overtook and captured a huge native trading canoe carved from a single log.[19] Ferdinand described this vessel as eight feet wide and as long as a galley, filled with exotic merchandise covered with a canopy of palm leaves, and carrying a crew of twenty-five (F. Columbus, 1947:274). Amid the cargo were maize, roots, and "victuals like they eat in Hispaniola," along with woven cotton fabrics, all from Mesoamerica. In fact, there was such a wide selection of native goods aboard that Ferdinand's father, exclaimed, "Thanks to God, that he has given us a sample of all the things of that land without danger or fatigue to our people." Recalling Dr. Chanca's letter, in which he reported the Indians eating *ají (Capsicum)* on everything they ate, I like to believe that capsicums were in that canoe along with the other native foodstuffs[20] (Cohen, 1969:156). For certain, the Amerindians would not have left the fiery pods behind!

In a letter titled "Christopher Columbus Viceroy and Admiral of the Indies, to the most Christian and Mighty King and Queen of Spain, our Sovereigns, notifying them of the events of his voyage and the Cities, Provinces, Rivers and other Marvels, also the Situation of the Many Goldfields and other Objects of Great Riches and Value," we learn that on his final

Although Columbus had discovered peppers January 1, 1493, on Española during his first voyage, he gives a better description of them on his second voyage. "In those islands there are also bushes like rose bushes which make a fruit as long as cinnamon full of small grains as biting as pepper; those Caribs and the Indians eat that fruit as we eat apples."

voyage in the fall of 1502, soon after the Honduran landing, the explorers reached the coast of Nicaragua, where they spent some time repairing and refitting their ships (Ibid:283). During that sojourn Columbus questioned the natives about gold and other things. Afterwards he wrote to their majesties, "According to reports they are all acquainted with red pepper" (Ibid:288). It was his practice to collect a sample of all things new and different to take back to show to the King and Queen. There is no doubt in my mind he collected some of those "red peppers" for his sovereigns, and based on the pre-Columbian distribution maps (map 3, page 11), the Mesoamerican peppers would have been *Capsicum annuum* var. *annuum* (Heiser 1976:266; Pickersgill 1984:113; Andrews 1984:17).

A little later in 1502, when the Spaniards arrived in Panama, they found corn, beans, squash, and perhaps peppers, where they had been carried from Mexico gradually, down through Central America (F. Columbus, 1947:296). From there the pre-Columbian trade route went east across Tierra Firme (Spanish Main), and thence north into the Lesser Antillian islands (Sauer, 1966:54) (map 3 page 11). With the post-Columbian help of the Spanish, these foods, including the Mexican turkey, quickly traveled from the isthmus to all of the West Indies. Although it is certain that Mesoamerican capsicums like those described by Martyr had already reached some parts of the Greater Antilles at the time of Columbus's first

voyage, we can be assured they spread rapidly after the contact on the mainland in 1502.[21]

Fray Bartolomé de Las Casas, the Apostle of the Indies, spent many of his ninety-two years in the New World, first arriving in 1502. He recorded his careful observations in his *Apologetica Historia,* believed to have been drafted in Hispaniola between 1526 and 1529[22] (Fernandez, 1971:84). Two of the three capsicums he describes as being cultivated in the West Indies fit Martyr's descriptions and the illustrations found in Fuchs's herbal (Casas, 1967:58). One *ají* was long, red, and finger-shaped; a second was globular like a cherry and more pungent. A third was a wild *Capsicum* that bore very small fruits. The first matches the description of Fuchs's finger-type.

A look at the Portuguese enterprise will address our previous question regarding their responsibility for the distribution of peppers. During the early seventeenth century, botanical writers, including Charles L'Escluse, reported that some of the capsicums in India were called "Pernambuco pepper" and "Brazilian pepper." Evidence such as this supports the Portuguese introduction of the first *Capsicum* peppers to India, but gives no clue as to what species, though Pernambuco was a Portuguese province on the eastern point of Brazil, and it would therefore seem that those peppers were *Capsicum chinense* (map 1, page 6). By early in the sixteenth century the Portuguese had also introduced what they called "Spanish pepper" to Pamrukan, Java (Meilink-Roelofsz, 1962:151). The origin of

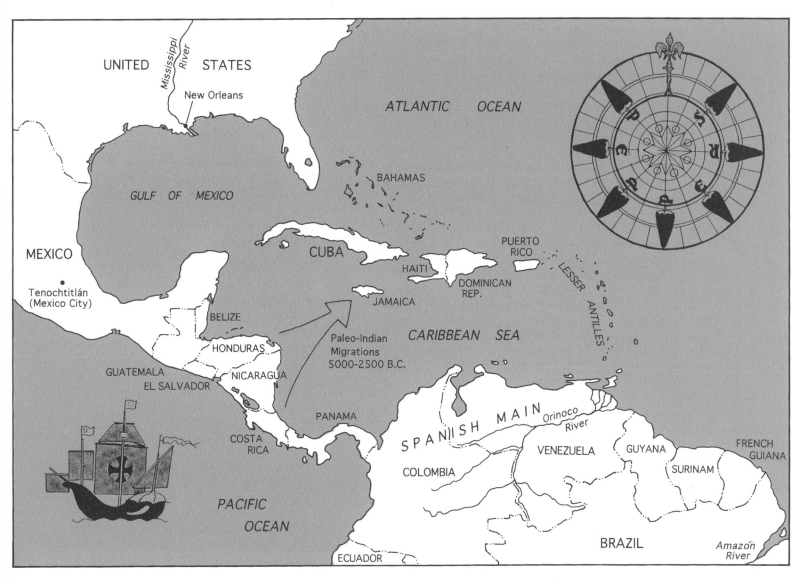

that common name for a *C. annuum* var. *annuum* poses another question. Why "Spanish" and not "Brazilian" or "Pernambuco"? Where had the Portuguese acquired "Spanish pepper"? The Spanish did not become active in the Pacific until 1565, and neither they nor other Europeans were permitted to trade in Indian and Indonesian ports during the century of Portuguese supremacy (1497–1600) in the Far East. This would indicate that the Portuguese first obtained *Capsicum* pepper from the Spanish, but where?

An attempt to answer that very significant query will require looking at some obscure facts and circumstances regarding the goings-on of the Spanish and Portuguese during the fifty years before and after the discovery. More than half a century before Columbus discovered the Americas, the Portuguese, under the auspices of Prince Henry the Navigator, had begun their exploration and occupation of the west coast of Africa.[23] At that time the rulers of both Portugal and

Map 3 (Caribbean Region)

This map is designed to help locate the various routes which capsicums followed before and after the region was first discovered and overrun by colonizing Europeans and their nefarious slave trade, which acted together to bring about the Columbian Exchange: the biological and cultural consequences of 1492.

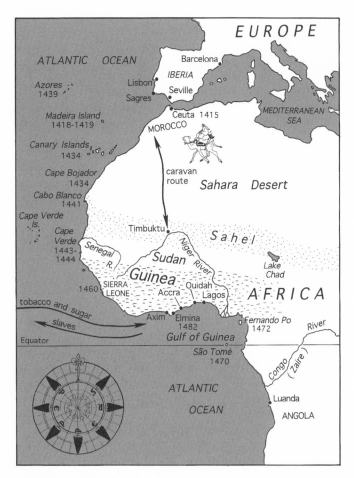

Map 4 (The Portuguese Enterprise)

For more than half a century before Columbus made his first voyage, the Portuguese had been sailing down the west coast of Africa establishing trading posts and sugar plantations. Their Atlantic islands became important way-stations for sailing ships on voyages to America. The West African coastal area, then known as Guinea, became the most significant region affecting the Columbian Exchange during the long period when Portugal dominated (1415–1600) world trade. Before finding the New World, Columbus had voyaged along the Guinea ("Ginnie") coast where he visited Elmina, the first European "castle" in Africa. The modern country of Guinea is but a small section in the northern part of this once vast territory, and Elmina is now in Ghana.

Spain knew that the valuable spices came from the Far East, but both countries were dependent on Venice as their source, and Venice was the eastern Mediterranean middleman for the hated Moslems at the caravan terminals of Aleppo (now Halab, Syria), Ragussa on the Adriatic, and in Alexandria, Egypt. As soon as the Iberian powers independently won their freedom from the forces of Islam in 1492, they each set out to find a way to the fabled Indies that would bypass those centers. Spices in general, and the pungent black seed of a botanically unrelated Indian vine, black pepper *(Piper nigrum)*, in particular, were not the only motivation for the Portuguese venture, but they were a predominant factor.[24]

Before the feats of Columbus, an Arab-speaking Portuguese, Pero de Covilha, reached India by way of the Mediterranean and the Red Sea. Although his was a shorter route to India, Islamic barriers made it unfeasible. Therefore, the Portuguese continued cautiously coasting[25] south along western Africa. The discovery of the uninhabited Cape Verde Islands in 1441, 300 miles off the coast of Senegal and immune to attacks from Africa, proved to be the most promising refitting stop on the voyage from India and America—a caravanserai of the seas. Continuing down Africa and rounding the Cape of Good Hope, the Portuguese captain Bartolomeu Dias sighted the Indian Ocean in 1487–88. With that, the rivalry between the two great Iberian powers came to a head. The Portuguese, experienced navigators with colonies in the Azores (1439), almost one-third the distance across the Atlantic, suspected that it was possible to reach the Indies by sailing west, but they believed that it was closer to sail around Africa, where they had already established many safe places to put ashore along its western coast (Morison, 1942:76). Early in the last quarter of the fifteenth century they had begun colonization and sugar plantations[26] on the uninhabited tropical islands of Cape Verde, São Tomé, and Principe, the last two with better conditions for agriculture. In 1482 they constructed Elmina Castle and Fort St. Jago, the first of their trade castles and forts on the Gold Coast.[27] As Portugal was about to reach the Malabar coast of western India, Spain chose to play her trump card, Christopher Columbus. No one dreamed that Columbus would stumble into a new world as a result of his voyaging off into the sunset, even though most seamen suspected that land lay

Christopher Columbus, after an engraving by P. Mercuri

The arms of Columbus, Admiral of the Ocean Seas

toward the west. Nor did they envision that the eating habits of the inhabitants of that New World—America—would change those of the known world. Consequently, after the discovery, the Portuguese hastened their exploration of the west African coast in an effort to reach the far eastern spice lands in order to catch up with Spanish achievements. Soon thereafter, a Portuguese ship under the irascible, brutal Vasco da Gama, with the guidance of the finest Arabian navigator in Malindi, Ahmad-Ibn-Madjid, arrived in India in 1497. Now the Iberian feud became testy.

Shortly after the discovery of America, the Borgian Pope Alexander VI decided to put an end to the squabbling between those two Catholic powers. In 1493 and 1494, with the Treaty of Tordesillas,[28] he drew an imaginary longitudinal line 370 leagues west of the Cape Verde Islands[29] which continued around the globe, even though no one knew what route it would take in the Far East. Then he proclaimed that Spain could explore and trade in the area to the west, while granting Portugal the eastern half, effectively barring to Spain the route around southern Africa (Map on end pages). This Catholic proclamation remained effective until Protestant nations of Europe chose to ignore it, challenging the two great Catholic powers.

The Canary Islands and the Cape Verde islands, especially the Canaries,[30] were to become the principal "stepping stones" to India, the West Indies and South America. These served as half-way houses between the ports of Europe, the Far East, and the New World

(Duncan, 1972:23). For four centuries those islands capitalized on their position as staging points for trans-Atlantic and Indian voyages and are, therefore, key locations in the Columbian Exchange. In its initial period, Santiago in the Cape Verdes served as a cardinal point for the gathering and dispersal of plants and animals, relaying them from one continent to another (Ibid:168).

The Portuguese did not leap into power in the Far East immediately (Elton, 1962:594). Pedro Alvares Cabral followed da Gama in 1500; his fleet of thirteen ships contained two vessels laden with trade goods, which could have included the New World capsicums from their West African trading posts.[31] In 1502, at the same time Columbus was exploring the coast of Mesoamerica, da Gama returned to India. He, too, could have carried maize and peppers. After a new trading post was set up at Cochin, a better harbor, he went back to his rewards in Portugal. But, it was not until the Portuguese seized Moslem-dominated Goa in 1510 that their Far Eastern efforts under governor Afonso de Albuquerque showed any results (Dames [Barbosa], 1918:170). By the time of Albuquerque's death in 1515, the Portuguese were shipping spices regularly from the Far East to Lisbon and thence to Antwerp, making Lisbon the greatest commercial city in Europe.

Although Cabral had discovered Brazil on his voyage to India,[32] no exploration was attempted (Hart, 1950:210). For the first thirty years after his landfall, the Portuguese, fully occupied in the Far East, made no use of pristine Brazil except as a source of brazil-wood for dye.[33] Salvador was founded in 1502, but no other colonies were established until after 1532, with the introduction of sugar plantations organized on the half-century of experience in their Atlantic Islands (Freyre, 1966:43, 197).

Meanwhile, to the north of Brazil, the Spanish were dominating the scene. Spanish mercantilism dictated that her colonies should exist for the sole benefit of the mother country. Although there ensued rapid envelopment of the areas considered to be economically alluring—those with gold deposits, ample labor supply, easy access, and abundant land for agriculture and grazing—total occupation of these territories never took place. Hispaniola, in the heavily populated West Indies, became their first center and served as a base for the conquest and settlement of the other islands, while Cuba became the base for exploration and conquest of the mainland. But the Caribbean as the center of Spanish interest persisted only until 1530, when the gold and the labor force became depleted. After that, Spanish immigration to the West Indies came to a standstill following their conquest of Mexico, Guatemala, and Yucatán. African slaves began to be imported through the Portuguese to replace the Amerindians, who verged on extinction by 1540[34] (Means, 1935:38).

The imported European domesticated pigs, cattle, and horses did so well on the islands that the archipelago became the suppliers of those animals to the conquistadors. Their traditional grains and olives did not prosper, however, as the Spaniards had little understanding of the nature of the Antillean environment, which was tropical with short days and had a seasonal cycle of rainfall reversed from that of Iberia. As a result, the settlers urgently needed foodstuffs from the mother country during the early years. This need was compounded by a persistent emphasis on European crops and a rejection of the native food from the *conucos* (mounded gardens).[35] Although the Spaniards introduced sugar cane to the West Indies, they had only limited success with it. The great Caribbean sugar plantations came in the seventeenth century with the advent of other Europeans.

The famed Spanish convoy system, which existed as the only legal link between the Caribbean and the rest of the world, was not implemented until 1561, long

after capsicums had become established in the Old World. Although two fleets supposedly departed from Spain each year for the Caribbean, several years could pass without New World ports hosting a single Spanish ship (West & Augelli, 1976:63). Even less shipping took place during our critical time frame, despite the need to supply the approximately ten thousand residents of the newly established Spanish colony. This paucity of Spanish shipping allowed the daring Portuguese to enter the region surreptitiously with their African slaves and other trade goods. This illicit trade was aided by Spain's own subjects in the Americas—not from disloyalty, but rather from dire necessity (Means, 1935:61).

In the first half of the sixteenth century only a thin trickle of exchange existed between Seville and the New World. Portuguese trade between Lisbon and the New World was greater. At the same time, back on the Iberian peninsula, relations, including commerce, between the two Iberian powers were surely cordial if not friendly, since the royal houses were now linked by marriage. That match was evidence of communication between Lisbon, Seville, and Barcelona that could have contributed to the rapid spread of *Capsicum* (Walsh, 1939:496).

The grain trade in Iberia was another contributing factor. At the time of the discovery and throughout the early movement (1492–1550) of New World economic plants—maize, tomatoes, tobacco, squash—bread grain in Portugal was deficient and the little country depended on a well-established trade with neighboring Spain and North Africa for its cereal supply (Pounds, 1979:63). Surely, the traders would have been aware of the new maize and its attendant plants—squash, beans, and capsicums. In 1498 Columbus wrote of maize when he said "it is a seed which makes an ear, of which I brought some back and of which there is now a great quantity in Spain" (Weiner, 1920: 120). In remote Galicia, adjoining Portugal, maize became common food and a possible source of seed quite early (Sauer, 1952:152).

By the 1550s the Portuguese merchants had penetrated all of Spanish America and in particular its capital cities and its important ports: Mexico City, Santo Domingo, and Cartagena. A considerable Portuguese trading network which spread throughout the New World in a matter of twenty years was centered on

Lisbon, and extended to both the African and the American sides of the Atlantic, with connections in East Africa and the Far East (Braudel, 1979:161). Even though there was a direct trade route between Portuguese Africa after 1535, (Elmina in present Ghana and Luanda in Angola) and Portuguese Brazil (Bahia in Pernambuco), throughout the sixteenth and seventeenth centuries, by royal decree, nothing went to India from West Africa, the Atlantic Islands, or Brazil, without going to Lisbon first (Marchant, 1941:450).

Very few Spanish ships actually made the West Indian trip even though the demand for European goods was so great in the Indies that Spanish merchants could not meet it. That neglected Indies trade, therefore, was a standing temptation to slavers, smugglers and illicit traders, mostly Portuguese, in the first half of the sixteenth century. From the early years of the century, African slaves had been employed in the sugar production of Hispaniola, and later throughout the Spanish Main and in coastal Mexico.[36] Portuguese slavers supplied other slave traders licensed by the Spanish government, and often ran cargoes across on their own account. That slave trade presented opportunities to acquire Mesoamerican foods, including capsicums.

Slaving was not the only opportunity. The Mesoamerican plants could have been available on the Iberian peninsula,[37] or at requisite refitting stops in the Spanish Canary Islands and the Portuguese Cape Verdes and Azores, where sailing ships were resupplied with local foods. Those Atlantic islands were frequented by both Spanish and Portuguese caravels sailing with the prevailing trade winds to and from New World ports, and the Azores were the last port of call for homeward-bound European ships (Duncan, 1972:17). Even Columbus sailed to Lisbon via the Azores before he returned to Seville at the end of his first voyage.

Scholars have studied and written copiously about maize, as you can see in the bibliography, so I started looking at its early movements because of its close association with capsicums. Without going into all the details, I have concluded that the Portuguese started growing maize and capsicums (*C. annuum* var. *annuum*) in the Azores, Madeira, and the Cape Verdes, as well as Guinea from the Senegal River on the Gold Coast of western Africa to the delta of the Niger River, as soon as they acquired the seed from a yet undetermined Spanish source late in the fifteenth century.[38]

From Guinea (Senegal River to the mouth of the Niger), where they were grown in the gardens of the trade castles and forts (Lawrence, 1964:37), the New World crops arrived on the islands of São Tomé and Principe beginning in 1502[39] (Jeffereys, 1954:193; 1975:35). The climate[40] along the Gold coast and on those Portuguese Atlantic Islands—Madeira, Azores, Cape Verde, and São Tomé—proved to be more compatible to the cultivation of tropical New World produce than either Iberia or the western Mediterranean.

The date of 1502 is very interesting because that is the same busy year that Columbus began his fourth voyage, taking him to the mainland of Mesoamerica for the first time, and da Gama made his second voyage to India. When maize was introduced to the island of São Tomé in 1502, the seed could not have come from the first Columbian landfall on the North American continent (1502–1504). The seed would have had to come to the Portuguese through the Spanish from an earlier Antillian source, because the Portuguese are not known to have been in the West Indies before 1509. Even though they discovered primitive Brazil in 1500, we have seen that it was much later before they began exploration or actually established themselves there.

After the introduction of those New World plants to Portuguese eastern Atlantic holdings, it was no longer necessary to return to the Western Hemisphere for them. The Portuguese added the new agricultural products to their regular cargoes while carrying on their long-established and highly profitable European trade in sugar, slaves, gold, ivory, and "ginnie pepper" (grains of paradise). It is highly probable that *Capsicum* seeds were transported from this area to India via Mozambique as soon as they were obtainable. An abundance of American maize *(Milho grosso)* was being exported from Gujarat, India, by 1516 (Barbosa, 1918).[41] If there had been an early introduction of the Caribbean/South American *ají* along with that maize, preference for the Mesoamerican chillies has caused them to be replaced long ago.

In the 500 years since the discovery, the dominant Caribbean/South American capsicums such as Scotch bonnet and habanero *(C. chinense)*, have yet to become popular in Spain, Mexico, and the United States, or in Africa, where the Portuguese had direct trade routes to Brazil. In fact, they are only now gaining acceptance in those places and are not common in the markets. *Capsicum chinense* is a native of the tropics and therefore harder to grow in temperate and subtropical climates. Its ripe fruit does not keep well, and it does not dry readily for year-round storage and use. Whole or ground, it does not travel satisfactorily, or have the versatility of its multifaceted sub-tropical cousin, *C. annuum* var. *annuum*.

The one-hundred-year Portuguese monopoly assured by the Treaty of Tordesillas resulted in their becoming the primary carriers of New World plants to the Old World. Not only could the Portuguese receive credit for the introduction of American flora and fauna to Africa, India, and the Far East, but also directly and indirectly to parts of Europe. As a result of those Portuguese introductions to India and/or East Africa, long-established Arabic-speaking Moslem traders were able to transport the American exotics from the Malabar coast and/or East Africa to the Middle East, whence they traveled along existing trade routes to eastern Europe via Constantinople and Venice. In addition, Portuguese convoys returning from India could have transported those introduced American foods, along with indigenous Asian spices, in cargoes from their new colonies east of the Pope's line back to Antwerp via Lisbon, as we shall see.[42]

Old World peasants, whether in the Balkans, Venice, India, or Indonesia, never grew black pepper, cinnamon, cloves, nutmeg, or cardamom in their gardens—the cultural requirements made it impossible. Once capsicum seed became available, they had an inexpensive spice that they could grow for their own use.

Using the distribution of coffee[43] as an analogy, I feel it would have taken only a few seeds from only a handful of blistering pods to introduce the spice which eventually burned its way through the kitchens of the Far East. Having found coffee growing wild in Ethiopia before 1000 A.D., the Arabs assured their monopoly by heating the coffee beans to prevent germination and by guarding their plantations. It took but seven viable beans stolen by a seventeenth-century pilgrim to Mecca from Mysore, India, to introduce coffee cultivation to India (Watt, 1889:465). It took but one smuggled plant from French Guiana to start

the world's greatest coffee empire in Brazil (Roden, 1983:78). Think of what a few "stolen" dried chilli-pepper pods would produce!

Considering that capsicums of the type that went to India have approximately twenty-five to sixty seeds in one pod, and that in the tropics they begin producing fruit within two and a half to three months and continue throughout the year, it takes little imagination to project a few seeds into enough capsicums to change the cuisines of much of the world's population.

As ecological historian Alfred W. Crosby, Jr., who coined the phrase "The Columbian Exchange," says, "The most important changes brought on by the Columbian voyages were biological in nature" (Crosby, 1972:xiv). If the effect of New World capsicums on Old World cuisines is any gauge, their transfer must have been one of the most significant achievements of the Admiral of the Ocean Sea. Inconceivable as it may seem today, at that time the Old World was without turkeys, corn, potatoes, squashes, common beans, peanuts, sweet potatoes, lima beans, cacao (chocolate), vanilla, avocados, tomatoes, pineapples, manioc (also called yucca, cassava, and tapioca), and *Capsicum* peppers, but not for long. Within the lifetime of the conquistadors, most of these foods were established throughout the world except for the Pacific Islands, New Zealand, and Australia. By 1542, only fifty years after their discovery by Columbus, three varieties of capsicums were recognized on the Malabar coast of India (Purseglove, 1968:526).

It is still difficult to perceive the rapidity of the spread of New World foods, especially corn, beans, squash, sweet potatoes, and capsicums, throughout the world.[44] Meanwhile, in the Americas, Old World plants and animals were also quickly assimilated.[45] In combination with the great variety of native American foods, their addition triggered a dynamic nutritional change. Food historian John C. Super (1988:80) asserts that during the sixteenth century, it is unlikely that any other area in the world had such a multiplicity of staples and abundance of animal protein as Spanish America, making possible the rapid expansion of the Spaniards in the Americas during the first half of the sixteenth century.

The Ships that Carried Peppers Around the World

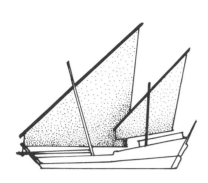

1. Arabian Dhow

Origin unknown. Until the thirteenth century this small, lanteen rigged (triangular sail) ship was exclusively Mediterranean. It could not beat against the wind; consequently it ran one trip a year, going out with the favorable winds of the northeast monsoon and returning with the southeast monsoon. It is still used today in the Persian Gulf, the Mediterranean, and the Red Sea.

2. Caravel

A fifteenth- and sixteenth-century southern European lanteen rigged sailing ship with smooth planking. It was later square rigged. The "Santa Maria" was a caravel and Da Gama's 4-masted "San Gabriel" was almost one.

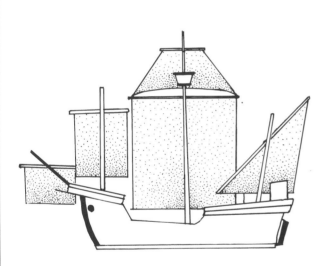

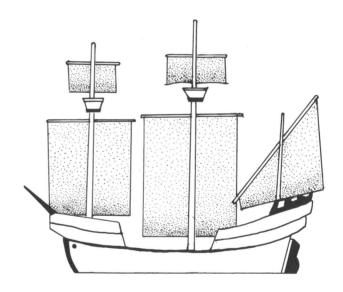

3. Nao

A fifteenth- and early sixteenth-century European sailing ship with smooth planking on heavy framing plus inside supported decks. It was larger than a caravel. The annual Portuguese ship from Goa to Macao and Japan was a nao.

4. Carrack or Galleon

A large, smooth sided sailing vessel, longer for its breadth, with a lower superstructure than the caravel and galleon from which it evolved. For 100 years, up to the seventeenth century, it was the major ship type.

The First Hot Spots

he hot spots are the locations throughout the world where the peripatetic, tropical pepper settled into the local culinary regime after having been carried from Columbus's New World by the Iberians. The principal areas form a broad pan-tropical belt within the boundaries of the Tropics of Cancer and Capricorn and widening through the sub-tropics (see map on end sheets). As varieties adapted to temperate climates have been developed, that pepper belt has continued to widen. We have theorized on how the Spaniards first acquired peppers, then examined the conceivable ways the Portuguese obtained the pod which they introduced to their African and Indian possessions; now let's follow the probable trail of the wandering pod through that ever broadening belt.

Latin America

The original pepper place in the world was a spot about midway in the immense area of the Western Hemisphere now referred to as Latin America (map 1, page 6). As we learned in the previous chapter, Europeans first encountered chilli peppers on the islands and shores of the Caribbean, then Mesoamerica—

Central America and Mexico—on south through the tropical and sub-tropical areas of South America. As the Spaniards moved through the vast area, peppers moved with them. Soon thereafter the Portuguese came to Brazil bringing with them ginnie pepper-loving Africans, who reintroduced those finger-shaped chilli peppers to the New World and its native pepper-loving inhabitants. The new African Americans soon acquired a taste for the local peppers which were being consumed with customary regularity and much gusto by the native Americans they encountered. Much of the pepper trail through the Latin American places has been covered in "Which Way Did They Go?".

CARIBBEAN

In the first chapter we discussed how peppers came to the West Indies of the Caribbean where they were found by Columbus and recorded in the journals of his first two voyages.

MESOAMERICA—MEXICO INTO
CENTRAL AMERICA

In 1502 the fourth voyage of discovery took the Iberians to the mainland coast of Central America where they again found the Mesoamerican red peppers. Mexico was not discovered for another fifteen years, then two years later it was invaded from Cuba by Cortés. He and his Indian allies conquered armies of the Aztecs in 1521 and soon thereafter the Spaniards began abandoning the torrid, humid West Indian tropics for the more compatible climate of temperate Mexico. From the central highlands they moved north and south carrying Old World flora, fauna, and western European civilization, as well as the exceptional Mesoamerican plants and the Mexican turkey with them. Today all the domesticated species of capsicums are cultivated commercially in this area with the exception of *Capsicum baccatum* var. *pendulum*.

TIERRA FIRME

Scholars believe that, after domestication in the vicinity of capsicum's original homeland, *Capsicum chinense* and the semi-wild *C. frutescens* moved northward into Amazonia and were the only chilli peppers found in the South American countries along the Caribbean before the arrival of the Spaniards (map 1, page 6). It was from those humid tropics the burning berries moved with early humans and birds into the Antilles and throughout the tropical and subtropical regions of South America long before the discovery. Mexican/Mesoamerican seed crops had almost reached the southern limits of Panama when their southern migration over ancient Amerindian trade routes was halted by European invasions. Soon after the European takeover of that area the Columbian Exchange began in earnest, and Mesoamerican and South American plants intermingled. In the first five hundred years following the discovery, *C. chinense* was not readily accepted in Mesoamerica except in Yucatán, a phenomenon which gives weight to my third scenario based on an exchange between Cuba and Yucatán.

ANDEAN

The original home of chilli peppers is thought to have been in southeastern Bolivia or nearby Brazil (map 1, page 6). It was natural for pepper-eating birds to have distributed the wild peppers throughout the Andean area before humans arrived. In the Andean countries—Peru, Ecuador, Bolivia, and Chile—the Pre-Columbian agriculturists domesticated two species of peppers, *C. pubescens* (*rocoto/locoto*) and *C. baccatum* var. *pendulum* (Andean *Ají*) and many other plants which were to make a difference after their introduction to the Old World following the conquest of their place of origin by the Spaniards. It was in 1533, twelve

years after Spanish triumphs in Mexico, that other Spanish conquistadores, led by the Pizarro brothers, Francisco the Conquerer and Hernando, entered Peru to begin their five-year abolishment of the Incas and their armies. Spain held control of that difficult terrain until Peruvian independence in 1821.

Probably because of that terrain, *C. pubescens* did not travel widely from its Andean homeland until early in the twentieth century, and it is still comparatively unknown outside the Western Hemisphere. It does not dry well, so it is not a good traveler. The rocoto prefers high altitudes and cool climate but cannot stand freezing. *Capsicum pubescens* is now grown in Costa Rica and the Mexican highlands.

The Andean *Ají* has ventured further afield throughout the central area of South America but until quite recently has not gone beyond that zone, although some of its varieties dry well enough to be carried about. Bolivia and Peru favor the rocoto, but the Andean *Ají* is number one in Ecuador. For the most part, Chile is beyond the tropical and sub-tropical zones naturally favored by capsicums.

THE EASTERN REGION

Before the discovery, only *Capsicum baccatum* var. *pendulum* grew naturally in parts of this area, which extends through Argentina to southern Brazil, but even then it did not extend south of the Tropic of Capricorn. In general the climate is not one that favors peppers and in pre-Columbian times the primitive natives were not agriculturists. For the most part the Europeans who have settled the area since that period came from countries where chilli peppers were not cultivated until quite recently, if at all.

BRAZIL

At the time of the Portuguese discovery of Brazil in 1500, the huge country was sparsely inhabited by stone-age people who did not practice agriculture. However, they did gather and eat wild chillies. Around 1535 the Portuguese introduced sugar plantations to the Pernambuco region where they settled first. Soon they were importing slaves from Africa because the natives proved to be unsatisfactory labor. An extensive and continuing exchange of plants and animals between the two continents began.

From its inception Brazil and Portuguese Africa had

the most intimate relations. These relations—ethnic, geographic, and cultural—continued for over three hundred years, to the time the African slave trade ended. The enormous migrations of Africans transformed Brazil into a second Guinea (Rodriques, 1965:7). In Amazonia, Portuguese policy was different from their African policy, and three of their practices transformed Brazil. They were: early imposition of the Portuguese language, interracial mixture, and conversion of the natives to Catholicism and with it social, moral, and intellectual values that are characteristic of Brazil. The Dutch captured northern Brazil in 1624 and were not driven out for about twenty years. During that period they also took the Portuguese colonies in West Africa. Without the help of the Mother Country, Brazil regained Angola and its source of slaves, and Angola became subordinate to Brazilian interests. During the eighteenth century direct commerce between India and Brazil via Angola, eliminating Lisbon, commenced. Brazil became independent of Portugal in 1822.

Africa

You will recall our discussion in the first chapter of a growing Portuguese presence on the West Coast of Africa dating from 1415 as their search for gold, slaves, and spices led them farther south along that long, uncharted coast towards the southern tip. Amid civilizations strikingly different from their own, they set about to exploit the continent in order to trade in slaves and ivory. The slave trade with the Americas, coupled with the introduction of New World foods, inaugurated a yet uncompleted cultural and economic revolution within Africa.

SUB-SAHARAN AFRICA

West Africans could have obtained the American peppers by several means. In writing about African agriculture, Marvin Miracle (1967:232) tells us that the Portuguese established friendly relations with the ruler of the Kingdom of Congo after their arrival in 1482, and

Within twenty years (1502) the Kingdom of Congo was sufficiently influenced by the Portuguese for the Pope to recognize it as a Christian state. In 1521 the son of the king of Congo, who as a boy had been sent to Portugal for education, was made the first bishop of Congo. Thus any superior crops that the Portuguese knew about at this time could easily have been introduced either by the Portuguese or by Africans sent to Portugal during this period.

The Africans, already accustomed to using the burning seeds of *Aframomum melegueta* (grains of paradise; [footnote 16, page 222]) in their food, readily accepted the fiery American capsicums, which soon supplanted that West African spice both at home and abroad (Freyre, 1966:469). After the early establishment of capsicums on the coasts of West Africa in the gardens of their trade castles and forts and on their Atlantic sugar islands, the Portuguese probably carried African grown chillies, along with the Far Eastern spices, to Lisbon and their mercantile colony in Antwerp, where much of their spice cargo was marketed (Meilink-Roelofsz & Godinho, 1962:132). In 1597 John Gerard, the English herbalist, reported that "ginnie" peppers were in England (Gerard, 1597:292). That he was not referring to *A. melegueta* is evident as he clearly describes capsicums, adding that they went from "Ginnie, India, and those parts, into Spaine and Italy: from whence wee have received seede for our English gardens." Today the most used capsicums in Africa are *Capsicum annuum* var. *annuum* of the finger-type, while *C. chinense* and the small, spontaneous *C. frutescens* are less common.

EAST AFRICA

The East African littoral is *otra cosa* (something else). Very early the Portuguese established garrisons in Mozambique and along the Swahili coast to refit and service the ships engaged in their Far Eastern seaborne trade. The Swahili coast, Somalia, and the Cape of Good Hope, however, will be considered as part of the Far East or, as the Portuguese called it, *Estado da India*.[1]

MEDITERRANEAN NORTH AFRICA

In 1492 Arabic-speaking Moslems of Mediterranean stock occupied a broad band of territory from the Black Sea to Morocco, thereby isolating Christendom from direct communication with the peoples of Asia. North Africa, a cultural world far apart from the Sub-Saharan region, was crossed by the highly cultivated Saracen Moors as they overran Spain. After their seven-hundred-year occupation of Spain, they were finally defeated by the armies of King Ferdinand and Queen Isabella. Following their loss of Spain, the routed Moors could have introduced the New World plants during their century-long flight from Spain into the Moslem world of western North Africa and from there into the rest of that domain around the Mediterranean, but it is unlikely (Wright, 1949:64).

As evidence of the early arrival of American plants in northern Africa, we find maize being cultivated in Ethiopia by 1547, and it is entirely possible the Portuguese introduced it in Ethiopian Massawa as early as 1520 via the Red Sea (Ibid:68). In the southern Balkans maize was known as Egyptian or Arabic grain. Writing in 1966, Traian Stoianovich, a Balkan economist, expressed the opinion that maize did not travel alone—where it went so went beans, squash, and I would add capsicums. The Moors' long-standing trans-Sahara gold, slave, and *melegueta* pepper trade provided another possible, but less likely, opportunity for contact with West Africa, and the American plants introduced to that coast.

The Middle East

The Middle East, a term not always satisfactory to some geographers, encompasses an area little comprehended and largely unknown by those of us in the United States. It is a territory extending from Iran to Libya and from the Sudan to Turkey, having a characteristic Mediterranean climatic regime of summer drought and winter rain (except in the extreme north and south) that sets it apart from its neighbors (Bullard, 1961:1). Until the twentieth century, this seemingly measureless area has been largely isolated from the main currents of economic and political activity, but the discovery of oil in the twentieth century changed all of that—rapidly.

Arabic, the dominant tongue, is the language of the Koran, and as such is one of the great unifying forces of the Moslem/Islamic world (Fisher, 1978:109). Long before the advent of the Portuguese, Arabic-speaking

traders and seamen were the great explorers of the Indian Ocean south to the Cape of Good Hope and north to the China Seas, as their far-flung bases on the southern China coast witness. Following the fall of the Roman Empire, the Arabs developed a vast empire with a rich scientific, literary, and artistic culture. They expanded knowledge while the lights of civilization and learning burned low in Europe during the Dark Ages. After 622 A.D., a Moslem flood raged through North Africa all the way to Spain, where it persisted for seven hundred years. It was the Moslem obstruction of the old routes to the Far East that drove the peoples of Europe to seek new directions to reach the oriental luxuries they craved, and in so doing encountered a new world. The traders of the Middle East played a leading role in the distribution of capsicums and other New World plants.

TURKEY AND THE ARABIAN CARAVAN ROUTES

Strategically situated as a bridge between Europe and Asia, ancient Turkey (Anatolia) and the courses of the Tigris and Euphrates Rivers have served as channels for the stream of humanity flowing between the East and West for ages. Barley, wheat, onions, peas, lentils, and dates are some of the important food crops first domesticated in that region, confirming a preoccupation with agriculture since prehistoric times (Barraclough, 1982:7).

The area was overrun by central Asiatic Turks riding down from Asia, who were in turn invaders, slaves, mercenaries, and adventurers, but who eventually ruled the land. Following the thirteenth-century Mongol invasion, the Turkish dynasty of the house of Ottoman, ruling through a military and religious autocracy, rose to become the major power in the fifteenth-century western world. It was they who built a unified political system on the foundation of the Arabic language and the Islamic religion.

A Turkish document, written between 1498 and 1513, mentions a New World plant, the common bean, for the first time, and by 1539 New World maize was already playing a pivotal role in that area (Johnson, 1981:130; Parry et al., 1976:89). It could have been that these first Columbian foodstuffs, including capsicums, came to Turkey from Spain via the Ottoman contacts with exiled Spanish Moors or expelled Spanish Jews, who conceivably distributed them throughout North Africa all the way to Egypt. The majority of those Jews settled in Turkey. Due to the nature of trade and the extent of warfare in that critical period, I suspect Jews were not the most likely carriers. The clandestine firearm trade between Spain and the Turks is another plausible answer.[2] The procurement of firearms caused nations that were uncompromising rivals before the world to become "blood-brothers in the privacy of the counting-house," according to anthropologist John Witthoft (1966:40).

Yet another possibility, and the most likely, is that capsicums arrived in Turkey from India or Egypt[3] via Ottoman agents traveling well-established medieval seaborne trade routes through the Persian Gulf and/ or the Red Sea, then to Venice and/or Istanbul. The northern route went from the Indian Ocean by way of Muscat, Ormuz (now Hormuz), and the Persian Gulf to Basra (al Basrah, Iraq) to Baghdad, then followed the Euphrates River to Aleppo, on to Antioch (Antakya, Turkey), and from there across or around Turkey to Istanbul or from Aleppo to the Syrian (not Libyan) port of Tripoli (later Alexandretta, now Ishenderum) and then by sea to Constantinople (Istanbul), Ragussa, or Venice. The southern route began at Aden, passing through the Red Sea to Suez and Cairo, from there by a riverless overland course to Jerusalem, Damascus, Aleppo, and on to Istanbul and/or Venice; or overland to Alexandria and thence by land or sea (Barraclough, 1982:58–59) (map 5, page 23). By whichever route, Aleppo was a key point. In 1600 Venice operated sixteen trading houses and a consular office in Aleppo, with quays at Tripoli to service the Adriatic shipping (Braudel, 1976:567; Lane, 1940:584). European traders rarely went beyond the cities at the edge of the desert (Braudel 1979:163). The realm of caravans[4] was dominated by Moslem traders.

Since Hormuz, at the strategic entrance to the Persian Gulf, was a Portuguese colony and center for trade in Arabian horses, oriental goods, Indian cottons, and spices from 1515 to 1662, there is the possibility that European and Turkish traders drawn to that center carried capsicums and other New World plants, and even the American turkey, to Anatolia. Although any of these traveling merchants could have brought them to Europe, the exchange probably resulted from

Ottoman armies following ancient trade routes of those merchants through the Persian Gulf, across Asia Minor to the Black Sea and on into the Balkans and Greece. I think the fact that Turks, like others were to do later, quickly recognized the value of American maize as food for livestock,[5] and required peasants in the occupied lands to grow it and other new food plants as provisions for both animals and men of their armed forces, explains the rapid movement of the American maize complex (Stoianovich, 1966:1039) (footnote 17, page 223).

Since Hormuz[6] was a Portuguese colony and center for trade as previously suggested, European and Turkish traders going to that center certainly took capsicums and other New World plants to Turkey. Later they were transported to Greece, Venice and the Balkans during the Ottoman invasion of Europe.

Another entryway was the ancient Malabar spice route through the Red Sea to Alexandria, Egypt, and on to Greece, Venice, and Germany. The Portuguese blockades were not completely effective in halting the trade in that narrow body of water. It was difficult to outmaneuver such ancient mariners as the skilled Moslem seafarers, who easily sailed their agile little boats across the Indian Ocean with alternate monsoons, guided by their substantial knowledge, and the use of the astrolabe or Jacob's staff. Their significant navigational skills led Islam to dominate a large part of the Old World until the fifteenth century (Braudel, 1982:412). The area around the Red Sea was part of the Turkish Empire during our period of 1492 to 1542, throughout which there was a marked revival in the Red Sea spice trade.

It is most important to note that the Flemish botanist Matthias de Lobel (1538–1616) observed that the Portuguese had introduced capsicums into Goa at a very early date and possibly began exporting them in competition with black pepper (*Piper nigrum*).[7]

For seventy-eight years Hormuz was the principal Portuguese export center[8] in Asia. In that length of time, even without motorized transportation, a lot can happen. From the conquered lands Moslem pilgrims went to all parts of the expansive Islamic world spreading their foodways. The conquerors, requiring food for their soldiers and mounts, brought seed to be grown in local gardens.

Beginning with the Italian Pietro Andrea Matthioli,

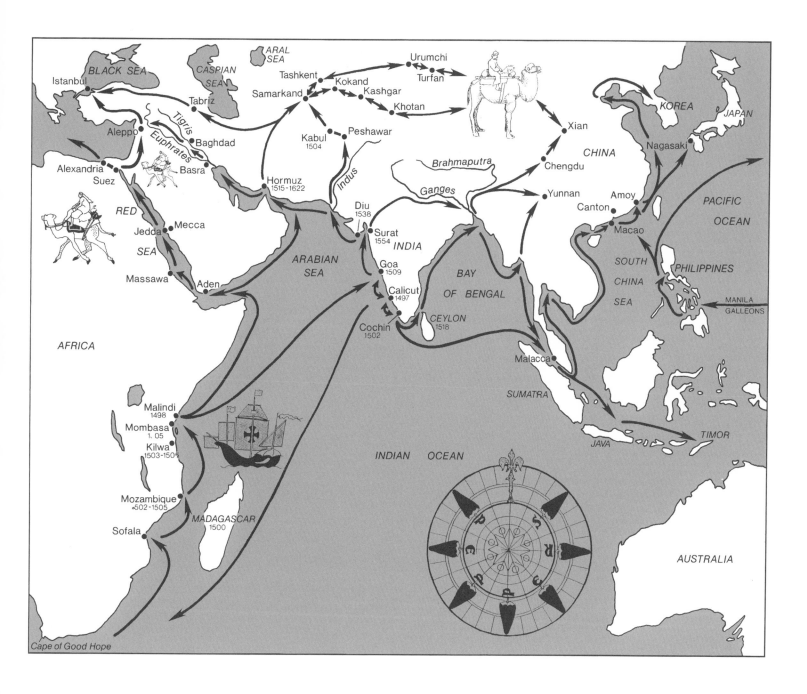

Map 5 (Diffusion Across Asia)

Once the readily accepted American capsicums had arrived with the Portuguese on the east coast of Africa and the Malabar coast of India, it was no problem for them to become a part of regular spice shipments which traveled over ancient trade routes meandering across all of Asia and the Middle East.

botanists, including Charles L'Escluse, Georg Rumpf, Carolus Linnaeus, and Phillip Miller, all considered the Americas to be the chilli pepper's place of origin. Nevertheless, Europeans in general held to an Eastern origin until Alphonse de Candolle (1827) published his reasons—linguistic and other—for accepting a New World birthplace for capsicums.[9] After the Portuguese, the Ottoman Turks[10] were probably more responsible for the early distribution (before 1565) of New World foods than any group of people. My question is not whether the Turks brought peppers to the Eastern Mediterranean and Eastern Europe. It is instead: Where did they get them?

I suggest several possibilities. The first proposed is

an improbable route from Spain via exiled Spanish Moors to Morocco, thence over Arabian trade routes through North Africa to Egypt; second, from Portuguese East Africa and India via Arabian Middle Eastern trade routes to Istanbul and Venice; third, the mysterious Albanian gun flint trade (footnote 2, page 227) fourth, from the pilgrims to Mecca; or a combination of all proposals. From my own research and travels I favor the second scenario, but to draw conclusive resolutions to the probable avenue by which peppers penetrated this area necessitates a detailed knowledge of the fifteenth- and sixteenth-century Middle East and eastern Mediterranean beyond my own.

The Far East

MONSOON ASIA

The southern and eastern part of the distant Far East is referred to as Monsoon Asia even though seasonal monsoon wind conditions do not apply to the entire area. It covers less than a seventh of the earth's land surface, yet embraces half its population and almost a third of the cultivated land in the world (Dobby, 1961:15). Some of the world's oldest civilizations are found within its boundaries, and everywhere millennia-old customs, food-habits, dress, and farming methods still prevail among the peasants. This land held the vaunted "riches of the Orient" that drove the western rulers and merchants of the fifteenth century to send their frail ships into the unknown. Those ships brought with them to the Far East the recently discovered food plants of the New World tropics which were readily established and incorporated into the cuisines of the area.

INDIA

India was a long time coming for the Portuguese. It had taken many years for them to work their way around Africa. More than three-quarters of a century had passed since they got their first toe-hold on the northwest African mainland, but now their goal had been reached. The audacious entrepreneurs would lose no time in establishing a monopoly over the Far Eastern spice trade, which they were to exploit to their advantage for the next one hundred years. Their King

Manuel[11] added to his title of "King of Portugal and of the Algarves on this side of and beyond the sea, in Africa," the pretentious rank of "Lord of Guinea and of the Conquests, Navigation, and Commerce of Ethiopia, India, Arabia, and Persia" (Hart, 1950:202).

After first landing at Calicut on the Malabar coast of India in 1498, the Portuguese quickly determined that Cochin, to the south, was a better harbor for their purposes. A bit later, they captured Goa (1510), long an important Moslem trading entrepôt, and installed their Far East headquarters in that more favorable location. As the capital of Portuguese India, Goa remained in Portuguese hands from 1509 to 1961—more than four centuries. It is visibly different from Mother India even today. Asian shipping was permitted to continue as before, provided a license was purchased and customs on the cargo were paid to the Portuguese.[12] New World economic plants—tobacco, pineapple, peanuts, henequen (source of sisal for rope), tobacco, and capsicums, to name a few—soon became a vital part of that cargo.

Coasting between Goa, Diu, Surat, or Hormuz to the Persian Gulf, or in convoys across the Arabian Sea to the Red Sea, American capsicums quickly joined the other spices following those two ancient medieval trade routes—the Aleppo and the Alexandria routes—long used by the Turks, Arabic-speaking mariners, and other Moslems to carry the lucrative trade from Monsoon Asia to the Levant; in toiling caravans the *Capsicum* travelers followed tributary Silk Roads from the Ganges delta over the Burma Road, or from the commercial center of Kabul on the caravan road from Turkey and Persia at the head of the Indus River to China; and they also sailed the sea lanes to Malacca and Indonesia used by coasting Chinese, Gujarati, and Arabic traders—these were some of the routes over which the New World foods traveled. Those new foods melded into the principally vegetarian cuisines of China, India, Indonesia, and other areas of the Far East.

Unlike Spain, Portugal did not yearn to establish an empire on land; her goal was a seaborne empire based on control of the seas and friendly relations with rulers (Greenlee, 1937:xxxiii). They made no attempt at extensive inland conquests; yet, such an empire as they coveted still required garrisons, factories, and support facilities at strategic spots along the various coasts.

Within their Goan headquarters, India's Portuguese invaders had among them not only conquerors and traders but also missionaries who set forth to make good Roman Catholics out of the local "heathens" (Elton, 1962:609). Those faithful Jesuits carried seeds for their mission gardens wherever it was their fate to be sent and we can rest assured they didn't forget them when they went to India, for one of their routines was to introduce the cultivation of maize, and surely its *Capsicum* companion, as a means of gaining the trust of the indigenous peoples (Boxer, 1952:179). The missionaries were also involved in trade as a means of supporting their work.

The pungent new American spice was welcomed by Indian cooks who, at home with biting black pepper and piquant ginger, were accustomed to sharp, spicy foods. The easily cultivated and naturalizing varieties of *Capsicum annuum* var. *annuum* and *C. frutescens* were, for them, a lot more heat with a lot less grinding and expense; they also grew readily and fruited abundantly in a sympathetic environment. Into the curries they went.

CEYLON, MALAYSIA, INDONESIA, THAILAND

The Buddhist island of Ceylon (Sri Lanka), populated today with Sinhalese, was of strategic importance on the oceanic trade routes of early Monsoon Asia. It has, in turn, been Portuguese, Dutch, and British before gaining its independence; however, the latter two occupying forces did not put out the fire that the Portuguese had ignited. Food in Sri Lanka is very pungent.

Islam, introduced by Arab traders at an early date, reached the eastern monsoon area long before American capsicums. Although it seems at least twenty years tardy, 1540 is the only recorded date I have yet to find for the arrival of New World capsicums in the East Indies (Indonesia) by way of the Arab and Gujarati traders—who had been active in Southeast Asia for a thousand years—and/or the overpowering Portuguese (Ridley, 1930:396). Moslem ships, sailing between Malaccan waters and the Persian Gulf or Red Sea, regularly frequented Atzeh, at the tip of Sumatra. Since 1511, Malacca had served as a forward base for Portuguese trading and missionary expansion into China, Japan, Thailand, and eastern Melanesia, and by 1550 the Portuguese had a permanent base at Macao

on the south China coast. Their *Nao da Macao*, the trading galleon romanticized in the novel *Shogun*, ran from Goa via Malacca to Macao and thence to Nagasaki, Japan, until the mid-seventeenth century. From any of these Portuguese ports of call, local seagoing craft—Malaccan, Javanese, Siamese, Cambodian, and Chinese, as well as Indian and Arabic—could easily have carried American peppers throughout the East Indies and the Spice Islands (Moluccas)—even to the Philippines and China. The chillies might also have been found about the same time at the Arab and Persian trading colonies which had been established during the seventh and eighth centuries in Canton and Hangchow, on China's southeast coast.

It has been suggested that dried or fresh chillies were taken as a condiment or food by sailors and inhabitants of the monsoon area, who inadvertently spread the seed when they stopped for meals (footnote 25, page 224). Native navigators who found the New World plants in Portuguese and later Spanish ports of Melanesia, Indonesia, the Philippines and Guam carried them from island to island. Not to be outdone, the birds hopped in. Even today flocks of pigeons descend from the mountains to feed on ripe red capsicums, thus carrying seed to remote places (Ridley, 1930:396). Though some Pacific islands were inaccessible to early sailors, few are so remote that chilli seeds could not have been deposited there by birds (Proctor, 1968:321). In any case, the capsicums soon spread in cultivation throughout that tropical area and then escaped from gardens to become naturalized in the wild, where they have been so successful and their adoption by the inhabitants of the zone is so complete that only recently do present occupants of the region even consider the suggestion that chillies are not indigenous to that area. Today, these people are born with capsaicin in their veins.

After the Dutch ousted the Portuguese from the Far Eastern spice world they were in command of the area for almost 350 years. During that time an early Dutch governor, Georg Rumpf, made significant observations of the peppers on Amboine (Rumphius, 1741–50(5):248). There was, however, no significant Dutch influence on the local cuisines.

Southwestern China[13]

The Chinese are considered by anthropologist Berthold Laufer to be the foremost masters of plant economy in the world, with all useful plants of the universe being cultivated there (Laufer, 1919:189). During the Ming dynasty of the sixteenth century, the Chinese were contemplative, intelligent, and broadminded people with an active foreign policy, who seldom rejected whatever good things foreigners offered. Considering communications and travel time in the sixteenth century, it took but a brief time for the American economic plants newly introduced to India by the Portuguese to have been added to the baggage carried northward so laboriously from the Gangetic Delta at the Bay of Bengal through Burma to Chendu in Sichuan over what is now known as the Burma Road, or to have followed the Brahmaputra River (Gode, 1960:290) from the Ganges to Sikkim, Bhutan, and Tibet, and finally from there across the border into Sichuan without interference of European nations (Laufer, 1907:224). They also could have traveled from the Indian Ocean up the Indus River to Afghan Kabul, to join the historic course followed by Marco Polo, winding its toilsome way through northern Pakistan to China. Yet another perilous route from the Indian Ocean began at Portuguese Diu and Surat on the Gulf of Cambay, from which the path followed rivers that were tributaries to the Ganges, winding its course to the mountainous bed of the Brahmaputra River, which flowed up and across the Himalayas to Sichuan (map 5, page 23).

It was over these torturous trails that emissaries, emperors, Arabic and Indian traders, religious pilgrims, and ordinary men came and went for centuries. Ancient Ming dynastic records show the origin of New World food plants in China to be the territory northwest of Tibet bordering Sichuan known as *Si-fan* (Hance & Mayers, 1870:523). Here again, within the lifetime of the conquistadors (about 1492 to about 1550), American food plants took root in Chinese soil. Alfred W. Crosby, Jr., declares that "No other large group of the human race in the Old World was quicker to adopt American food plants than the Chinese" (Crosby, 1972:199). American capsicums and tomatoes not only helped revolutionize the taste of cooking in the southwestern area of China, but they also supplied rich, new sources of vitamins C and A and specific minerals, thereby improving the diet. After their introduction, seasonal dietary deficiencies were no longer a major problem, as vital nutrients were now available during most of the year (Anderson & Anderson, 1977:329).

Southeastern China, with its ports in Fukien, including Canton and Amoy, had intimate trade relations with the Portuguese for at least thirty-five years before the founding of the Portuguese trading colony at Macao in 1550, and later with the Spanish colonies in the Philippines (Boxer, 1953:xx, xxxv). Coastal Chinese did not fail to notice and incorporate the valuable new plants the *Fo-land-chi* (Portuguese) had brought to Asia, but, during the Ming dynasty, there were no roads from their seaports to carry those new foodstuffs six hundred miles to Sichuan. As a consequence, peppers entered China two ways—to the east by sea, and to the southwest by overland routes (Ho, 1955:195).

East Asia

JAPAN

The Portuguese sailed to feudal Japan around 1549 and opened those islands to New World foodstuffs. With the annual voyage of the *Nao de Macao,* from Goa via Malacca to Macao and thence to Nagasaki, Japan, an interchange went on until 1636, nearly one hundred years, when Japan closed its doors to all except the Dutch and Chinese (Muroga, 1967:96; Latourette, 1964:234). Even if the Portuguese were not the actual carriers of the *Capsicum* to Japan, the Japanese themselves could have encountered it on their regular and long established trading forays into Southeast Asia. Modeling their ships after Spanish vessels seen in the Philippines, Japanese mariners even sailed across the Pacific to New Spain (Mexico) before Spain slammed that gateway in 1611, causing Japanese envoys to return from missions to Mexico from the port of Acapulco aboard Spain's Acapulco-Manila galleon (Nuttall, 1906:46).

KOREA

From its isolated location on a peninsula west of Japan, you would hardly think of Korea as a hot spot, but according to the per capita consumption of chillies it is the hottest spot on the *Capsicum* trail (Govindarajan, et al., 1987:189). Korea took no part in the spice trade either before or during the era of that exotic commerce. The first account of Korea was brought to the outside world twelve years after a 1653 Dutch shipwreck on the coast of Korea by some of the crew who finally made their way to Japan (Winchester, 1988:19). We still know little of daily life in Korea.

The first inkling the Koreans had that an advanced and civilized world existed beyond China was a map brought to Seoul from Peking by a Korean diplomat in 1606. The first physical contact Koreans had with Europeans was also in Peking, where Portuguese Jesuit missionaries were hard at their job of converting the "heathen" to the Roman Catholic form of Christianity. A lone Dutch seaman was shipwrecked on the Korean coast in 1627. He lived there and taught the military how to make cannons but he never had contact with another European. Books were the first European import into Korea in 1644 by way of Peking, but later the missionaries themselves went. New World plants would have had to come the same way.

Europe

I feel certain that chillies came to Europe from several directions and by various carriers, but after I present a few more puzzling facts of the case, you can decide for yourself or use the information to ferret out a better solution.

Unlike the peoples of Africa and the Far East, the Europeans first saw the American food complex—maize, beans, squash—as feed for livestock. I propose that the Middle Eastern traders recognized the new "corn" as potential fodder. After the Turks acquired maize, they had it grown in garrison gardens by peasants in the expanding Ottoman Empire as feed for the vast numbers of animals required to transport their huge armies and essential supplies, then later for the troops and peasants themselves. As a result it became established in the newly conquered territories—Arabia, Greece, the Balkans, Egypt, North Africa, and Sicily. After the Turkish armies departed, the peasants in those lands continued to grow these crops in their own gardens, not only because they produced more

than their native crops, but also because they were still unknown to the noble landowners and hence untaxed. *Capsicum* peppers traveled in the same baggage train and were grown in the same gardens as the traditional Turkish staples.

Keep in mind that in early sixteenth-century Europe, the peasant majority received its basic food supply from communally cultivated cereal crops. These were supplemented by new "garden" crops. New crops could be tried out in gardens around the house. Only after a crop proved successful in the garden was it allowed space in the communal fields. Virtually no records of garden crops were kept, so this important part of agriculture is a dark spot in the early history of agriculture (Pounds, 1979:34). It is highly probable that the New World plants such as maize, sunflower, potato, and tobacco were first grown in the peasant's home garden. Peppers were, and still are for most of the world, a garden crop.

THE BALKANS

The Turkish military conquest, led by Suleimán the Magnificent, of the wealthy but divided Balkan peninsula, was the prelude to the introduction of the pungent red pepper which is known as spice-paprika in that region. During our "critical period" in *Capsicum* history, the Ottomans took Belgrade (1521), Rhodes (1522), Hungary (1526), and stood before Vienna (1529) before being stopped. A vast area that included not only the Balkans but North Africa, Egypt, and Syria, as well as Asia Minor, was under the domination of the Ottoman Empire until the Mediterranean Sea battle of Lepanto (1571) ended its advances. As previously mentioned, Turkish military policy required the peasants of occupied lands to cultivate garrison gardens which produced the food needed for the multitude of men and herds of animals in the army, and it was no different here.[14] Some authors believe maize was being grown in the Balkans by 1520–1530. This may well be so, for maize had become entrenched in the folklore of the region by the beginning of the eighteenth century (Stoianovich, 1966:1035). We are told by the French historian Fernand Braudel (1976:665) that the establishment of a system to provision the army was followed by another equally important, but less rigid requirement, which was "the construction of roads and fortified posts, the organization

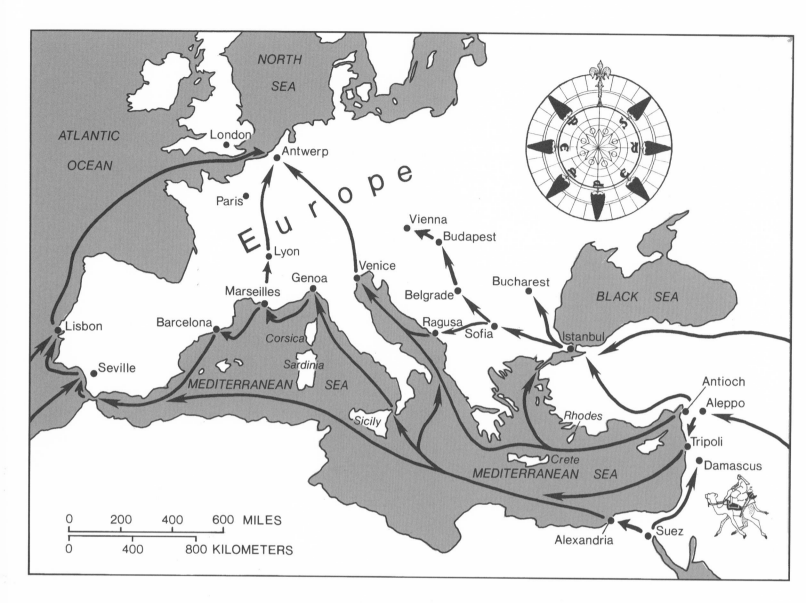

Map 6 (The Spice and Silk Trade Routes
to Europe 1492–1600)

*The sixteenth-century eastern routes from Asia to
European markets traversed by New World foods which
had been introduced into India by the Portuguese after
1497.*

of camel trains, the setting in motion of all the supply
and transport convoys," and finally the transmission of
Turkish civilization to the conquered. Over these supply routes came the treasures of Asia, as well as New
World foods.

By the middle of our critical time frame (1492–
1542), the Portuguese dominated the sea lanes of the
Indian Ocean and Hormuz—which functioned as the
center for the seaborne goods destined for Persia and
the rest of the Middle East. At the same time, the Venetians considered the hazardous sea voyage from the
Adriatic to Egypt to be the main impediment to their
trading endeavors in the Turkish dominated Mediterranean (Braudel, 1976:668). Thus, it would seem the
Persian Gulf route, or overland from the Red Sea to
Aleppo, would be the more likely *Capsicum* trails to
the Balkans. Aleppo was the great spice center which
supplied Istanbul and Venice.

Contrary to what appears to be the obvious route—America to Spain to Europe—I suggest that capsicums arrived in Europe by two separate routes. The first was the traditonal western route used by the Iberians going directly to Antwerp from the peninsula by sea. The Portuguese brought goods to Lisbon from the Far East, Africa, and their Atlantic islands, then took them to market in Antwerp; while the Spanish took their shipments from America to Seville, then on to Genoa or Antwerp. The second course went to eastern Europe via Venice or Istanbul, having been brought to those centers from the Far East by Moslem traders following ancient pathways (map 6, page 28).

Iberians and Western Europeans may have been familiar with American peppers, but they did not appreciate their spice value until long after the pod's mid-sixteenth-century introduction to the Balkans. It took the Napoleonic blockade of European ports in the first decade of the nineteenth century to put them on the table when they were reintroduced from Hungary and the Balkans as a substitute for more favored imported spices being denied entrance.

As the sixteenth century began, Pounds informs us, Europeans obtained their spices in this way:

> They came from south-eastern Asia either by the overland or the oceanic route to respectively Venice or Lisbon. Venetian spices were distributed mainly by the Alpine routes to central and western Europe, and only occasionally by galley to western ports. The Portuguese spices were distributed by sea, most going to Antwerp for redistribution in northern Europe. (Pounds, 1979:58)

Cane-sugar from India or Arabia was sold along with spices which usually passed through Venice to Germany on the way to markets in Flanders (Antwerp). Such reports would appear to reaffirm one of our proposed eastern Mediterranean entry routes. The western route is not in doubt.

The Venetian fleet, Europe's link with the Levant,[15] controlled the entire Adriatic after 1000 A.D. By virtue of the first three Crusades, Venice[16] acquired exclusive trading rights in the Near East, and the crusaders acquired a craving for spices and other Oriental goods.

Venice became owner of the strategic island of Corfu in 1386, thereby gaining control of the Adriatic because to enter or leave the Adriatic meant sailing past Corfu. As a consequence, shipping tended to concentrate there (Braudel, 1976:126). The major part of the spices and other oriental goods going to Venice was obtained at Aleppo. Recall that by the seventeenth century, Venice had a consular office and many trading houses in Aleppo, along with quays at Tripoli to service her cargo ships. The risky voyage to the more distant Alexandria was undertaken less frequently. Whether the source was Aleppo or Alexandria, Venice got her spices and trade goods from the Turks, who got them directly from India or from the Far East via India or Egypt over the Red Sea or North Africa. Peppers did not appear in Venice as an immaculate conception. From the twelfth century until the sixteenth, when the Portuguese arrived in India, Venice had a long-standing monopoly on the transport and distribution of black pepper, the basic spice, picking it up in eastern Mediterranean ports after its arrival from India and sent over the Alps to Germany or by mule-train across the Italian peninsula to Genoa.[17] But between 1520 and 1542 the Portuguese were in a position to prevent passage through the Straits of Gibraltar to Venetian galleys on their way to the Atlantic ports of Europe (Parry, 1953:143). Consequently, trade between the eastern and western Mediterranean was practically nil during our critical time frame. The shrewd merchants of Venice were no figment of Shakespeare's imagination.

The Turkish control of the eastern Mediterranean and the Middle East was so complete and her market so large that it prompted a Portuguese spy in Egypt to report, "there being so much which comes to the dominion of the Turks, it is no wonder that so little comes to Lisbon." In fact, towards the middle of the century the Portuguese even considered contracting with the Turks to have the spices for the king of Portugal brought through the Levant (Lane, 1940:585).

In 1535 Gonzalo Oviedo (1851:551) wrote that capsicums had been carried to Italy and Spain, and in 1542 Leonhart Fuchs (1543:cclxxxi) was the first herbalist to report that capsicums were cultivated in Germany, where they were grown in pots. According to English herbalist William Turner (1538:63), they were in England before 1548; author Zoltan Halasz (1963:24) finds them in the Balkans before 1569; and botanist Carolus L'Éscluse (1611:104) found them in Moravia by 1585. Evidently believing that the foreign *Capsicum* plants had come to Europe from India, Fuchs called a long finger-type *Indianischer pfeffer* (Indian Pepper), a bulbous-shaped one *Greyter Indianischer pfeffer* (Greater Indian Pepper), and a more or less conical pod *Calechutischer pfeffer* (Calicut Pepper). He also made one reference to *Piper Hispanum*, Spanish pepper, which was not illustrated. Could the *Hispanum* have come with the Spanish-Albanian gun flint trade and the others with Indian spices? These names imply that he considered them to be native to that port where the Portuguese first entered India. Even today, in Calicut, the Tamil-speaking populace call the dry, red finger-type chillies *kappal molakai*,[18] which translates as "the pepper from the ship" or "the ship's pepper." In a letter written in 1569 they were referred to as *Türkisch rot pfeffer* (Turkish red pepper) (Hálasz, 1963:24). Fernand Braudel (1976:543) affirms that Fuchs's Germany received spices and pepper from Venice. The Venetians got them from the Middle Eastern spice centers which, in turn, got them from India.

To repeat as emphasis, it is here proposed that Europe received capsicums through more than one avenue in addition to the long-held assumption that the Spanish brought them to the Iberian peninsula in 1492, from whence they traveled to all of Europe, the Mediterranean area and the world. The second possibility is here proposed that the Portuguese acquired pepper seeds and other American seeds very soon after the discovery from an as-yet undocumented source, either in Iberia, the Azores, or the Canaries—one of those wind-determined points where sailing ships of all nations must go when crossing the Atlantic Ocean. The Portuguese then introduced them to their outposts in tropical West Africa and the nearby islands where they were growing sugar, and there the new seed immediately took root. From there they carried them to the Malabar Coast of India and thence throughout their Far Eastern trading sphere. Although the geographer Carl Sauer was on a different chase, his statement supports my thesis:

We may therefore consider the alternative that the German herbalists were competent describers and did know what they were talking about.

The South German towns were intermediaries in the great trade from North Italian ports, especially Venice, across the Alps to the Rhine and its tributaries; knowledge as well as goods flowed mainly out of the South into High Germany. Venice in particular was built on the Levantine trade, through which it rose to greatest wealth and power in the fifteenth century, at which time there were Venetian factories and colonies in number extending from the Adriatic to the easternmost Mediterranean. Venice had the closest contacts with the Ottoman Empire both before and after the fall of Byzantium. Nowhere in Europe were things "Turkish" so well known as in Venice. Nowhere north of the Alps was Venetian knowledge as well disseminated as in South Germany. . . . Cultivated seed plants originating in the New World are more significant in the eastern end of the Mediterranean and in Italy than they are in Spain, and seem to have been so as far back as there is knowledge of them. (Sauer, 1952:150–51)

If Sauer had continued by saying that the Ottomans acquired their cultivated New World seed plants through the long established trade with the west coast of India and the east coast of Africa, or from Egypt[19] and the north African route after they had been introduced to those regions by the Portuguese and Spanish Moors, I could rest my case—if it were not for the annoying complication posed by all those Amerindians lying dead in their homelands from shots fired with Albanian gun flints during my "critical period" (footnote 2, page 227).

In England during the Middle Ages, the Indian peafowl (*Pavo cristatus*) was called "turkey-cock," probably because it had been introduced to eastern Europe by the Turks. Some writers have proposed that any large bird that spread its tail like a peafowl was called "turkey." Accordingly, the large, spreading American bird (*Meleagris gallopavo*), which was introduced to western Europe through Spain, would have been dubbed turkey.[20] I don't completely agree, because the French name for that noble bird is *dinde,* from *d'Inde* meaning "from India" (not from the West Indies),[21] and the Turkish word for the same bird is *hindi* (from India), which may or may not be similar misapplications. Those names, however, point towards the west coast of India as being where the Turks got the big bird (footnote 20, page 228). Because the distribution of the turkey from Spain, after its introduction there in 1511, is well documented, many are unable to accept any other point of distribution (Schorger, 1966:11, 464). But couldn't the big bird have arrived by both eastern and western routes? The French words for peppers—*poivre d'Inde* and *poivre du Brézil*[22]—used at the time the turkey words arose, are not considered inappropriate. My guess is that the French acquired many new American foods, including peppers, not only from Spain but also from the Venetians, who got them from the Turks, who got them from India where the Portuguese had brought them.

In addition to spices, Venetians bought grain from the Turks. Warring Venice, in urgent need of the grain supplies from Ottoman lands, "was suffering from a dearth of corn"[23] (Parry et al., 1976:89). New World beans, maize, and squash were established in Ottoman lands before 1542 (Johnson, 1981:131). Why not capsicums too? They probably were, but because they were not as important to the economy as those staple crops, their presence was not recorded in the highly organized tax records kept by the Ottoman Turks.

SPAIN AND PORTUGAL

Fifteenth- and sixteenth-century Spanish and Portuguese peoples had differing attitudes toward agriculture, which may have contributed to the Portuguese having a greater influence on the world-wide distribution of American food plants than the Spanish, even though the Spanish received them first. According to ethno-botanist Edgar Anderson, "The Portuguese had a highly specialized horticulture, an enthusiasm for unusual vegetables in fine variety, and a special flair for agricultural botany; while the Spanish exhibited aristocratic disdain for the dirty details of vegetable growing" (Anderson, 1958:16). ¿*Quien sabe*?

The early French botanist, Carolus L'Éscluse, on a visit to Spain in 1564, saw the "American *Capsicum* where women had pepper plants hanging in the entrance to their gardens throughout the entire year. The fruit has various shapes and is used both fresh and dry as condiments." In Portugal he also found many types being cultivated at the monastery of Ulysitton on the banks of the Tagus River. Some of those were "en-

dowed with a yellow color," and were so hot that "the sharpness would burn the jaws for several days" (L'Éscluse, 1611:104).

ITALY AND THE MEDITERRANEAN

Although in 1535,[24] thirty-seven years after the discovery of America, at a time when Spain was in control of western Italy and traded in Genoa, the chronicler Gonzalo de Oviedo recorded that capsicums were "carried to Spain and Italy," they were not actually used there as food to any extent until much later. At first most were grown in pots as rarities. Later the larger sweet *Capsicum* probably went to the Italian peninsula along with the tomato, which was recorded by the Italian herbalist Pietro Matthioli in 1554. *Capsicums* were shown in a painting by an anonymous follower of the Italian painter Meresi da Caravaggio in 1607[25] (Spike, 1983:41–42).

During the reign of Charles V (1519–1558), the people of Spain did not eat capsicums as did their more adventurous kinsmen in America, so it is unlikely that they carried those first capsicums with them in their journeys throughout the Spanish kingdom of the Hapsburgs, which encompassed not only Spain and the Netherlands but also the southern half of the Italian peninsula, including Naples. Although the Mediterranean peoples could have cultivated capsicums sometime after the introduction of the more acceptable Mexican varieties, they did not adopt them or the tomato as a part of their cuisine for two hundred years (Grewe, 1987:73–74).

Geographically and, at the time of the discovery, politically, the Mediterranean was effectively divided into two parts by Sicily and the Italian peninsula. The eastern half was dominated by Islamic peoples and the western half by Christians. Venice was dependent upon the Turks for her spices and wheat, while Florence and Genoa relied on the Iberians for imported goods (Braudel, 1976:557). Communication between the two halves was slow because Venice had few commercial connections to Lisbon, and trade between the eastern and western basins of the Mediterranean was at a virtual stand-still. In the Western Mediterranean, Genoa traded with Bruges in Belgium. The two poles of Western European commerce were Italy and the Netherlands, the latter with Antwerp as its market center (Braudel, 1982:419).

For centuries the Mediterranean, bustling with maritime commerce along its littoral, had been the highway to the Levant, with long-established trade and affiliations. The ships of the western Christians used the Straits of Messina to enter the eastern part, while the eastern Islamic ships passed through the Sicilian Channel to go west. There were also continuous mule trains transporting goods across the Italian peninsula from one coast to the other. In spite of this exchange, the two halves of the sea maintained their sovereignty, and their own spheres of influence organized into closed circuits. Between the middle of the fifteenth and sixteenth centuries Spanish imperialism gained control of the western sea. By contrast, the eastern Mediterranean was the Ottoman sea. These two parts of the Mediterranean, commanded by warring rulers, were physically, economically, and culturally different from each other (Braudel, 1976:135).

Trade and travel brought Catalans into contact with people in other parts of the western Mediterranean. Naples, Sardinia, Sicily, Spain, and much of the western Mediterranean were unified under Ferdinand the Catholic after his fleet captured Naples in 1516. From this strengthened position Ferdinand could stand as a bulwark against the advance of Islam. As a result of the Ottoman naval offensive within the fixed time limits of our survey (1492–1542) there was virtually no trade or interchange between Spain—including the eastern coast of its Neapolitan Territories—and those areas under the Ottoman empire (Coles, 1968:92). I contend that such a situation precluded the introduction of peppers to Venice and the Balkans directly from Spain during this period. Interchange between the eastern and western halves of the Mediterranean slowly resumed with the decline of the Ottoman Empire, but capsicums had been in Europe more than a quarter of a century by then.

The daughter of Ferdinand and Isabella, Joanna, married the short-lived Hapsburg, Philip I. Joanna's son was Charles of Ghent, King of Spain (1516–1556), who became Charles V, Emperor of Austria and Spain (1519–1558), grandson of the Spanish sovereigns. He had little time for Spain, but after 1535 the riches of his grandparent's New World, pouring in through Seville, became a major consideration of the Austrian Hapsburgs. (Now you understand why I saw Moctezuma's feathered headdress and other Aztec treasures in the museums of Vienna and not in Madrid.) Although the contacts between Spain and Germany were strong during the long reign of Charles, they did not produce any recorded plant introductions from Spain to Germany. In 1580 Spain and Portugal were united under Phillip II, the son of Charles V and great-grandson of Columbus's sponsors—Ferdinand and Isabella. The two Iberian powers were merged for the following sixty years.

Although the Turks got a grip on the heel of the Italian boot during this same period, I do not think that they introduced capsicums to the Italian Peninsula or acquired capsicums from Italy at that time or place. I believe sweet capsicums and tomatoes[26] came to western Italy from Spain[27] for several reasons. First, the historic record of western Mediterranean trade links Seville and Barcelona with the southern half of Italy (formerly Naples) and Sicily. (This is the part of Italy where the use of sweet capsicums and tomatoes predominates today.) Second, the pungent capsicums (spice-paprika) the Turks carried to the Balkans were not that sweet *Capsicum* type which came to be favored by both Italian and Spanish cooks. Finally, the method of cooking with capsicums and other spices in the Balkans is more Indian in nature, while that of the western Mediterranean is unique to that region (Parry et al., 1976:86).

ENGLAND

Although during the Victorian age spicy Indian food was in vogue, England does not have a peppery cuisine. It was nevertheless a vital stop on this round-the-world journey of the pod. It has not been possible thus far to determine through documented evidence how it was that capsicums arrived in England by 1548. We know that British[28] trade with either the West or the East Indies was not established at that time, so capsicums must have been exported to England from Europe. The English could have acquired the seed from Spain or in the nearby port of Antwerp, the crossroads of Europe, where considerable Portuguese and Spanish mercantile enterprises flourished at that time. Spain and the Netherlands, which included Antwerp, were united in the Hapsburg Empire. We have seen that sugar and spices came from India, through Germany and Antwerp on their way to Great Britain, so why not peppers? In 1548 the English herbalist William Turner mentions capsicums: "In englishe Indishe [from India] peper, and the duche indisshouer [from India] pfefer." John Gerard, a later British herbalist, wrote in 1597 that the peppers being grown in pots in England were "ginnie peppers," indicating they had come from west Africa. Evidently, the peppers which came to England were not directly of American origin.

Capsicums straight from Spain were also a prospect. The first of Henry VIII's wives was Katharine of Aragon, another daughter of Ferdinand and Isabella. Although the widowed Katharine did not marry Henry until 1509, she had come to England in 1501 to marry his short-lived brother, bringing with her a retinue of one hundred and fifty, which included cooks, bakers, and carvers. This Spanish connection continued for more than thirty years, until her death.[29]

John Frampton, an English merchant, in his translation of the Spaniard Nicholas Monardes's herbal, refers to the close relationship that existed between England and Spain when he remarks, "the afore saied Medicines . . . are now by Marchauntes and others brought out of the West Indias into Spaine, and from Spain (Iberia) thether into Englande, by suche as dooeth daiely traffike thether" (Monardes, 1574:4). Also, the Portuguese could have brought them via Iberia to England, as there is a report of five Portuguese ships tied up at Falmouth, England, in 1504, heavily loaded with black pepper and spices from Calicut (Braudel, 1976:544). It was, regardless, from English gardens that our world-traveling *Capsicum* returned to the Western Hemisphere.

Anglo America

Except in the two Spanish colonies of Santa Fe, New Mexico, and Saint Augustine, Florida, the introduction of domesticated capsicums into Anglo-America north of Mexico—which at that time included Texas and the southwestern states—took place after the early years of distribution, 1492–1600. Nevertheless, I think we would be remiss not to look at our own territory. Today we can enjoy a wide variety of capsicums in a plethora of peppery dishes offered by our indigenous Tex-Mex, Southwestern, Creole/Cajun, and nouvelle cuisines, about which reams have been written. A number of our contributing chefs are among those who have pioneered and/or written about the peppery foods of the United States.

Both the British and the Dutch had ample sources for capsicums by the time they began to colonize continental Anglo-America in 1607. Red peppers, along with other food plants, arrived in Bermuda from England on the good ship *Elizabeth* in 1613. On December 2, 1621, Captain Nathaniel Butler, governor of the Bermudas, sent the governor of Virginia large cedar chests, "wherein were fitted all such kindes and sortes of the country plants and fruicts, as Virginia at that time and until then had not, as figgs, pomegranates, oranges, lemons, plantanes, sugar canes, potatoe, and cassada rootes, papes [papaya], **red-pepper**, the pritle peare [prickly pear], and the like" (Laufer, 1929:242, emphasis added). Peppers were also brought into the Dutch settlements in Pennsylvania early in the eighteenth century by Dutch trading vessels plying between their West Indian and North American colonies. Also, the French brought peppers from their Caribbean colonies and Guiana to their American territory at the mouth of the Mississippi River. In spite of these early records, capsicums did not take hold in the thirteen colonies until later, when the plantation system and African slavery were introduced. Chillies were still curiosities in 1785 when George Washington grew two kinds of them in his Mount Vernon, Virginia, botanical garden. The plantations in the southern colonies had a climate more suitable for the cultivation of capsicums, and the African slaves, both from the West Indies and directly from Africa, had already developed a diet that demanded chillies. Chillies probably came with shipments of slaves or on trading vessels from the West Indies.

A small still-life painting by the American artist Raphael Peale records green bell peppers in Philadelphia in 1814. And so capsicums traveled from the New World to the Old World and back again to the western hemisphere. My account is incomplete, and like all chronological reports may mistake appearance for reality. It cannot be claimed that all the questions concerning the circulation of chillies are settled, but they have been highlighted. It is hoped someone will accept the challenge to further trace the perilous passage of the peerless pod. In the meantime, let's see how that peregrination affected the cuisines of the lands it touched.

Hot Spots Today

he real hot spots in today's world of peppery food are Mexico, Guatemala, much of the Caribbean, most of Africa, parts of South America, India, Malaysia, Thailand, Indonesia, southwestern China, the Balkans, the United States (Louisiana, Texas, and the Southwest), plus Korea. In these places capsicums are consumed on a meal-to-meal basis. In fact, a fourth of the adult population of the world uses pungent chillies in their food daily. There are other areas—in North America and parts of Europe—where sweet or mildly pungent capsicums are commonly used as part of the daily fare, but more as a vegetable or an occasional condiment. The popularity of peppery foods is growing so much throughout the world that suppliers find it difficult to keep up with the demand.

We have followed the probable trail of the captivating *Capsicum* and can see that it forms pathways girdling the equator and spreading north and south through the tropics and subtropics in a wide pan-tropical belt (map on end pages). To understand why intensive use of the tropical peppers is typical in those warm climes requires a look at the food patterns of the inhabitants of *Capsicum's* natural habitat—the tropics. I won't go into a detailed account of the cuisine of each hot spot; that has already been done in other food books,

but I will look at some generalized patterns of cuisines and meals, resulting, I hope, in a better understanding of why *Capsicum* cookery is the way it is.

Culinary behavior, the deliberate processing of a foodstuff for the purpose of changing it in some calculated manner, has occurred in all cultures throughout human history, yet everyone does it differently. This personal method or style of culinary behavior is what we call cuisine (E. Rozin, 1982:190). Partaking of a cuisine different from your own is, in essence, a culinary handshake introducing you to another culture.

A cuisine is one of the most characteristic and least complicated expressions of a culture. It consists of a limited number of foods; there is an established and repetitive way of flavoring the basic components; it prefers certain methods of preparation; and it is eaten according to prescribed rules, revealing the beliefs of a society, both positive and negative (Sorre, 1962:450). Some limitations, such as food taboos, result in the group not utilizing all the food that nature has placed at its disposal. A cuisine is essentially very conservative and resistant to change (Farb & Armelagos, 1980:190). Notwithstanding that conservatism, new foods are regularly added by preparing the new food with the habitual seasonings, and/or using time-honored cooking techniques. For example, Indian curries had been around for hundreds of years before America was discovered, but chillies were readily incorporated, becoming the dominant seasoning in a rather intricate flavor principle.[1]

In my travels through the lands where peppery cookery dominates, I have noted a pattern in every locale, be it Africa, Mexico, India, China, Sri Lanka, Indonesia, South America, Thailand, Yemen, or Bhutan. What I began to realize—and want to emphasize—as I savored the local dishes, is that there is always a basic starch which governed the local cookery (Super, 1985:2–3). It is difficult for those of us in the modern Western World to comprehend that the cookery of most of the rest of the world is based on a single, staple food, which is eaten every day at every meal (Coe, 1994:115). The dominant starch could be rice, maize, yams, manioc, wheat, barley, potatoes, or whatever starch food was native to the area, that is eaten with a sauce (stew, gravy, ragout, curry) containing legumes, vegetables, and occasionally a little meat. The sauce differed from place to place according to the spices, herbs, and amount of chilli used to season it. The meals were primarily vegetarian, either by choice or by necessity.

Based on evidence of their cultivation as early as 7,000 to 5,000 B.C., or at least seven thousand years ago, capsicums are apparently the earliest spice used by humankind. The use of Middle Eastern saffron came a little later, and black pepper, ginger, and turmeric in India did not begin for another 3,000 to 4,000 years (Govidarajan, et al., 1987:185). Plants of the genus *Capsicum,* indigenous to the American tropics, were introduced to the subtropics in the western hemisphere in pre-Columbian times. At the beginning of the sixteenth century, when capsicums were introduced by Europeans to similar environmental conditions in the tropics and subtropics of the Old World, the American pepper quickly became pantropic.

The natives of those torrid regions were accustomed to eating spicy foods to spark up their bland starch and legume diet, but their own spices were costly to produce and to use. The new spice was welcomed because it produced fruit within a short time and it yielded practically year-round. In addition, the seeds had a relatively long period of viability and were very simple to transport. The dried fruit also shipped and stored easily and was therefore inexpensive and readily available, even to the poorest; also it could be grown in the home garden. A little went a long way. These factors helped it to quickly spread worldwide throughout the tropics and subtropics.

Food Taboo Chart

	Buddist	Hindu	Judaism	Islam	Roman Catholic	Eastern Orthodox	Coptic
Alcohol		A		X			
Beef	A	X					
Coffee / Tea				A			
Eggs / Dairy	O	O	R		R	R	
Fish	A	R	R			R	
Meat & Dairy at Same Meal			X				
Meal, All	A	A	R	R		R	R
Pork	A	A	X	X			A
Shellfish	A	R	X			O	
Ritual Slaughter of Meats			P	P			
Moderation	P			P			
Fasting*	P	P	P	P	P	P	P

Common Religious Food Practices
A—Avoided by the most devout
O—Permitted, but may be avoided at some observances
P—Practices
R—Some restrictions regarding types of foods or when foods are eaten
X—Prohibited or strongly discouraged

*Fasting varies from partial (abstention from certain foods or meals) to complete (no food or drink)

Based on a chart by P. G. Kilther & K. P. Suchen in *Food & Culture in America*, 1998.

Much has been said about the cooling effect of evaporating sweat that results from eating capsicums as being the reason they are consumed with such gusto in hot lands (Lee, 1954:539). Yes, they make you sweat when you eat them in the tropics—and also in an air-conditioned room—but you don't see tropical inhabitants munching on peppers as they sweat in the cane fields and rice paddies in order to cool off. Rather, pepper eaters eat them in their food because they like the taste and because they are convenient.

The common denominator in pepper cookery, a starch base, which I observed in my travels, is the "core" of the principal meal as defined by anthropologist Sidney Mintz (1988:41), and is accompanied by a periphery, or "fringe," composed of foods of every sort, which provide flavor and sauce for the core. The fringe makes it possible for people to eat with zest large quantities of the monotonous core food by providing some supplementary contrasting flavor. This meal model holds for most of the Third World countries day in and day out.

Legumes (pulses)—beans, peas, lentils, chickpeas, peanuts—are almost invariably cooked to make a sauce (page 171) to spoon over the starch when served. To the sauce may be added a little meat or fish, pickled vegetable, spicy condiment, or other taste enhancers—chillies being a prime example.

Capsicums were a welcome addition to such monotonous and often dry diets because the pungent element (capsaicin) in chillies increases the production of body fluids (page 55). First, the appetite is aroused, next an increased flow of saliva facilitates chewing and swallowing the starchy food, then digestion of those starches in the stomach is aided by stimulation of the flow of gastric juices.

Throughout the past five centuries, creative cooks in Turkey, India, Sichuan, Indonesia, Bhutan, Hungary, Thailand, the Caribbean, and Africa took up the New World pepper and used it to skillfully embroider new designs on their cuisines with its vivid *Capsicum* threads. Today our own inventive chefs are creating daring new culinary combinations to delight our senses and titillate our taste buds. The recipes of many of the pioneers of *Capsicum* cookery are presented in this book.

Latin America

Now that scientists have determined that peppers originated in South America, one might think that all of those countries would have equally peppery foods; however, that is not the case. According to Professor of American Studies, Alfred W. Crosby, Jr. (1986:3), "More than three of every four inhabitants of the southern temperate zone are entirely of European ancestry." He classifies Argentina, Uruguay, southern Brazil, and Costa Rica, plus the United States and Canada, as "Neo-Europes." It is principally these countries that do not have traditional fiery cookery. The other Latin American countries where the populations are largely mixtures of European-Amerindian-African stock are the places where pungent peppers are used routinely in cookery.

The basic starch staples of pre-Columbian America—maize, bitter and sweet manioc, potatoes—are still being grown and used, but in many areas, food staples from the Old World have been accepted as well. When the Europeans came to America, they brought with them plant and animal foodstuffs never imagined by the Native Americans and they found plant and animal foodstuffs never imagined by denizens of the Old World. Cows, horses, sheep and large, barking war dogs[2] were but several of the wonders that arrived with Columbus on his second voyage, as well as wheat, chickpeas, barley, and sugarcane. Then came onions, garlic, citrus, apples, peaches, cucurbit melons, grapes, rice, chickens, pigs, and on and on. Although the Amerindians were forced to grow and prepare Old World food for their conquerors, in the beginning they rarely added those foods to their traditional meals, which at the time of the conquest were mainly vegetarian with the addition of occasional game, domesticated dogs, insects, and seafood.

Of those post-Columbian plant introductions to the Americas, the one that probably had the most far-reaching and longest-lasting effect, not only on cookery but also on demographic and sociological events, was sugarcane (page 203). In Europe, at the time of the discovery of America, sugar had come into normal use, but it was still the luxury it had been since the Crusaders (eleventh through thirteenth centuries) first returned with it from the Holy Land. In the previous chapter we related that in their drive to bypass Venice and any dealings with the hated Moslems, the Portuguese introduced sugarcane and its related slave labor to their new colonies on the eastern Atlantic islands—Madeira, Cape Verdes, São Tomé, Principe, the Azores—soon after 1473. This gave them a head start of at least sixty years to acquire far-reaching experience with sugar plantations by the time they introduced that institution to Brazil in 1535 (see page 19). Columbus brought sugarcane from Spain and the Canary Islands to the West Indies on his second voyage and soon thereafter Native Americans were forced to labor in its cultivation. The tragedy of that effort is only too well known (footnote 34, page 225). The introduction of sugarcane culture, with its attendant African slave trade, had a significant influence on the movement of New World plants, including *Capsicum*, that is evident even today in Latin America.

When the Spaniards arrived in continental North America, they soon realized the Incas, Aztecs and Mayas were accomplished gastronomes who had a wide range of ingredients at their command and ate with a high level of refinement. After the Spanish occupation of the new lands, the European and American cookery melded to produce unique cuisines.

CARIBBEAN

Although some Spanish influences can still be recognized in Caribbean cookery, today it is mainly a mix of Amerindian and African, as a byproduct of the plantation system with its European overlords. To this early melting pot have been added the tastes of more recent migrants—East Indian, Asian, and South European. The many migrations, voluntary or forced, to the Caribbean area have created one of the most ethnically heterogeneous areas in the modern world (Mintz, 1988:36). Each group has brought its influence to bear on the starch-based cookery—now rice and beans—resulting in a true fusion cuisine. Peppers, principally the habanero type (page 69) and Scotch bonnet (page 77), both *C. chinense*, are used more as condiments than as seasonings.

MEXICO

Elizabeth Lambert Ortiz, an authority on Latin American cooking, remarks that Mexican (Meso-american) cooking, resting firmly on its Amerindian origins and interwoven with Spanish cookery, is the

most exotic of all Latin American cookery. Maize, beans, squash, tomatoes, avocados, and chillies are vital in Mexican cuisine, which is characterized by sauces featuring the rich flavors of the varied *Capsicum annuum* var. *annuum*. The flavor principles of modern Mexican food are tomatoes, chillies, and cumin (*comino*) with maize and beans, while those of Central America are lime (*limòn*), coriander, garlic, and chillies with rice and beans. (Cumin, coriander, garlic and lime came with the conquerors.)

TIERRA FIRME

Venezuela has no identifiable cookery but has been influenced by other Latin American countries. In Colombia the cuisine is less traditional, with peppers appearing primarily in the daily table sauces. Rice, potatoes, manioc, seafood, poultry, and coconut milk are used extensively, and *arepas* (biscuit-sized cornbread) are more common than tortillas.

ANDEAN

The foodways of the Andean countries—Peru, Ecuador, Bolivia, and Chile—have a certain similarity to each other. Because several species of capsicums were domesticated in that area by the pre-Colombian inhabitants, there is long history of pepper usage. In fact, chillies were so important in the lives of the Incas that on certain occasions they were required to abstain from both peppers and sex, sort of a pre-Columbian version of Lent or Ramadan (Coe, 1994:62). Each of those countries has a broad native culinary base on which Spanish and other more recent influences have been built, making them delightfully different from the cookery of other South American countries. Peruvian cuisine is *picante* and cooks are extravagant in their use of peppers (*aji*) while preparing food and in pungent table sauces to add to those dishes according to one's own taste. These are made very peppery with their native *ajís*—*C. baccatum* var. *pendulum* (see page 51) and *C. chinense* (see page 51), and the indecently pungent rocoto, *C. pubescens* (see page 76) plus a couple of the more recently introduced milder Mexican *C. annuum* var. *annuum*. The Amerindians of Peru had domesticated the potato, quinoa, lima beans, squash, and divers peppers which they combined with the meat of wild game or the several domesticated animals and birds—llamas, alpacas, muscovy duck, and the guinea pig. The city of Arequipa is famous for the traditional pungent Peruvian dish, *Rocoto Relleno*, a meat-filled pepper delicacy (recipe, page 132). Seafood is also prominent in Peruvian cookery and it is here that *seviche* (seafood "cooked" in lime or lemon juice) originated (recipe, page 111).

In Ecuadorian cookery, potatoes and vegetables are important and there is always *salsa de ají,* a peppery table sauce (usually made with *ajís*, tree tomatoes [*tamarillo*], leeks, and cilantro), which is used generously, but little chilli pepper is incorporated in the preparation of the main dishes. My favorite Ecuadorian concoction is *locro*, a thick potato soup served with farmer's cheese, avocado slices and annatto (recipe, page 117). Their version of shrimp seviche, in which Seville oranges (bitter) or a mixture of orange and lime juice is used to cook the seafood, runs a close second (recipe, page 110). The completed dish is served with fluffy, white popcorn. In fact, popcorn is used in soups and other dishes as you would use croutons.

The food of Bolivia is less known than that of the other Andean nations, but is no less deserving of our attention. The altitude in that somewhat bleak land is a challenge to both tourists and cooks. Here the rocoto pepper reigns supreme in the ubiquitous, pungent, table sauce called *llajwa* (ya-wha) (recipe, page 173). It was surprising to me how many delectable vegetable soufflés and casseroles are served in Bolivia and throughout the Andean lands—a well-adapted colonial introduction.

The long coastline of Chile provides a great variety of seafood that is prepared in interesting ways and served with delicious Chilean wines but, as a whole, the cuisine is not peppery. Its strong European influence is easily recognized.

EASTERN REGION

In Argentina, renowned for its beef and wine, Spanish cooking has been modified by the large influx of Italians and Germans. Uruguay, Paraguay, southern Bolivia, and southern Brazil are characterized by a mixture of *caboclo* (Amerindian or Amerindian/European), Portuguese, with a slight trace of African.

BRAZIL

Brazilian cuisine, one of the most varied in Latin America, has been influenced by the early introduc-

tion and assimilation of great numbers of Africans, who readily adopted the local peppers—which they named *malaguetas* after the *melegueta* pepper of their Guinea homeland—to form the predominant Afro-Bahian cookery of northern Brazil. That hybrid cuisine began to change when Europeanization followed independence in 1822. Bread came in with the nineteenth century and French recipe books took their toll on traditional Brazilian cookery (Freyre, 1966:468). Introduced rice has virtually supplanted the root starches—manioc-yam-sweet potato—as the primary carbohydrate base. Today the three styles of cooking—Bahian, Cariocan, and Paulista—are a mixture of Portuguese, African, and Amerindian, with the Cariocan of Rio de Janeiro leaning heavily on pepper sauces made from varieties of *Capsicum chinense* and the *malagueta* pepper (footnote 16, page 222). The northern coastal area of Brazil, where sugarcane and slaves were first introduced, is the region of heaviest pepper usage. In writing about Amerindians and Africans of that zone, colonial writers reported that "both groups abuse peppers," and they still do.

Africa

Africa is so immense that it is not fair to generalize, but for the most part the main dishes of many African countries combine grains with legumes into a one-dish vegetarian meal. Porridge made of a cooked starch that may be manioc (cassava) (page 97), sorghum, millet, rice, yams, or maize, according to region, is served with a great variety of stews (sometimes called relishes) seasoned with tomatoes, onions, chillies, or other available vegetables. Most of the peppers and other vegetables used in these stews come from gardens cultivated near the huts. Legumes are the primary source of protein, while meat, beef in particular, is an exception in the traditional diet (Coetzee, 1982:64).

Today, food in Africa covers a wide range of tastes, but chillies are the common denominator. Whether you are using the pungent pepper seasoning *berberé* in Ethiopia, the *piri-piri* sauce and stews of Ghana, Nigeria, Senegal, and the Ivory Coast, or curry in Kenya and South Africa, you will be eating the American pepper and, most likely, at a concentration that is not easy for beginners to tolerate. *Pili-pili*,[3] a sauce made of chillies, onion, garlic, lemon juice, tomatoes, and horseradish, is used throughout Africa.

For some reason, the capsaicin content of peppers grown in most of Africa is higher than that of peppers grown in most other places. Pharmaceutical companies that use capsaicin in their products have known this for a long time and consequently, most of the chillies they use have been imported from Africa; however, India and China have taken the lead recently (Trease & Evans; 1983:375; Maga, 1975:180). Nevertheless, one bite and you'll agree that African chillies are hotter than their American counterparts.

SUB-SAHARAN AFRICA

On their arrival in coastal Africa below the equator, the Portuguese found a culture strikingly unlike their own, but one that offered a rich prize in raw materials and slaves. "It was a new world on the old earth, and a new man in that world" (Rodriques, 1965:4). Initially the Portuguese control of the coasts of Africa had little effect on the food habits of its people. Only after the discovery of Brazil in 1500 and the introduction of sugar plantations there in 1535, which impelled the importation of huge numbers of African slaves to its shores, did a significant exchange of plants between South America and Africa occur (Crosby, 1972:106). Approximately a third of the principal commodities produced today in African tribal economies were not known to its peoples before the arrival of the Portuguese (Miracle, 1967:231). West African palates were not only accustomed to food made pungent with grains of paradise (*Afromomun melegueta*) (footnote 16, page 222), but their humid, tropical climate with its warm, short days was a ready-made environment for most of the New World plants .

EAST AFRICA

The entire east coast of Africa also readily accepted the New World plants, using them in a cuisine heavily influenced by the food-ways of India.[4] Highly spiced curry-type dishes are prominent throughout the area. The fiery Ethiopian curries and its *berberé* condiment reflect less European influence compared with those of other nations in that area, as a result of greater isolation. Ethiopia was never colonized and was only relatively recently ruled by Italy for a brief time. New World foods came into Ethiopia quite early over the traditional Red Sea spice route, and its cuisine reflects those ancient contacts.

MEDITERRANEAN NORTH AFRICA

There is a greater variety of peppers available for cooking in Mediterranean North Africa because the countries in that area not only have the pungent types that made their way north with the Arabic trans-Sahara slave trade from the west coast, but they also had the advantage of the busy Mediterranean commerce and Arabian traders. The excellent Moroccan paprika is made from the types of peppers used for Spanish paprika, probably a relatively recent introduction. The Mediterranean food style of Morocco is based on spices, falfal (peppers), the savor of herbs, a variety of vegetables, and the natural bounty of the land. *Cous cous*, the traditional Berber grain dish of the Maghreb area—Morocco, Algeria, Tunisia—is served with legume stews flavored with the pungent *harissa* sauce (page 92), in a communal bowl (*kasaa*) from a round table, usually on Friday. It is but one example of a culinary tradition handed down orally from mother to daughter.

Modern invaders of another type are bringing about a fiery change in these areas, if the growing sales of pungent red pepper products from Louisiana and Texas are indicators. When the oil boom in North Africa and the Middle East began, oil field workers from the vast fields in Louisiana and Texas went by the thousands to man the rigs until the locals could be trained to do the new work. With them went their indispensable pungent pepper sauces which have caught the fancy of the Arabic-speaking world.

The Middle East

TURKEY

Originally from the north and west of China, the varied people now known as Turks were a nomadic group who shared a common culture with the Mongolians. Their language is an offshoot of the Ural-Altaic cluster distantly related to Mongolian, Finnish, and Hungarian. They wandered into Central Asia, becoming one with the Iranian nomads through annihilation and absorption. Famed as warriors, the Seljuk

Turks became the mercenaries of the Near Eastern and Mongolian armies that initiated the fall of the Byzantine Empire, allowing the emergence of the Ottomans. Intermarriage was so common between the Mongol ruling class and the Turkish troops that after a time, the rulers became Turks in language and culture. The Turks of Anatolia (now Turkey) and the vast Ottoman Empire were mainly farmers. Although today industrialization is spreading, the remaining Turkish nation is still largely a rural country of small villages.

The peasants' diet has changed little throughout the ages. The main meal is a bulgar (wheat) or rice pilaf served with vegetable stews, yogurt, and lots of wonderful crusty bread. Lamb is the most important meat; however, meat is not regularly eaten in the villages. The evening meal of the urban upper classes usually has two or three vegetable dishes, a pilaf, and increasingly some meat or fish. Islamic taboos include alcohol, blood, and the flesh of horses, pigs, asses, and carrion eaters. Tediously wrapped or stuffed vegetables are favorites. Preparing a Turkish meal takes patience and a lot of hard work. Most urban workers eat restaurant food at noon; consequently, the restaurant meals in Turkey are very much like home food. Both groups have a taste for very sweet sweets but don't ordinarily eat them with meals. There has been a considerable Persian influence, resulting in a cosmopolitan cookery.

Peppers of the finger (cayenne)-type are abundant. Unlike our current peppers in this country, the shorter Turkish peppers are very flavorful but only mildly pungent. Fresh green ones (*yesil biber*) are chopped into salads and stews or roasted whole and served with meat, on kebabs, or with stews. Pickled green peppers are a familiar condiment. Ripened and air dried, the very flavorful conical, dark red ones (*kiemiz biber*) are carefully seeded and veined, then crushed into small flakes which are served in little bowls to be sprinkled liberally on prepared food.[5] It is also ground into a fine powder, like our paprika, and used during cooking to add a rich flavor and color. When in season, another very flavorful, pale green bell-type (only used fresh) is stuffed with seasoned rice and steamed. Turkish food is not pungent, but is very delicately flavored with herbs such as parsley, thyme, dill, dried mint, and fennel. The shallot-like onions are more subtle than ours, and garlic is not allowed to overpower the herbs.

Turkish grain-based cookery is one of the seminal cuisines of the world, and Ottoman conquests carried that cuisine's influence into Persia, Greece, the Balkans, Asia Minor, and North Africa, while the Moghuls delivered it to India, where it persists to this day. It predominates in the eastern Mediterranean. Wheat bread, yogurt, kabobs (cooked on skewers), the sunken tandir/tandoor oven, pilaf, Arabic coffee, olive oil, and oriental spices are but a few of the foods and food practices that the Ottoman invaders carried with them to their new territories. The Asiatic Turks began to arrive in the Middle East during the eleventh century. As they conquered the Saracen lands of the Arabian region, Islam conquered them. The new converts spread their doctrine with zeal and fury. Through the ages, the Turks have so intermixed with the people they conquered that the physical Mongoloid traits have practically disappeared, but their yogurt hasn't.[6]

THE ARAB WORLD

The culinary traditions of the Middle Eastern countries are highly blended. Although there are a few recognizable "national dishes," the cuisines of Turkey, Syria, Lebanon, Iran, Egypt, Iraq, Saudi Arabia, Egypt, Tunisia, Algeria, Morocco, the Palestinian part of Israel, and Greece are a closely related complex that has been passed down from mother to daughter. The Moslem invasions within the region introduced Arabic dishes throughout. Peasant food was brought by the soldiers and court cuisine by their generals (Roden, 1983:13). The best of the two sources became the melting pot for a new culinary tradition, and trade between the Arabic and then the Ottoman empires made the ingredients available.

The literature dealing with the spice trade in the fifteenth and early sixteenth century is filled with references to the exploits of "Arabs and Moslems" and their influence on the arts, trade, and technology of that world. It is important to remember that about the time of the birth of Christ, Arabs were involved in complex trading patterns to the east with India, to the north with Europe, and throughout the Roman Empire. When Islam began (632 A.D. is usually the date given), the Arabs quickly became an international force, conquering most of the present-day Middle East and much of Spain, Sicily, and east to India. The high culture of the Arab Moslem Empire was approximately 632 to 1000 A.D.

With the rise of cities, a complex cuisine developed. *The Baghdad Cookery Book of 1226* contains 160 recipes, some very intricate. The nomadic Bedouins in the Arabian peninsula continued to eat as they had always eaten—primarily dates, bread,[7] with camel and goat meat and milk. Settled agricultural peoples had available to them a wider variety of foods and spices. The new starch plant, rice, entered from India via Syria, Iraq, and Iran, and was cultivated throughout the Arabic world all the way to Spain. In the cities, a different cookery developed, using products from the traders as well as what was grown locally.[8] A big change came with the introduction of plants from the New World—especially tomatoes and red peppers.

Although Arabs were active in the spice trade at an early date, spices were not used in their food until later because trading with them was much more profitable than eating them. Sugar, an East Indian product, went first to Iran and then spread throughout the Mediterranean. Increased transport and travel brought foodstuffs from one part of the empire to another. With the Crusades came some European ("Franc") influences. Iran's had been the most distinguished culture in the Middle Eastern area and at one point things Iranian, such as a taste for sweet and sour, were "in." Presentation was, and still is, paramount, evidenced in the use of turmeric, *bixa* (*achiote*), and saffron to add color to the very complex dishes. Meat, rice, and sugar were for the rich—lentils, beans, and honey for the poor. Pork and wine were, and still are, taboo to all. The fall of Baghdad to the Mongols in 1258 marked a decline in the interest in the culinary arts. As religious puritanism grew, preoccupation with gastronomy shrank (Roden, 1980:13).

Today lamb is still the favored meat; preferred vegetables are eggplant, cauliflower, okra, cucumbers, spinach, onions, and garlic; favorite fruits are pomegranates, apricots, dates, oranges, grapes, apples, and melons. Lemon juice is used profusely. Fresh mint, dill, and parsley are the chief herbs, and cinnamon is the most frequently used spice. Foodways have changed little in the centuries that elapsed since the Mongols galloped their shaggy ponies down from the steppes of Mongolia.[9] Chicken is still eaten with nuts, rice with legumes, and meat with fruit; however, for the most part, tomatoes have usurped fruits in meat dishes. Herbs, spices, flower waters, and color are loved by all. Rice and yogurt play important roles. Ingredients are finely ground or pounded, rolled into little forms, simmered in broth, drowned in syrup, or cooked with yogurt as they were long ago. Desserts may be pastries filled with ground nuts and sticky honey, or thickened milk puddings. It is a delightful, but laborious and time-consuming cookery, in which capsicums play little part.

Monsoon Asia

The majority of the people in the world live in Monsoon Asia. That mass of Oriental humanity is still rural and agricultural in nature. Their foodways went unchanged for hundreds of years until the strange plants from the New World arrived five hundred years ago. American peanuts, sweet potatoes, corn, squashes, tomatoes, and chillies were hungrily adopted into their traditional eating patterns.

INDIA

The dramatic culinary change that spread throughout the Far East began in India. Who could have dreamed that a few innocuous red pods from the cargo of a lumbering Portuguese carrack unloaded at Calicut, Cochin, or Goa,[10] would literally fire the imaginations of the cooks of the Far East? At the very same time that the seaborne Portuguese were introducing entirely new foods from the New World to the coastal regions of the subcontinent, a Moghul[11] invasion was sweeping across the northern passes from Afghanistan. Those invaders brought new foods and cooking techniques from the Old World to a mixed race of people who, with time, would assimilate and modify both into their own unique and varied cuisine. The Portuguese enriched themselves, while the Moghuls enriched the culture of India.

When one thinks of Indian food, curry comes to mind. Today, it is impossible to imagine a curry without *Capsicum* peppers. Curries are dishes with a varying amount of gravy-type liquid (see page 171) to which is added legumes, meat, fish, and/or vegetables along with a quantity of bruised spices and chillies. The term curry, first applied by the British, has become a generic one for that Indian gravy or sauce. A little "curry" gives a lot of flavor to a large mess of rice or *chapatis* (soft, flat, griddle-fried bread). Various sour, bitter, sweet, or astringent dishes are served with it. The side dishes are presented either directly on a platter (*thali*) or on a large leaf around the central pile of rice or bread, or in small containers served on the *thali* and little piles on the leaf. The diner helps himself to the various items, mixing these with rice or folding them up in pieces of flat-bread. This is often accompanied by a cooling yogurt *raita* (pages 57 and recipe 116). Sweet dishes are eaten separately at the end. Indian recipes are very flexible, presenting only the basic ingredients and methods to be used. The rest is up to the cook.

In most Indian cooking the bruised, whole spices are put in hot oil to release the flavors into the oil (mustard oil, sesame oil, coconut oil, or ghee—clarified butter—but never olive oil).[12] Although other ingredients are added to this spice mixture, the whole spices are not meant to be eaten but are to be set aside unobtrusively by the diner. Even when the spices are ground into a powder (*masala*) (recipe page 217), they are frequently heated in oil first. Onions,[13] garlic, and ginger pastes, along with several basic gravies/sauces, are prepared and kept on hand for use with various combinations of spices in the cooking of curries. Much cooking is done in a *kadhai* (a deep frying pan). The Indian flavor principles are garlic, cumin, ginger, turmeric, coriander, and cardamom, along with chilli and black pepper.

Although their origins may be long forgotten, many ancient religious taboos may have been originally designed to keep devotees from eating unfit animal flesh (page 35). Today refrigeration and rapid transportation have caused some changes. Those groups are beginning to overlook old restrictions and are consuming small amounts of lamb, fowl, mutton, and seafood with their curries; however, one still does not offer pork to a Moslem or beef to the others. Other types of meat preparation derive from Persian cookery initiated by the Moghuls in northern India and almost always involve yogurt,[14] except in certain kebabs (Westrip, 1981:73). Hindu cooks are more inventive when preparing fish than meat dishes. The labor intensive Moghul cuisine, with origins in Iran and Turkey, is the *haute cuisine* of India (Tannahil, 1981). The Moghul overland invasions of northern India were contemporary with the Portuguese

seaborne incursions to the south on the Malabar Coast.

Because the ancient Gujarati of western India were a seafaring and shipbuilding people who conducted a flourishing trade with the Indonesian archipelago, their very pungent, spicy cookery was not only incorporated into Indonesian foodways, but was also influenced by them (Meilink-Roelofsz & Godinho, 1962:21). As a consequence of early trade contacts with Indonesia, the dishes of eastern and southern India, as well as those of Gujarat, are probably closer in taste to Indonesian and Malaysian dishes than to the Central Asian Moghul meat dishes. Also, for reasons of trade routes, the tandoori roast meat of the northwest has closer links with Central Asia through Afghanistan than with the rest of India. Those coastal areas encountered chillies first, which may account for their greater popularity in those localities. In 1900 Goa was the principal *Capsicum*-growing region in India and the fiery pods were known as Goa peppers (*Gowaí mirchi*) in Bombay (Watt, 1972:135). From India, the peppery cookery progressed through Burma to Thailand.

BHUTAN AND NEPAL

Bhutan and Nepal, two small Oriental countries tucked in the Himalayas adjoining India's northern borders, probably should not be considered together because their cultures are quite different as a result of their long isolation. The factors that have influenced their basically vegetarian cuisines, however, are similar enough to be discussed jointly. Chinese and Indian influences and religious food taboos are about equal in the kitchen and so is the quantity of peppers—plenty. Nepalese Hinduism has absorbed Buddhism and imposed its food taboos on its followers. As a result, no beef is eaten in Nepal and only male sheep, goats, and water buffalo are slaughtered (in the prescribed ways) for food. A succulent Nepalese water buffalo fillet was one of the best pieces of meat I have ever eaten anywhere.

Bhutanese waiters become greatly distressed and are quick to point out if they consider your order to have too much starch or if you choose two preparations nearly alike. This idea of balance between the starch, *fan,* and the vegetable and meat, *ts'ai*, is a typical Chinese food attitude (page 45). In late October the rooftops of the already colorful Bhutanese homes are ablaze with scarlet peppers spread on roof tops to dry, and long red clusters punctuate the gaily painted eaves.

THAILAND

If asked the main characteristic of Thai food, you would not be wrong in saying "hot." Although many influences can be detected in modern Thai cooking, it is the Indian that prevails. There is good reason for this, because Indian culture and Buddhist religion were dominant in ancient Siam. In the twelfth and thirteenth centuries, migrations of Thai peoples followed the rivers leading to Siam from the Central Asian regions of Hunan and Sichuan. The influences of Hinduism, Buddhism, and Confucianism formed the character of Southeast Asian civilization. Although there were Portuguese, English, and Dutch trading posts, no European power ever colonized Buddhist Siam.

Predominately vegetarian, Thai cookery is highly refined and presentation is important. You will be served many curries and curry-type dishes, but you will never encounter the use of yogurt or beef in traditional Thai cooking. A large quantity of many spices and chillies of the finger (cayenne)-type are used. Instead of following that Indian practice, a Thai cook grinds the spices, herbs, and chillies into a paste and then stirs that paste into hot coconut oil to which the other ingredients are added.[15]

Until quite recently, only very pungent chillies, like those cultivated in India, were grown and used in Thailand. In fact, there is no Thai word for sweet pepper. In the last few years a sweet pepper has been introduced for consumption by foreigners, and several chillies, including the yellow 'Santa Fe Grande' ('Caribe'), have found their way into gardens, but the typical populace does not use them. It would be hard to convince most Thais that capsicums are not native to their country.

INDONESIA

Indonesia, the world's most populous Moslem country, is made up of over thirteen thousand islands, some quite large, populated with one-fifth of the world's inhabitants. The fabled Spice Islands are among these islands. Throughout history, spices have drawn traders and adventurers to these tropical islands, and as a consequence the food is less distinctive than in some of the other countries in that part of the world. The strongest culinary influence is Chinese, which is to be expected when you recall that Chinese traders had sailed here for spices by the first century A.D., centuries before the first Europeans set foot in the area. Large-scale immigration from India is usually ruled out even though Hinduism and Buddhism became established as early as the third century A.D., and the food bears the effects of that contact. The ancient and steady flow of Arab traders injected large doses of Islam into the veins of Indonesians. The formative influences of Mohammedanism, Hinduism, Buddhism, and Confucianism defined the distinctive character of Southeastern Asia and spilled over into Indonesia.[16] The offspring of the Arab traders and native women acquired their fathers' food taboos, which they spread among their mother's people. Again, the Portuguese, bent on commerce and not colonization, introduced peppers, peanuts, and pineapples along with other American food plants that were absorbed into the native rice-based cuisine.

Each ethnic group uses its own combination and intensity of spices—cardamom, cinnamon, fennel, cumin, and coriander, but seldom, if ever, cloves, nutmeg and mace. Fresh aromatic seasonings to which coconut milk is added are the basis of a sweet and sour combination which defines Indonesian cooking. For the most part, the fresh spices and chillies are ground into a paste, then mixed with the dry flavorings before the leaf seasonings are combined with the cooking liquid. The results are very aromatic.

Many foods are cooked with coconut and/or wrapped in banana leaves. *Satay*, skewered meat which is barbecued, is served with the popular peanut sauce. All the islanders use chillies, utilizing them more as a condiment than as a seasoning, and no meal can be eaten without a *sambal* (page 94)—searing table sauces that are mixtures of tomatoes, garlic, onion, chillies, lime juice, and often a touch of fish or shrimp paste, ground together daily in small amounts. However, those in a hurry can buy sambals in bottles like our catsup, but there the resemblance ends. Soy sauce, garlic, molasses, and New World peanuts are the defining Indonesian flavor principles.

Many young Americans may not remember that the seven thousand Philippine Islands were governed by the United States following the Spanish-American War of 1898—when Cuba and the Philippines were ceded to the United States—until they were granted independence in 1945 at the end of World War II. They might be surprised that English is the language that the Filipinos in the various islands resort to in order to overcome local language barriers. Westernization from that forty-seven-year tenure was extensive but not complete. Spanish is the other language that a Visayan Filipino might use when trying to speak with a Tagalog Filipino, because Spain owned the islands from the day Fernando Magellan[17] planted Spain's flag and cross in 1519 until the day the Americans took over, 379 years later. Calling those years the period of Spanish domination is, in reality, quite misleading. In actuality it was a period of Mexican influence because the so-called Spaniards were natives of New Spain in the Americas and the Philippines were governed by the Spanish Viceroy of Mexico. Not until Mexico won its independence from Spain in 1821 was the governing of the Philippines directed from Spain by "real" Spaniards.

At the coming of the Spaniards, the Philippine Islands, from the standpoint of geography and ethnicity, were really a part of the East Indies. The inhabitants were mostly Moslem Malays only a little removed from the primitive stages of culture. To the Spaniards and also the Portuguese, so recently out from under the Moorish yoke, anyone who was dark and Moslem was a Moor, so they called the local Moslem folk *Moros*. The Moros are dominant in the southern islands. Even though Indonesian traits are evident, the culture of the Philippines evidences a greater Chinese influence than from any other society, and nowhere greater than in the Cantonese-style cookery which makes great use of soy sauce, rice wine, ginger root, garlic, and/or meat broth, and/or fermented black beans. After almost four hundred years of Spanish-Mexican influence, one would expect significant vestiges to be evident in the local cookery because peppers, along with other New World plants, entered the islands after 1565, when the Acapulco-to-Manila galleon (map 5, page 23) became an agent for the distribution of goods between the Orient and New Spain

for over 250 years.[18] As a whole, Filipino food is not peppery, and the rich, dark red sauces of Mexico made with ancho pastes are nowhere to be found. With soy sauce replacing *anchos, adobo,* the national dish, has little resemblance to its Spanish or Mexican ancestor. Today, either small bowls of vinegar-based chilli-pepper sauces or bottled hot sauces are served as table sauces to be added at the diner's discretion. Peppers appear as vegetables in Chinese-style dishes. Although menus in the Philippines may be peppered with Spanish words, the food is not peppered. The Filipinos accepted the new foods only by adapting them to their traditional cookery.

However, several dishes were carried over from the Mexicans, such as filled pastry or *empanadas*, tamale-like *sumans* of squash or rice wrapped in banana or palm leaves, beans, corn-on-the-cob, and several others. The hot chocolate drunk there is exactly like that of Mexico, even down to the *batidor*, a flanged, wooden beater twirled between the palms of the hands to make it. It was fascinating for me to recognize Amerindian words for foods being used in the native dialects, because this affirms that the plant was not present before the Spanish brought the plant and its name.

English	Spanish	Viscaya	Origin
avocado	aguacate	abokado	Nahuatl (*āhuactl*)
chocolate	cacao	cacao	Nahuatl (*cacahuatl*)
corn	maiz	mais	Arawak
papaya	papaya	kapaya	Arawak
peanut	mani	mani	Arawak
pepper	chilli/chile	sili	Nahuatl (*chilli*)
pineapple	piña	pinya	Latin (*pinus*)
potato	papa	papa	Quechua
squash	calabasa	calabasa	Arabic via Spain
sweet potato	camote	camote	Nahuatl (*camohtli*)
tobacco	tabaco	tabaco	Arawak
tomato	tomate	kamati	Nahuatl (*tomatl*)

The cookery of Moslem Malaysia is very similar to that of Indonesia, but the Malaysians were even more influenced by the Chinese, who constitute a majority of the racial stock. A special Chinese-based cuisine is the *nonya* cooking of Malaysia and Singapore (*nonya* is Malay for a well-to-do Chinese lady). Sri Lanka and India have both had more input in Malaysian cookery than in Indonesian. Their transplanted curries and *biryanis* (rice with meat or vegetables) are very evident in Malaysia. The food is often coconut-based and also made very pungent with peppers.

Southwestern China

Food in China is a cultural obsession. Few other cultures are as food oriented as the Chinese. The Chinese fare, using preparation methods based on the duality of things (Tao), is very different from western food (J. Newman, 1981:39). It is a cuisine which emphasizes variety of preparation, a blending of small pieces, short cooking time (fuel is precious), and the use of whatever foods are available except for dairy products. It is chiefly vegetarian as a consequence of centuries of population pressure on the food supply. The basis of the Chinese way of preparing food from raw ingredients to morsels ready for the mouth is the division between *fan* (grains and other starch foods), and *ts'ai* (vegetable and meat dishes). A balanced meal must have appropriate amounts of both (Chang, 1977:7).

China, so long isolated from the world, is divided into four regions on the basis of geographical features that separated the ancient peoples, allowing them to develop differently in each area. Each of these geographical units evolved a distinct, highly refined cookery which began to intermix regionally during the Han dynasty.[19] For the purpose of our pepper discussion, only one region, referred to by Chang as the southwest—including Yunnan, Guizhou, Sichuan, Hunan, and Hubei—are of concern.

Southwest China, like the southwestern United States, favors pungent and spicy foods prepared with vitality and zest. The hot and humid climate of the Chinese southwest is a companion to a cuisine that features a pungent, peppery taste combined with delicate flavors. Although there are more similarities than differences in Chinese culinary practices, why is that area so different from the other regions?

For whatever reason, it was only in the landlocked areas of the southwest, communicating with India and the Middle East through the plodding silk caravans, that chillies markedly influenced the cookery. Once there, peppers were readily available at little cost. Sichuan-Hunan cuisine is characterized by a passionate use of chillies, pepper-like *fagara* (page 96), garlic, and fermented soybean products, vinegar, sugar, and peanut or rape seed oil are common. Wise and complex use is made of nuts and poultry, and pungent flavors of all sorts are harmoniously blended and quickly cooked. As yet, milk and dairy products have not taken a prominent place. The flavor principles of southwestern China are soy sauce, brandied wine, and ginger root plus sugar for "sweet" dishes, vinegar for "sour," chillies for "hot." If American Chinese restaurants are any measure, we know that in restaurants featuring Sichuan or Hunan menus we can expect the food to be "hot." I found only two or three pepper cultivars of the finger (cayenne)-type (*Capsicum annuum* var. *annuum*) in the markets of those two Chinese territories, but what they lacked in variety they made up for in quantity.[20]

East Asia

Nowhere was Chinese influence more direct than in Japan. With the introduction of Buddhism about A.D. 645, Japanese society was modeled on T'ang China. This influence carried over into cookery and became the basis of Japanese cookery, which relies on seafood and rice, with soy sauce, saki, sugar, and sometimes ginger root as flavor principles. The Portuguese were the first Europeans to come to Japan, then later came the Spaniards and the Dutch. First among them were their merchants, then their missionaries. Although the Portuguese Jesuits did not cooperate in missionary activities with the Spanish Franciscans, Augustinians, and Dominicans from the Philippines, they all had good luck with conversions for a while, so much so that around 1637 the Japanese closed their doors to all foreigners, except for contact with the Dutch and Chinese. They were not reopened until the second half of the nineteenth century. It was these missionaries who introduced peppers to Japan.

Japan produces peppers for export, but they are not used in their own classic cookery. Japanese food emphasizes raw and colorful dishes requiring only a minimum of cooking and served with cereal foods and the ever-present pickled vegetables. Although the Japanese have a long historical involvement with the chilli, it was the American occupation forces and their catsup and pepper sauce that really got the Nipponese into nipping peppers. Douglas MacArthur's introduction of American ideas of nutrition to Japan after World War II has changed not only the eating habits of that people, but also the physiques of postwar generations, as witnessed by a comparison of the heights of young native-born Japanese today with those of their grandparents. Post-World War II affluence and westernization have taken their toll on Buddhist beef avoidance in the home of Kobe beef steaks, and it will probably affect their life expectancy, which presently is the longest in the world. Until recently, wine and olive oil were unknown in Japan.

KOREA

It came as a great surprise when I learned that Korea has the world's highest per capita consumption of chillies per day. Northern China has had the greatest influence on the rice-based, vegetarian-by-necessity cookery of Korea. Next to cereal foods, vegetables provide the bulk of the diet. Here the rice is eaten plain, without sauce or condiments, but at the same time as the soup and crispy-tender stir-fried vegetable dishes, or with a soupy one-dish meal. Fresh red or green chillies are cooked in the vegetable, seaweed, and fish dishes rather than as part of separate condiments. When meat is eaten, it is skewered and cooked on small grills. Along with chillies, the flavor principles are soy sauce, brown sugar, sesame seeds, and garlic. Spices and herbs are not customarily used. A long, narrow, red finger (cayenne)-type is the most commonly used *Capsicum*. *Kim ch'i*, pickled Chinese cabbage, combined in a thousand ways with such things as ginger, chillies, turnips, cucumbers, and/or shrimp or fish, is served with *every* meal. This ubiquitous fermented condiment is usually made every September at harvest time. Although Korea was dominated by the Japanese for many years, their food is more highly seasoned, and more elaborate cooking methods are used than in Japan.

Europe

Today we do not think of Europe as a place where peppers are incorporated into the cuisine; however, some countries have done so, particularly those in the Balkans. As an outcome of the long Dutch tenure in Indonesia, following their capture of the Portuguese Indonesian spice empire at the beginning of the seventeenth century, a taste for spicy Indonesian foods was taken home. Today Indonesian restaurants serving *rijstaffel* (rice table) are not uncommon in Holland, but typically, food there is anything but picante. However, modern Dutch horticultural skills are producing those dazzlingly colorful bell peppers that enhance our tables and challenge our growers.

For the most part peppers, sweet or pungent, are not used in most of Western Europe. In England, France, or any of the old European colonial powers, one would have to go to a restaurant which is typical of its former colony, in order to partake of pungent foods. Today the numerous immigrants from those colonial areas, along with many of the returned colonials, have created a limited demand for the exotic native dishes flavored with red peppers, which has resulted in ethnic restaurants and food shops to meet their demands. As a result, peppery food can be found, but it is still not commonplace in home cooking.

A surprising exception is Sweden, where several recent books about cooking with peppers have been published. If *Eat the Heat* and *Arctic Heat: Modern Swedish Hot Cooking* by Jonas Borssén are any indication, a warming trend in Scandinavian cookery can be anticipated in the new century.

THE BALKANS AND HUNGARY

The arrival of our bright red pod did indeed cause a revolution in the eating habits of the Balkans, but the change was not overnight. The peppers that first landed in the Balkans, where they are known as *paprika,* were of the finger (cayenne)-type, having a mild to potent pungency, and are used more as a seasoning or spice paprika.

Among crops introduced directly to the Balkans by

the Turks during the period of occupation (fifteenth to nineteenth centuries), or by North Balkan Christian market gardeners working abroad or in other parts of the Turkish empire, or diffused due to population migrations within the Empire, were five cultivars of *Capsicum annuum* var. *annuum* (Johnson,[21] 1981:132). The Greeks called this new spice *peperi* or *piperi* after the Latin *piper*, meaning black pepper, which may have derived from *pipali (peepul)*, a Sanskrit word meaning "sacred fig tree." The Bulgarian people modified it to *piperke, peperke, paparka*. When the so-called "Turkish pepper" reached Hungary, the name was slightly altered to become *paprika*. It was in Hungary, during the sixteenth and seventeenth centuries, that paprika slowly but surely altered the cookery as the plant itself was changed. The original fiery peppers were bred to reduce the capsaicin content and to increase the flavor and coloring power of the tapering, elongated cone-shaped pods used for "spice-paprika." Later, blocky, sweet types were introduced from the Mediterranean area. Today platters of quartered, fresh, pale-green, sweet bell-type peppers are served on buffet tables—even at breakfast, and are eaten like apples.

Zoltan Halasz,[22] in his book on Hungarian paprika, tells us that the spice-paprika is added to typical Hungarian stews and goulash (*gulyas*) and is prepared in two basic ways: (1) the paprika is added to a roux made of heated lard and flour, to which various spices are added, and is used to thicken the dish; and (2) onions are cooked in hot lard, paprika is added to the hot mixture, and then the meat and other ingredients are incorporated (Halasz, 1963:127). Dishes prepared by the second method are called "paprikas." It is important to dissolve the paprika in hot, but not burning, fat. One cannot fail to notice that this method of preparation is more akin to the Indian and Persian method of sautéing spices in hot oil before adding the other ingredients than it is to the Mediterranean use of peppers as a vegetable or table sauce, which supports the scenario of origin via India. Balkan cookery has two strong influences: Turko-Middle Eastern and Austro-European. The techniques of East and West are combined and passed from mother to daughter. Yogurt, herbs, and chillies are characteristic of Balkan kitchens.

Western Europe

SPAIN AND PORTUGAL

Many Americans equate Spain and Portugal with Mexico when they think of food, and expect it to be full of chillies, but in fact their dishes are not spicy. The stay-at-home Spaniards and Portuguese never did develop the taste for chillies that their more adventurous kin who immigrated to the Americas did. In spite of shared territory and origins, the two Iberian cultures are not alike. Although both of their cuisines are simply cooked, the Portuguese use market produce more inventively and with more herbs and spices than the Spaniards. A paste, like the Mexican *adobo*, made of sweet red peppers used by the Portuguese as a dry marinade to season meats and poultry, is one of the things that sets Portuguese meat cookery apart from the Spanish. Both chillies and sweet peppers are used in cooking, and a sauce made of *piri-piri* (recipe page 174) peppers is kept in a bottle on the table to use over almost everything the Portuguese eat. These caustic little peppers are said to have first come to Portugal from Angola, Africa.

Reflecting long years of foreign domination, many Spanish cooks use a lot of Phoenician-introduced saffron, garlic, and parsley, along with Moorish cumin and Roman olive oil. Protein comes more from seafood than from red meat in their cookery. Spanish cookery is very regional. The first peppers that arrived from New Spain were looked upon more as curiosities and ornamentals than as something to be eaten. The tomato met the same fate. The Moorish *gazpacho* (soaked bread), brought to Andalusian kitchens from Morocco, began as a soup of bread soaked in olive oil, garlic, almonds, and vinegar thinned with water. Much later some of the new American foods such as tomatoes and sweet peppers, along with local onions and cucumbers or whatever might be in the garden, were incorporated into the traditional mixture.

When the Moors returned to Morocco from Spain after their final defeat in 1492, they carried the new American tomatoes and peppers home with them. The famous Spanish *paellas*, based on short-grained rice introduced by the Moors, use only a little chopped sweet pepper.

When West Indian peppers first arrived in Spain, their need for a hot, humid habitat and short days made them difficult to grow. It was not until the more readily cultivated varieties of *Capsicum annuum* var. *annuum* arrived from highland Mexico that any culinary interest in peppers developed. In Spain I found fields where some of the biggest, brightest red bell peppers I have ever seen were growing. Others produced smaller tomato-like peppers for paprika. I saw no chillies growing, although they are cultivated to a lesser degree. *Chilindrón* dishes blending red bell peppers, tomatoes, onion, garlic, and succulent ham with other meats—except beef—are typical of northeastern Spain. *Sofrito* (page 94), with a *Capsicum* base, is a traditional Spanish seasoning mixture. The use of chillies in table sauces such as *romesco* (page 175) and *piri-piri* (page 93) is reasonably commonplace. The tomato has had greater effect on Spanish and other Mediterranean cuisines than have peppers. In the past, the Iberians have not favored a peppery cuisine, but usage of chillies is growing.

THE MEDITERRANEAN

After the decline of the Ottoman Empire, interchange between the eastern and western halves of the Mediterranean cautiously resumed. One would expect such interchange to have some effect on the cuisines of the Mediterranean region, and it did. Although there are differences from country to country, there is a similarity that makes Mediterranean cookery distinctly different from that in other parts of Europe.

Since ancient times, Mediterranean cuisines have been based on fish, bread, goat meat, olive oil, and later, citrus and tomatoes were added. Spaghetti and the maize dish called *polenta*,[23] considered so typically Italian, are foreign introductions. The sweet, highly flavored, strong-colored, tomato-shaped pepper that is grown today and used to make a high-quality paprika in both Spain and Morocco is not like those long-podded types favored in the paprika regions of Yugoslavia. Therefore, it was probably not introduced to Morocco by the Ottomans, but instead later by the Spaniards. Pungent peppers are grown to a limited degree in the Mediterranean area, especially the North African countries, but they are the exception rather than the rule, and are used primarily as table sauces such as *rouille*, *harissa*, and *romesco* rather than as a seasoning. Mediterranean cookery favors the type of sweet pepper we call "ethnic peppers" and uses them as vegetables more than as seasoning and condiments as Balkan cooks do.

North America

The foodways of North or Anglo America are not as peppery as other American countries we have discussed because its history is completely different. When the first Anglo and Western European colonists arrived in temperate North America they encountered an abundance of wild game and Amerindian agriculturists growing the "three sisters"—corn, beans, and squash—but not the tropical "little brother" chilli. From the Amerindians the colonists learned to grow the new crops using local methods, finding them easy to cultivate, simple to prepare, and easy to store—just the thing to take when the new Americans gathered their families and moved farther west. The familiar European staple, wheat, was demanding to grow and took too long to mature, while a crop of maize could be ready in six weeks without plow or horses. To this they added hogs and chickens, which could fend for themselves in the wilderness, as supplements for the abundant wild game, fishes, and native foods from the land.

A major influence on North American cuisine was the diversity of cultures. Not only were many of the foods of the Native Americans adopted, but also their methods of preparation, such as making hominy, succotash, and maple syrup. Successive groups from other European societies brought their foodways to enrich those found in the new continent, each making its own contribution. Among other things, the British gave us apple pie; the French influenced the making of soups, chowders, and fricassees; the Spanish brought sugarcane, oranges, and wine-making, as well as the technique of barbecuing, which they learned from the native Caribbeans; the Dutch added cole slaw; the Scotch brought oatmeal; the Irish returned the potato to the New World; Germans contributed sausages; Italians gave us pasta, and on and on. To all of these has been added the touch of the African slave, who brought us okra and watermelons (Farb & Armelagos, 1980:195–200). Later events resulting from our twentieth-century wars, along with increased travel and immigration, brought added Mediterranean, Oriental and Middle Eastern influences—and pizza. A willingness to experiment and borrow from these other cultures is yet another characteristic of North American cookery.

Cultural diversity was significant, but the more important North American tradition of plenty was based on a primeval abundance which became the basis of the emerging cuisine. That abundance made a virtue of large helpings simply served. Lack of domestic help eliminated foods that required careful preparation. The food was nutritious, and the dishes were simple and served separate from one another, without sauces or garnishes to mask the flavors. Pork was the principal meat in the South and West until this century, because the self-reliant pig was an ideal meat source for those pioneers. Maize in its myriad forms, from corn-on-the-cob to porridge to cornbread, was the plant staple. The new enthusiasm for democracy made a virtue of simple and often tasteless food.

The spicy seafood, rice and cayenne pepper (see page 61) dishes evolved after the French-Canadian paddled down the great Mississippi River and met his countrymen who had sailed up from their Caribbean colonies into the crawfish- and oyster-filled bayous of southern Louisiana; the flavorful blending of French, Spanish and Afro-American influences with a love for peppers merged into Creole cooking; the pungent, tortilla-based cookery that Mexicans brought with them north of the Rio Grande and combined in their Texas kitchens with the new ingredients to create Tex-Mex cooking, still full of chillies, and only faintly resembling anything in Mexico—but good!—those are the exceptions. To them is added the new Southwestern cookery in which daring young chefs have borrowed from the Mexican, the Amerindian, the cowboy, and newcomers from the rest of the United States to produce a flavorful and color-filled piquant mélange unique to the area—such are the taste-teasing pepper pockets where pepperphilia predominates.

The Tie That Binds

In all the places we have discussed, the chillies that prevail over all the others are the Mexican native, *Capsicum annuum* var. *annuum* and all its varieties, and, to a much lesser degree, *C. frutescens*. There are many cultivars of the first species, especially in Mexico and the southwestern United States, but few of the second, which is semi-wild. The two varieties of those species that dominate the eastern hemisphere are a finger (cayenne)-type and a tabasco-type. A generalized comparison of the usage in the West (Mexico, the U.S. Southwest, and Guatemala), with the East (Africa and Monsoon Asia) might go like this: In both worlds, East and West, a meal lacks a certain spirit without chillies. In the East and the Balkans, peppers are an integral ingredient of the sauces and goulashes that go over the starch. Pulverized peppers go into the meat, and small ones are eaten as a side dish or in condiments. The West fills large sweet or pungent pods with cheese or meat and fries them in fat or bakes them. The East fires up its curries and stews with chopped, ground, or whole small pods. Both regions like pungent sauces to slosh over cooked dishes. In both the East and the West, peppers are combined with other spices and herbs in side dishes or sauces more than served alone. The meals of the East and the West may not be alike in the makeup of the dishes, but the biting taste of each suggests the other. The tie that binds is the pungent chilli.

If you had to serve a dinner that was acceptable to all and balanced nutritionally to the entire populations of the places we have discussed—Latin America, Monsoon Asia, southwestern China, Japan, Korea, and Africa—what would you serve? That universal menu could be: chicken, rice, squash, and chilli sauce, with tea for a beverage and a banana for dessert (Moore, 1970:219). Of course, each locale would use its characteristic flavorings to make the dish palatable from its own point of view.

What is a Pepper?

ow do you account for the popularity of the pepper pod[1]—neither pepper nor a pod? The genus *Capsicum* is a rather mixed-up group of plants. Not just the name *pimiento* is cause for argument but also the defining characteristics of that genus are still being debated. However, there are some things on which all agree. To begin with, *Capsicum* is no relation to its namesake, black pepper, which is the seed of a woody vine, *Piper nigrum*, a native of India. Nor is it any kin to *Pimenta diocia,* allspice, the seed of a native American tree of the myrtle family.

The confusion in names arose as a result of the confident Columbus, who was so certain he had landed in some part of the East Indian Archipelago when his search for black pepper and other spices prompted him to sail west from Spain over five-hundred years ago, that he called the pungent spice the natives used on everything they ate "pimiento" after the pimienta for which he was searching. Later the Spanish explorers added to the chaos by also calling the second unrelated indigenous spice they found pimienta, or pepper. This one was the aromatic allspice, or Jamaican pepper. Capsicum "peppers" are also not related to what was known before the discovery as the Guinea or ginnie pepper, *Aframomum melegueta* (footnote 16, page 222), a pungent African

spice from Guinea known as "grains of paradise," or melegueta pepper which, along with its kin, cardamom, is a member of the ginger family (footnote 16, page 222). True grains of paradise were brought to the Americas with African slaves, who loved it; but they learned to like a fiery little American *Capsicum* even more. The variously named ancient African spice—melegueta- "ginnie pepper" grains of paradise—is no longer used in Brazil but a form of its name is. Malagueta, a corrupted version of melegueta, has become the name by which the little native Brazilian pepper is known. To add to the confusion, after the Portuguese introduced the finger-like American capsicums to Guinea they not only largely supplanted the native melegueta pepper but also expropriated one of its names—"Ginnie" pepper.

If it is not the pimiento, then just what is the *Capsicum*? The genus *Capsicum* is in the family Solanaceae, as is the deadly nightshade, potato, tobacco, petunia, and others. Thousands of years ago some tropical Amerindians cultivated, improved, and developed the ancestral *Capsicum* into a wide variety of fruits that grow from sea level to an altitude of ten thousand feet, but are killed by frost. The genus *Capsicum* consists of perennial herbaceous to woody shrubs native to the American tropics. In areas subject to freezes, it is grown as an annual. Scholars are not in agreement as to its place of origin—either somewhere in southwestern Brazil or in central Bolivia. Long before humans migrated across the Bering Strait to America, and before that migration reached Mesoamerica, it had been carried by birds, its natural means of dispersal, to other parts of South and Middle America (Pickersgill, 1984:110). Centuries later, when the Europeans arrived, birds and/or pre-Columbian Amerindians had not only carried the indigenous spice to Mesoamerica and the Caribbean, but they had also domesticated[2] the four or five species which are cultivated today. Each of the domesticated species had been developed independently in different geographical regions from the small-fruited wild species (Ibid: 112). No new species have been developed since Columbus first stumbled onto the red and green capsicums of the New World.

All species of the wild *Capsicum* have certain common characters: small pungent, red fruits which may be round, elongate, or conical; the fruit is attached to the plant in an erect position; the fruit is readily removed from the calyx; and the seeds are dispersed by birds. Wild *Capsicum* flowers have a stigma-bearing

style that extends beyond the anthers to facilitate pollination by insects. Domesticated cultivars have short styles which promote self-pollination. Once people began to grow the *Capsicum* plants, they—unconsciously or perhaps even consciously—selected seed from those fruits more difficult to remove from the calyx because these would remain attached until harvest, making it harder for birds to pluck. They also observed that if the capsicums hung down and remained hidden among the leaves, the hungry birds had trouble extracting them. As a result, pendent fruit became more desirable, and today most domesticated capsicums have pendent fruit instead of erect. Size increased as larger and larger fruits were selected, and the weight of those larger and heavier fruits also helped the capsicums become pendent.

In the case of many domesticated plants, the color, flavor, size, and shape of the part of the plant most valued by humans was changed through the user's selection for the desired characteristic (Harlan, 1975). All mild and sweet capsicums are the result of such domestication. All wild capsicums are pungent—mouthwarming. This pungency, unique in the vegetable kingdom, results from the presence of a group of closely related alkaloid compounds.

According to botanist W. Hardy Eshbaugh (1993: 132–39), there are approximately twenty-five species of *Capsicum*, four of which have been domesticated. Many of the wild capsicums are harvested and one, *Capsicum annuum* var. *glabriusculum (chiltepín)*, is cultivated[3] to a limited degree, and is the only wild *Capsicum* widely used in the United States. There are four or five domesticated species: *C. a.* var. *annuum, C. frutescens, C. chinense,*[4] *C. baccatum* var. *pendulum,* and *C. pubescens*. Studies to be reported in a forthcoming monograph on the genus *Capsicum* may call for the merging of the first three closely related species, or, at least, the second and third. The status of *C. frutescens* as a valid species is definitely questionable (Eshbaugh, personal communication 1991).

I feel a capsule of *Capsicum* taxonomy will not be hard to swallow, and will be good for you.[5] Judging from the 1988 scholars' map (page 6) that shows what was then thought to be the distribution of each of these species at the time of the discovery, Columbus should have first encountered only domesticated *C. chinense* and *C. frutescens,* although the wild *C.*

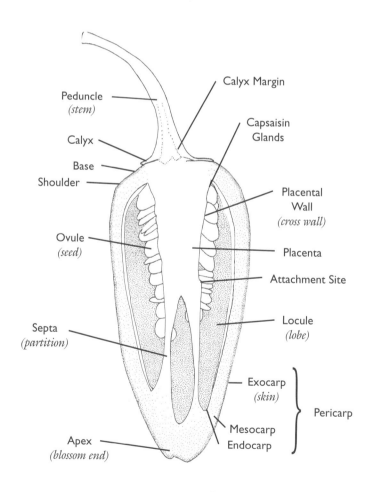

Peduncle
(stem)

Calyx

Base

Shoulder

Ovule
(seed)

Septa
(partition)

Apex
(blossom end)

Calyx Margin

Capsaisin Glands

Placental Wall
(cross wall)

Placenta

Attachment Site

Locule
(lobe)

Exocarp
(skin)

Mesocarp

Endocarp

Pericarp

Cross-section of a Pepper

annuum might have been around. However, as in my earlier writings and in previous pages of this book, I have theorized that *C. annuum* var. *annuum* had already been introduced to the West Indies despite that (map 1, page 6). Twenty-seven years after the discovery, when the relentless Hernando Cortés invaded Mexico, he encountered *C. a.* var. *annuum*. Later conquistadors would meet *C. baccatum* var. *pendulum* and *C. pubescens* in the Andean regions of South America. *Capsicum annuum* var. *annuum*, *C. frutescens*, and *C. chinense* are the only ones that diffused to become established in the Old World where the dubious *C. frutescens* now grows spontaneously or semi-wild. All three are known to grow in Africa, but only *C. a.* var. *annuum* and *C. frutescens* are significant in India and the Far East. It is thought that near the beginning of the twentieth century, *C. pubescens* was introduced from its Andean homeland to the highlands of Central America and Mexico, athough it could have moved into Mesoamerica with the conquistadors much earlier (Pickersgill, 1984: 118). It requires a cool, freeze-free climate with a long growing season, but the fleshy fruit deteriorates rapidly; as a consequence, its distribution is more limited than the others. For some reason, the widespread Andean *C. baccatum* var. *pendulum* has never caught on outside South America. I had good luck growing several varieties of these flavorful Andean *ajís* in my Texas garden, but perhaps their sprawling habit makes them undesirable commercially.

Virtually all of the capsicums found in markets around the world are *C. a.* var. *annuum*. If you plant seed saved from a garden where several cultivars of that variety are grown, you can expect considerable variation in the offspring. Consequently, there are untold numbers of varieties of this species. Interspecific sterility barriers prevent it crossing at all with *C. pubescens*, and only under special conditions will it cross with *C. b.* var. *pendulum*. It will cross with the other two, *C. frutescens* and *C. chinense*, and some of the resulting hybrids have produced viable seeds. Some scholars have thought that *C. annuum*, *C. frutescens*, and *C. chinense* have a common ancestor, and that the latter two are closely related. In fact, recent evidence has caused the pioneering *Capsicum* scholar, Charles B. Heiser, Jr., (1985:151) and others, to conclude that from both practical and biological standpoints there is no justification for recognizing *C.*

frutescens and *C. chinense* as separate species. When and if they are combined, the name used will be *C. frutescens* by nomenclatural priority, which may bring about another period of confusion in *Capsicum* names. However, whatever the name, they'll taste the same.

The only way you can reliably differentiate between the various *Capsicum* species is by the corolla and its calyx (the flower) and not the fruit. Let's start with the easy ones. The flowers of *C. b.* var. *pendulum* and *C. pubescens* are so different from the flowers of the other three species that if you saw those plants in bloom you would have no doubts. *C. b.* var. *pendulum* has a white flower with yellowish spots and white anthers that turn brownish yellow with age. *C. pubescens* has a beautiful purple flower with a tiny white border, and to make recognition even easier, its seeds are black. The flowers of the other three have white to greenish-white petals and purple anthers. *Capsicum chinense* and *C. frutescens* flowers are slightly greenish, while those of *C. annuum* var. *annuum* are milky white. Occasionally the annual pepper will have two flowers per node, but never more than two so don't confuse it with *C. chinense* which *always* has two or more. Unless you are growing the plants yourself, you will probably not be confronted with the problem of flower identification.

For the most part, it is impossible to positively identify a species by the fruit alone. But don't worry, only three cultivars that are not *C. a.* var. *annuum* are grown commercially in the United States at this time. One is 'Tabasco,' a *C. frutescens,* and the others are both *C. chinense*—*dátil*, and *habanero*. Your problem in the kitchen or market will be in distinguishing one *C. a.* var. *annuum* cultivar[6] from another.

If you purchase seeds or plants for your garden, record the cultivar name. The common names frequently vary from place to place and will often be different for the same cultivar depending on whether it is fresh or dried. The cultivar name should be the same everywhere, because it has been registered.

When Columbus first came upon capsicums, the Arawaks of the West Indies called it *axí,* which the Spaniards transliterated to *ají* (*ajé, agí*). That language is extinct now, and so are the Arawaks (page 7). As I've said earlier, it is highly probable that capsicums traveled from South America to the West Indies in prehistoric times with the South American name *ají* already attached. Today in the Dominican Republic and Haiti (formerly *Española*) and a few other places in the Caribbean along with much of South America, the pungent varieties are still called *ají*. However, *uchu* and *huayca* are ancient words used for capsicums by some Amerindian groups in the Andean area. Spanish called it *pimiento* or *pimientón* (depending on the size) after *pimienta* or East Indian black pepper. The Spanish names traveled with the plant to Spain, but not through Europe; it is called *peperone* in Italy, *piment* in France, and paprika by the Slavic peoples in the Balkans.

At the time the Spaniards arrived in Mexico, the Nahuatl-speaking natives called their fiery fruit *chilli*. The Nahuatl stem word *chilli* refers to the *chilli* plant. The root of *chilli* is *chil-*, which also means "red" but not "hot." To the generic word *chilli*, the term that described the particular *chilli* cultivar was added (e.g., *Tonalchilli* = chilli of the sun or summer, *Chiltecpin* = flea chilli). The term *chilli* first appeared in print in 1651, when the work of Francisco Hernandez was published. It is his interpretation of the sound of the word he heard the Nahuatl-speaking natives calling peppers. This was probably similar to "chee-yee," hence the Spanish double L, which sounds like y. According to Francis Karttunen, author of *An Analytical Dictionary of Nahuatl*, "when Nahuatl nouns ending in *-lli* have been borrowed into Spanish, they have changed *-lli* to *-le*, which is why *chilli* in Nahuatl has become *chile* in Spanish." It refers to both pungent and sweet types and is used in combination with and placed before a descriptive adjective, such as *chile colorado* (red chilli) or a word that indicates the place of origin, such as *chile poblano* (chilli from Pueblo). The same variety can have different names in different geographic regions, in various stages of maturity, or in the dried state. Consequently, the names of capsicums in Mexico can be very confusing.

The Portuguese language uses *pimenta* for capsicums and qualifies the various types—*pimenta-da-caiena*, cayenne pepper; *pimenta-da-malagueta*, red pepper; *pimenta-da-reino* or *-da-rabo*, black pepper; *pimenta-da-jamaica*, allspice; while *pimentão* is pimento, red pepper or just pepper. *Ají* and chile are not found in a Portuguese dictionary, nor did they carry the words chile or *Capsicum* with them in their travels.

The Dutch first, then the English, were probably responsible for carrying the current *Capsicum* names to the Eastern part of the world because in Australia, India, Indonesia, and Thailand chilli (chillies) or sometimes "chilly," is commonly used by English speakers for the pungent types, while the mild ones are called capsicums. However, until very recently only mild varieties were to be had in Australia, while Indonesians and Thais don't yet use sweet capsicums so they have no word for them. Each Far Eastern language has its own word for chillies—*prik* in Thai, *mirch* in Hindi, to name but two.

The United States is where the most confusion exists. Here we find both the anglicized spelling, chilli (chillies) or chili (chilies) and the Spanish chile (chiles) used by some for the pungent fruits of the *Capsicum* plant, while chili (minus one *l*) is also used as a short form of chili con carne, a variously concocted mixture of meat and chillies. *The Oxford English Dictionary* gives "chilli" as the primary usage, calling "chile" and "chili" variants. *Webster's New International Dictionary* prefers *chili*, followed by the Spanish chile and the Nahuatl chilli. In the American Southwest, the Spanish chile refers to the long green/red chilli that is/was known as the Anaheim or the long green/red chilli, but is now preferably called the New Mexican Chile by the folks there. New Mexicans even went so far as to enter the name in the *Congressional Record* of November 3, 1983 (misidentified as *C. frutescens* instead of *C. annuum* var. *annuum*). In an English-speaking country, it seems somewhat inconsistent to choose the Spanish chile over the anglicized chili, or chilli. It would be so much less confusing if they were called what they are—capsicums—but getting Americans to call peppers capsicums would be like getting us to use the metric system, but chilli instead of chili or chile is more realistic. To make matters even more confusing, pimento, an anglicized version of pimiento, has been adopted by the Georgia Pimento Growers Association for their mild product, but that word is not always used.

Not because one name is right and another is wrong, but for the sake of consistency and clarity, in this book *Capsicum* or peppers will be used when speaking of the fruit of the *Capsicum* in general, both sweet and pungent; chilli for the pungent types; chili for the spicy meat dish; and pimento for the sweet, thick-fleshed, heart-shaped red *Capsicum*. If *chile* in italics is used, it will refer to a native Mexican cultivar or, unitalicized, to the long green/red New Mexican

Chile type. Whenever possible the name of the specific fruit type/group[7] or cultivar name will be used. It is hoped that the reader will follow suit, thereby helping to stabilize the troublesome situation.

The important thing to remember is that each variety has its own character and if another variety is substituted, the flavor of the dish will change. Therefore it is essential that not only the specific *Capsicum* but also its specific form (fresh, dried, canned, pickled, etc.) be used and not just hot pepper or green pepper. Reading the cultivar descriptions starting on page 59 will make this easier.

Nutritional Considerations

Capsicums are not only good, they are also good for you. They contain more vitamin A than any other food plant; they are also an excellent source of vitamin C and the B vitamins. One jalapeño contains more vitamin A and C than three medium-size oranges. Capsicums also contain significant amounts of magnesium, iron, thiamine, riboflavin, and niacin. Even though chillies are not eaten in large quantities, small amounts are important where traditional diets provide only marginal vitamins.

In *Peppers,* I give a detailed account of the nutritional value of capsicums along with the story of their use by the Hungarian scientist Albert Szent-Györgyi in his discovery of vitamin C. Vitamin C is a very unstable nutrient. It is readily destroyed through exposure to oxygen in the air, by drying, and by heating, and it is soluble in water. In other words, cooking is very damaging to it. Keep cut or peeled capsicums well covered to prevent contact with oxygen and don't allow them to stand in water for more than one hour. Nevertheless, considerable vitamin C is retained in cooked and canned green capsicums. Green capsicums are higher in vitamin C than ripe red capsicums because vitamin C diminishes with maturity. Vitamin A is just the opposite; it increases as the *Capsicum* matures and dries. Also, vitamin A is not lost when exposed to oxygen, and is quite stable during the cooking and preservation process.

Pepper seeds are primarily carbohydrates with some protein and fat. They also have a little manganese and copper, but otherwise add little nutritionally. In Anglo-America they are traditionally removed but in other countries that is seldom customary—especially in the small chillies. Removing seeds from fresh green or red chillies reduces the pungency to some extent because the seeds absorb capsaicin from the placental wall where they are attached. In dry chillies or any peppers that have large, mature seeds (ex. ancho and New Mexican Chile types), they have become woody in texture and some find that texture undesirable; however, others grind them up to give a nutty flavor to sauces (ex. *chile cascabel*). Higher grades of paprika and pepper flakes have had the seeds and veins removed before grinding. Whether you leave the seeds in or remove them is strictly a matter of personal preference having little effect on nutritional value.

1 Gram Uncooked	Vit. A (ICUS)	Vit. C (MG.S)
Bell pepper	50	1.20
Fresh orange	2.24	.538
Carrot	30.5	.35
Potato	.375	.016
Tomato	8.49	.22

Weight conscious readers may be happy to learn that capsicums and a few other pungent spices cause one's metabolic rate to increase after eating them. This diet-induced thermic effect requires six grams of chilli combined with three grams of prepared mustard to burn off an average of forty-five calories in three hours (Henry & Emery, 1985:165).[8]

In recent years much has been written concerning the nutritional and medical attributes of capsicums as reported in scientific studies. During this same period the public has become more health conscious, which has led to increased nutritional awareness. The terms low-calorie, low-cholesterol, complex carbohydrates, high-fiber, low-sodium, unsaturated oils, and low-fat have become part of our daily vocabulary, and food growers and processors are responding to public demand by providing for these nutritional requirements. Health authorities are in agreement that a change in our traditional American food-style is vital to good health. Capsicums conform to these food restrictions and at the same time their distinctive flavor peps up an otherwise bland, creamless, butterless, eggless, saltless meal. Capsicums are a real health food!

Capsaicin, The Pungent Principle

People don't eat capsicums for the vitamins and fiber; they eat them because they are pungent. Take away the vitamins and the fiber and people would still eat chillies, but take away the capsaicin and they don't want them. A unique group of mouth-warming amide-type alkaloids containing a small vanilloid structural component is responsible for the burning sensation associated with capsicums by acting directly on the pain receptors in the mouth and throat.[9] This vanilloid element is present in other pungent plants used for spices such as ginger and black pepper. For some time capsaicin was believed to contain only one active pungent principle, but more recently, studies have added other compounds to form a pungent group of which capsaicin is the most important part. Three of these capsaicinoid components cause the sensation of "rapid bite" at the back of the palate and throat, and two others cause a long, low-intensity bite on the tongue and midpalate. Differences in the proportions of these compounds may account for the characteristic "burns" of the different *Capsicum* cultivars. In both sweet and pungent capsicums, the major part of the organs secreting these pungent alkaloids are localized in the placenta, to which the seeds are attached, along with dissepiment, which is the part of the placenta that divides the interior cavity into sections or lobes (page 51). The seeds contain only a low concentration of capsaicin. Historian Bartolomé de Las Casas made an astute observation about the pungency in capsicums four and a half centuries ago: "This is what one should know. The part that burns are the seeds and the veins (*rayas*) that form inside the compartments where the seeds appear. All that is between these and does not come in contact with the veins is not pungent, it is sweet and smooth."

The response to some additives in food used at optimal levels is the perception in the mouth of a warm, mouth-watering quality. A sensory analyst and *Capsicum* authority from India, V. S. Govindarajan, insists that this response should be defined by the term "pungency," rather than the other less desirable connotations routinely used—hot, stinging, irritating, sharp, caustic, acrid, biting, burning. He also suggests that pungency be given the status of a gustatory characteristic of food as are sweet, sour, bitter, saline, astrin-

gent, or alkaline. I try to say "pungent" instead of "hot" but long-standing habit interferes just as it does when I try to use "centimeters" instead of "inches."

The capsaicin content is influenced by the growing conditions of the plant and the age of the fruit, and could possibly be variety-specific. Dry, stressful conditions will increase the amount of capsaicin. Beginning about the eleventh day, the capsaicin content increases, becoming detectable when the fruit is about four weeks old and reaching its peak just before maturity, then dropping somewhat in the ripening stage. Sun-drying usually reduces the capsaicin content, the highest retention being obtained when the fruits are air-dried, with minimum exposure to sunlight.

Many people swear to me that sweet capsicums in their garden have crossed with hot ones, resulting in their sweet ones producing pungent fruit the same year. With the evidence hot in their hands it is hard to make them believe that a cross will not evidence itself in the same growth cycle. What actually happened to their bell or banana pepper is something called sequestering (accumulating) by botanists, and it is not a phenomenon particular to *Capsicum*. Even though the cultivar planted had been bred until it was non-pungent, non-poisonous, etc., it still held some of the original genes that would produce capsaicin or a particular poison. Occasionally, climatic factors combine with the aging process, causing those latent characteristics to build up so that towards the end of a stressful season they have compounded to produce a marked pungency or increase in toxicity in the otherwise non-pungent or non-poisonous fruit.

Ethnobotanist Gary Nabhan explains that the distasteful and sometimes poisonous alkaloids found in plants serve to keep the seed out of the wrong animals and get them in the right ones in order to guarantee seed dispersal as the animal moves from the feeding place. Once dispersed by the animal, the seed must be able to germinate. If a chilli seed is to germinate, it must pass through the creature's digestive tract undamaged. Birds have a digesive tract that softens the seed without significant damage. The capsaicin discourages other animals from eating chillies, while the red color attracts the birds to the ripe fruit. Many small animals cannot see red. Birds, the only other animal besides man thought to eat chillies on purpose, lack appropriate pain receptors and are therefore untouched by the chillies they consume with such relish. They miss the fun!

Capsaicin is hard to detect by chemical tests. It has virtually no odor or flavor, but a drop of a solution containing one part in 100,000 causes a persistent burning on the tongue. The original method for determining the heat in capsicums is the Scoville Organoleptiac Test, which is a taste test developed in 1912 that relies on the physiological action of the compound. It is a highly subjective method and has been largely replaced by the use of high-pressure liquid chromatography (HPLC), a reproducible technique for quantifying capsaicinoids in products using capsicums; however, the results are still given in Scoville Units. HPLC only measures the relevant amount of capsaicinoid compound of one particular pod, from a particular location, particular season, and particular plant. The same cultivar may test differently when grown under different circumstances. The results of such procedures can only be considered to be a general guide. In your kitchen, you should taste a tiny portion to estimate the pungency and adjust your usage accordingly. Don't be afraid; just do it. Instead of rating the pungency of the various cultivars described in "What Is a Pepper?" in Scoville Units, a simple scale of one to ten has been used here because I was not able to find two published Scoville Unit rankings in agreement.

Capsaicin is eight times more pungent than the piperine in black pepper, but unlike black pepper, which inhibits all tastes, capsaicin only obstructs the perception of sour and bitter; it does not impair our discernment of other gustatory characteristics of food. Capsaicin activates the defensive and digestive systems by acting as an irritant to the oral and gastrointestinal membranes. That irritation increases the flow of saliva and gastric acids. Eating capsaicin also causes the neck, face, and front of the chest to sweat in a reflexive response to the burning in the mouth. Very little capsaicin is absorbed as it passes through the digestive tract, an uncomfortable consequence of which is jalaproctitis or burning defecation (Diehl & Bauer, 1978). This is probably the basis for the Hungarian saying "Paprika burns twice." Capsaicin irritates the intestinal lining and augments its movement, thereby reducing the transit time of food. It has the same effect of fiber as a restorer of "regularity" (McGee, 1984:557).

There is little evidence that constant consumption of chillies has an effect—either positive or negative—on the average person. If stomach ulcers are present or developing, the stimulation of gastric acid secretions caused by eating chillies is a potential hazard.

Eating capsicums not only increases the flow of saliva and gastric secretions, it also stimulates the appetite. These functions work together to aid in the digestion of food. The increased saliva helps ease the passage of food through the mouth to the stomach, where it is mixed with the activated gastric juice. These functions play an important role in the lives of people whose daily diet is principally starch-based.

Emotional upsets, nicotine, or caffeine greatly increase the amount of acid in the stomach, and ulcers are often the result. It is only common sense to recognize that eating stimulating chillies while emotionally tilted, smoking, sipping coffee, or having a few margaritas will really fill your stomach with acid. The good news is, our body has a complex physical-chemical barrier to protect your stomach lining from the acid. The bad news is that alcohol and aspirin will readily penetrate that barrier. One aspirin causes the loss of only a small amount of blood, but in conjunction with alcohol it can bring on excessive bleeding.

There is a preventive measure you can take if you dearly love to mix chillies with margaritas or some other alcoholic imbibement. Fat takes hours longer than carbohydrates or proteins to digest. Stimulants such as alcohol take longer to affect someone who has eaten a fatty snack such as cheese before drinking. Cheese serves to coat the stomach. If you have a finicky stomach, eat some cheese or drink some cream before indulging in food highly spiced with chillies and washed down with wine, beer, or margaritas.

There are several ways to put out the fire. Capsaicin is not soluble in water. Although no amount of water will wash it away, cool water will give temporary relief by changing the surface temperature. In 1984 I discovered that the addition of a small amount of chlorine or ammonia ionized the capsaicin compound, changing it into a soluble salt (Andrews, 1984:127). This works miracles on your hands but, of course, you can't drink chlorine or ammonia. Like many organic compounds, capsaicin is soluble in alcohol. Again, this works on the skin, but caution must be noted when you drink it because we have already seen that alcohol penetrates the barriers nature has provided to protect your stomach lining—as well as being intoxicating. For your burning mouth, try using vodka as a mouthwash and gargle, then spit it out—great for the dedicated driver. Cheap vodka works just as well!

Recently it was determined that oral burning can be relieved by lipoproteins such as casein that remove capsaicin in a manner similar to the action of a detergent, thereby breaking the bond the capsaicin had formed with the pain receptors in your mouth. Milk and yogurt are the most readily available sources of the casein. It is the casein, not the fat, in milk that does the job, therefore, butter and cheese will not have the same effect. *Raita*, the traditional cool yogurt and chopped vegetable accompaniment to fiery curries, has served this function for generations in India (recipe page 116).

Capsaicin, or the burning sensation produced by it, may prove to be a non-habit-forming alternative to the addictive drugs used to control pain. The fact that the vanilloids occur in most pungent plants has led neurobiologists to conclude that the mammalian nervous system has specific neuroreceptors for those compounds. Birds and other non-mammalian creatures such as snails or frogs do not have similar neuroreceptors. Studies of capsaicin and its relationship to substance P, a neuropeptide that sends the message of pain to our brains, has led investigators to conclude that capsaicin has the capacity to deplete nerves of their supply of substance P, thereby preventing the transmission of those hurt-filled signals. Already this ability of capsaicin is being used to treat the pain associated with shingles, rheumatoid arthritis, and phantom-limb pain. Obviously, Native Americans had a sound basis for treating toothaches and the pain of childbirth by eating chillies, that the rest of the world has been slow to recognize.

Aroma, Flavor, and Color

I am often asked if certain capsicums, especially ornamentals, are edible. Yes, all capsicums are edible, but, like the Orwellian pigs, some are more edible than others. Flavor makes the difference. The flavor compound of capsicums is located in the outer wall (pericarp). Very little is found in the placenta and cross wall, and essentially none in the seeds (page 51). Color and flavor go hand in hand because the flavoring principle appears to be associated with the carotenoid pigment: strong color and strong flavor are linked. For example, the red bells are far superior in flavor to the less expensive greens. Unfortunately, most people don't consider anything but the price or pungency when they select a cultivar. *Capsicum pubescens* (rocoto) and the varieties of *C. chinense* (habanero) are more aromatic and have a decidedly different flavor than those of *C. annuum* var. *annuum,* but for most Anglo-Saxons (*Gringos*) those two species are too pungent to enjoy. Being able to recognize the differences in flavors of the various cultivars is most important in cooking. Using a different variety can completely change the character of a dish. You cannot substitute an ancho for a guajillo or a bell pepper for a banana pepper without a noticeable difference.

Color in a painting is the most compelling element, and it is an important adjunct in foods as well. Few foods are more stimulating to our visual sense than an array of brilliant red, yellow, green, orange, purple, and brown capsicums.[10] Even if you don't eat capsicums, their use as garnishes can enhance the total appearance of your dish or table. The carotenoid pigments responsible for the color in capsicums make them commercially important as natural dyes in food and drug products throughout the world. Red capsanthin, the most important pigment, is not found in immature green capsicums. All capsicums will change color as they mature from green to other hues. Green capsicums are simply gathered before they are fully ripe. Brown-colored capsicums result from the retention of the green chlorophyl, which mixes with the red pigment to make brown in the mature fruit. Unripe capsicums have better keeping quality and are less difficult to transport than ripe ones; consequently, they are more available and less expensive in the market. Unfortunately for the consumer, the distinctive *Capsicum* flavor develops only as the fruit ripens, reaching its peak at maturity.

Taste and smell are separate perceptions. If you are not conscious of the distinctive aroma of a *Capsicum* you should be—it adds to the pleasure of eating it. Americans are learning to appreciate aroma in capsicums as Asians and Africans have long done. Several aroma compounds produce the fragrance. The taste buds on the tongue can discern certain flavors at dilutions up to one part in two million, but odors can be detected at a dilution of one part in one billion. The more delicate flavors of foods are recognized as aromas in the nasal cavity adjacent to the mouth. Sensory cells with this function are much more discerning than the tongue. Compare the aroma of a jalapeño with that of habanero—you'll recognize the specific odor of each immediately. The enchantment of peppers is like that of a lovely woman whose charm of shape and subtle perfume entice you to her and whose inner fire creates mystique and desire.

Why Chilli Lovers Love Chillies

What is it about a fruit that makes one-quarter of the adults on the earth eat it every day in spite of the fact that nature designed it to burn in order to protect it? They can't all be capsimaniacs suffering from chilliphilia, can they? Psychologist Paul Rozin has probably looked into that question more completely than anyone else, writing numerous fascinating papers detailing the results of his studies. I can do no better than to summarize his findings.

Rozin looks first at the adaptive/evolutionary explanations commonly offered. One by one he has shot them down for lack of demonstrable evidence. Nor has he found any antibacterial effect; capsicums do not help preserve food and capsicums weren't used to disguise spoiling food in their original New World setting. The fact that the chilli is used in greatest quantity in mild climates such as Korea and highland Mexico negates the claim for a sweating/cooling effect. There are, however, other more probable theories. The extremely high vitamin A and C content give them a nutritional advantage that early man may or may not have recognized. By activating the flow of saliva, capsicums aid in chewing dry, starchy foods and increase their flavor. Capsicums have a wide range of aromas, flavors, colors, and pungencies to provide variation to monotonous diets. The burning in the mouth gives a feeling of fullness (a meat quality) to repetitious, bland meals. In Europe the initial adoption of the chilli was medicinally and socially motivated. Of these modifying values, flavor enhancement and salivation are the most likely to have been realized and utilized. The burning effect produced by capsaicin is a principal reason for liking capsicums. The initially negative feeling becomes positive. Regular consumption of chilli has only a slight desensitizing effect, good news for the chilli lover who craves the burn (Rozin, 1990:248).

Liking to eat chillies is definitely an acquired taste unique to human mammals. Young children do not care for them. In the first stage, the initial exposure to chilli, few like it. The second stage is liking it—not everyone does. Preference comes about initially from the enhancement of the flavors of other foods. This progresses into a liking for the burn. Professor Rozin concludes, "Chilli is currently consumed for one reason: it tastes good."

What is a *Capsicum*? An old dictionary of "Aztequismos" defined chile as "*el miembro viril*" or virile member (Robelo, 1904:131). However, since this book concerns food and why we like to eat capsicums as a food, I'll not go into the medical or physiological aspects that concern responses to such sensations, as its aphrodisiac potential, opponent-endorphin responses, and benign masochism. If you want to know more about capsaicin-stimulating endorphins scurrying about in your brain or how the enjoyment of constrained risks brings out the thrill-seeker in you, I suggest reading the work of Paul Rozin and Andrew Weil, or looking at my *Peppers*. Happy mouth-surfing!

Look at Me
Cultivar Descriptions

he peppers you are about to see are shown off the plant and without foliage, just as you will find them in the market place. They have been drawn in the same scale relative to each other so that you will not be seeing fruit that is tiny drawn large in order to fill the space on the page.

Banana Pepper and 'Hungarian Wax'

Capsicum annuum var. *annuum* Linné

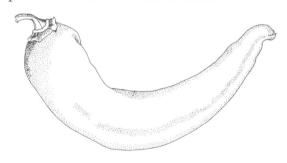

COLOR: Pale yellow-green to yellow, maturing to bright red

SHAPE: Elongated cylinder, tapering to a point. Wax-type

SHAPE: 5½ to 6 inches long by 1½ inches wide

PUNGENCY: Sweet; 0. Hot; 5

SUBSTITUTES: 'Cubanelle' for sweet; 'Caloro', or 'Santa Fe Grande' for hot

OTHER NAMES: 'Sweet Banana', 'Hungarian Yellow Wax'

USES:

FRESH: in salads, as garnishes, stuffed like in celery, in vegetable dishes and stews, fried

PICKLED: as garnishes, in salads, sandwiches, as a condiment

SOURCES:

FRESH: Home garden, farmer's markets

DRIED: Not used dried

PROCESSED: Pickled banana peppers available in food stores

SEEDS: Most seed suppliers

AVAILABLE CULTIVARS: 'Early Sweet Banana', 'Giant Yellow Banana', 'Hungarian Yellow Wax', 'Long Sweet Yellow'

This beautiful, flavorful pepper is a crisp addition to an hors d'oeuvre tray, but its availability depends on your location. It is a favorite of the home gardener, so look for it in a farmer's market. The sweet form is known as the Banana Pepper and the hot is called Hungarian Wax. Both are long, tapered, yellow fruits that cannot be distinguished until you take a bite. They are commonly used in their immature yellow state. The ripe red Banana Pepper is good in salads and vegetable dishes, but the fully ripe 'Hungarian Wax' is almost too hot to eat. This cultivar was introduced from Hungary in 1932.

Bell Pepper

Capsicum annuum var. *annuum* Linné

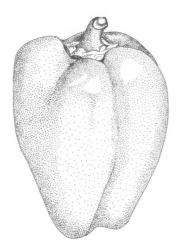

COLOR: Green to red, orange, yellow, brown, or purple

SHAPE: Blocky. A few cultivars, such as the tomato-shaped 'Sunnybrook' or the long, narrow 'Ruby King,' do not conform. Bell-type

SIZE: 4 to 6 inches long by 3½ to 4 inches wide

PUNGENCY: Sweet; 0, except for Mexi-bell; 3 to 5

SUBSTITUTES: Banana, 'Cubanelle', pimento peppers

OTHER NAMES: Capsicums, mango, *morrón*, *pimentón*, or any one of the hundreds of hybrid cultivar names

USES: Stuffed (parboiled 2 to 3 minutes first), fried, in casseroles, vegetable dishes, salads, garnishes, relishes, soups, crudités, sauces

SOURCES:

FRESH: Food stores, farmer's markets, home garden

DRIED: Bell peppers are not dried whole. Dehydrated flakes can be found in the spice section of food stores

PROCESSED: Ripe red ones are canned as a pale substitute for pimento

SEEDS: There is a multitude of cultivars; any seed company will have one or more. Popular cultivars: Ace Hybrid, 'Argo', 'Big Bertha', 'Cal Wonder', 'Klondike Bell', 'Ma Belle', 'Oriole', 'Staddon's Select', 'Yolo Wonder'

Who can't recognize a bell pepper? Sweet peppers of the type known as bell peppers are the most used *Capsicum* in the United States. Sweet peppers were developed through the process of selection by the Amerindians before Columbus discovered America and were known as bell peppers as early as 1681. A lobed pepper of the tomato-type was probably the precursor of the ubiquitous bell. In a small still-life painted in 1814, Raphael Peale depicts green bell peppers, thereby recording their early presence in the markets of Philadelphia. Since that date American growers have developed several hundred different bell cultivars with such fanciful names such as 'Bull Nose' and 'Big Bertha.' 'Calwonder' ('California Wonder') was introduced in 1928, and is the most popular.

The bell, a thick-fleshed, sweet pepper used primarily as a vegetable, is consumed most frequently in the unripe green stage even though they may ripen to red, orange, yellow, brown, and deep purple. In recent years pepper breeders have developed cultivars that remain green when fully mature. In the midwestern United States the bell-types are frequently called "mangoes" even though they are in no way related to that tropical fruit. The food historian William Woys Weaver explains that seventeenth-century merchants in England imported stuffed pickled mangoes from India. English cooks, with no source for that tropical fruit, substituted such things as cucumbers and unripe peaches in their efforts to reproduce the delicacy. When the recipe arrived in their American colonies, baby muskmelons and bell peppers replaced the exotic mangoes and the name was transferred to the peppers (recipe page 213). Most older cook books call for bell pepper when a recipe requires sweet green pepper.

The fruit can grow erect or pendent and there may be from two to four locules or lobes. For some reason the four-lobed fruits sell better. When selecting bell peppers, choose those that are well-shaped, firm, and thick fleshed. Pale, blemished, wrinkled, limp specimens are not desirable. The fully ripe red or colored fruit is much more flavorful and digestible than the common unripe green ones. Holland is producing beautiful, colorful, large bell peppers for the American market which are quite delicious but expensive. Some American growers are beginning to compete for the market the Dutch have created. Those colorful, tasty bells have become favorites of American chefs. Bells are also grown in Mexico for export to the United States; however, they are not commonly eaten in Latin America.

The bell does not need to be peeled before using; however, in recipes for stuffed peppers it is advisable to parboil them. This can also be done in the microwave by putting them in a covered microwave-safe dish with a tablespoon of water for a minute or two, depending on the number of peppers. Roasted and peeled ripe bells impart a new flavor dimension to salads and casseroles. Store the fresh peppers in the vegetable drawer of the refrigerator.

Cascabel
Capsicum annuum var. *annuum* Linné

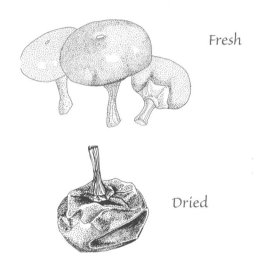

Fresh

Dried

COLOR:
   FRESH: Dark green to reddish brown
   DRIED: Dark reddish brown with translucent, glossy skin
SHAPE: Oblate. Cherry-type
SIZE: 1 inches deep by 1 to 1½ inches wide
PUNGENCY: Hot, 4
SUBSTITUTES: *Catarina*, cayenne, *guajillo, japonés*
OTHER NAMES: *Bolita, bola, chile trompo, coban, trompillo*
USES: Ground/powdered in sauces, tamales, sausages, casseroles; as a seasoning; toasted or untoasted
SOURCES:
   FRESH: Not used
   DRIED: Imported; Mexican food stores, border markets
   PROCESSED: Probably not imported
   SEEDS: Mexico or specialty seed suppliers.
      Cultivar: 'Real Mirasol'

The Mexican *cascabel* is a cherry pepper look-alike when it is fresh but there the resemblance ends. When the ripe fruit dries to a dark reddish brown color, the skin becomes translucent and the seeds rattle around inside, hence its name cascabel, or jingle bell. Its look-alike, the thick-fleshed cherry pepper, does not dry satisfactorily. At times the smaller elongate *catarina* and the larger *guajillo*, which also dry with a translucent skin and seeds that rattle, are incorrectly labeled *cascabel*. This round red pepper may grow erect or pendent. It is cultivated in the Mexican states of Durango, San Luis Potosí, and Coahuila. When ground—seeds and all—the nutty flavor of the roasted cascabel makes a wonderful sauce. Smaller varieties such as *bolita* (little ball) and *bola* are pickled.

Do not confuse the round *cascabel* with the smaller, conical 'Cascabella'.

Cayenne
Capsicum annuum var. *annuum* Linné

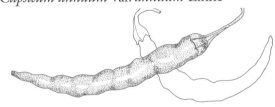

COLOR: Dark green to red; new yellow and orange
SHAPE: Elongate cylinder, wrinkled, curved. Cayenne-type
SIZE: 5 to 6 inches long by ½ to ¾ inches wide
PUNGENCY: Hot to very hot; 7 to 8
SUBSTITUTES: Jalapeño, *serrano*, Thai
OTHER NAMES: A pepper of the cayenne-type was one of the first, if not the first, capsicums introduced to the Far East. It has become the most common type of *Capsicum* grown in the world, with different names in every country.
USES: In Creole and Cajun dishes, Indian, Indonesian, Thai, Pakistani, Hunan, and Sichuan cooking. In meat and vegetable dishes, salad dressings, and as a table spice
SOURCES:
   FRESH: Farmer's markets, home gardens, and some food stores throughout the country
   DRIED: In any ethnic or supermarket spice section, powdered or whole

PROCESSED: Powdered in the spice section of almost any food store; used in some pepper sauces; used in some Cajun seasonings

SEEDS: Most seed suppliers carry one or more varieties

AVAILABLE CULTIVARS: 'Cayenne Langer', 'Cayenne Large Red Thick', 'Cayenne Pickling', 'Golden Cayenne', 'Hades Hot', 'Hot Portugal', 'Japanese Fuschin', 'Jaune Long', 'Long Red', 'Long Slim', 'Mammoth Cayenne', 'Ring of Fire'

The cayenne chilli could be called the Cajun or Creole pepper because it is such an integral part of those cuisines. In the past many have said this pre-Columbian cultivar probably originated in French Guiana on the northeastern coast of South America and was named for the Cayenne River there, but my recent travels and research have shown that to be wrong.[1] I am now convinced it came to Brazil from West Africa, and the Cayenne River was named for the pepper. Actually the Portuguese obtained the Mesoamerican domesticate from Spanish sources soon after Columbus had found it on his first voyage to the Greater Antilles (page 8). It was described by Peter Martyr as finger-like, but the name cayenne came later.

The Portuguese immediately introduced it to the gardens of their established trade castles and forts on the Guinea and Gold coasts of West Africa where it found the tropical climate required for its propagation. From there the pepper went to their Atlantic sugar islands. These bases provided the source for a rapid, world-wide dispersal of that long, red, finger-like pepper. In those days, all things—plant, animal, or man—from that West African area carried the name "Ginnie" with it. (Map 4, page 12)

By the time the Portuguese introduced sugar plantations and slavery to Brazil, "Ginnie Peppers" had become requisite to the diet of the slaves, so to Brazil they went. In fact, capsicums became an indispensable adjunct to the slave trade by all participating nations from its inhuman inception to its merciful conclusion.

In northern Brazil the dominant Amerindians were the Tupians. Their language, Tupi, became the *lingua franca* in the Valley of the Amazon. In their effort to transform "Ginnie" to fit their Tupi language, the word became *kyinha, quiya,* or *quiynha,* pronounced "Kee-e-ña," but corrupted by Europeans to cayenne

(Martius, 1863:419). In Brazil, the new pepper, *Capsicum annum*, became *Quiya uca,* and moved north with the Tupians to their river valley homelands between the Amazon and the Orinoco. At some time after this, an island off present day French Guiana acquired the name,[2] as did a river and a town. Following the Dutch capture of northern Brazil in 1624 (held to 1654) and the sugar islands off West Africa (1625–1630, 1641) from the Portuguese, they became the dominant slave and pepper traders between Africa, Brazil, and the Lesser Antilles, thus the new Tupi name went with the finger-like pepper from Brazil to the Guianas then to French and Dutch Antillian sugar plantations. Hence the pungent red pod returned to its West Indian homeland after more than 150 years of world-wide travel.

In 1682, René de LaSalle claimed the Mississippi River and all the land drained by it for France. Louisiana was founded in 1699 and New Orleans located in 1718. For some time after its organization, Louisiana experienced many difficulties in getting and establishing her domestic plants and animals (Post, 1933:584). The properous French West Indian sugar plantation island of St. Domingue served as the principal distribution point for imported domesticated plants and animals to their southernmost North American colony. Cayenne pepper conceivably arrived in Louisiana with African slaves via the trade routes from French West Indian colonies. The exact period in which the cayenne pepper arrived in Louisiana has not been determined, but it had probably been introduced by the middle of the eighteenth century while the French were in control. (Map 3, page 11)

With the Treaty of Paris in 1763, after one-hundred years of French ownership, the Spaniards were awarded New Orleans and Louisiana west of the Mississippi. They took command in 1766 and held sway in Louisiana until 1802. During that period the Spanish cuisine melded with existing French cookery and a "native born" or Creole cuisine was launched. From 1756 to 1785 the arrival of French Acadians (Cajuns) exiled by the British added a new facet to the local culinary scene, but the cayenne pepper remained a fundamental ingredient. No Creole or Cajun specialty is complete without its special bite.

Soon after the discovery of America, the same cayenne-type pepper from Portuguese West Africa was distributed to India and the Orient after introduction by the Portuguese. This long, curved, sharp pointed fruit with its wrinkled skin and biting pungency is the fruit-type for a group of peppers often called "finger peppers," "ginnie peppers," "chilli-peppers" or "cayenne-peppers." It ranges in size from three to twelve inches in length with a narrow shoulder. In the United States it is cultivated commercially in Louisiana and is grown in home gardens throughout the country. Although the long, slender, curved fruit is typical, a blocky and shorter type has been developed in recent years. In Mexico, peppers of the cayenne-type are *mirasol/guajillo* and *chile de árbol,* but they are not the same cultivar as our cayenne pepper. Although the Far Eastern cultivars have been grown for centuries, they have neither common nor cultivar names.

In commercial circles, the dried cayenne is known as "ginnie pepper."[3] What is sold as powdered cayenne pepper may or may not contain cayenne peppers (page 61). It is usually made from one or more very pungent, small red varieties grown in India, Japan, Africa, Louisiana, South Carolina, and Mexico. This is the red chili powder called for in Indian, Pakistani, and Indonesian recipes. Cayenne pepper has become synonymous with dried chili powder or packaged "red pepper." If a dish has been seasoned with cayenne pepper or is very pungent, it is said to be "cayenned."

SOURCES:
FRESH: Home gardens, farmer's markets
DRIED: Not used dried
PROCESSED: Pickle section in food markets
SEEDS: Most seed suppliers have at least one cultivar
AVAILABLE CULTIVARS: 'Bird's Eye', 'Cerise', 'Cherry Jubilee', 'Cherry Sweet', 'Christmas Cherry', 'Super Sweet', 'Red Giant', 'Tom Thumb'

This rotund pepper has been around since before Columbus discovered America. Portrayed by such early herbalists as Fuchs (1543) and L'Éscluse (1611), its shape is similar to that of a cherry, hence its name. This name is applied to a group or type of pepper that has fruits which are globose or oblate. They can be sweet or hot, large or small, erect or pendent, and they are grown as often as ornamentals as they are for food. The cherry pepper does not dry satisfactorily and is used almost entirely as a pickled condiment. There are many cultivars of the cherry-type.

In Mexico, the pungent *cascabel* has the outward appearance of a cherry pepper; however it has very thin flesh which dries readily and becomes translucent. The *cascabel* is only used when dried.

Cherry
Capsicum annuum var. *annuum* Linné

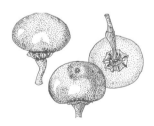

COLOR: Medium green to red
SHAPE: Oblate. Cherry-type
SIZE: $\frac{3}{4}$ to 1 inches long by $1\frac{1}{4}$ to $1\frac{1}{2}$ inches wide
PUNGENCY: Sweet or hot; 0 to 4
SUBSTITUTES: Any pickled pepper
OTHER NAMES: Hot cherry, Hungarian cherry, sweet cherry
USES: Pickles, relishes, jams, salads, garnishes, condiments

Chile de Arbol
Capsicum annuum var. *annuum* Linné

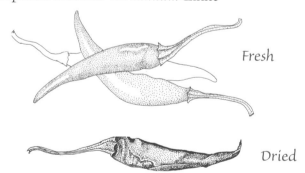

Fresh

Dried

COLOR:
FRESH: Green to red
DRIED: Bright red
SHAPE: Elongate conical, narrow shoulders; pointedapex. Cayenne type
SIZE: 3 inches long by $\frac{3}{8}$ inches wide
PUNGENCY: Hot; 7

SUBSTITUTES: Cayenne, *chiltepín*, *japonés*, dried Thai

OTHER NAMES: *Alfilerillo*, *bravo*, *cola de rata*, *cuauhchilli*, ginnie pepper, *pico de pájaro*

USES: In table sauces

SOURCES:

    FRESH: Seldom used fresh; home gardens in the United States

    DRIED: Found packaged in the spice section of many supermarkets and ethnic food stores

    PROCESSED: Not processed

    SEEDS: Catalogs of specialty seed companies; from packaged dried fruits

This very narrow, curved chilli keeps its bright red color when dried. It is used with the seeds, as all chillies are in Thailand. Although it is not very flavorful, it is very, very picante, making it desirable for sauces or as a capsaicin pickup with less pungent, but more savory, varieties.

Chiltepin (Chiltecpín)

Capsicum annuum var. *glabriusculum* (Dunal, 1852) Heiser & Pickersgill, 1975

COLOR:

    FRESH: Green to red, some nearly black; glossy

    DRIED: Brownish red

SHAPE: Ovoid

SIZE: $\frac{1}{4}$ inch long by $\frac{3}{4}$ inch diameter

PUNGENCY: Very hot; 10+

SUBSTITUTES: Really nothing, but try cayenne pepper, Thai peppers, Tabasco peppers (not the sauce)

OTHER NAMES: *Amash*, *amomo*, bird, bravo, *chilillo*, *chilipiquin*, *chilpaya*, *chilpequin*, *chiltipiquín*, *del monte*, *huarahuao*, malagueta, *max*, *piquén*, to name but a few

USES: Fresh or dried they are mashed together with anything on your plate; table sauces; seasoning meats, vegetables, soups, and stews. Mash some of the peppers in a little hot water and allow to sit a few minutes, then use the water for seasoning.

SOURCES:

    FRESH: In the lower part of the Southwest, grows wild in backyards, fencerows, anywhere birds stop; in the rest of the country, found in some markets

    DRIED: Ethnic food markets, Native Seeds.SEARCH, home gardens

    PROCESSED: Some pickled in the Southwest; erratic availability in markets

    SEEDS: Native Seeds.SEARCH; specialty seed houses, friends in the Southwest. They are slow to germinate. Ask your friendly neighborhood birds to help you.

A little dish of this tiny fireball always stays on my kitchen counter. I use at least one in almost everything from salad dressings to cream sauces to kill the blandness. There are many names for this wild little chilli. Two of the most common ones are *chiltepín* for the ovoid type, and *chilpequin* for the longer, more acute form. The variously spelled common name is a corruption of the original Nauhatl name, *chiltecpín* (pronounced chill-tech-peen). Many South Texans call them all *chilpequin* or *chilipequin*; however, in Mexico *chiltepín* (prounounced chill-tey-peen) is more commonly used. Previously I have referred to this pepper as *Capsicum annuum* var. *aviculare* (Dierbach, 1829), D'Arcy and Eshbaugh; 1973 *Phytologia*, 25(6):350; but the International Board for Plant Genetic Resources has adopted *C. annuum* var. *glabriusculum* (Dunal, 1852) Heiser & Pickersgill, 1975; Baileya, 19:156. Since the board is striving for worldwide consistency, it would seem best to use their choice even though I like *aviculare*, which refers to birds.

Many think they have discovered a new pepper when they find a slightly different *chiltepín*, but there are so many intergrades in size, shape and color—some are even black—throughout its range from the American Southwest to Colombia, that there is no use getting excited. To add to the confusion within this extensive range, the tiny forms of *C. frutescens* are also commonly termed "bird peppers." Birds eat tiny peppers greedily because, unlike mammals, they don't have the neuroreceptors affected by capsaicin. Birds become the primary agents for the dispersal of this native pepper when they expel the seed of the digested fruit they have picked and swallowed whole from the bush. It would appear that the germination rate of native chiltepines benefits from their passing through the gut of certain birds; at least they are not harmed by the ingestion (J. J. Tewksbury, Personal Communication, 1999). Otherwise, the germination time is longer than that of a domesticated pepper.

Unlike most chillies, the *chiltepín* prefers partially shaded to shady locations. This is probably a result of the noted relationship with their avian disperal agents and a bird's affinity for trees. It also does well in pots. I've had the same plant in a big clay container for over ten years. Older plants become quite woody. The difficulty in harvesting this little fruit, combined with the fact that most are only found in the wild, makes it *very* expensive: ten dollars or more per pound. But a little goes a long way and you have to be quick—the birds are waiting!

One of the favored ways to use *chiltepíns* is to fill a small sauce bottle about three fourths full with the whole fruits, then fill the bottle with vinegar, sherry, or tequilla. Let it sit awhile, then douse vegetables, soups, or what-have-you with it. I use kitchen sherry or tequila instead of vinegar for a mellow sauce; refill as needed. When cooking with them, crush the peppers in a mortar or a custard cup, and add a little water; use this pepper water to season with instead of throwing whole peppers into your stew. It is less of a shock to the guest who might get a whole pepper in a mouthful of stew. Use it to season roasts, turkey, and capon before baking by making holes in the meat with a larding tool or ice pick and poking *chiltepínes* deep inside.

For deeper insight into the bird chilli, read Gary Nabhan's chapter named "For the Birds: The Red-Hot Mother of Chiles" in his delightful, award-winning *Gathering the Desert*.

'Cubanelle'

Capsicum annuum var. *annuum* Linné

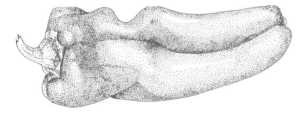

COLOR: Pale yellow-green, to orange, to red; at times all those colors at once; glossy

SHAPE: Elongated cylinder, undulating; sunken apex; Cuban or ethnic-type

SIZE: 6 inches long by $2\frac{1}{4}$ inches wide

PUNGENCY: Sweet; 0

SUBSTITUTES: Red, yellow, or orange bell (green, if hard pressed); banana; 'Szegedi' or any sweet ethnic-type

OTHER NAMES: Italian pepper

USES: Always used fresh: fried, in salads; as a vegetable, stuffed, in any recipe calling for a bell pepper

SOURCES:

FRESH: Home gardens, farmer's markets, some ethnic food stores on the East Coast

DRIED: Cannot be air-dried; perhaps can be dehydrated as you would bells

PROCESSED: Not processed

SEEDS: Commercially available but you may need to search the catalogs

AVAILABLE CULTIVAR: 'Biscayne', 'Cubanelle', 'Cubanelle PS'

The name Cubanelle is derived from Cuba; however, it is thought to be of Italian origin, having been introduced to Anglo-America in 1958. With the addition of the Italian diminutive ending *-nelle*, the meaning is presumably "little Cuban." Possibly, the Italians first acquired it from Cuba or vice versa. This large-fruited, very colorful cultivar of the wax-type is characterized by a thick, sweet flesh that is much more flavorful, but not quite so thick, as those of the bell-type. The 'Cubanelle', and other peppers of the ethnic-type, such as 'Shepherd', 'Laparie', 'Sweet Hungarian', 'Romanian', 'Szegedi', and 'Gypsy', have long been popular where there are large populations of people of Italian or Slavic descent; recently they have gained considerably in popularity. It is delicious when used for the same dishes as the less flavorful green bell pepper, and will become more readily available with public demand.

Italian cooks cut this pepper into $\frac{1}{2}$ to 1 inch strips, which they sauté in olive oil. More olive oil and garlic are added to the cooled pepper strips. Covered bowls of this are always kept in the refrigerators of Italian homes for snacks on French-type bread or for sandwiches at suppertime (page 218).

Dátil

Capsicum chinense Jacquin

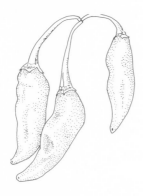

COLOR: Yellow-green to golden yellow

SHAPE: Elongated with a slight neck; pointed apex; shallowly wrinkled. Long wax-type

SIZE: 2 inches long by ¾ inches wide (mid-way)

PUNGENCY: Very hot to very, very hot; 10

SUBSTITUTES: Habanero

OTHER NAMES: *Mindoran*

USES: In sauces, relishes, as a seasoning

SOURCES:

> FRESH: Seasonally in home gardens, farmer's markets, food stores in and around St. Augustine, Florida

> DRIED: Heat-dried fruits available packaged in same area

> PROCESSED: Numerous sauces and relishes bottled in same area

> SEEDS: From growers in the St. Augustine, Florida, area

This little-known pepper has the same potential as the 'Tabasco' and probably originated in much the same fashion. The 'Tabasco' came to Louisiana in the 1840s from Mexico and through isolation and selection became a cultivar so different from its original Mexican parent that no *Capsicum frutescens* variety like it occurs in Mexico today. It is thought the first dátil was brought to the United States from the West Indies even earlier than the Tabasco, but it has remained in and around the area to which it was originally introduced. There it still awaits widespread recognition.

In 1763, after two hundred years of occupation and trade, Spain lost her Florida territory to England. Four or five years later Dr. Andrew Turnbull brought fourteen hundred indentured laborers—mostly male, but a few with families—to his indigo plantation in New Smyrna, Florida, from Greece, Italy, Corsica, and English (formerly Spanish) Minorca. Five hundred died during the first five months, and at the end of nine years only six hundred of the original group were living. He also brought African slaves to work on his indigo plantation.

Tradition has the dátil pepper being brought to St. Augustine, Florida, around 1776 when the surviving Minorcans fled to that city to escape the abuses at Turnbull's plantation. It is my educated guess that the Minorcans did not bring the dátil with them from Minorca to Anglo-America because *C. chinense* did not grow in the Mediterranean at that time (or now, for that matter); instead, the pepper appeared in Florida as a result of the convenient and long-standing trade in slaves and other goods between St. Augustine and the West Indies—Havana in particular—during the Colonial period (1565–1821) or shortly thereafter. Though they probably didn't bring them to this country, I do not hesitate to credit the Minorcans with giving the new pepper its name. In the Minorcan language, a Catalan Spanish derivitive, dátil means date. Mediterranean peoples knew the date because it had been introduced to that region by the Phoenicians long before. It is unlikely the Spanish residents in colonial Florida would be familiar with dates; nor would the African slaves brought from the West Indies, most of whom were of Mande-speaking tribes from the Guinea region, to whom the word dátil was alien. The original Minorcans would have to have named it, because their American-born children had not seen dates on date palms. Unless further research provides some additional documentation, its precise origin will remain clouded by the haze of time. No matter how the original Minorcan immigrants pronounced dátil, today Floridians call it "dat-el," rhyming with "that." For a full story, see my exploration of its origins in the Fall 1995 issue of *The Florida Historical Quarterly*.

About forty to fifty commercial growers cultivate small plots of dátils, making it the first *C. chinense* to be grown for profit in the United States, though recently commercial farmers have begun growing habaneros. This commercial production has been going on for at least seventy years.

The wrinkled, golden little fruits look somewhat like fresh dates while they are still on the palm tree, hence their name. Like its cousin, the habanero, the dátil is quite aromatic and very, very *picante*. A little goes a long way.

The dátil is used by food processors in the green state because the fully ripe fruit will not keep more than two or three days; consequently almost everyone uses it that way. However, it is much more fragrant and flavorful when golden. For that reason I'd recommend growing some of your own. Try it; you'll like it.

'Floral Gem'
Capsicum annuum var. *annuum* Linné

COLOR: Yellow to orange to bright red; glossy; calyx yellow

SHAPE: Elongated cylinder; indented blossom end; wax-type

SIZE: $1\frac{1}{2}$ inches long by 1 inch wide at shoulder

PUNGENCY: Hot; 6 to 7

SUBSTITUTES: Cascabella

OTHER NAMES: None

USES: Pickled, fresh in table sauces

SOURCES:

    FRESH: Home garden, farmer's markets; uncommon

    DRIED: Not dried

    PROCESSED: Pickled in food stores; supply irregular

    SEEDS: Hard to locate, try catalogs of specialty seed houses

    AVAILABLE CULTIVARS: 'Floral Gem Jumbo', 'Floral Grande'

Even though it is bright red when mature, 'Floral Gem' is known as one of the yellow wax-types because it is processed only in the yellow stage. Home gardeners, of course, can use it in any of its color phases. The cultivar was first released in 1921. Later, it was one of the chillies used to develop the 'Caloro', which came out in 1966. The plant's spreading, almost vinelike habit is responsible for its name. It is the only yellow

chilli cultivar with an indented end and for years was processed by the Trappey Company of New Iberia, Louisiana, for their brand Torrido Chili Peppers. Unfortunately, these are no longer always on the shelf. Trappey provided the growers with seed, but it was difficult to get them gathered because pickers never care to pick the small peppers. For a period the company was owned by the McIlhenney Company. If you are lucky enough to find a jar, use them in salads or chopped and cooked with meats, sauces, or beans.

'Fresno'
Capsicum annuum var. *annuum* Linné

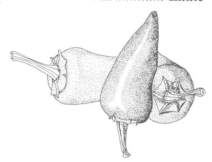

COLOR: Yellowish green (never yellow) to red; glossy

SHAPE: Conical; pointed apex; wax-type

SIZE: 3 inches long by $1\frac{1}{2}$ inches wide at shoulder

PUNGENCY: Hot; 5 to 7

SUBSTITUTES: Jalapeño, 'Santa Fe Grande', serrano

OTHER NAMES: Hot chili

USES: Used green; as a seasoning, in sauces, pickled; same uses as for the jalapeño

SOURCES:

    FRESH: Home gardens, farmer's markets, some food stores in the Southwest

    DRIED: Never dried, flesh too thick

    PROCESSED: Pickled, but not found regularly in food markets

    SEEDS: Catalogs of a few specialty seed houses

This very glossy, medium-size, wax-type that stands erect amid dark green foilage was released in 1952 by Clarence Brown, who named it in honor of Fresno, California. It is used only fresh because the thickness of the flesh precludes drying. Its resistance to tobacco mosaic, a disease fatal to peppers, resulted in its use to develop 'Caloro' in 1966. A seed company in turn used 'Caloro' to develop 'Fresno Grande'. 'Fresno' turns a bright red when ripe, but it is used in the unripe green stage. Off the bush, the mature red fruits look very much like the ripe 'Santa Fe Grande'; however 'Fresno' is green and red, never orange or yellow, and 'Santa Fe Grande' is never green. In the Southwest, where it is grown, it is often called hot chili. 'Fresno' should not be overlooked as an ornamental in beds or pots.

Brown also developed the smaller conical 'Cascabella'.

Guajillo, dried; Mirasol, fresh
Capsicum annuum var. *annuum* Linné

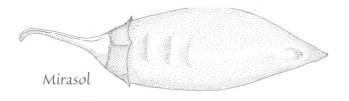

Mirasol

Guajillo

COLOR:
  FRESH: Green to red to brownish red
  DRIED: Translucent reddish brown
SHAPE: Elongate conical; pointed apex; Cayenne-type
SIZE: 3 to 5 inches long by $\frac{1}{2}$ to $1\frac{1}{4}$ inches wide, very variable
PUNGENCY: Hot; 4 to 5
SUBSTITUTES:
  FRESH: serrano, jalapeño, Thai
  DRIED: cascabel, New Mexican Chile
OTHER NAMES:
  FRESH: *Miracielo*
  DRIED: Cascabel, *puya, pullia, travieso, trompa*, perhaps *costeño* and *chilhuacle*
USES:
  FRESH: In table sauces, used like the serrano
  DRIED: In sauces, seasonings, for color
SOURCES:
  FRESH: Not yet available in markets in the United States; home gardens
  DRIED: Primarily in the Southwest or in ethnic food stores

PROCESSED: Not processed
SEEDS: Catalogs of specialty seed catalogs
AVAILABLE CULTIVARS: 'La Blanca 74', 'Loreto 74', 'Real Mirasol'

The *mirasol/guajillo* is one of the most variable chillies. Not only can the thin-skinned fruit vary from small to large, smooth to wrinkled, erect to pendent, but also the plant is quite inconstant in its growth patterns. Next to the *ancho*, the *guajillo* is the most used dried chilli in Mexico, and there is good reason. The flavor is very distinctive, and only small amounts of the dried fruits are required to both flavor and color the dishes prepared with them. The coloring quality is exceptional.

Mirasol means "it is looking at the sun," yet most of the fruits are pendent, except in the earliest stages (a variable characteristic). Since this cultivar is pre-Columbian in origin, it may well be that the attachment position has changed from erect to pendent through selection for larger, heavier fruit over hundreds of years, while the name stayed the same. Gourds (*guaje*) are used for rattles; therefore the dried form of this chilli, with seeds that rattle when shaken, are called *guajillo* or "little gourd." One of the most used capsicums in Peru is known there by the name *Mirasol*. However, it is not the same as the Mexican cultivar described here, but is instead a larger fruit whose species identity is not known to me—probably not *Capsicum annuum* var. *annum*. Author Amal Naj, my New Yorker friend from India, told me he knew a chilli in India called the same thing. It's an obvious name for a fruit that points towards the sun.

The *guajillo* is often called cascabel; however, the true cascabel is a globular shaped chilli with a completely different flavor and coloring quality. Dried New Mexican Chiles (page 71) are sometimes mislabeled *guajillos*. *Guajillos* are used in stews, soups, as a condiment with chicken dishes, and in *chilaquiles* (a traditional Mexican dish using stale tortillas). They are wonderful for chili con carne or any dish that you want to be a rich, red color. There are two other very localized chillies in Mexico that may be only regional variations of the *mirasol/guajillo*—*costeño* and *chilhuacqui*. Both are used dried in the same manner as the *guajillo*. I grow my own *guajillos*, and let them dry on the bush.

Habanero

Capsicum chinense Jacquin

COLOR: Green to yellow-orange, or orange, or orange-red

SHAPE: Round to oblong, undulating; pointed apex; Habanero-type

SIZE: 1 to 2½ inches long by 1 to 2 inches wide

PUNGENCY: Very, very hot; 10+

SUBSTITUTES: Nothing can match its flavor and aroma, but try 5 jalapeños for each habanero, or one dátil, one Scotch bonnet or one rocoto

OTHER NAMES: Congo, bonda man Jacques, bonnie, ginnie, Guinea pepper, *pimenta do chiero, siete caldos,* Scotch bonnet, and *pimienta do cheiro* in Brazil

USES: In table sauces, cooked sauces, as a seasoning

SOURCES:

FRESH: Some markets on the East Coast catering to Caribbean people, home gardens; increasingly in supermarkets and specialty food stores.

DRIED: Will not dry well on the bush. The dried ones being sold have only heat; the flavor that distinguishes the fresh habanero is all gone

PROCESSED: Bottled sauces, canned; in specialty shops and some supermarkets

SEEDS: Catalogs of some specialty seed companies, not easily found

Wow! Handle the habanero, meaning from Havana, with care! Some folks equate Yucatecan habanero and the West Indian Scotch bonnet, as I did in the past. Although they are not the same cultivar, they are the same species. The habanero is consistently lantern-shaped, while the other golden pepper has no neck and is regularly inverted at the apex when mature, giving it the form of a Scotsman's tam-o'-shanter, or "bonnet," hence its name. The pointed apex of a glossy, smooth, mature habanero is never inverted into a basal fold to produce the appearance of the Scotsman's headpiece. There are other varieties of *C. chinense,* as well as *C. annuum* var. *annuum*, and *C. baccatum* var. *pendulum,* that have the inverted shape of a Scotch bonnet when they are pale yellow-green and immature, but they don't stay that way. These balloon out when mature into a somewhat crinkly, lobed, blocky fruit the size and color of a golden habanero. Also called Scotch bonnet and habanero, they are too irregular and crinkly to be either; nevertheless, people unfamiliar with *C. chinense* call them by those names because they recognize a similarity. They are only crossed-up cousins, however.

To add to the confusion is another *C. chinense*, the West Indian Hot, a habanero-type. This blocky pepper is always red and not quite as aromatic and flavorful as its glowing orange cousin in Yucatan, yet it is often referred to as a red habanero. In fact, in a West Indian farmer's field of mixed peppers there can be found several habanero look-alikes.

The habanero holds a claim to being one of the hottest chillies in North America. It was developed and grows in Yucatan, Mexico, but there are other habanero-types throughout the Caribbean, most of which are incorrectly called habanero. After *Peppers* was published, I learned about another *C. chinense*, the dátil (page 66), which is probably an equal to the habanero in pungency. Some brave soul will have to make a comparative test of the dátil, habanero, Scotch bonnet, West Indian hot, and *C. pubescens.* The habanero is highly aromatic, with an unmistakable flavor. Do wear gloves when working with any *C. chinense*. I especially like to cook black bean soup with a habanero, and it is an agreeable companion to lamb in stews and curries. A fresh table sauce made with chopped habaneros, lime juice, and salt is a staple throughout the Caribbean.

Habaneros can be grown in home gardens; however, the germination period is quite long. It requires a warm, moist environment to produce a compact plant filled with clusters of glowing orange lanterns. A sight to behold, it is well worth the wait, both aesthetically and gastronomically. A new super pungent cultivar, 'Red Savina' has been registered in California, supposedly five times the Scoville count of a regular habanero—WOW!

Jalapeño

Capsicum annuum var. *annuum* Linné

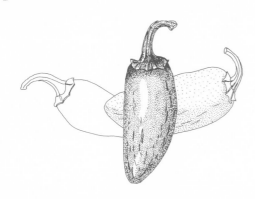

COLOR: Bright to deep blackish green; matures red

SHAPE: Cylindrical; blunt apex; jalapeño-type

SIZE: 3 inches long by 1½ inches wide

PUNGENCY: Hot to very hot, according to season, soil conditions, and state of maturity; 5

SUBSTITUTES: 'Caloro', 'Caribe', 'Fresno', 'Santa Fe Grande', serrano,

OTHER NAMES: *Acorchado, bola, bolita, candelaria, cuaresmeño, de agua, gorda, huachinango, jarocho, mora, morita*

USES: In condiments, sauces, soups, stews, meat and vegetable dishes, appetizers, desserts, as garnishes

SOURCES:

FRESH: Most supermarkets (it's becoming more readily available throughout the United States); although some commercial growers in the Southwest raise jalapeños, most are imported from Mexico; home gardens

DRIED: Will not air dry; must be smoked. Smoked peppers are called *chipotles* and when *chipotles* are canned with vinegar they are *adobado* (page 91)

PROCESSED: Canned sliced or whole, pickled (*en escabeche*), prepared with other canned and frozen foods; in cheeses, sauces, candies, etc.

SEEDS: Most seed suppliers will have at least one cultivar

AVAILABLE CULTIVARS: 'Early Jalapeno', 'Espinalteco', 'Jalapa', 'Jalapeno M', 'Jaloro' (yellow), 'Jarocho', 'Jumbo Jal', 'Mitla', 'Papaloapan', 'Peludo', 'Pinalteco', 'Rayado', 'San Andres', '76104', 'TAM Mild Jalapeno-1'

It is probably safe to say that the jalapeño is the best known chilli of all in Anglo-America, and its popularity and celebrity continue to grow. A jalapeño even soared to outer space on an early manned space flight, becoming our first "astro pod." This fiery fruit originated in Mexico and was named for the city of Jalapa in the state of Veracruz. In Mexico only the pickled form of this cultivar is called jalapeño; the fresh green fruits are called *cuaresmeño* (Lenten chilli). A shorter, fat variety is known as chile gordo (fat chilli). The flesh of the jalapeño is too thick to air-dry satisfactorily; therefore, the ripe red ones are dried (*ahumado*) by smoking in an oven similar to a Chinese smoke oven. This smoked jalapeño is called chipotle, as is any pepper when it has been dried by smoking. *Chipotle* is the common spelling for *chilpotle* which is from the Nahuatl word *pochilli* or smoked chile. The *chipotle* is sold dried or pickled (*adobado*) in cans. *Chipotles* are much hotter than the green jalapeño because the amount of capsaicin in all peppers increases with maturity.

The skin is usually marked with corky (*acorchado*) striations. The food industry has found that consumers want jalapeños to have these lines and will pick striated ones over the unlined fruits even though the striations have no effect on the flavor. There are more than a dozen named jalapeño cultivars, including one out of which researchers at Texas A & M University have bred most of the heat. The idea behind that new cultivar was to provide a processor with a neutral jalapeño so a specific, controlled amount of capsaicin could be added, thereby regulating the degree of pungency in order to be able to label the product accurately—mild, medium, hot. The only problem is that no grower will plant a tame jalapeño. Obviously, the public likes to play jalapeño roulette.

Store fresh jalapeños in the refrigerator in heavy plastic zip-lock bags or tightly closed jars, from which all air has been expelled. They freeze well. Blanching for two minutes before freezing helps preserve capsaicin. Spred them in a flat pan and freeze. When frozen, bag them loosely, seal well, and use as needed. Dried *chipotles* can be stored in tightly closed plastic bags in a cool, dry place.

Jalapeños can be pickled and canned Mexican style with vinegar, oil, and spices, or in the American style without spices. If you have to substitute a pickled jalapeño when a recipe calls for a canned or fresh one, you must rinse out the vinegar lest you change the flavor of the dish.

New Mexican Chile (Anaheim)

Capsicum annuum var. *annuum* Linné

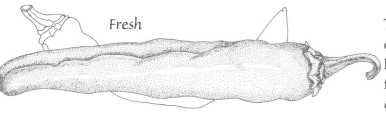

Fresh

Chile Colorado
(dried)

COLOR:
  FRESH: Bright green to red
  DRIED: Brownish red
SHAPE: Elongate, flattened, tapering to a blunt point;
  New Mexican/Anaheim-type
SIZE: 7 to 10 inches long by $1\frac{3}{4}$ to 2 inches wide
PUNGENCY: Mild to hot, depending on cultivar;
  1 to 4
SUBSTITUTES: Poblano for fresh, *ancho* or *guajillo* for
  dried
OTHER NAMES: Anaheim, California long green
  chile, *chilacate, chile college,* chile colorado, *chile de
  ristra, chile verde*, 'Chimayo', 'Hatch', long green/red
  chile, 'New Mexico No. 9', *pasado,* and many other
  cultivars. Frequently packaged dried fruits are in-
  correctly labeled *guajillo*
USES: Stuffed (relleno), in soups, stews, sauces, casseroles, fried, as a garnish, in souffles, etc., as well as
  for decoration
SOURCES:
  FRESH: Most food stores in the Southwest, but
    becoming more available throughout the country
  DRIED: Same as fresh
  PROCESSED: In the spice section of food markets;
    sold as pizza pepper; red pepper flakes; pow-
    dered (sometimes as paprika and also in commer-
    cial chili powder), as well as pure, also sold as
    canned green chiles, whole or chopped.
  SEEDS: Most seed suppliers will have one or more
    cultivars such as: Anaheim, 'Anaheim M', 'Ana-
    heim TMR 23', 'Big Jim', 'California', 'Chimayo',
    'Colorado', 'Coronado', 'Eclipse', 'Española Im-
    proved', 'New Mexico No. 9', 'NuMex', 'R-Naky',

'Red Chile', 'Sandia' (hot), 'Sunrise', 'Sunset',
'TAM Mild Chile', 'TMR 23', etc.

This is the beautiful, long green or red pepper that originated in New Mexico. The ancestor of this popular cultivar was probably brought to New Mexico from Mexico in 1597 when Captain General Don Juan de Oñate colonized that territory for Spain.[4] In 1896, almost three hundred years later, a California rancher, Emilio Ortega, who had been raising cattle in New Mexico, took some of the local pepper seeds with him when he returned to Oxnard, California. He started a pepper cannery in Anaheim, California. The first New Mexican Chile cultivar developed from this seed was named Anaheim, a cayenne-type. Some consider the New Mexican Chile-type (same as Anaheim) a type apart from the cayenne, because the number of its cultivars has multiplied so.

Meanwhile, back in New Mexico, Dr. Fabian Garcia was working with fourteen strains of a similar pepper. Of the fourteen strains being studied, number nine proved to be the favorite. In 1917 Garcia released 'Improved No. 9' which became the most widely grown long green/red pepper for many years to come. Today there are many cultivars. After the fall harvest the bright red strings of the mature fruits are hung to dry. These *ristras* have virtually become the symbol of the region, where they are not only consumed in enormous quantities but are also celebrated in art, song, and pageantry.

Several years ago, the scientists of the National Pepper Conference recommended that the official name be designated as the long green/red chile, instead of calling the pepper by one of the many cultivar names or the Anaheim-type. This did not satisfy the New Mexican growers, producers, and pepper fanciers, who wanted it to be known as the New Mexican Chile. The New Mexicans did not stop until they got that designation into the Congressional Record in Washington, D.C. So it must be official, and hereafter various cultivars will be called the New Mexican Chile-type.

Unless very young and tender fruits are available, the fresh fruits must be roasted and peeled before using. In the fall, throughout the Southwest, you may see roadside chile roasters being patronized by the New Mexican Chile lovers as they prepare to stock their freezers with the new fall crop. You can't believe the amount those folks consume. Select firm, bright colored, unwrinkled fresh fruits and clean, pliable dried ones.

The most popular dish prepared with the New Mexican Chile is chile relleno. The chile is filled with cheese, dipped in a batter, and fried (I use a beer batter recipe on page 186 for a super relleno). Although this is the most commonly used pepper in the Southwest, it has not played a significant part on the Mexican food menu in Mexico or Texas; however, interest in them is growing.

The fresh green chiles are dehydrated after being roasted or smoked to make a product with a flavor completely different from other chile flavors. Called *pasados* or *chile pasados*, they are rehydrated (page 89) and used in stews and sauces.

Store New Mexican Chiles in the refrigerator for immediate use, and freeze or dry them for future use, but DO NOT attempt to put up this non-acid vegetable at home except in vinegar and salt-based relishes and sauces—to do otherwise would be risking botulism. The recipes in the preserving section are quite safe if followed accurately (page 203).

Pasilla, dried; Chilaca, fresh
Capsicum annuum var. *annuum* Linné

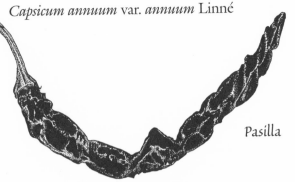

Pasilla

Chilaca

COLOR:
  FRESH: Dark blackish green ripening to dark brown
  DRIED: A warm black
SHAPE: Elongate, flattened, irregular, wrinkled; pointed apex; New Mexican Chile/Anaheim-type
SIZE: 6 to 12 inches long by $\frac{3}{4}$ to $1\frac{3}{4}$ inches wide
PUNGENCY: Medium to hot; 3 to 4
SUBSTITUTES:
  FRESH: Poblano
  DRIED: New Mexican Chile, *poblano-mulato*
OTHER NAMES:
  DRIED: *Chile negro*/black chile, *chile de Mexico, chile para deshebrar, quernillo, pasa, prieto*
USES:
  FRESH: In sauces and as a vegetable after charring and peeling
  DRIED: In table sauces, as a garnish and condiment in soups, and is essential to *mole* and other cooked sauces
SOURCES:
  FRESH: Probably not found outside Mexico; home gardens
  DRIED: Many supermarkets in the Southwest; some ethnic food stores
  PROCESSED: Not processed
  SEEDS: Catalogs of specialty seed houses.
  AVAILABLE CULTIVARS: 'Apaseo' and 'Pabellón 1'

This long, narrow, curved pepper with its dark, chocolate color is very distinctive. In Spanish, such a brownish black color is termed *achocolatado*—chocolate colored. The brown color results from the mixing of green and red pigments when the plant retains the green chlorophyll into the mature stage, at which time red pigments are produced. This pepper dries into a very wrinkled fruit the color of a raisin, consequently it is called *pasilla*—diminutive of *pasa* (raisin). The fresh form of this variety is known as *chile chilaca*, which derives from the Nahuatl *ácatl* meaning gray hair or old, a good description of the long, wrinkled, bent form.

There is too much confusion over the name of this uniquely formed and colored chilli. In Baja California and the northwestern Mexican states, the name *pasilla* is given to the much wider and shorter *ancho* and *mulato*. Unfortunately this practice has carried over into southern California, where I found them being sold in the fabulous Tianguis Latin American food markets as *chile negro*, while the *mulato* and *ancho* bore the name *pasilla*. At Tianguis I was told the labels bore the name by which the grower called the pepper whether it was correct or incorrect. It would be helpful if Californians would not perpetuate a misnomer begun in northwestern Mexico. To further complicate the issue, a Oaxacan chilli with the same color but an entirely different appearance and flavor is called *pasilla*. That Oaxacan *pasilla* is very likely the progenitor of the long green/red New Mexican Chile which is said to have had the pasilla as an ancestor. In the Oaxaca area, the true *pasilla* is known as *pasilla de Mexico*, while the local cultivar is the *pasilla de Oaxaca* or just *pasilla*.

The fresh *chilaca* is used primarily in the central and northwestern regions in Mexico. The more popular dried *pasilla*, with its rich, mellow flavor, is desirable in cooked sauces, or toasted and crumbled, or ground into a table sauce.

'Pepperoncini'
Capsicum annuum var. *annuum* Linné

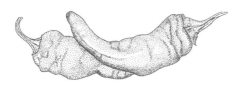

COLOR: Green to red
SHAPE: Elongated cylinder, pointed apex, wrinkled; New Mexican Chile/Anaheim-type
SIZE: 3 to 5 inches long by $\frac{3}{4}$ inches wide at shoulder
PUNGENCY: Sweet to mild; 0 to 1
SUBSTITUTES: Golden Greek or any pickled pepper
OTHER NAMES: None

USES: Green fruit pickled with salads
SOURCES:
  FRESH: Home gardens, farmer's markets
  DRIED: Not dried
  PROCESSED: Pickled, in most food stores
  SEEDS: Most large seed company catalogs, specialty seed suppliers.
  AVAILABLE CULTIVARS: 'Golden Greek,' 'Pepperoncini'

Little is known of the origin of this sweet cultivar, from which only the green fruits are used to make the pickled pepper usually found in Italian salads. The name comes from the Italian word for chilli, *peperone*. It was probably developed from a cultivar of Italian origin, but we don't know for certain. It is grown in Louisiana and some of the southern states. There is a very similar yellow form, 'Golden Greek', originally grown in Greece and pickled in the same manner.

Pimento
Capsicum annuum var. *annuum* Linné

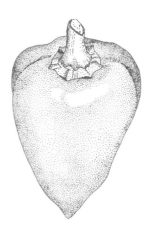

COLOR: Green to red; glossy
SHAPE: Conical, pointed apex, often heart-shaped; Pimento-type
SIZE: $4\frac{1}{2}$ inches long by $3\frac{1}{2}$ inches wide at shoulder
PUNGENCY: Sweet; 0
SUBSTITUTES: Red bell pepper, tomato pepper
OTHER NAMES: *Pimiento*
USES:
  FRESH: In salads or in any recipe calling for bell; canned, in casseroles, cheese spreads, garnishes, to stuff olives

SOURCES:

FRESH: Home gardens, farmer's markets, occasionally in food markets

DRIED: Not dried

PROCESSED: Canned, common in supermarkets

SEEDS: Catalogs of most large seed companies

AVAILABLE CULTIVARS: 'Bighart', 'Canada Cheese', 'Mississippi Nemaheart', 'Perfection', 'Pimiento Select', 'Pimiento-L', 'Sunnybrook', 'Truhart Perfection', 'Truhart, Perfection-D', 'Yellow Cheese'

Most of the commercially grown pimentos are found in the South and in California. The name comes from the Spanish word for pepper, *pimiento*. The second *i* was dropped when the Georgia Pimento Growers Association adopted that spelling for this sweet, heart-shaped fruit; however, many processors still use *pimiento*. Its aromatic flavor and distinctive red color make it highly desirable. When red bell peppers or the tomato peppers are canned, their color is not the alluring, bright red of the pimento. It is peeled before canning, but fresh ones can just be sliced or chopped for salads or as a garnish. Now that ripe red bell peppers can be purchased regularly, most of the pimento processors have shut down.

Poblano, fresh; Ancho and Mulato, dried
Capsicum annuum var. *annuum* Linné

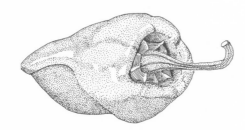

Poblano

COLOR: Dark green; matures red or brown

SHAPE: Tapered to a blunt point; wrinkled; ancho-type

SIZE: 4 inches long by 2½ inches wide

PUNGENCY: Mild to hot; 3

SUBSTITUTES: Mexi-bell, New Mexican/Anaheim chile

OTHER NAMES: *Ancho, chile para rellenar, joto, mulato, pasilla*

USES: Stuffed or *relleno*, strips or *rajas*, in soups and sauces. Roast, seed, and peel before using.

SOURCES:

FRESH: Food stores throughout the Southwest. More food stores in other parts of the country are carrying it in the imported produce section.

DRIED: See *ancho* (page 74) and *mulato* (page 75)

PROCESSED: Not processed

SEEDS: Specialty seed suppliers. *Poblano* does not always produce typical fruit in the United States, except in the area around Oxnard, California

AVAILABLE CULTIVARS: 'Ancho', 'Ancho Esmeralda', 'Chorro', 'Miahuateco', 'Mulato Roque', 'Verdeño'

The *poblano* or *chile poblano,* as it is known in Mexico, originated near the city of Pueblo, southeast of Mexico City; hence its name *poblano* or pepper from Pueblo. It is one of the most popular cultivars in that country. The fruit is undulating and more or less triangular in shape. The flesh is moderately thick, but not as thick as the bell pepper; therefore it dries well. Several similar cultivars are known as *poblanos* when in the very dark, dusky green immature stage, but when they are fully ripe and dried they each have another name. These are the *ancho*, *mulato*, 'Miahuateco', and 'Chorro'. These cultivars vary from a mild to a medium pungency. Growers have found that in the United States, the *poblanos* seldom attain their typical form; consequently, those found in our markets are virtually all imported from Mexico and are not always readily available. Select firm, unwrinkled, rich dark green fruits.

In Baja and southern California, both the dried forms and the fresh green fruit are incorrectly known as *pasilla* (page 72); however the flavors and shapes are different. In that area, if a stuffed pepper recipe calls for a *pasilla*, it probably means *poblano* because the true *chilaca/pasilla* is too long and "skinny" to be stuffed. This is very confusing, for a true fresh *chilaca/pasilla* cannot be substituted for a fresh *poblano*.

Ancho (dried)
Capsicum annuum var. *annuum* Linné

COLOR: Dark brown, brick red after soaking

SHAPE: Flattened, wrinkled; ancho-type

SIZE: 4 inches long by 2½ inches wide

PUNGENCY: Mild to rather hot; 3 to 4

SUBSTITUTES: *Mulato*, New Mexican Chile (*chile colorado*), *pasilla*

OTHER NAMES: Chile Colorado (in Texas), *mulato*, *pasilla*

USES: In sauces for enchiladas, chili con carne, *adobados* (meat prepared with a sour seasoning paste), commercial chili powders

SOURCES:

FRESH: See *poblano* (previous entry)

DRIED: Most food stores in the Southwest, ethnic specialty stores

PROCESSED: Sold as chili powder in spice section

SEEDS: Specialty seed suppliers

AVAILABLE CULTIVARS: 'Chorro', 'Esmeralda', 'Flor de Pabellon', 'Verdeño'

In Mexico the unripe, green pepper is never referred to as an *ancho* (which means "wide"), but in the United States many growers and seed suppliers call it *ancho* from the seed on, making no distinction between the fresh and dried state. The dried *ancho* is a type of poblano that is a deep red when fully mature and dries to a very wrinkled, blackish brown, flattened form. After it has been soaked, it becomes brick red. Soaking for more than an hour is usually unnecessary and will reduce the flavor and food value of the pepper as the nutrients dissolve in the water. Save the soaking water for sauces and soups (remarks under *mulato* [page 75]).

The three robust, dried Mexican chiles—*ancho*, *mulato*, *pasilla*—are ground separately and made into a paste which is sold in little blocks that look rather like baking chocolate. This paste is known as *pisado chile*—not *pasado* (page 72).

Mulato (Dried)
Capsicum annuum var. *annuum* Linné

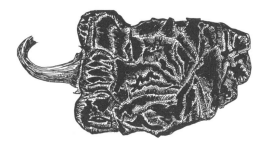

COLOR: Dark brown

SHAPE: Flattened, wrinkled; ancho-type

SIZE: 4 inches long by 2½ inches wide

PUNGENCY: Mild to hot; 3 to 4

SUBSTITUTES: *Ancho*, *pasilla*

OTHER NAMES: *Ancho*, *pasilla*

USES: In sauces like *mole poblano*

SOURCES:

FRESH: See *poblano* (page 74)

DRIED: Imported from Mexico, sold in food stores throughout the Southwest, usually in mixed lots with *ancho*

PROCESSED: Canned *mole* sauce is now available where Mexican products are sold

SEEDS: A few specialty seed suppliers carry it, but the *poblano/mulato* does not produce typical fruit when grown in the the United States.

AVAILABLE CULTIVARS: 'Mulato V-2', 'Roque'

The *mulato* (in the U.S.A. a person of mixed white and black ancestry; in Spanish the word means tawny-colored) ripens to a deep, chocolate brown color which is called *achoclatado*. Like the *ancho*, it also becomes blackish brown, very wrinkled, and flattened when it is dried. The two are difficult to distinguish until soaked, but the *mulato* retains its brown color after soaking while the *ancho* rehydrates to red. The chocolate-like flavor of the *mulato* is sweeter, richer, and a little more pungent than that of the *ancho*. The *ancho*, *mulato*, and true *pasilla* are ground into a paste and sold as *chile pisado*, and one square is equal to one tablespoon of powdered dried chillies.

Because the dried *anchos* and *mulatos* are so difficult to distinguish before soaking, they are often used interchangeably. Not only are they difficult to identify in the marketplace, but the confusion is compounded in Baja and southern California, where both the dried forms and the fresh green fruit are mistakenly referred to as *pasilla* (page 72). In that area caution must be used in recipes calling for *pasilla*; they very likely mean *ancho* or *mulato*, and it will make a difference in the final flavor of the dish.

Select clean, flexible, insect-free fruits. Store in an airtight container in a cool, dry place. Wash and soak in boiling water for no more than one hour before use. Longer soaking removes both flavor and nutrients. Reserve the soaking water for sauces and soups.

Rocoto
Capsicum pubescens Ruiz & Pavon

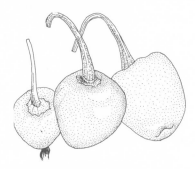

COLOR: Green to golden yellow or red

SHAPE: Globose to oblate

SIZE: 1½ to 2 inches long by 1½ to 2 inches wide

PUNGENCY: Very, very, very hot; 10+

SUBSTITUTES: Nothing really, but try 1½ to 2 habaneros or 6 to 8 jalapeños for 1 rocoto.

OTHER NAMES: *Caballo* (Guatemala and bordering Chiapas, Mexico), *canario, manzana,* and *perón* in Mexico; in Costa Rica it is *manzana* but more often jalapeño.

USES: In table sauces, as a seasoning, stuffed, in vegetable and meat dishes

SOURCES:

FRESH: Not readily available in the United States

DRIED: Not dried

PROCESSED: Not available

SEEDS: Perhaps a specialty seed catalog

Although this species is not available commercially in the United States (as of 1999) except in a few ethnic food stores which import it, you need to know about it because it probably will be soon. This chilli is different, unmistakably so. To begin with, the stems are very hairy, hence the Latin name meaning "pubescent"; the flowers are always purple; the irregular seeds are coal-black; and it requires a cool climate at altitudes of thirty-five hundred to six thousand feet. On top of that, to some people, it must be one of the hottest chillies going. It would take a lot of getting used to, and here's why. Although the Scoville rating for the capsaicin content is less than the habanero, its nordihydrocapsaicin is three and a half times that of the habanero. Those two alkaloids do not cause pain in the same place in your mouth. Obviously, I am more sensitive where the "nordi" hits, because I cannot eat an uncooked rocoto. I used to buy it in the

market in San Jose, Costa Rica, where it is called "jalapeño"—pungent/hot foods are not traditional there, so all hot peppers are called jalapeños.

There are many varieties of *C. pubescens* in the Andean region but, unlike the cultivars of *C. annuum* var. *annuum,* they do not have individual names. Down there, all are called rocoto but are distinguished by size—the larger are called *rocoto del huerta* (garden) and smaller hot ones are *rocoto del casa* (house). The garden ones are used for the *Rocoto Rellenos* for which Arequipa, Peru, is renowned. Peruvian cooks remove all veins and seeds, boil the whole pepper for a little while, then rinse, before adding the filling and cooking it. The rocoto was a latecomer to the lower part of the North American continent, perhaps as late as the twentieth century. The fruit spoils rather quickly. If you find some, wash and seed them (with gloves); cut in strips, blanch for 1 to 2 minutes, and freeze. Use as you would habaneros or dátils.

Santa Fe Grande
Capsicum annuum var. *annuum* Linné

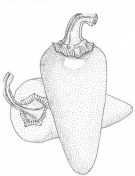

COLOR: Pale greenish yellow to orange to red; glossy

SHAPE: Conical, pointed apex; wax-type

SIZE: 3½ inches long by 1½ inches wide at shoulder

PUNGENCY: Medium hot to very hot; 6

SUBSTITUTES: Any hot yellow pepper, such as *caricillo,* 'Cascabella', 'Floral Gem', 'Hungarian Wax'

OTHER NAMES: 'Caloro', 'Caribe', *cera, güero*

USES:

FRESH: in table sauces, pickled, as a seasoning

SOURCES:

FRESH: Many food markets, home gardens, farmer's markets

DRIED: Not dried

PROCESSED: Pickled, infrequently found in food stores

SEEDS: Catalogs of specialty seed houses; some of the larger seed company's catalogs.

AVAILABLE CULTIVARS: 'Caloro PS', 'Caloro', 'Caribe', 'Grande Gold' (sweet), 'Hybrid Gold Spike', 'Santa Fe Grande', 'TAM Rio',

This is a beautiful pepper plant when full of fruits in all their stages—yellow, orange, and red. This prime example of a yellow wax pepper is the same pepper as the 'Caribe' in Mexico and the 'Caloro' in California. The ripe red fruit is difficult, if not impossible, to distinguish from the ripe red 'Fresno', but try to remember that the 'Fresno' never passes through yellow or orange stages, nor the 'Santa Fe Grande' through a green stage.

Like other peppers with fairly thick flesh, the 'Santa Fe Grande' will not air dry satisfactorily. In Mexico all yellow peppers are called *güeros* or blondes, even though some of them may be red when mature. In the northern part of Mexico the 'Santa Fe Grande' is grown for export to American food markets, but it is not used to any degree in Mexico. When Americans sent Mexican growers seeds of the bitingly hot 'Santa Fe Grande', the Mexicans called it 'Caribe' after the cannibalistic Amerindians who inhabited the Caribbean Islands at the time of Columbus. It can be used in any recipe calling for jalapeño, but will not have the typical jalapeño flavor.

Scotch Bonnet
Capsicum chinense Jacquin

COLOR: Green to yellow-orange or orange

SHAPE: Stem end (base) is depressed. The deeply inverted, always rounded apex folding into a crimped periphery just below the base gives the rounded fruit the appearance of a Scottish tam-o'-shanter, a cap with a tight headband and a full flat top with a large pompom, or like a small unidentified flying object. Scotch bonnet-type

SIZE: 2 to 2½ inches in diameter; 1¾ to 1½ inches deep

PUNGENCY: Very, very hot; 10 +

SUBSTITUTES: Habanero, dátil, West Indian hot, several serranos

OTHER NAMES: Scot's bonnet, bonnie

USES: In table sauces, cooked sauces, as seasoning

SOURCES:

FRESH: Markets catering to West Indians, home gardens

DRIED: Does not dry well; retains pungency but loses flavor

PROCESSED: Bottled sauces in specialty shops

SEEDS: Catalogs of some specialty seed companies, not easily found

The Scotch bonnet was first mentioned in *The Gardener's Dictionary* by Phillip Miller in 1768, when he listed a West Indian pepper with wrinkled leaves and bonnet shape. There has been much confusion between this cultivar and other cultivars of *C. chinense*, especially habanero. In the first three editions of *Peppers* I held it to be another name for habanero, but my West Indian visit with Brian Cooper, agronomist with Caribbean Agricultural and Development Institute (CARDI) in Antigua, convinced me that they are two distinct cultivars and that the habanero is a Mexican cultivar not widely grown in the West Indies, although many look-alikes of the same species grow there. "Look for the rounded apex and depressed base," Dr. Cooper stresses. There are many intergrades, but the purest strain is found in Jamaica. Even though they look like Scotch bonnet, the squash pepper (*C. annuum* var. *annuum*), and the rocotillo, (*C. chinense*) both have a neck and a very pointed apex.

Both the Scotch bonnet and the habanero, along with the dátil and West Indian hot (a habanero-type), probably derive from the same Amazonian ancestor brought to the West Indies before the arrival of Columbus by migrating Amerindian farmers. Its primary use is in table sauce (page 173).

Serrano
Capsicum annuum var. *annuum* Linné

COLOR: Green to red, glossy

SHAPE: Elongated cylinder; blunt apex. Serrano-type

SIZE: $2\frac{1}{4}$ inches long by $\frac{1}{2}$ inches wide

PUNGENCY: Hot to very hot; 6 to 8

SUBSTITUTES: Chiltepín, 'Fresno', jalapeño, Thai

OTHER NAMES: *Balín, chile verde, cora, serannito, típico*

USES: In table sauces, guacamole, relishes, vegetable dishes, as a seasoning or garnish

SOURCES:

FRESH: Most food markets, but less common than the jalapeño; home gardens, farmer's markets

DRIED: Does not dry well. The dried *japonés* (page 81) are *not* dried serranos.

PROCESSED: Mexican pickled (*escabeche*) serranos are occasionally found in specialty stores

SEEDS: Catalogs of most large seed houses and specialty seed companies

AVAILABLE CULTIVARS: 'Altimira', 'Cuauhtemoc', 'Cotaxtla Cónico', 'Cotaxtla Gordo', 'Cotaxtla Típico', 'Huasteco 74', 'Panuco', 'Serrano Chili', 'Tampiqueño'

The slick little serrano is the favorite green chilli for table sauces and guacamole in Mexico and my kitchen. Its crisp, fresh flavor makes it quite distinctive. It is also wonderful in uncooked fruit chutney. The name comes from *serranias* (foot hills), because it is believed that it originated in the foothills north of Puebla in Mexico. Although the serrano has very adaptable growth habits, it is not grown commercially to any extent in the United States. It is not necessary to peel or seed them, just slice thinly. Serranos freeze well, and if you blanch them before freezing, their pungency is not lost. After blanching two minutes, freeze them in a shallow, metal pan, then quickly separate and bag them in plastic. Frozen this way you can reach in the bag for one or as many as you need for up to a year. Like the jalapeño, the serrano does not dry well.

'Tabasco'
Capsicum frutescens Linné

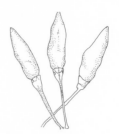

COLOR: Pale yellow-green to yellow to orange to red

SHAPE: Elongate cylinder; pointed apex; Tabasco-type

SIZE: 1 to $1\frac{1}{2}$ inches long by $\frac{1}{4}$ to $\frac{3}{8}$ inches wide

PUNGENCY: Very hot; 10

SUBSTITUTES: Chiltepín, 'Cascabella', 'Louisiana Sport', 'Mississippi Sport', Thai

OTHER NAMES: None

USES: In sauces, as a seasoning

SOURCES:

FRESH: Home garden

DRIED: Not dried

PROCESSED: Pepper sauces made with Tabasco peppers abound; occasionally pickled whole peppers are available in food stores

SEEDS: Specialty seed catalogs, a few major seed catalogs. The seed you get will probably be Greenleaf Tabasco

This little firebrand has been the subject of much litigation over the use of its name, and of much dispute over its origin. Whatever went before, the chilli we now know as 'Tabasco' was developed by the McIlhenny family of Avery Island, Louisiana, who fiercely protect its name. The cultivar was named after their fermented pepper sauce. All the 'Tabasco' peppers used in their Tabasco Brand Pepper Sauce® are grown from seed which the McIlhenny Company selects and furnishes to growers. Any seed you might find elsewhere is probably the 'Greenleaf Tabasco,' which is a little hotter and deeper red and was the result of a cross with *C. chinense* to resist infection by tobacco mosaic, a disease which was killing the 'Tabasco' plants. Other sauces may be made with the 'Tabasco' pepper, but you will have to read the fine print on the label because only the McIlhenney Company can use tabasco in the name. These sauces are used in soups, stews, bloody Marys, on oysters, in egg dishes, and anything needing a dash of fire. Use Tabasco Brand Pepper Sauce® only if you desire your dish or drink to have its characteristic flavor, which is the result of vinegar and the fermentation process by which it is made.

A detailed, documented discussion of this cultivar can be found in *Peppers*. The new-found popularity of peppers has brought a plethora of sauces to the market place to compete with Tabasco Brand Pepper Sauce®. So many, in fact, that for the first time in the long history of the Avery Island sauce, its makers have branched out into farm stores, a catalog, and many other products—even T-shirts flaunting their world-famous trademark. Tabasco peppers are not grown commercially to any extent in this country today because, like other very small chillies, no one will pick them. I had a huge one espaliered in a sun room for years. They make a beautiful potted plant.

The range of the wild and semidomesticated varieties of *C. frutescens* is more limited than that of *C. annuum* var. *glabrisculum;* however, throughout their ranges both tiny chillies are called "bird peppers" by the local people. This long-standing interchange of vernacular names for the two has caused much confusion to everyone but the birds—they greedily harvest them no matter what the name is.

Tomato
Capsicum annuum var. *annuum* Linné

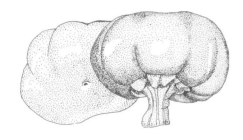

COLOR: Green to red
SHAPE: Globular, tomato-like, or squash shaped; tomato-type
SIZE: 3 inches in diameter
PUNGENCY: Sweet; 0 to 1
SUBSTITUTES: Pimento, red bell pepper
OTHER NAMES: Paprika, Spanish paprika, squash pepper

USES:
  FRESH: same as for bell pepper (page 60); powdered sold as paprika; canned as pimento (page 73); food and industrial coloring agent
SOURCES:
  FRESH: Home gardens, farmer's markets
  DRIED: Not used
  PROCESSED: Canned sold as pimento; pickled; commercial coloring agent; powdered
  SEED: Catalogs of most large seed companies.
  AVAILABLE CULTIVARS: 'Canada Cheese', 'Early Sweet Pimento', 'Sunnybrook', 'Tomato Pimento', 'Yellow Cheese Pimento'

Few tomato peppers, if any, are grown today in Mesoamerica where they originated. This thick-fleshed, sweet *Capsicum* is thought to be the precursor of the ubiquitous bell pepper. It is highly extolled in Spain and Morocco for the high quality paprika produced from it, although it is not the only *Capsicum* used for paprika. For the most part, the tomato pepper is grown in the southern United States, where it is not only sold for making paprika and as a coloring agent, but also as a substitute for the true pimento. When canned it is more yellowish red than the canned true pimento.

Miscellaneous Cultivars

These varieties of *Capsicum* are not commonly available in this country; however, you might read about them occasionally or see them in a farmer's market or ethnic food store or a seed catalog. I predict that some will soon enter the market as "gourmet peppers." If there are large cultural groups living in a community, you can be sure there is at least one food store to supply the ingredients their traditional cuisines require.

CARIBBEAN ISLAND PEPPERS.
As related earlier, Columbus first encountered the *Capsicum* pepper on Hispaniola in the Caribbean region, where only the *C. chinense*, *C. frutescens*, and possibly *C. annuum* were thought to have been established at that time. Most of the varieties found there today are of the first two species, which are known for their extreme pungency. They have taken many forms

and carry many local names which vary from island to island. The Scotch bonnet-type and West Indian hot (a habanero-type), along with a duke's mixture of *C. chinense* such as congo, bonnie, Peggy mouth, St. John's market, Jamaica red, and *ají gustos* are grown in the West Indies for local use and export to Great Britain, Canada, and Holland, where large populations of West Indians can be found. They are also occasionally found in ethnic markets and farmer's markets in the United States. They are used primarily in table sauces; however, they may be used in the same manner as other similar chillies. In the Caribbean area, West Indian farmers have a different attitude about growing peppers than *Capsicum* growers elsewhere. Keeping one *C. chinense* cultivar separate from the other is not important to them or their customers. Their fields of mixed *C. chinense* are allowed to cross at will. People who are familiar with peppers in the United States and Mexico recognize that the interbred Caribbean chillies are different from those jalapeños, bell peppers, and other types of *C. a.* var. *annuum* they are familiar with. The only similar pepper that chilli fans from mainland North America may have seen is a habanero—so, they tag the name habanero onto any similar looking Caribbean *C. chinense*. Indeed, many are habanero-types, but not the cultivar habanero, which is a native of Yucatan, Mexico (page 69).

The only *C. a.* var. *annuum* I saw being cultivated was a poor specimen of the bell-type. The "bird pepper," a tiny, pointed, elongated cone-like *C. frutescens,* grows spontaneously in gardens and under trees. This is probably very similar to the malagueta of Brazil. If you travel in the West Indies, please collect seed and *the local name*, make notes on how they are used, and send them to me, because I have only visited Antigua, Jamaica, and St. Croix.

ETHNIC PEPPERS

These are large, thick-fleshed, undulating, sweet fruits known in the trade as frying or ethnic peppers. The 'Cubanelle' and 'Romanian' are typical of this type. People from the Balkans, Greece, and Italy favor these as a fried vegetable dish or with meats and sliced fresh with bread for breakfast. Look for them in ethnic food markets where there are concentrations of people of those origins.

INDIAN PEPPERS

The two most common chillies (*mirch*), one 2 to 4 inches and the other $1\frac{1}{2}$ to 2 inches, are *C. a.* var. *annuum* of the cayenne-type, and are used both fresh and dried. They are long, slim, curved chillies that go from green (*hari*) to red (*lal*). When used fresh, only the green ones (*hari mirch*) are selected. Pepper venders can be seen carefully removing from the pile any pepper that has begun to turn red (*lal mirch*). Cayenne, serrano, Thai, *japonés*, other small cayenne-types, or ground cayenne pepper may be substituted. Before mixing them with other ingredients, Indians toss the unseeded dried peppers into hot oil for a few seconds, along with other spices, in order to bring out the flavor. In India not many varieties are found, but those few are used in great quantity. Fields dotting the countryside are accented by huge, bright red squares of chillies spread to dry. A little round variety is also used dried, but to a lesser degree. In India the more recently introduced sweet bell-type peppers are called "capsicums" and are used as a vegetable, while the pungent varieties are chillies or chillys. Another rather recently introduced Hungarian wax-type is used in the pale yellow-green stage as a vegetable.

INDONESIAN PEPPERS

These are used more as a condiment (*sambal*) than for seasoning the main dishes. Although some are used in cooking, the food is not as blistering as Thai and Indian victuals can be. The variety of capsicums in Indonesia is more limited than in Thailand and India and those few cayenne-types found in the markets vary from island to island. Most are grown in home gardens instead of large commercial plantings. Kalimantan (Borneo), Java, Irian Jaya (western New Guinea), Sumatra, Sulawesi (Celebes), Bali, and the islands of the Lesser Sundas use a small ($\frac{1}{2}$ inches to $\frac{3}{4}$ inches), elongate-cylindrical *C. frutescens* and a couple of larger ($1\frac{1}{2}$ inches to 4 inches) *C. a.* var. *annuum* of the cayenne-type. In addition to these, I found a bright red habanero-type *C. chinense* being used in Sulawesi, but did not find it elsewhere. As in Thailand and India, no common names are used. Until the Dutch came to Indonesia and applied the Nahuatl-Mexican name chilli to the peppers introduced by the Portuguese, the most common name was *cabé* for *C. a.* var. *annum* and *cabé rawit* for *C. frutescens*, the tiny "bird pepper." *Cabé hijau* are green and *cabé merah* are red. *Lombok* is a Javanese word for peppers. The "bird peppers" are known as *cabé burong* in Malaysia and *lombok rawit* in Indonesia.

JAPONÉS, SANTAKA, AND HONTAKA

Three small (2 inches by ½ inch), very pungent chillies of the cayenne-type. Green ones, like the hawk's bill (called *hontaka* in Japan) are used in sauces, and the dried red ones are made into a powder for seasoning. These cultivars may be of Japanese origin. No matter what you may read in books or on labels, the *japonés* is *not* a dried serrano. I know because I grew plants using seed from several different brands of *japonés* peppers and I can say that the resulting plant was *C. a.* var. *annuum* of the cayenne-type, not serrano. Let me know if you learn where this pepper got its name and where it comes from. Surely someone who buys it to sell will know where it is being grown.

MEXICAN PEPPERS

These are almost too numerous to list, each region having its own variety that is usually not grown or shipped elsewhere. These local types are called *criollos*, a creole person being one born in the Americas of Spanish or French parents. When the term is applied to a *Capsicum* cultivar, it means a very local type, native to a particular land area and not widespread. They are also called *chile corriente* (common chile) and *chile casero* (household chile). In Mexico each of these varietal names would be prefaced with the word *chile*, i.e. *chile amarillo, chile carricillo*, etc. In Mexico, the locals claim no *gringo* can truly comprehend the *chile* mystique, and scoff at those of us *gringos* who profess to be *chile* authorities. All of the following are *C. a.* var. *annuum*. Some of the less familiar are:

AMARILLO. A beautiful, deep gold-colored, elongate chilli about 2 inches long and quite narrow and pointed. It dries to a translucent ochre color. These dried fruits are comparatively expensive in the markets of Oaxaca. Save the seed, as it will do well in your garden.

CARRICILLO. A pungent, pale yellow, narrow-shouldered, wrinkled, curved fruit of the cayenne-type that ripens into vermillion. It is not used fresh or dry, but rather is pickled in its yellow stage and used in fish dishes. This *güero* (page 77) is also called *chile cristal, chile largo, and x-cat-ik.*

CATARINA. Shaped like the beak of the parakeet, or *catarinita*, this small (¾ to 1 inch), green to red, very pungent chilli is used dry. The dried translucent red fruits allow the seeds to rattle. It is favored for tamales and is used green in table sauces, as is the serrano. The fresh green form is sometimes called *mirasol* because it grows erect or "looking at the sun." It is also called *cascabelillo*.

CHILACATE. This is the Mexican name for the dried long red New Mexican Chile (page 71). It is also called *chile del norte, chile colorado, chile largo colorado,* and *chile magdalena.*

CHILHUACQUI. A very variable chilli that looks like the *guajillo* in some areas; in others it produces a wider red fruit, *chilhuacqui negro*, which dries black and is more like the ancho. Another, *chilhuacqui amarillo*, is yellow with narrow shoulders. These are grown on the Pacific coast of Chiapas and bordering Guatemala.

CHIPOTLE. Any chilli dried by smoking (*ahumado*) is a *chipotle*. Although *chile moros* and *chile bolitos* (two small jalapeño-types), serranos, and others, are smoke dried to a wrinkled, tough, fairly dark brown fruit, it is the jalapeño that is most commonly used for *chipotles*. Its varieties are known as *típico, meco*, and *morita*. They can be purchased dried or lightly pickled and canned (*adobado*). Picked ripe red, they are hotter than green jalapeños. Most *chipotles* are produced in the region of the Gulf of Mexico.

COSTEÑO. A medium-sized (very variable, up to 6 inches), green to red, narrow-shouldered chilli, that dries a translucent, reddish brown, is grown in the state of Guerrero, Mexico. It may be a variation of the *guajillo*. The dried fruits are used.

DE AGUA. The large, thick-fleshed water (*agua*) *chile* comes from Oaxaca and Guatemala. Looking like a pale green, longer poblano, it matures to vermillion and is roasted and peeled before being made into sauces. It is too succulent to dry.

DE ONZA: This is a cayenne-type, bright red chilli that is used dried like the *chile costeño*. In fact, it looks like a little fatter version of that cultivar. It is grown in Oaxaca.

GÜERO. This is not any cultivar in particular. It means "blond" and is the name given to any yellow pepper or any pepper used in the yellow stage.

MORO/MORITO. A small variety of jalapeño, it is often smoked for *chipotles*. Some Mexicans call all pickled *chipotle* (smoked) jalapeños by this name.

PULLA/PUYA: A 3 to 4 inch, elongate cylinder with narrow shoulders and pointed apex. This chilli becomes a translucent deep red when dried. It is probably a local variation of the *guajillo*, and is used in the same way.

THAI PEPPERS

Peppers are indispensable to Thai cooking, which is my favorite of the Far Eastern cuisines. To me it is more subtle than Indian and more flavorful than Indonesian. The larger varieties are *C. a.* var. *annuum* and appear to be almost the same as the Indian varieties and used in the same quantity, if not more. There are at least ten kinds of varying size and pungency in the markets. Even after attending a cooking school in Bangkok, I am not able to assign distinct flavors to the different varieties, but they do have different degrees of pungency. Some are pale green, others yellow or red, but all are pungent. They are not seeded before being put in a dish. The various colors are used to enhance the dishes—presentation is important in Thailand. Both fresh and dried fruits are often used whole with the stems on. Substitute serranos, chiltepínes, or jalapeños for fresh Thai peppers, and for the dried ones, fill in with ground cayenne pepper or *japonés*. I did find a tiny cylindrical red pepper that was *C. frutescens*. It was semidomesticated and used like our *chiltepín* (page 64). In rural and tribal villages, baskets of scarlet peppers drying on rooftops or porches made already colorful scenes even more vibrant. Most common names are only the word for pepper, *prik*, with some additional descriptors such as: *hang* = dried, *yuk* = fresh. The practice of giving each variety a name like jalapeño or bell pepper does not seem to be prevalent. 'Santa Fe Grande'/'Caribe' and some sweet bell-types have been recently introduced, but their use is not widespread as yet. English-speaking Thais use the word chillies for pungent peppers.

Several small varieties that have limited distribution need to be defined because they have been significant in the pepper industry from time to time. They are all *C. a.* var. *annuum*.

'CASCABELLA.' This small ($1\frac{1}{4}$ inch by $\frac{3}{4}$ inch), wax-type fruit is similar and closely related to the larger 'Fresno' (page 67); both cultivars were developed in California by the same plant breeder. It grows on a very bushy plant and is yellow at first, turning orange and becoming red upon maturity. The conical fruit with a pointed apex is usually used in the yellow state for hot pickled peppers. The small size makes it highly desirable to pickle packers. The Spanish *cascabella* is formed from two words—*cascara* (skin, husk), referring to the waxy outer covering, and *bella* (beautiful). The name sounds and looks similar, but is not related to another Spanish word, *cascabel* which is used as the name of a round, red Mexican chile (page 61).

PAPRIKA. You may find a paprika pepper listed in seed catalogs; however, there is no single paprika pepper used for making paprika (page 46).

SPORTS. Two hot sauce and pickling varieties, 'Louisiana Sport' and 'Mississippi Sport' are small (1 to $1\frac{1}{2}$ inches by $\frac{1}{4}$ to $\frac{1}{3}$ inch), erect-growing, elongate-cylindrical, green to red peppers. They were used as substitutes in vinegar-packed whole fruits when a disease threatened the 'Tabasco' pepper crop. Neither is used to any extent today.

SQUASH. This beautiful red or golden pepper splashed with purple, about 2 inches in diameter, is shaped like a pattypan squash. Although it is a *C. a.* var. *annum*, many call it *rocotillo* because the red form looks very much like that mild South American *C. chinense*, and the seeds are frequently sold as such. The squash pepper is pale green when young and very hot but with little flavor. It is great for garnishes or used as an ornamental in the garden or in pots.

PART II

Preparation & Recipes

Cooking with Peppers
How to Choose 'Em and Use 'Em

ow that we know where chillies came from, and where they went, and what they are or are not—let's eat them. As I said in my earlier book *Peppers*, before cooking with or eating capsicums you should familiarize yourself with the methods for selecting, preparing, and handling our precious pods in order to ensure an enjoyable experience. Please, in your rush to become a pod fellow, take the time to follow instructions. Peppers are expensive. You don't want to waste them, but most of all, you don't want to get burned. Wear protective gloves if preparing more than one or two chillies. Work in a well-ventilated area—the fumes are tearjerkers. Do not put your hands in your eyes, or any bodily orifice for that matter. If you get too much on your hands, wash them in one part household bleach to five parts water. Do this at the start—don't wait until you are burning beyond relief. Repeat if necessary (Andrews, 1995:137). It really works! An ammonia mix will also work, but it smells worse. When making relish or anything requiring quite a few chillies, I keep a small bowl of the chlorine solution by the sink to dip my hands in as needed, a practice born of sad experience.[1]

Keep peeled and cut peppers well covered because vitamin C is destroyed by contact with oxygen. According to food scientist Harold McGee (1990:64), the only plastic food wrap that does not let in too much oxygen is polyvinylidene chloride (Saran Wrap). Press all the air out before sealing (fresh storage page 86).

Selection

Fresh

Capsicums are a fruit that is used like a vegetable. The chilli *aficionado* will either grow his or her peppers or buy them in a supermarket, ethnic food market, or farmer's market. By whatever means they are come by, you should be aware of a few points when selecting peppers. Capsicums of any type can be picked when they are green or when a fully mature red, though they can also mature to orange, yellow, purple, or brown.[2] Both the compounds that furnish the flavor (page 57) and the pungency (page 55) of peppers do not develop immediately, rather increasing gradually with maturity. Consequently, the immature fruits are less pungent and less flavorful than the fully mature ones. This accounts for a jalapeño *chipotle* being so much hotter than the familiar green jalapeño, because only the fully mature red fruits of any chilli are smoked to create *chipotles*. It also justifies my opinion that green bell peppers are a poor excuse for a pepper. Now that the big, brightly colored, flavorful bells are in the supermarkets on a regular basis, I don't ever have to buy the green ones except for garnish or decoration, and I burp less. That opinion is probably not acceptable to the bell pepper growers, but I feel better.

In your gardens, choose fruits that have smooth, glossy skins and are firm to the touch. If you have to really tug to get it off the stem, it is not quite ready. These same qualities should be looked for by those who must buy peppers in the marketplace. Except for those insipid, obsequious, omnipresent green bell peppers, which grow in some places year round, peppers are a seasonal crop, and the best selection will be in the summer and fall. In the store you are often met with a bin of chillies that are wrinkled has-beens. In that case, all you can do is pick around for those with the fewest wrinkles. Try buying them in season, when they are bright, shiny, and crisp, to freeze for later use (page 88).

Dried

Not all peppers will air-dry or sun-dry satisfactorily. Those that dry well have thinner skins than the succulent ones such as the bell pepper, jalapeño, serrano, 'Santa Fe Grande', 'Fresno', and many sweet ethnic varieties. If possible, select dried peppers that are unpackaged, because you can pick the better ones. Look for clean, insect-free (tiny holes in the skin are made by bugs; also, powdery dust may be a sign that insects have been present), peppers that are still pliable, not brittle. There should be no light-colored blotches or transparent spots. Many packaged dry chillies are tagged with incorrect names. Pay no attention to those labels, but do look at the size, shape, and color and determine the variety for yourself after studying pages 59-82.

Storage

Fresh

If you are not going to use the peppers immediately, they may be stored in the refrigerator for four or more weeks by drying fresh pods with a clean cloth, then placing them in an airtight container or a *tightly* sealed heavy zip-lock plastic bag from which you have expelled all air.[3] Place the tightly closed container in the refrigerator (optimum temperature 45° to 46°F). Each time you use peppers from the container, dry the unused pods before removing the air and resealing—a home vacuum-packer would be ideal. Every six days remove the container from the refrigerator and allow the peppers to come to room temperature, dry them, return to container, remove air, and seal. This is a method of storage that I recently discovered. If you cannot store them this way and are not going to use them within a week, it is best to freeze them and use them for cooking (page 88).

If peppers are to be shipped, or kept out of the refrigerator, or if you don't have time to withdraw the air, put them in a paper container. *Never* put them directly into an air filled plastic bag before packaging them, as they will spoil rapidly.

Dried

Dried peppers will keep almost indefinitely if stored properly. Make certain they are dry and put them in tightly closed, heavy plastic bags or jars of glass or plastic in a cool, dry place, preferably the refrigerator or freezer. Check them from time to time to be certain they are not deteriorating or beginning to mold. Mildew will usually start on the inside where the seeds attach to the placenta (page 51). Peppers with traces of mildew should be disposed of right away. Remember, only thin walled/skinned peppers will air dry satisfactorily.

Using Fresh Peppers

The best way to use peppers is right off the bush; unfortunately that is seldom possible. However you acquire them, they will need to be washed, stemmed, deveined, and seeded before they are chopped or otherwise utilized in a favorite dish. All this business of roasting and peeling peppers before you cook with the precious pod is enough to scare most novice pepper cooks away. (The only fresh peppers that really need to be skinned are the poblano and the longer, tough-skinned New Mexican Chile—whichever of its cultivars you may be using—and even that ritual can be forsaken with certain of its cultivars if the recipe calls for chopped, minced, or pureed chillies; experiment with one pod first.) However, this blistering and peeling is all part of the pepper mystique. Pepper buffs just like to get right in there with their charismatic pods.

The big bell pepper, 'Cubanelle', poblano, and others of these types should be parboiled or blanched for 2 to 3 minutes before they are used whole for stuffing, if the filling is not to be cooked in the pepper shell. If you have a microwave, put them in a covered microwave-safe container with a couple of tablespoons of water and cook them for a minute or two on high, depending on the size and quantity. Either way, care must be exerted not to cook them to a point that they cannot hold their shape. As soon as they are removed from the heat, plunge the peppers into cold or iced water to stop the cooking.

Small chillies can be washed, stemmed, seeded, and deveined without skinning. In Mexico, India, Indonesia, and the Orient, none of those steps are followed before the fiery fruit is plopped into the pot or wok, whole or chopped. It is recommended that, if you do decide to clean more than one or two pods, you wear plastic or rubber gloves and keep the tissue box handy. When seeding only a couple, handle them gingerly, taking care not to touch the cut surface, and use a small tool to remove the seeds. I have designated the cupped end of a metal cuticle pusher for the job; try it! The principal reason for removing the "innards" of a chilli is to reduce the pungency. In Mexico, peppers that have had the veins and seeds removed are called *capones*, which, like the caponized chicken, means they have been castrated. *Chipotles capones*, which require more preparation time, naturally bring a much higher price than those left intact.

Usually, if a recipe calls for a pepper to be roasted, it is not only to remove the peel, but also because that charred flavor is desired. When you roast and steam them to remove the skin, there is considerable risk of overcooking your peppers to the point that they become too soft to stuff or chop. Like skinning a cat, there is more than one way to roast and skin a pepper.

Blister Methods for Peeling

Before peeling a batch of New Mexican Chiles or poblanos, test one to see if the skin is so tough that all that work is necessary. If you have very fresh, young peppers and plan to grind or chop them, they may not require peeling. However, I tried the lazy way one time (and only one time) with some supermarket New Mexican Chiles, cultivar unknown. I did them in the food processor without peeling, and ended up having tiny pieces of cellophane-like skin in my chiles. I had to cook and strain them before I dared use them in my sauce. The New Mexican Chile presents the most "skin" problems, and some of its myriad cultivars are worse than others. I repeat, test one to see if yours have tough or tender skins.

Peeling peppers can be done by "blistering" the pods, using one of several methods, or by using a hot paraffin dip. We won't go into the troublesome paraffin dip here (see my *Peppers* book on page 128). The actual blistering or roasting can be done in a number of ways. Your choice will probably be determined by your source of heat. Don't forget to keep that little bowl of chlorine solution handy!

STEP I:

Before blistering the skin, always pierce or make a tiny slit in the pod to vent it so that it will not explode.
BURNER ROASTING. If you have a gas stove, set the flame at medium and place your peppers on the burner trivet. If the openings in the burner are too large or if you have an electric stove, place a cake rack, hardware cloth, steel cooling rack, or one of the new stove burner racks designed for stove-top grilling over it. Never let the skin of the pepper touch the electric element. Set the burner on high. Use kitchen tongs to rotate the pods as they start to char. Continue turning until the entire pepper is blackened and blistered. Remove as soon as they are charred to prevent cooking.
BROILER ROASTING. Arrange the peppers on an aluminum foil-covered broiler pan or cookie sheet and place it 3 to 5 inches under the broiler. As in the burner method, keep turning the pods until completely charred. This method allows the peppers to cook more because the oven holds the heat. If shape and firmness are required in your peeled pepper, do not use this method; however, it is a quick way to blister a number of pods at the same time for making stews and sauces. Constant attention is required.
OVEN ROASTING. Preheat the oven to 550°F. Place the peppers on the oven rack and roast until blistered, for 3 to 7 minutes. No turning is required. Note: For blocky peppers like the bell, cut the stem end off flat and stand the cut end on the rack.

MISCELLANEOUS METHODS. The same principles of roasting as in the three previous methods can be used with a charcoal grill or barbecue grill; or in a heavy griddle or skillet on top of the stove. Roasting in hot oil in a saucepan is not recommended. Commercial roasters using revolving cylindrical cages set over gas flames have become commonplace in New Mexico and parts of the Southwest, where New Mexican Chiles are sold in bulk.

STEP 2:

Steaming. Remove the blistered pod from the heat and cool immediately in one of the following ways:
1. Place in a paper bag for 10 to 15 minutes.
2. Wrap in a cold, wet cloth and allow to steam 10 to 15 minutes.
3. Plunge into ice water. This method will give a crisper pepper because it stops the cooking process immediately.

STEP 3:

When the peppers are cool, begin peeling at the stem end while holding one under running water. A small knife will help. Wear rubber or disposable plastic gloves to protect sensitive hands from the fierce capsaicin. For freezing, *do not peel,* in order to retain more flavor, color, and vitamins. The charred skins will slip off easily when the peppers are thawed. Don't forget the chlorine water for your hands!

STEP 4:

Slit the pod; remove veins and seeds by cutting and washing. For more attractive stuffed chillies, leave the stems attached.

Freezing

Frozen peppers may be used in cooking for seasoning, or as stuffed peppers; they are too soft for salads. Most of the nutritive value is retained if care is taken not to expose the peeled or cut fruit to the air, as oxygen destroys vitamin C rapidly. Leave the blistered and steamed peel on the pods as long as possible to guard against this loss. When freezing pungent chillies, parboiling before freezing will prevent capsaicin loss.[4]

For New Mexican Chiles and poblanos:

1. Blister and steam in a damp cloth but do not peel. When thawed, the skin comes off readily.
2. If space is a problem, remove the stem and seeds; otherwise, freeze the entire pod to prevent exposure to oxygen.
3. Flatten the whole pods to remove air and fold once for easy packing and handling.
4. Pack in a moisture-vapor-proof package, excluding as much air as possible. Double layers of waterproof paper between the pods will facilitate separation when peppers are needed.

For bell peppers and large sweet peppers:

1. Wash, core, seed, and dry the peppers. Cut in half; place the halves on a metal pan or baking sheet and freeze.
2. Stack the frozen halves one inside the other and pack in a moisture-vapor-proof package, excluding as much air as possible. Freeze. Use from the bag as needed.

For chillies (jalapeños, serranos, etc.):

1. Wash and dry the peppers. Blanch and dry. Place the whole pods on a metal pan or baking sheet and freeze.
2. Place the frozen pods in a moisture-vapor-proof package, excluding as much air as possible. Freeze. Use from the bag as needed.

Drying Peppers

Sun-drying.

Sun-drying is an ancient method best adapted to arid climates, but it is not feasible in humid areas.

FOR GREEN NEW MEXICAN CHILES

1. Select full-grown but immature pods. Wash, peel, and slit the pod and remove the seeds, veins, and stem.
2. Spread the peppers in single layers on trays or racks. Cover with cheesecloth to exclude pests and dust. Tilt the rack to face the sun. Turn the pods occasionally. A clear plastic or glass covering will increase the heat. Dry for 2 to 3 days, bringing the trays in at night to prevent moisture from condensing on them. The product should be crisp, brittle, and medium green.

1. Allow the pods to remain on the plant until fully mature. Select only ripe red pods. Using heavy twine, run a string through the stem end and hang in the shade to dry. Or,

2. Let the pods ripen and remain on the plant until deep red; place on trays or heavy paper to dry in the shade. Bring in at night. Or,

3. Allow the fruit to mature on the plant; place the pods on a cool, dry window sill to complete drying. Store the whole pods in tightly-closed jars or well-sealed heavy plastic bags in the refrigerator.

Oven-drying (This works for ripe bell peppers.)

1. Core, seed, and remove the ribs/veins from the peppers. Quarter the peppers, or cut them into $\frac{3}{4}$-inch strips.

2. In a large steam basket, steam the peppers for 20 minutes, then dry on paper toweling.

3. Place the peppers, cut side down, on cheesecloth-covered racks. Set the racks on baking sheets. Dry the peppers in a preheated 140°F oven until just short of being crisp, or to crisp if desired, 8 to 10 hours or more. Turn the pepper pieces once about midway through the drying time, and keep the oven door propped open slightly to allow moisture to escape.

4. Let the peppers cool completely before packing.

Smoking

Another method of artificially drying peppers is to smoke them. Although this practice is not followed commercially in the United States, it is the procedure by which *chipotles* (page 70) are produced in Mexico. Fully ripened red jalapeños or any other types of chilli are placed on a bamboo grate over a pit in the ground. A tunnel carries the smoke from the fire pit to the grate. This is very similar to the workings of a Chinese smoke oven (Laborde, 1982:69). The chillies may be processed with or without the seeds. The smoky flavor imparted by this pre-Columbian method is a subtle addition to sauces and mayonnaise. You can do it at home on a small scale in one of those cylindrical smokers like Mr. Smoky.

Dehydration

Dehydration is drying with heat from a man-made source. Studies show that not only is the job done faster but also the product is cleaner, retains more of the nutritive value, and has better color than chillies dried in the sun.

1. Peel the fruit if necessary (page 87).

2. Place the pods in a colander and blanch in boiling water for ten minutes to destroy the enzymes that cause changes in color and flavor. This step can be omitted with New Mexican Chiles but not with jalapeños, bells, or poblanos because their flesh is thicker.

3. Cut the pods in half.

4. Spread the pods in a single layer between two pieces of cheesecloth on racks, nylon screen, or trays. Place in a dehydrator at 130° to 135°F for about eight hours.

Using Dried Peppers

The dehydrated product can be placed in a blender or processor and flaked or powdered. The ground product will keep better refrigerated. Whole pods may be used in recipes that require a long cooking time and a large amount of water such as stews and soups.

A whole fresh green chilli can be smoked (page 89) or roasted (page 87) before it is dehydrated. This imparts a unique flavor to the dehydrated chilli—called *chile pasado* in Mexico.

Rehydration

Anchos, *pasillas*, *mulatos*, *guajillos*, cascabels, *chipotles*, and other dried peppers are usually rehydrated (plumped with water) before being used in food preparation. To do this, either place the chillies in a pan, cover with water, bring to a boil, remove from heat and let stand for an hour, or place in a bowl and cover with boiling water and let stand for an hour. Drain the chillies and reserve the soaking water for use in sauces, soups, stews, etc. You can leave the chillies in the water for more than an hour if necessary but you must realize that the longer they remain in the water, the more the flavor and nutrients are dissolved. Try not to leave them more than one hour. After they have been drained, remove the stems, seeds, and veins. Now they are ready to be used as they are, shredded, chopped, or puréed.

Making a paste

Rinse the chillies in cold water. Remove the stem and seeds and break the pods into pieces. Soak in enough warm water to cover for 30 to 40 minutes but never more than one hour. Place them in a blender with some of the soaking water and purée. Add water as needed to make the desired consistency. The paste can be cooked in hot oil with other ingredients to make a sauce. Store in a covered jar in the refrigerator until needed (recipe, page 179). For a variation use toasted chillies.

Toasting chillies

Rinse the chillies under cold running water and pat dry. Heat a heavy skillet over medium-high heat until a drop of water will sizzle. Place a few chillies in the skillet and toast until just fragrant, turning frequently to avoid scorching. Large types such as the ancho

should be pliable; if not, soak them in a bowl of boiling water for a few minutes. Remove the seeds and veins from the larger types, but this is not necessary for small chillies. Rehydrate the toasted chillies as directed previously.

Another option is to rinse and dry the chillies, then fry them in ½ to 1-inch of hot oil in a skillet over high heat until aromatic and puffy. Drain on paper toweling and proceed as above.

Making a powder

Dried peppers can also be made into a powder by removing the stems, seeds, and veins and grinding 4 to 6 pods at a time in a blender until pulverized. Sift and regrind the larger pieces. Store in a covered container in the refrigerator and use when the recipe calls for powdered red pepper or chilli powder. One tablespoon is equal to one dried *ancho*, *mulato*, and *pasilla* or two New Mexican Chiles. One-eighth teaspoon of ground dried chillies like cayenne can be substituted for one *chiltepín*, *chile de árbol*, or *japonés*.

Let's Come to Terms

 **Pepper Products**
(Condiments and pepper preparations)

An uncontested claim could be made that no other cultivated plant has such a multiplicity of fruit types with such diverse uses over such an expanse of the world as does *Capsicum*. The publication of *Peppers* in December of 1984 coincided with an increase in the acceptance of the pretty, pungent pod. As that popularity has continued to grow, I've been delighted, and so are the burgeoning number of producers of peppers and pepper products.

Peppers have many uses as comestibles—as vegetable, spice, and condiment—and the list is growing. Let's look at a few of the types of products found on

the shelves of the supermarket. The important attributes valued in *Capsicum* products are: color, pungency level, and aroma. Within these types of pepper products are so many variations and brands that it would not be possible to include them all.

ACHAAR (ACAAR). A pickled, oily Indian condiment, often—but not necessarily—very hot. Limes, lemons, mangoes, ginger, eggplant, and other things might be used to make an *achaar*, but the decisive ingredient is chilli. It is served with curries. Contrary to the origin of the word *achaar/achar* given in the first edition of my book *Peppers* (page 5), *achaar* is Persian, not Portuguese, and it does not mean "chilli." The word, and probably the pickle, came to India early in the sixteenth century with the Moguls from the northwest at the same time the Portuguese entered the southwest coast bringing the hot element—chillies. The pickles and peppers met and melded on the subcontinent to become *achaar*, the favored hot pickle in India. It can be bought in Indian food stores or gourmet food shops. No substitute.

ADOBO. A pickle sauce; also a dry marinade for meats made by puréeing together peppers—pungent and/or sweet, garlic, salt, pepper, spices, and lime juice or vinegar. Meat is rubbed with the *adobo* and allowed to sit for several hours or overnight, then it is *adobado* (pickled/preserved) and ready to cook. *Adobo* originated in pre-Columbian Mexico and moved on with the Manila Galleon to the Philippines, where only the name remained the same (page 44). No substitute.

CAYENNE PEPPER. A ground product made from small peppers which contain large amounts of capsaicin. It is not obligatory to make this seasoning from cayenne-type peppers, although it may contain some, along with African, Mexican, and Louisiana chillies. The name cayenne is derived from Tupi, an Indian language of northern Brazil and the Amazon basin (page 62). The powder ranges in color from orange-red to a deep red; as a result it is sometimes labeled simply "red pepper," a term the American Spice Trade Association considers to be inappropriate. Substitute ground or powdered red pepper.

CHILLI OIL. A seasoning oil made with pulverized dried red chillies. Make your own by heating ½ cup vegetable oil in a small skillet over medium heat; add 4 teaspoons ground cayenne pepper (page 91), ground dried red New Mexican Chiles, hot paprika, or ground dried small red chillies. Remove from the heat and carefully add ½ cup hot water while guarding against spattering. Simmer over medium heat for 10 minutes, then cool. After the oil rises to the top, skim it off and put it in a tightly sealed jar. Discard the chilli sediment. Use when a recipe calls for chilly oil, chilli/chili oil, Chinese chilli/chili oil, etc.

CHILI POWDER. (Note the one *l* with *i* at the end.) Dried pods of milder cultivars such as the long red

New Mexican Chile and/or the *ancho* are the principal ingredients of this blend of several peppers and other spices—oregano, cumin, cayenne, garlic powder, paprika. It was first produced commercially by Willie Gebhardt, a German Texan in New Braunfels, Texas, in 1892, to be used in making chili con carne. A popular brand still bears his name.

Reams have been written about chili con carne, so those who want to know more can refer to such books. Purists would never dream of using a commercially prepared chili powder in their chili pot. **Warning.** Chili powder **cannot** be substituted for ground *ancho*, *mulato*, or *pasilla* if they are called for in a recipe because the spices in the powder would alter the recipe. Chilli/chile powder is pure ground dried chillies (next entry).

CHILLI/CHILE POWDER OR PEPPER. This contains only ground red chillies (one or more types) and is **never** a blend of ground peppers and other spices, as is chili powder. They cannot be interchanged. Some chilli powders are finely ground, others may be coarse, while others have seed ground with the flesh. The pungency is dependent on the types of peppers used. You can make your own (page 90) or buy some. Do not substitute chili powder.

CHILLI/CHILI SAUCE. The name is misleading; commercial chilli sauces have few or no chilli peppers in them. Instead they are seasoned crushed tomato catsups with tomato seeds, onion, garlic, sugar, vinegar, some spices, and perhaps a little chilli. They are usually more textured than catsup. This sauce is one of a breed of sauces and catsup that were developed from chutneys and pickles when English cooks found the liquid in the pickle bottle was more interesting than the pickled vegetable. Many manufacturers have dropped it.

CHINESE PEPPER MIX. A freshly ground mixture of whole black, white, and Sichuan peppercorns (*Zanthoxylem piperitum*) that have been roasted in a dry skillet over medium heat until fragrant before grinding. Make your own.

CHUTNEY. The principal type of this delightful Indian accompaniment to curries and meats usually has as its basis two fruits or two vegetables or a fruit and a vegetable, plus onions, tamarind, ginger, garlic, and chillies cooked with vinegar, sugar, and salt. Many of these are "put up" as you would preserves; however, today we are enjoying many innovative uncooked fresh chutneys. Create your own combination!

CRUSHED RED PEPPER. The acceptance of this product has grown in recent years along with the fame of pizza. The long red New Mexican Chile is the primary, although not necessarily the only, pepper to be dried and crushed—including the seeds—then used in this product. It is also available as pizza pepper or *pepperoni rosa.*

CURRY POWDER. This condiment originated in India from *garam masala* (freshly ground dry spices; page 217) and spread to other areas under Indian influence, where it is used to prepare a variety of sauces (curries) to be mixed with meat, seafood, and/or vegetables and served with rice and condiments. Since the eighteenth century, when English interest in and occupation of India began in earnest, curry powder has been used in Great Britain and Europe. A standardized, prepared curry powder does not exist in India, and what we buy here is a poor substitute for a freshly ground batch of spices. In the home of the curry, combinations of spices are ground with peppers specifically for the dish being prepared. It might consist of as few as five or as many as fifty ingredients.

The pungency of curry powder depends on the amount of chilli used. Commercially prepared curry powders are made by grinding slightly roasted chillies to a powder and mixing that powder with ground turmeric for color, then adding coriander along with other spices, which may be one or more of the following; allspice, anise, bay leaves, caraway, cardamom, celery seed, cinnamon, cloves, dill, fennel, fenugreek, garlic, ginger, mace, mustard, nutmeg, pepper (white and black), poppy seeds, saffron, mint, cubeb berries, sumac seeds, juniper berries, zeodary root, and salt. After my extensive travels in the curry belt, I can only say that the product on our food market shelves pales by comparison to the freshly ground spices.

Get a spice mill, mortar, or electric blender and try the mixes on page 217. Store tightly closed in the refrigerator with air removed.

FISH SAUCE. A Southeast Asian sauce made from layering fresh anchovies and brine. It is used as the Chinese use soy sauce. There is no substitute. Buy in an Oriental food store.

FIVE-SPICE POWDER. A blend of various spices including fennel, Sichuan pepper, cloves, cinnamon, and anise; used for chicken, fish, and marinades. No substitute. Buy in Oriental food stores.

GARAM MASALA. A blend of dried spices that have been roasted just before they are ground into a fine powder by a *masalchi* (the person who grinds) and used sparingly toward the end of cooking a dish, or sprinkled over the cooked food as a garnish. There are as many versions as there are chefs. Make it yourself (page 217).

HARISSA. The Maghreb—Tunisia, Algeria, Morocco—in north Africa is the home of this fiery blend of dried red chillies, lemon juice, olive oil, garlic, salt and spices. Harissa paste both flavors and colors such dishes as its traditional companion *couscous,* a steamed grain dish. Look for it in specialty or ethnic food stores or make it yourself (Recipe page 176).

HOISIN SAUCE. A thick, spicy, sweet, dark brownish-red Chinese condiment made of soy bean flour, garlic, chillies, ginger, and sugar, used in stir-fried dishes, on *mu shu* pork, and in Chinese barbecue sauce. It is sold in cans or bottles at Oriental food stores, and will keep for months in a tightly closed jar in the refrigerator. There is no substitute.

NAM PRIK. This Thai hot sauce is a very hot mixture of ground shrimp, garlic, sugar, and dried red chillies mixed with lime juice, fish sauce and chopped Thai or serrano peppers. Used on chicken or grilled meats. Look for it in Oriental food stores. No substitute.

PAPRIKA. No single cultivar of pepper is used to make paprika. Paprika is a ground product prepared of the highly colored, mild red fruits of one or more cultivars of *Capsicum annuum* var. *annuum*, and it is used to season and color food. Sweet paprika is primarily the flesh with more than half of the seeds removed, while hot paprika contains seeds, veins, calyces, and stalks, depending on the grade. *Paprika* is also the name by which all peppers are known in the Balkans. Pungent Hungarian paprika is prepared from a long cayenne-type pepper they call 'spice paprika' and is somewhat pungent, while Spanish and Moroccan paprikas are prepared from a milder, tomato-shaped pepper. Paprika is produced in Bulgaria, Czechoslovakia, Yugoslavia, Hungary, Spain, Portugal, Morocco, Chile, and Arizona and California in the United States (Govindarjan, 1986:212–16).

PEPPER JELLY. Not long ago pepper jelly could only be found at the county fair or those other places where ladies brought in their jams and jellies to sell, but now it can be found in every large food market. Most of it is made with a combination of bell peppers and a chilli, such as jalapeño, or habanero. It is eaten as an accompaniment to meat and poultry, as mint jelly is with lamb, and it is nice over cream cheese on a cracker for the snack tray. Perk up an old fashioned jelly roll cake with it (recipe page 220).

PEPPER SAUCE (BOTTLED). In 1992, on the shelf of a supermarket in a Texas city of 250,000, I counted at least forty different pepper sauces. Six or seven years before that there would have been six to ten. Today, I don't have time to count them all. No matter how many you may find, there are two basic types of pepper sauce:

(1) That which uses whole fruits of very hot varieties preserved in vinegar or brine. It is used to douse cooked vegetables, especially greens. The liquid can be replenished with more vinegar or brine (this can be done several times).

(2) Mashed or puréed chillies that either have or have not been allowed to ferment and are then used as is or mixed with vinegar and spices.

These sauces are generally put up in small bottles designed to dispense the fiery liquid one drop at a time. "Shots" of hot pepper sauce are added with caution to stews, eggs, soups, oysters, and Bloody Marys, to mention a few. Although Tabasco Brand Pepper Sauce® has almost become generic for the second type of pepper sauce, its makers are justifiably vehement in their insistence that the others are not **THE** "Tabasco Sauce," and that there is but one original fermented sauce made of Tabasco peppers and it is to

be known as Tabasco Brand Pepper Sauce®, not simply Tabasco sauce (page 78). I get announcements of new pepper sauces made from all kinds of chillies—dátils, jalapeños, habaneros—in many styles—Malaysian, Thai, Jamaican, Yucatecan—regularly. Try them until you find one you like, or design your own.

Tabasco Brand Pepper Sauce® is made from a pepper mash that is packed into fifty-gallon Kentucky white oak barrels, covered, layered with salt, and allowed to ferment for three years. At that time the mash is filtered, homogenized, diluted one to three with vinegar, and bottled in the world-famous bottle with its cherished trademark.

Vinegar or sherry pepper sauce is a simple favorite. Fill a sterile bottle with whatever small chillies you might have—chiltepínes, tabasco, sports, Thais, 'Floral Gems'—then fill the bottle with a good vinegar, tequila, or sherry. Let it sit for several weeks before using and refill when necessary. Use on vegetables, eggs, soups, and what have you.

PICKLED AND PROCESSED PRODUCTS. Today you cannot keep up with the growing array of pepper products appearing in our food markets. Pepper processors are hard put to keep up with the increasing popularity of the captivating *Capsicum*. We now have canned peppers, pickled peppers, sauces, dips, cheeses, vegetables with chillies, chilli-flavored potato chips, chilli con queso soup, hot corn chips, candy, jellies, stuffed olives—the list goes on and on. A commonly used Spanish term for "pickled" is *en escabeche*. These products are used in place of fresh or dried chillies to add zip to any recipe or to prepare traditional dishes requiring them. Pickle processors like to use little bite-size chillies to eliminate the danger of "spurting" that may occur when biting into a large pickled pod. Many an unwary bystander has been temporarily blinded when a careless *aficionado* put the bite on a pickled jalapeño.

PIMENTO/PIMIENTO. (See page 73)

PIRI PIRI. The dried red piri-piri pepper is called *jindugo* in former Portuguese Africa. It is sold in Portugal in two sizes, the tiny 1-inch long type that is like the Brazilian malagueta pepper (probabaly *Capsicum frutescens*, not to be confused with melegueta pepper or Grains of Paradise from Africa's west coast) and a larger variety, about 3 inches long. Both are extremely hot. Many Portuguese and African households simply put the whole, stemmed, dried red peppers in a glass jar, filling it about a third full of peppers then topping it off with olive oil. The sauce is left to mature for a week or so (recipe page 174.)

RED PEPPER POWDER AND FLAKES. (See entries for crushed red pepper, chile powder and cayenne pepper)

SALSA PICANTE OR MEXICAN HOT SAUCE. The standard Mexican table sauce can now be purchased in bottles in any food market. This once humble preparation made fresh daily by every Mexican homemaker is a mixture of chopped tomatoes, onions, and chillies with a few herbs—mainly cilantro and garlic with some salt and sometimes a little vinegar or lime and a pinch of sugar. Picante sauce, or *salsa picante*, is used as a dip for toasted tortilla chips (*tostadas*) in and on Mexican dishes, as well as on eggs, tacos, and hamburgers. The market for this salsa is growing at a rate of fifteen to twenty percent annually, and it now outsells catsup. There are literally hundreds of variations of *salsa picante*. *Pico de gallo* (rooster's beak) is a name occasionally given to this hot sauce; however, the original Mexican dish by that name is more like a salad made with *jícama*, oranges, onions, and a dash of powdered red pepper or chopped serranos (see sauces in recipe section).

SATAY (SATÉ) SAUCE. An Indonesian sauce, which can be bought in Oriental food stores or gourmet shops, made of chillies and peanuts ground with lemon grass, shrimp paste, lemons, coconut milk, sugar, and salt, to be used on grilled meat. No substitute.

SAMBAL. Sambals are any kind of fiery-hot or spicy relish or condiment served with food. Of Malaysian/ Indonesian origin, the burning sambals are found wherever that influence is felt. The basis is always chillies plus a range of such ingredients as garlic, shallots, shrimp paste, tomatoes, tamarind, and even peanut butter. In East Africa sambals are mixtures of chillies with vegetables, such as cucumbers or carrots, which accompany curried dishes. Southern India is known for a coconut sambal. Many are often in the form of a

paste or a thick sauce that varies in degree of pungency. Some are sour, while others are sweet. They can be likened to the *salsa picante* of Mexico and some are virtually the same as *salsa cruda* (uncooked). They are best when made fresh daily in small amounts; however, for a sambal fan in a hurry, a reasonable facsimile can be bought in Oriental food stores and some supermarkets in bottles like American catsup.

On a houseboat trip lasting several days on a river in Kalimantan (Borneo) the native cooks let me prepare a fresh sambal for each meal. They are quite simple (recipes, page 176).

SOFRITO. A traditional Spanish seasoning mixture of onions, garlic, capsicums—sweet and/or pungent—herbs, annatto, and sometimes ham, sautéed in olive oil or lard. Canned sofrito is now available.

WHOLE PEPPERS, DRIED. There are numerous types of chillies sold in bulk or in packages as dried whole pods. The varieties most commonly sold in this manner are the long red New Mexican Chile, *pasilla*, *mulato*, *ancho*, *cascabel*, *guajillo*, *de árbol*, *japonés*, *chiltepín/pequin*, *catarina*, and others.

WHOLE PEPPERS, FRESH. In the United States and Canada, the peppers most easily found commercially are the various bell pepper-types, long green/red New Mexican Chile, and the yellow wax-types. Some of the Mexican favorites found in U.S. markets on a fairly regular basis are jalapeño, serrano, and poblano. In ethnic food stores, varieties favored by the ethnic group served there are often found. These are used fresh as vegetables, in sauces, and as seasoning.

MISCELLANEOUS. In 1984 I wrote about jalapeño lollipops, jalapeño jelly beans, olives stuffed with jalapeños, "armadillo eggs" (deep-fried jalapeños stuffed with Italian sausage dressing), and the "Martinez" (martini made with jalapeño stuffed olives or an olive and a piece of jalapeño on a toothpick). Now the list could go on and on because chillies are put in almost anything you can think of, and as we travel more, our earth gets smaller and our tastes broader. To such old standbys as Jamaican Pickapeppa sauce, which is similar to Worcestershire sauce but pungent, can be added sauces from all parts of the world. Now on the market are new imports like mandram, a West Indian stomachic made of ground *chiltepínes*, cucumber, shallots, chives or onions, and lime or lemon juice; the Arabic *ras el hanout*, a mixture of spices—black pepper, chilli, turmeric, lavender, etc.—used in Moroccan dishes; the list goes on and on. If you go to various ethnic food shops and poke around for new things, you will find others too numerous to mention, but you can be certain they will have one thing in common—they are HOT!

Ingredients

Many of the recipes included in this book have had foreign inspiration or sources, and the ingredients called for are often exotic, with names that vary from country to country. I have included the scientific names because those are constant the world over and can be used if further information is desired.

ACHIOTE/ANATTO BIXA ORELLANA. *Achiote* is the Spanish and Anatto the English name for a beautiful, small, pink flowered, tropical tree, which is a native of the West Indies, with fruit that looks like bright red castor bean pods. The seeds are a powerful coloring agent and are used to color foods more than to flavor them. The seed itself is not eaten, but boiled in oil then strained. The colored oil or the oily paste takes the name of the seed. The little pots used to make and store *achiote* are called *achoteras*. They are designed to strain the seeds from the oil while the seeds stay inside to be used again several times (make one with a tuna can). Look for the seed or preparations of it in supermarket spice sections or Latin American and Indian food stores. Substitute turmeric.

Pre-Columbian Amerindians living in the tropics used powdered *Bixa* to paint their bodies, probably the source of the epithet "red Indians" (Sauer, 1966:56). Sometimes Eurasians substitute achiote for henna (*Lawsonia inermis*) as a dye stuff.

AVOCADO. *Persea americana*. In Mexico it is called aguacate after *ahuacatl*, a Nauhatl word meaning testicle in reference to its shape. In South America it is *palta*. It is also referred to in Mexico as "poor man's butter." Sometimes known as the alligator pear, this buttery, high calorie, vitamin rich fruit turns dark when exposed to oxygen, but can be protected with citrus juice, prepared citric acid, vinegar, and/or by excluding oxygen with closely wrapped plastic wrap (Saran is best). To peel easily, cut the fruit in half, take a tablespoon and insert it just under the skin and scoop the entire avocado half out of its shell in one motion. No substitute.

BLUE CORN MEAL. *Zea mays*. Corn meal made from grinding the dry kernels of a blue-colored corn, favored by the Hopi Indians of Arizona. Available in southwestern supermarkets, or order from Native Seeds/SEARCH or hot food catalogs. Substitute yellow or white corn meal.

CANOLA OIL. *Brassica rapus*. Name is an elision from Canada oil; also known as rapeseed oil; comes from the rape plant, a relative of the mustard plant. Lowest in saturated fat of all oils and second highest in mono-unsaturated fat after olive oil. Substitute for any cooking oil or salad oil.

CARDAMOM. *Elettaria cardamomum*. This very aromatic seed of a member of the ginger family is native to India. It has not gained the acceptance it deserves in America, but is an Asian, Arabic, and Scandinavian favorite. Do not buy it in powdered form. Get the small gray-green pods, remove the seeds and grind them yourself. Or throw the pods in whole as done in India, but be sure not to eat them. Very expensive as a result of very specialized growing requirements—a little goes a long way. Store tightly closed in the refrigerator or freeze. No substitute.

CHAYOTE. *Sechium edule*. A pre-Columbian Mexican squash. The green, pear-shaped fruit with only one large seed is eaten boiled, fried, stuffed or in soups and salads.

CILANTRO. *Coriandrum sativum*. Although a native of the eastern Mediterranean, it is sometimes called Chinese parsley, culantro, or coriander. The leaves (cilantro, fresh coriander), the seeds (coriander), and, occasionally in Indonesia, the roots are used. It has gained in popularity because it is a component of many Mexican, North African, and Oriental dishes. Does not keep well. Put stems in water, cover, and keep in the refrigerator for two to three days. At times bunches of cilantro in the supermarket will have the roots in place; however, the only dependable source is a home garden. Substitute parsley for color but no substitute for flavor. Many people can't stand it.

COCONUT MILK. *Cocos nucifera*. The liquid found in a fresh coconut, called coconut water, is drunk as a refreshing beverage in the tropics. It is not coconut milk. Coconut "milk" is man-made by soaking grated coconut meat in hot water and squeezing out the liquid, as follows: Place 1 cup of grated coconut to 4 cups of boiling water in a blender and blend for a minute or two. Strain through a mesh or cheese cloth. Store in the refrigerator or freeze if not to be used in a day or two. It will keep one to two weeks. The same coconut meat can be used to make two batches, but the second will not be quite as rich as the first. Feed the remaining coconut to the birds.

CORIANDER. See Cilantro.

CRÈME FRAÎCHE. A thickened, nutty flavored matured cream, not sour cream. To make it: stir 1 tablespoon of buttermilk into 1 cup of whipping cream and heat until lukewarm. Remove from the heat, loosely cover, and allow to stand at room temperature until it thickens, 8 to 36 hours, depending on the temperature of the room. Store, covered, in the refrigerator for up to 2 weeks.

CUMIN (COMINO). *Cuminum cyminum*. The flat, oval brown seeds of this eastern Mediterranean and Egyptian annual herb of the parsley family look like caraway or fennel seeds, but are very different in flavor. Essential to Thai, Indian, Middle Eastern, North African, Mexican, and southwestern U.S.A. cooking. Often toasted before using. No substitute.

EPAZOTE. *Chenopodium ambrosioides*. From the Nahuatl *epazotl*, this Mexico and Central American native is an annual herb with deeply serrated leaves and a strong, camphor-like odor. A few chopped leaves of this almost weed-like plant give character to squash, blackeyed peas, and other vegetable dishes. Several sprigs added to a pot of beans are said to alleviate the problem of flatulence. It works! Use fresh or dried.

Store the dried leaves in a tightly closed jar. Purchase it in Latin American food markets or grow your own, but be careful—it is like a weed and will take over your herb bed. Seed may be labeled *pazote* (saltwort) or Jerusalem Oak Pazote. No substitute.

FAGARA. *Zanthoxylum armatum* and/or *Z. planispinum*. In China the peppery seeds play the role of black pepper in our own cuisine. Look for them in an Oriental food store. Substitute black peppercorns.

FRUCTOSE. See Sugars.

GALANGA. *Allpinia galanga*. Siamese ginger. A ginger-like root from Southeast Asia. Used in Thai and Indonesian cooking. Buy in Oriental food stores. Substitute fresh ginger.

GINGER. *Zingiber officinale*. The spice commonly called ginger is actually a rhizome. The "root" of this tropical, Southeast Asian native is indispensable in Oriental cookery. Select plump, smooth roots, scrape off the thin skin, place the roots in a jar, fill with sherry wine, cover and store in the refrigerator, where it will keep for weeks. Do not freeze. Ginger is also preserved in syrup or candied and coated in sugar to be used as is or chopped and sprinkled over desserts. Most supermarkets and all Oriental food stores sell both fresh and preserved ginger. There is no substitute.

JICAMA. *Pachyrhizus erosus*. Jicama is the large, turnip-like, brown-skinned root of a native Mexican legume with a crunchy, slightly sweet white interior. Use fresh, as crispness is lost when cooked. Store in the refrigerator for up to two weeks. More and more supermarkets carry this in their special vegetable section. Select firm roots. Substitute peeled and seeded cucumber.

KAFFIR LIME. *Citrus hystrix*. Substitute juice from fresh limes for the juice and any citrus leaf for the leaves of this Asian citrus. Oriental food stores may have the leaves if you don't live where citrus trees grow.

LEMON GRASS. *Cymbopogone citratus*. A fairly tall, clumping grass. The bulbous, white base and the leaves are essential to Thai, Vietnamese, and Indonesian cuisine and probably native to that area. It is easy to grow, but a hard freeze will kill it. If you don't grow it, try an Oriental food store. You can substitute lemon peel.

MANGO. *Mangifera indica*. The fruit of a large tropical tree that is native to India. It is eaten ripe or green, raw or cooked, dried or made into preserves and chutneys. There are many varieties of this aromatic fruit—some good, some stringy. The juice may cause problems to the skin of some people hypersensitive to irritants in the sap. As a precaution, use one knife to peel the fruit, and a clean knife to slice the flesh to avoid contaminating it with the resin in the peel. Most supermarkets have mangos, at least part of the year. Select rather firm partially ripe fruit blushed with red or yellow on a taut skin. Smell the stem end to make certain it has not begun to ferment. Substitute fresh peaches.

MANIOC. (Cassava, Yuca). *Maniot esculenta*. This food plant is of New World origin but now an extremely important food starch of the tropical lowlands in both hemispheres. The edible part is the large, tuberous root. There are two groups—sweet and bitter. The latter requires special preparation through labor intensive grating, pressure, and heating to make it safe to eat by removing the poisonous cyanogenetic glucosides. In temperate areas it is used in the form of tapioca for puddings or commercially as a starch or sizing.

MASA HARINA. *Zea mays*. A very finely ground yellow hominy (lime-treated dried corn) used to make tortillas and tamales. The pre-Columbian discovery of nixtamalization, whereby ripe maize grains are soaked and then cooked with lime or wood ashes, enhanced the protein value, making it a superior foodstuff. A diet of properly processed maize and beans furnishes all the protein requirements of a working male (Coe, 1994:30). Available in food stores in the Southwest and Latin American food stores elsewhere. It is being made by the Quaker Oats Company. No substitute.

MENNONITE CHEESE. A white farm cheese made by Mennonites. Substitute a white farmer's cheese, white cheddar, or Monterey Jack.

MEXICAN CHEESES. Before the arrival of Columbus, people of the Americas had no dairy animals. The domesticated Andean llamas were milked, but the milk was not drunk. It is thought some sort of cheese may have been made. There are now many, many cheeses in Mexico but few of them are available in U. S. food markets. *Queso fresco* (fresh) and/or *Queso blanco* (white) are mild, fresh cheeses used to crumble over the various tortilla dishes. Feta makes an adequate substitute. *Queso añejo* (aged) is a dry cheese similar to Parmesan. *Asadero* (roasting) is a cheese to be melted, such as mozzarella.

MEXICAN CHOCOLATE. *Theobroma cacao*. The name for chocolate derives from two Nahuatl words, *xoco* (bitter), and *atl* (water). In pre-Columbian Mexico, a chocolate drink was made with cold water, sweetened with honey, and spiced with vanilla, then beaten until foamy with a *molinillo* (a wooden beater that is twirled between the palms). Today the drinks are made from small cakes of sweetened chocolate. In the U. S., it can be purchased at most Latin American food stores. Substitute sweet chocolate.

MUSTARD. *Sinapis alba* (white); *Brassica nigra* (black). The seeds of this Mediterranean native, ranked with salt and sugar as our most common spices, were used by the ancient Greeks and Romans. The flavor develops only when the aromatic seeds are crushed and mixed with water. Many mustard preparations are available, or you can prepare your own. No substitute.

MUSTARD OIL. *Brassica* spp. A yellow oil made from mustard seed—pungent when raw but sweet when heated slightly. It is used in Indian cookery to prepare vegetables, fish, and for pickling. Peanut oil can be substituted. Look for it in Indian food stores.

NOPALES. *Opuntia engelmannii* (or a similar species). New or very young green pads (these are flat stems, not leaves) of the prickly pear cactus, a New World native. The fruits, *tunas*, can be eaten when ripe. Many supermarkets now carry *nopales* in season (spring). Look for the *opuntia tunas* to be the next Kiwi fruit. No substitute.

ONION. *Allium cepa*. Probably originated in central or southwest Asia and eaten before recorded history. The pungent onion and its relatives, garlic (*A. sativum*), leeks (*A. ampeloprasum*) and chives (*A. schoenoprasum*), are not only used for flavor but also for nutrition and medicine. In markets in India and South America you will not find anything but red onions—in their recipes use only red onions or substitute leeks or shallots but *do not* use strong yellow or white onions. Leeks are used extensively instead of onions in Andean countries. Raw red onion is "cured" or marinated, then the mellowed onion is used in salads or as a condiment in Andean nations—very good. To cure: peel and finely slice the onion then rub salt into it. Let sit for at least ten minutes. Rinse several times; squeeze out water. Add lime juice. Marinate at least ten minutes, then drain. Keep in an air tight container for at least a week. Works on white or yellow onions also.

PALM SUGAR. *Coco nucifera* or *Borssaus flabellifer*. The sap of either the coconut palm or the sugar palm is formed into light brown cakes and used in cooking. If it cannot be found at an Oriental food store, soft brown cane sugar can be substituted.

PAPAYA. *Carica papaya*. Sometimes called papaw, this large herbaceous herb grows to twenty feet tall and bears large, melonlike, green to orange fruits with pinkish orange flesh that emerge from the trunk-like stem. This native of tropical America was introduced to the Philippines by the Spaniards in mid-sixteenth century and from there became pantropic. Ripe fruit is commonly eaten fresh with lime or lemon, but unripe fruit is never eaten raw because of the latex content. It can be used in making pies, sauces, jams, and marmalades—alone or combined with pineapple. The fruit should be ripe and slightly soft. To ripen, put it in a paper bag in a dark place. Do not chill the fruit before it is ripe. Most supermarkets have papayas year round. Peaches or cantaloupe could be used in a pinch.

PEPITAS. *Cucurbita pepo*. Fruit seeds are called *pepitas*, but in Latin American recipes, it is the raw, hulled, unsalted pumpkin seeds which are referred to. These are greenish in color with a nutty flavor and are ground for sauces; used toasted or plain. Stored in the refrigerator in tightly closed containers they will keep several months. Toasted pumpkin "pepitas" can be found in the nut section of supermarkets. Substitute sunflower seed or pine nuts.

PILLÓNCILLO. A little loaf (*pilón*) of unrefined brown sugar from Mexico that can be in the shape of a cone, loaf, or cylinder. Substitute dark brown sugar (see Sugars).

PIMENTO/PIMIENTO. (*Capsicum annuum* var. *annuum*). Pimentos come in a variety shapes and colors—round, lobed, heart-shaped, yellow, red. The first pimento peppers grown in this country were from Spain. The large heart-shaped fruit is very aromatic. "Pimento" is the name adopted by the Associated Pimento Canners of Georgia instead of the Spanish *pimiento* for the thick-fleshed, sweet, bright red *Capsicum* that is usually cored, flame peeled, and canned whole or diced; however, *pimiento* is still used on many of the products on the grocers' shelves. Pimento (fresh or canned) is used for garnishes, in cheese spreads and bricks, in casserole dishes, and wherever bits of color are desired in food. The availability of fresh red Bell Peppers has put all but two of the pimento processors in the U.S. out of business.

RICE VINEGAR. *Oryza sativa*. A light amber, red, or dark black colored condiment or flavoring agent made from rice. The light type is used in sweet-and-sour dishes, the black is used to darken the color of sauces, and the red type is used mainly as a dip for meats and vegetables. Buy it at Oriental food stores; it will keep indefinitely. There is no substitute.

RICE WINE. *Oryza sativa*. There are two kinds of *Shaosing*, China's most popular wine—white and yellow. The sherry-like yellow is made from yellow rice and is warmed in tiny cups before drinking. In cooking, substitute Japanese sake, dry sherry or gin, but never cooking or cream sherry. The clear, vodka-like white wine from north China is used in cooking not as flavoring, but rather to neutralize strong odor. Purchase at Oriental food or liquor stores.

ROMA TOMATOES. *Lycopersicon esculentum*. A small, cylindrical, Italian-type tomato used for cooking and sauces. It has fewer seeds and less juice than regular tomatoes. Excellent for sauces and sun or oven drying. In my travels I have noticed that the Roma tomato has almost entirely replaced other types of tomatoes in the markets of Third World Countries in both hemispheres. It has still not taken over the Balkans, northern Pakistan and the other "-stan" countries which had at one time been in the U.S.S.R., but it probably will.

SESAME OIL. *Sesamum indicum*. The flat, white seed from this herbaceous annual have been ground for their oil in non-Hebrew cultures since a few thousand years before Christ. This non-pungent, nutty flavored oil, used for seasoning, not cooking, is consumed at or near the principal areas of production—Africa, India, China, and the Middle East. The oil will keep almost indefinitely in the refrigerator. The best can be found in Oriental and Middle Eastern food stores. The whole seed is used in cooking and baking. Tahini or sesame paste is an emulsion of seasame seed and oil. No substitute.

SICHUAN PEPPERCORNS. *Zanthoxylum piperitum*. Not kin to either black pepper or capsicums, these are the small red-brown seed from the prickly ash tree. Available in Oriental food stores. Substitute black peppercorns.

STAR ANISE. *Illicium verum*. The licorice-like flavor of the seed of this small Chinese evergreen tree is rather new to American cooks. It is entirely different botanically from anise (*Pimpinella anrsum*). Look for it in Oriental food stores. No substitute.

SUGARS. Sugars are the rudimentary carbohydrates. Granulated sugar is sucrose from a native of India, sugarcane (*Saccharum officinarum*) or the European beet (*Beta vulgaris*); glucose is sugar found in fruits and vegetables; and fructose is the major component of honey and corn syrup. Crystalline fructose is more refined and less natural than sucrose. Fructose must be used in its natural form to be a "healthy" substitute for sucrose.

TAMALES. Seasoned masa mixed with lard, and spread on corn husks or banana leaves (in the banana belt) and cooked; they may be unfilled or filled with any of a variety of seasoned fillings and rolled, ends folded, and steamed. The "shuck" is removed before eating. Canned (a very poor substitute often wrapped in flavorless paper) and frozen are in most supermarkets. Fresh in southwestern supermarkets or Latin American food stores. In Texas almost everyone has a favorite local "tamale lady" to make them for special occasions—a Christmas Eve tradition in south Texas (see Masa harina).

TAMARIND. *Tamarindus indica*. A tropical tree from India that produces a large brown bean pod. The seeds inside the brittle shell are enclosed in a sticky, brown pulp with a tart flavor. In India the pulp is an integral part of chutneys and sauces. It gives Worcestershire sauce its characteristic flavor. Soak the dried pulp in enough lukewarm water to cover until soft—25 to 30 minutes. Squeeze until the pulp dissolves in the water, then strain to remove seeds and fibers. A rather salty, bottled tamarind paste is available in Indian food stores. In the Southwest the dried pods are frequently available in supermarkets. Dilute the paste with water to prepare juice, or reserve the soaking water to use when tamarind juice is called for. Substitue dried apricots mixed with Worcestershire sauce.

TAMARILLO. *Cyphomandra betacea*. In the same family as the tomato, the "Tree Tomato" is the egg-shaped, red or golden fruit of a small tropical tree from Andean South America with skin similar to a pomegranate. It can be substituted for tomatoes in sauces and salsas or stewed with honey or sugar and a little cinnamon for a dessert. Ecuadorians use it for their *Salsa Ají*. Delightful! Substitute Roma tomatoes and a little fresh lime juice.

TOMATILLOS. *Physalis ixocarpa*. These little Mexican, green husk "tomatoes" are not really tomatoes, but rather are kin to the Cape gooseberry. Their tartness adds distinction to many Mexican-style dishes and sauces. Select firm, unblemished fruit and remove the husks before using. Fresh ones can be found in southwestern supermarkets and canned ones are available in most places. Drain the canned ones before using. Green tomatoes can be substituted.

TORTILLA. An unleavened, thin, flat, round bread made of cornmeal or flour, it is the basis of Mexican, southwestern, and Tex-Mex cookery. The ones made with wheat flour are handy substitutes for the typical breads of India and the Middle East. Available in the bread and/or refrigerator section of many supermarkets. Essential for enchiladas and tacos (see Masa harina).

 **Cooking Notes**

The cooking notes are few in number because most kitchens have a standard cookbook like *The Joy of Cooking*, which can serve as a reference. The notes included here are for your convenience because they have been used frequently in the directions for preparation of the recipes.

AL DENTE. To be firm to the tooth or to have a little bite. Cooked until tender but retaining an agreeable firmness.

BLANCH. To plunge food into boiling water and cook until softened, or partially or fully cooked. To do this in the microwave, place the vegetables in a recommended microwave-safe container, add a few tablespoons of water, cover, and microwave at high 2 to 5 minutes depending on the quantity; stir. If needed, repeat. It is very important to plunge into iced water to stop cooking.

CHOPPING HERBS. Wash and dry the herbs, as moisture causes sogginess. Remove any wood-like stems, then process in a food processor by pulsing on and off.

CLARIFY BUTTER. To melt chunks of butter in a small, heavy pan over low heat so that the fat can be separated from the solids. When the foam has risen to the top, remove from the heat, and skim off the foam. Pour the butter off carefully in order to leave the solids in the pan. Clarified butter keeps almost indefinitely when refrigerated in a tightly closed container.

DÉGLACE. To déglace a pan is to dilute the concentrated juices left in a pan in which meat, poultry, and fish have been roasted, braised, or fried. Use wine, clear soup, stock, sometimes cream, or, in a pinch, water.

DEMI-GLACE. A demi-glace is made in a saucepan by bringing 1 quart of brown stock to a boil over high heat; reduce heat and add 4 teaspoons of cornstarch mixed with 4 teaspoons cold water. Simmer until reduced by half and the mixture is thick enough to coat a spoon. Stir until it is cool to prevent separation. This will keep up to a week in the refrigerator or longer if frozen. Use in making sauces. Note: Canned beef or chicken bouillon can be substituted if homemade stock is not available.

GRINDING SPICES. Whole spices and herbs may be ground in a small electric spice or coffee grinder, or by using a mortar and pestle. In order to maintain the volatile natural flavoring compounds of the spice, grind only what is needed at the time. Do not overgrind. Between uses, clean grinder by grinding dry rice grains, then dispose of them.

GRINDING VEGETABLES. Can be produced with the coarse grind disk on an old-fashioned meat grinder (hand turned or electric) or a Braun type mixer/grinder (mine is 1970 vintage). It is almost impossible to get a comparable texture with a food processor—it will be either too coarse or too mushy. Ground vegetables have a distinct coarse texture as opposed to shredded or chopped vegetables.

NON-REACTIVE CONTAINER. A glass, enamel or agate coated, stainless-steel, or any other type container that will not set up a chemical reaction with the food placed in it. Especially important when the foods are highly acidic.

PARBOIL. See Blanch.

REDUCE. To decrease the volume of a liquid by boiling, thereby concentrating its flavor.

ROASTING VEGETABLES. (1) Place the vegetable (ex. tomatoes, garlic, shallots, eggplant) on an aluminum foil-lined pan 4 to 6 inches under the broiler flame. Broil until the skin is evenly charred, turning as needed. Remove only badly charred skin in order to maintain desired flavor. Squeeze the garlic or shallots from their skins. Or, (2) place the vegetables on an aluminum foil-lined pan in a preheated 550°F oven and allow to remain only until blistered, 3 to 7 minutes, being careful not to cook. Plunge into ice water for a crisper vegetable.

SAUTÉ. To cook and brown food in a very small amount of really hot fat, usually in an uncovered skillet. The secret is to have the fat or oil very hot, the food dry, and to sear quickly to prevent loss of juices.

STOCK. The broth from boiled bones, meat, chicken, or fish, used in preparing soups and sauces. A flavorful stock is important. When boiling a chicken or other meat, add onion, celery, peppers, garlic, carrots, bay leaves, peppercorns, and herbs. Cook over low heat until the meat is tender. (For a richer stock, remove the meat, debone, then return the bones to the stock and simmer for an hour or more.) Remove the meat (or bones), degrease, and strain. For a clear stock, never allow the broth to boil. Veal meat and bones produce stock with a neutral flavor. For a brown stock with a more robust flavor, cook the bones in a roasting pan in a 450°F oven, turning several times, until bones are golden brown on all sides. Add the browned bones to the stock pot along with the vegetables.

SWEAT. See Wilting/sweating.

TOASTING SEEDS. Place seeds—sesame (benne), cumin, pumpkin (pepita), sunflower, poppy, or whatever—in a flat pan and toast for about 20 minutes in a 350°F oven and stir frequently, taking care not to scorch. This can also be done in a microwave by spreading the seed in a shallow microwave container and cooking, stirring in $\frac{1}{2}$ to 1-minute intervals, until toasted. This brings out the nutty flavor. Prepare with or without a little vegetable oil. Yet another method is in a dry skillet over low heat on a stove, using little or no oil and guarding against burning by watching carefully and stirring frequently.

WILTING/SWEATING. Vegetables can be wilted (or sweated) in a covered skillet with a small amount of oil, over medium heat, stirring frequently to prevent any browning. Cook them to a barely limp state. This can be done in a covered dish in the microwave without using oil, a plus for the calorie-and health-conscious-cook.

YOGURT. An ancient milk product made from whole or skim milk to which a bacterial culture is added. Non-fat or lite yogurt can be used in place of sour cream and, when dripped, for creamed cheese to lower fat and calorie content. To drip yogurt, suspend it in a drip bag or line a strainer with 2 layers of cheese cloth, add the yogurt and place it over a bowl. Twist the top with a twistie. Let drain for 3 hours at room temperature.

Befores,
Soups & Salads

SERRANO BLOODY MARY

A Bloody Mary you can't beat from Mark Miller, the guru of Southwestern Cuisine. His pace setting restaurants—Coyote Cafe in Santa Fe, New Mexico, and Red Sage in Washington, DC—along with his books Coyote Cafe: Foods from the Southwest *and* The Great Chile Book *have made a difference in the way America eats.*

Makes 12 Servings

- ⅓ cup fresh lime juice
- 3 to 5 serranos (page 78), stemmed and seeded
- 1 bunch cilantro (fresh coriander), stemmed and chopped (reserve some sprigs for garnish)
- 1 46-ounce can tomato juice
- ¾ cup tequila, chilled
  Salt and freshly ground black pepper to taste

Blend the first 3 ingredients in blender. Mix with the tomato juice and tequila. Pour through a strainer into pitcher. Your may want to strain it twice. Serve over ice. Garnish with fresh cracked pepper, salt to taste, and a sprig of cilantro.

CHILE-CON-QUESO WITH RAJAS
Patricia Quintana, Chef/Author
Patricia Quintana lives and teaches in Mexico but often visits the United States, where she is a sought-after cooking teacher and restaurant consultant. She is one of the foremost authorities on her native cuisine and is employed by the Mexican Ministry of Tourism to promote the cooking of Mexico throughout the world. Her cookbooks, with photographs by Ignacio Urquiza, are outstanding.

Makes 6 to 8 Servings; more as a dip

- ¼ cup (½ stick) margarine
- 1 large red onion, finely chopped
- 12 poblanos (page 74) or green New Mexican Chiles (page 71), roasted, peeled, veins and seeds removed; cut in strips (*rajas*)
- 1 fresh or canned jalapeño, minced
- 2 cups Monterey Jack cheese, grated
- 2 cups Mozzarella cheese, grated
- 1 cup milk
- 1 cup heavy cream or yogurt thinned with milk to consistency of heavy cream
- 1 large ripe tomato, peeled, finely chopped, and well drained
  Salt and freshly ground black pepper to taste

Melt the margarine in a frying pan over medium heat, then cook the onions, stirring, until transparent. Add the poblano strips and jalapeños and cook, stirring, until softened. Add the cheeses and cook over low heat until the cheese begins to melt. Stir in the milk, heavy cream, and crème fraîche, and season with salt and pepper. Cook until a thick sauce is formed with the partially melted cheese, about 20 minutes. Add the tomatoes just before serving. Serve immediately in individual bowls or small plates with freshly made corn tortillas. In the southwest, chile con queso is served from a chafing dish or fondue pot as a dip with tostadas (toasted tortilla chips).

WHITE BEAN DIP

This healthy, low fat, dip is a variation of the Ecuadorian salsa de chochos, which are big dried lima beans, sort of an Andean humus. I found it easier to use our navy beans or baby limas because the big white lima must each be slipped out of its skin after soaking. They are wonderful that way, but tedious. Make it at least a day ahead.

Makes 2 Cups or More

Day Before:

1 cup dried navy, white, baby lima, or big lima beans; soak overnight in water to cover. If using big limas, remove the skins after soaking (they slip off easily).

Next Day or Day Before Serving:

Drain the beans and put in a large covered pan with water to cover by several inches. Bring to a boil, then reduce heat and cook covered until very tender. Add boiling water as needed. Drain. Set aside.

   2 tablespoons olive oil
   1 cup leeks or red onion, finely chopped
1½ cups chicken broth
   2 tablespoons fresh basil, minced
   2 garlic cloves, peeled and minced
   1 teaspoon lemon juice
   2 serranos, seeded and chopped; or to taste
      Salt and freshly ground black pepper to taste

Put the oil in a large sauce pan (2½ quart), over low heat, add the onion and garlic and cook until translucent. Add the broth and cook another 5 minutes. Add the drained beans, basil, serranos, and lemon juice; mix well. In batches put the mixture into a blender and process until smooth. Return the puréed mixture to the saucepan and cook over low heat, stirring, until it thickens (about like humus or peanut butter). Remove from heat. Season with salt and pepper. Chill overnight before serving. Use as dip for raw vegetables, chips or crackers. Keep well covered in refrigerator for a week or freeze for later use.

BABA GHANOUJ, TEXAS STYLE (EGGPLANT DIP)

Another healthy, low fat dip based on a Middle Eastern favorite. You won't even know you are eating eggplant. I use a little wooden cleaver found in a souq *(market) to chop the vegetable. It is like the ones I saw being used in homes throughout the Middle East and Central Asia. The texture is better than when chopped with a knife. In lieu of that, try a wooden spoon or wooden spatula. The food processor makes it too slick. Make the day before use so the flavors meld.*

Makes 2½ cups

   2 eggplants (about 1½ pounds each), baked until soft
   2 tablespoons sesame seed
   4 tablespoons olive oil
   2 serranos, seeded and chopped (or more to taste)
   3 garlic cloves, peeled and chopped
      Juice of 1 lemon
   2 tablespoons fresh parsley leaves
   2 tablespoons fresh mint leaves
   ½ teaspoon cayenne pepper, or to taste
      Salt and freshly ground black pepper to taste

Pierce the eggplants in several places. Wrap them separately in aluminum foil and place on a baking sheet. Bake in a preheated 450°F oven until soft, about 45 minutes. Unwrap and let stand until cool enough to handle. While cooling, place all the other ingredients, except salt and pepper, into a blender. Process until creamy smooth.

Halve the eggplants lengthwise and remove all the flesh, discarding the seeds and the skin. Coarsely chop the eggplant and place in a bowl. Add the creamed mixture and stir until well mixed. Season with salt and pepper to taste. Adjust other seasonings. Cover and place in refrigerator overnight to mellow. Serve at room temperature with flat bread, chips, or as a dip for vegetables. Keep well-covered up to a week in the refrigerator. Eggplant does not freeze well. If using only 1 eggplant, use only ½ the amounts of other ingredients.

THE PEPPER LADY'S CHILE-CON-QUESO

This is about as Tex-Mex as you can get, but an informal gathering wouldn't be the same without it.

Makes 8–12 Servings, More as a Dip

- 1 2 pound package Velveeta® cheese, cut into 1" cubes
- 1 pound sharp cheddar cheese, shredded
- 1 10 ounces can Rotel® diced tomatoes and green chiles
- 2 fresh poblano (page 74) peppers or New Mexican Chiles (page 71), roasted (page 87), skinned, deveined and chopped
   Salt and freshly ground black pepper to taste
   Ground cayenne pepper to taste

Melt the Velveeta cheese in a microwave or in a large double boiler or crock pot, being careful not to scorch. Add the cheddar cheese gradually, stirring until melted and completely mixed with the Velveeta. Drain off half of the liquid from the can of tomatoes and green chiles. Add the remainder with the tomatoes to the melted cheeses, mix well. Add the chopped fresh chillies. Stir until well mixed. Add seasonings to taste. Serve immediately with freshly made corn tortillas. In the southwest, chile con queso is served warm from a chafing dish or fondue pot as a dip with tostadas (toasted tortilla chips).

CREAMY CHILE DIP

A delightfully different dip for raw or parboiled vegetables, tostadas, or used as a stuffing for celery, banana peppers or cherry tomatoes as appetizers.

Makes 1 Cup

- 6 green New Mexican Chiles (page 71), peeled, seeds removed, chopped; or a 4-ounce can, drained, chopped
- 1 8-ounce package cream cheese or dripped yogurt (see note below)
- 2 tablespoons milk
- 3 tablespoons green onion (scallion), finely chopped

- 4 garlic cloves, pressed
- ½ teaspoon cayenne pepper or to taste
   Banana pepper halves and/or celery stalks

Combine all the ingredients and beat until creamy. Add more milk if necessary. Allow to sit for at least 1 hour at room temperature before serving. Serve as a dip with chips or fresh vegetables or stuff in banana pepper halves (page 59) or celery.
NOTE: Drip yogurt by placing plain, non-fat yogurt in a drip bag or filter. Suspend it over a bowl; allow to drip overnight in the refrigerator. This is a low calorie substitute for cream cheese in any recipe.

MACHO BUTTER

My mother used to hide peanut butter from me to keep me from eating the entire jar at one sitting. I wish she was around to hide this one from me. It's habit forming.

Makes about 5 Cups

- 3 chipotles, soaked in water, seeded and deveined
- 4 anchos (page 74), lightly toasted (page 90), soaked in water, seeded and deveined
- 1 garlic clove, peeled
- 3 cups chunky peanut butter
- ½ cup sesame seeds, more if desired
   Cayenne pepper to taste

Place the peppers and garlic in a blender jar and blend until well mixed; adding a little pepper water to make a paste. Gradually add pepper mixture to the peanut butter in a bowl and mix well. Add sesame and mix until distributed throughout. Serve as a spread with tortilla chips, bread rounds, or celery sticks.
NOTE: This should be creamy like peanut butter; if too dry and crumbly add a little peanut or canola oil and mix well until desired consistency. If chunky-style peanut butter is added to pepper mixture in the blender it will no longer be crunchy.
NOTE: If you want to make just one jar full, divide the ingredients by three.

HOT OLIVES

Prepare a jar of hot olives to have on hand for drinks, appetizers, or what have you.

    1 jar giant whole or stuffed olives
       Juice from the same-size jar or can of jalapeños
       (page 70)

Drain the juice from the olives and replace it with the juice from the jalapeños. Recap the jar and keep it in the refrigerator for 3 weeks before using. Replace the liquid in the jalapeño jar with equal amounts of vinegar and water. Recap and store in the refrigerator.

LILLIAN'S TANGY CHEESE BALL

Great for parties because it can be made ahead of time, and leftovers can be remolded and frozen!

Makes 1 Large or 2 Small Balls

    6   ounces Roquefort or blue cheese, at room
        temperature
    10 ounces very sharp, crumbly cheddar cheese,
        finely grated, at room temperature
    12 ounces cream cheese, at room temperature
    1   small onion, grated
    1   tablespoon Worcestershire sauce
    1   teaspoon cayenne pepper, or to taste
    1½ cups pecans, finely chopped
    1½ cups parsley, stemmed and minced

Place in a large bowl with the onion, Worcestershire, and cayenne pepper. Add ½ cup each of the nuts and fresh parsley, reserve the remainder. *With your hands*, blend all thoroughly. NO PROCESSOR! Shape into 1 large or several small balls and place each in a small bowl lined with plastic or aluminum foil. Refrigerate over night. Before serving, roll balls in a mixture of remaining parsley and pecans. Serve with unsalted or water crackers.

NOTE: Unused portions of the ball can be remolded and frozen.

PITA PEPPER CONFETTI HORS D'OEURVRES

Rollie Anne Blackwell, Chef/Owner

Rollie Anne Blackwell is the chef/owner of Gourmet Dallas in Dallas, Texas. She uses exciting regional ingredients and flavors to create zesty and delicious gourmet cuisine.

Makes 40 Hors d'oeuvres

    ¼ cup (½ stick) unsalted butter or margarine
    1 large red bell pepper, seeded and cut into very
       small squares
    1 large yellow bell pepper, seeded and cut into
       very small squares
    1 green bell pepper, seeded and cut into very
       small squares
    6 small green onions (scallions), chopped finely
       Salt and freshly ground black pepper to taste
    6 ounces grated Monterey Jack or Ancho-Chili
       cheese
    1 package pita bread, cut into triangles, brushed
       with melted butter or margarine and toasted in
       400°F oven until crisp
       Fresh cilantro (fresh coriander) sprigs, optional

Melt the butter in a frying pan over medium heat, then cook the red, yellow, and green bell peppers and onions, stirring, until translucent, about 2 minutes. Season with salt and pepper and add the grated cheese, stirring until melted. Mound onto the toasted pita triangles and garnish with a sprig of cilantro if desired.

PICKLED CHILE ANCHOS

Miguel Ravago, Chef/Author

Miquel Ravago, of Mexican descent, came to Texas from Arizona. He has been a most successful chef, restaurant owner, and the co-author of an award winning cookbook, Cocina de la Famila.

Makes 10 or 20 Servings

    4 cups red wine vinegar
    4 cups water
    5 cones *piloncillo* (Mexican sugar), or 1 cup brown
       sugar

12 garlic cloves, peeled
10 bay leaves
2 tablespoons black peppercorns
2 tablespoons allspice berries
½ cup vegetable oil
½ cup olive oil
20 Chile anchos (dry), one side slit, seeded, and deveined (page 90)
Sprigs of fresh herbs such as: thyme, sage, marjoram, oregano, mint, or tarragon

For the Filling

1 cup ricotta cheese
1 cup cottage cheese
Green onions (scallions), chopped; to taste
Cilantro (fresh coriander), minced; to taste

In a saucepan boil the vinegar, water, and *piloncillo* over high heat until the sugar dissolves; lower the heat. Add the garlic, bay leaves, and spices; allow to simmer for 10 minutes. Turn off the heat and add the oil, herbs and anchos; marinate overnight at room temperature.

To serve: drain the anchos and stuff with the cheese filling or use tuna salad, seafood salad, guacamole salad (page 113). Garnish with sprigs of herbs.

GRILLED QUESADILLAS WITH SMOKED CHICKEN
Reed Clemons, Chef/Owner
Reed Clemons trained at the New York Cooking School before settling in Austin, Texas, where he owns and operates several favored restaurants, among them the Granite Café and Mezzaluna. He features creative dishes in a combination of ethnic styles but with southwestern overtones.

Makes 8 Servings

3 cups black beans (see preparation below)
16 flour tortillas
1 pound smoked chicken, diced (can substitute grilled chicken)
1 pound Monterey Jack cheese, grate

3 poblanos (page 74), roasted (page 87), peeled and cut into strips
1 chipotle (page 70) *adobado* (canned), puréed, (use more if desired)

Spread the puréed black beans on eight of the tortillas and top with the smoked chicken, Jack cheese and poblano strips. On the other 8 tortillas, spread the puréed chipotle. Place these tortillas on top of the first 8, face down.

Place the *quesadillas* on a preheated grill or oiled skillet for a minute or so, and then, without turning the *quesadilla* over, turn them at a 45-degree angle for another minute or so, or until there is a good criss-cross pattern. Then repeat the same procedure for the other side. Be careful not to burn. Once they are done, take them off the grill and cut them into 6 to 8 wedges. Serve them hot with a tomatillo sauce (page 178) and guacamole (page 113).

Black Bean Preparation

1 pound black beans, picked over
4 tablespoons oil
2 large onions, diced
1 garlic clove, peeled and minced
2 tablespoons ground cumin (comino)
4 tablespoons fresh epazote (page 96), chopped optional
Salt to taste

Soak the beans in water for several hours or overnight. Heat the oil in a large saucepan (2¾ quart) over low heat and cook the onions and garlic, stirring, for 5 minutes. Add the drained beans and enough fresh water to cover, the cumin, and *epazote* and bring to a boil. Reduce the heat to medium-low and simmer until tender, about 2 hours, stirring occasionally and making sure there is enough water to cover the beans. If additional water is needed, add only boiling water. Purée the beans in a food processor (you may have to do this in batches). Season with salt.

CHEESE-STUFFED ANAHEIMS

Frieda and Karen Caplan,
Food Importing-Marketing/Owner

Frieda and Karen Caplan head up a Los Angeles-based wholesale produce business called Frieda's that pioneered much of the specialty produce market in this country. One of their introductions, the Chinese gooseberry, took off after they renamed it the kiwifruit. No cooking is involved in these stuffed peppers!

Makes 36 Appetizers

- 4 ounces sharp Cheddar cheese, shredded
- 3 green onions (scallions), chopped
- 2 fresh chillies, such as serrano, Caribe, 'Santa Fe Grande,' 'Fresno,' jalapeño (see index), seeded and minced
- ⅓ cup ripe olives, chopped
- 2 tablespoons fresh cilantro (fresh coriander), chopped
- 2 tablespoons milk
  Salt and freshly ground black pepper to taste
- 4 to 6 green New Mexican Chiles/Anaheim (page 71), stemed and seeded
  Lettuce leaves
  Fresh cilantro (fresh coriander) for garnish

In food processor or using a mixer, combine cheese, onions, the 2 chilli peppers, olives, cilantro, and milk until well-blended. Season with salt and pepper. Slit the Anaheims lengthwise. Stuff Anaheims with cheese mixture, packing in mixture with the back of a spoon. Chill several hours or overnight. To serve, arrange lettuce leaves on a platter. Slice stuffed Anaheims crosswise into ½ inch thick slices; arrange on platter. Garnish with cilantro, if desired. Serve cold or at room temperature.

ECUADORIAN SEVICHE DE CAMARONES SHRIMP SEVICHE

Seviche (say-be-chay), a marinated seafood classic, can be enjoyed at any meal. It was created in Peru and became an Andean favorite. Popcorn, the authentic accompaniment, must have also originated in the same region before Columbus because it is used there in so many different ways. It is not buttered and salted as we have come to expect at our movie theaters but is frequently used as we do croutons.

Makes 4 to 6 Servings

- 1 pound headless shrimp, cooked 1 minute in 2 cups of boiling water; drained, shelled and cleaned. Set aside 1 cup of the cooking water (shrimp broth)
- 6 tablespoons fresh lime juice
- 1 teaspoon salt
- 1 red onion, thinly sliced, separated into rings and cured (page 97)
- 1 teaspoon fresh lime juice for curing onion
- 1 serrano (page 78), seeded and chopped
- 1 Roma tomato, seeded and chopped
- ½ cup fresh orange juice
- 3 tablespoons ketchup
- 2 tablespoons olive oil
- 1 tablespoon cilantro (fresh coriander), minced
  Salt and freshly ground black pepper
- 1 quart of popped popcorn
  Lime wedges for garnish

In a large, flat, nonreactive container mix the lime juice and salt. Marinate the shrimp with the lime juice in the refrigerator for 1 hour or more, stirring occasionally. Add the onions, serranos and tomatoes to the marinated shrimp. Drain, then mix in the reserved cooking water, orange juice, ketchup, olive oil and cilantro. Chill thoroughly and serve in small bowls with a teaspoon. Garnish with lime wedges. Pass the popcorn.

NOTE: For seviche, shrimp of 40 to 50 count per pound are a nice size. If they are larger you might need to cut them in half and increase the cooking time slightly.

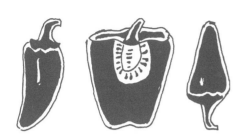

GRILLED SCALLOPS WITH A ROCOTILLO MANGO RELISH
Chris Schlesinger, Chef/Owner/Author
Grilling is Schlesinger's specialty. He owns restaurants in Cambridge, Massachusetts, and is co-author of The Thrill of the Grill. *Chris became challenged by peppers on a trip to Barbados. This tasty appetizer is really quite simple to prepare.*

Makes 8 Appetizers

- 2 pounds scallops
- 1 cup rocotillo peppers, small dice (fresh red pimento or red bells)
- 1 small red onion, small dice
- 1 green bell pepper, small dice
- 1 fresh jalapeño, small dice
- 2 mangos, small dice
- ½ cup orange juice
- ½ cup pineapple juice
- ½ cup fresh lime juice
- ¼ cup chopped cilantro
  Salt and freshly ground black pepper, to taste

The Scallops

Place scallops on a skewer and grill on a medium hot fire until scallops are golden brown outside and opaque color inside (approximately 2 to 3 minutes per side).

The Relish

In a mixing bowl, combine remaining ingredients into an uncooked relish. Season to taste. Serve scallops on a bed of relish.

NOTE: Rocotillos may be hard to find, so substitute pimento, red bell, or any thick fleshed pepper with a little dash of ground red pepper.

SEVICHE (CEVICHE)
Seafood seviche originated in pre-Columbian Peru. It makes a refreshing appetizer or a main course for a light summer meal. Lucky the cook who has a fisherman friend!

Makes 10 to 12 Servings

- 1½ pounds red fish, snapper, trout or a mixture (use any good fresh fish your favorite fisherman brings home), filleted and cut into very narrow strips.
- 2 cups mixed clams, oysters, shrimp, and/or snails, chopped (if none available, use more fish)
- 3 cups fresh lime juice (Mexican limes preferred but *no* bottled lime juice)
- 2 fresh green chillies (serranos, jalapeños, or Fresnos, see index), seeded and chopped
- 1 large ripe tomato, chopped
- 1 large red onion, finely chopped
- 3 to 4 cilantro (fresh coriander) sprigs, chopped
- 1 to 2 tablespoons olive oil
  Salt and freshly ground black pepper to taste.

Place all of the chopped seafood in a nonreactive bowl. Cover with half the lime juice, and marinate in the refrigerator at least 4 hours, preferably overnight. Drain and wash in cold water (important). Drain again. Return to bowl. Pour in remainder of lime juice and the remaining ingredients. Some like to add sliced stuffed olives. Adjust seasonings. Serve in cocktail dishes before dinner; from a bowl sitting in ice as an appetizer; or on a bed of lettuce as a luncheon entrée. Accompany with soda crackers.

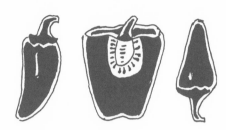

SOUTHWESTERN RAW VEGETABLE SALAD

Kurt Koessel, Chef

Chef Koessel of Ginger Island in Berkeley, California, created this salad which is excellent for a buffet table—no last minute lettuce.

Makes 10 Servings

- 1 medium size jícama (page 96), peeled and julienned
- 2 red bell peppers, seeded and julienned
- 2 poblanos (page 74), seeded and julienned
- 2 fresh green New Mexican Chiles (page 71), seeded and julienned
- 1 jalapeño (page 70), seeded and chopped
- 1 medium-size red onion, thinly sliced and separated into rings
- 1 cup red seedless grapes

For the Dressing

- 1 tablespoon cumin (comino) seeds, toasted (page 101) then ground
- 1 tablespoon fresh chopped cilantro (fresh coriander)
- 1 tablespoon red New Mexican Chile flakes
- 1 tablespoon fresh lime juice
- 1 teaspoon lime zest, grated
- 2 garlic cloves, peeled and minced
- ½ teaspoon salt
- ¾ cup extra virgin olive oil
- ½ cup red wine vinegar

Combine salad ingredients in a serving bowl. Combine dressing ingredients in a small bowl or glass jar; mix well. Just before serving, pour the dressing over salad and toss.

ENSALADA FAVORITA

Lucinda Hutson, Herbalist and Author

Austinite Lucinda Hutson is a cooking teacher, author, and herb expert—both as a gardener and cook. This native Texan is the author of Tequila: Cooking with the Spirit of Mexico *and* The Herb Garden Cookbook. *Wow! A salad that can be made ahead of time!*

Makes 6 to 8 Servings

For the Marinade

- ¼ cup mint vinegar or white wine vinegar
- 4 tablespoons fresh lime juice
- 3 garlic cloves, minced
- ½ teaspoon brown sugar
  Salt and freshly ground white pepper to taste
- ¼ teaspoon crushed red chilli pepper flakes
- 2 tablespoons fresh mint, chopped
- 6 tablespoons olive oil

For the Salad

- 3 medium sized zucchini, scored with a fork and cut into ⅜-inch slices
- 4 to 6 green chile GOURMET CHILES or fresh green New Mexican Chiles (page 71), roasted, peeled, cored, seeded, and cut into strips
- 6 green onions (scallions) with most of the green tops, chopped
- 4 ounces cream cheese, cut into ½-inch pieces
- 2 tablespoons fresh mint, chopped
- 1 tablespoon cilantro or parsley, chopped
  Salt and freshly ground black pepper to taste
- 2 ripe avocados, cubed and sprinkled with fresh lime juice
- 1 head red-tipped lettuce
  Fresh mint sprigs and cilantro sprigs for garnish
  Lime wedges

Make the marinade by combining the vinegar, lime juice, garlic, sugar, salt, pepper, chilli flakes, and mint; slowly whisk in the olive oil. Set aside. Bring a pot of water to boil; place the zucchini in a steam basket and steam for 2 to 3 minutes or until crisp-tender. Submerge in ice water immediately; drain. Pat the zucchini dry and place in a shallow glass dish. Add the green chile strips, onions, cream cheese pieces, chopped mint, and cilantro; sprinkle with salt and freshly ground white pepper. Drizzle the marinade over the squash mixture; gently mix together well. Marinate several hours or overnight, mixing occasionally. Before serving, add the avocados and mix well. Serve on chilled plates with crisp lettuce, mint and cilantro sprigs, and lime wedges.

Another way to serve this is to omit the green chile strips and serve each portion in a whole roasted and peeled green New Mexican Chile. Simply slit the chile down the middle, leaving the stem intact, and fill with the squash mixture. Serve on a bed of lettuce with a mint sprig, drizzling any remaining marinade over the chile.

NOTE: GOURMET CHILES are frozen New Mexican Chiles that have been roasted and vacuum packed with the skins on to insure year round freshness and vitamin retention. When thawed the skins slip off easily. P.O. Box 39, Mesilla, NM 88046

GUACAMOLE (AVOCADO SALAD)

It's a long, long road to guacamole and there are many variations of the dish along the way—most of them loaded with fat. After the traditional recipe are some suggestions for lessening the fat.

Makes 2 Cups

4	ripe avocados, peeled and mashed with a fork
1	small tomato, chopped
1	tablespoon minced onion
1	clove garlic, juice only
1 to 2	serranos, seeded and minced
2	teaspoons cilantro leaves, finely chopped
	Lime or lemon juice, to taste
	Salt and pepper to taste

Mix all the ingredients in a bowl. This mixture should have some texture. If a processor is used, care must be taken to keep the mixture from becoming too smooth. The addition of 1 teaspoon of Fruit Fresh® (ascorbic acid) will allow you to make this several hours ahead of serving time without fear of it turning black on top; cover it closely (no air space) with saran wrap. Other-

wise, make it at the last minute. Serve with toasted tortilla chips.

ALTERNATE 1: For each avocado blend in 1 cup low-fat cottage cheese and follow the directions as given above. This is about half the fat for the same size serving as the straight avocado guacamole recipe. Serve with baked low-fat tortilla chips or raw vegetables.

ALTERNATE 2: Substitute thawed and puréed frozen green peas for the avocado and proceed with the guacamole recipe. A little extra serrano may be needed or try half peas and half avocado the first time. Serve with baked low-fat tortilla chips or raw vegetables.

NOTE: To peel an avocado; cut in half and remove the seed. Using a tablespoon, insert spoon between peel and meat, working the spoon to the other side and scoop out entire half; dip quickly into a solution of water and ascorbic acid (use a commercial preparation such as Fruit Fresh) or wipe it with lemon juice to prevent darkening.

If avocado is not ripe, wrap in newspaper or paper sack; place in micro-wave. Using a half-minute to start with, and more or less as needed as you progress, heat the avocado until it is the desired consistency, taking care not to cook it.

AUNTIE'S PERFECTION SALAD

My Aunt Julia's specialty and my favorite congealed salad. She always made it for me during my annual summer visit to Seguin, Texas.

Makes 8 to 10 Servings

- 3 cups Hunt's tomato juice, or a substitute
- 2 tablespoons unflavored gelatin, softened in ½ cup cold water
- ¼ cup sugar or equivalent artificial sweetener
- ½ cup herb vinegar (page 215)
- 1 teaspoon salt
- ½ teaspoon freshly ground black pepper
- 2 tablespoons Worcestershire sauce
- ½ teaspoon Tabasco Pepper Sauce®
- 1 serrano, seeded and minced (optional) (page 78)
- 1 small jar pimentos, chopped
- 1 cup cabbage, finely chopped
- 2 small red apples, cored and chopped
- 2 cups celery, chopped finely
- 1 small red bell pepper, seeded and chopped finely
- 1 tablespoon onion juice
- 1 head Bibb or leaf lettuce, washed and crisped Mayonnaise (page 184), Chipotle Mayonnaise (page 184), or Creamy Serrano Dressing (page 183)

Soften gelatin in a little cold water. Heat 1 cup of the tomato juice to the boiling point and pour into a large mixing bowl. Dissolve the softened gelatin in the hot juice; add the sugar, vinegar, salt, pepper, Worcestershire, and Tabasco Pepper Sauce® and stir until well mixed. Add remaining juice and the chopped vegetables and onion juice. Pour into a large rectangular Pyrex dish or mold. Chill until firm. If you want, release from mold, cut into squares and serve on bed of lettuce on individual salad plates or serve directly from the pan. Top with a dollop of mayonnaise or Creamy Serrano Dressing.

GARDEN POTATO SALAD

When entertaining guests, it is always a blessing to be able to make some of the dishes well before the event. This is one which must be made ahead of time so that the flavors will meld and be absorbed into the potatoes.

Makes 6 to 8 Servings

For the Salad

- 2 pounds new potatoes
- 1 tablespoon canola oil
- 1 medium-size onion, thinly sliced
- 5 garlic cloves, peeled and minced
- 2 medium red bell peppers, seeded and julienned
- 1 to 5 jalapeños (page 70), seeded and sliced (depends on desired pungency)

For the Dressing

- 1 tablespoon dry mustard
- 1 teaspoon freshly ground black pepper
- ½ teaspoon ground cayenne pepper or to taste
- 2 teaspoons salt
- ¼ cup olive oil
- 2 tablespoons cider or herbed vinegar

Boil the unpeeled potatoes in water to cover until quite tender (this can be done in the microwave). Drain and cool until easy to handle, then slice each potato into large chunks. Heat the oil in a heavy skillet over medium heat and cook the onion, garlic, and both peppers, stirring until tender. Combine with the warm potatoes. In a small bowl, blend dressing ingredients with a wire whisk until smooth. Pour over warm vegetables, tossing gently. Refrigerate at least for several hours or overnight to let the flavors blend. Allow the salad to stand at room temperature 1 hour before serving.

PEPPER, ENDIVE AND SPROUTS SALAD

A painless way to eat your vitamin-rich vegetables.

Makes 6 to 8 Servings

- 1 head Bibb lettuce, torn into bit-size pieces
- 1½ cups sunflower sprouts
- 2 Belgian endives
- 1 red or yellow bell pepper, seeded and julienned
- 1 medium-size red onion, thinly sliced and separated into rings
  Creamy Serrano Dressing (page 183)

Wash the lettuce, sprouts, and endives. Drain in colander and shake off excess moisture. Wrap in paper towels, place in plastic bag and refrigerate for at least 1 hour. Cut the endives in half lengthwise, then cut each half into small strips. Place endive, pepper, lettuce, onion and sprouts in salad bowl and toss with Creamy Serrano Dressing.

ROMAINE SALAD WITH CRISP CHILE RINGS

Linda Lau Anusasananan, Food Journalist

Linda Anusasananan is a native Californian of Chinese descent who has been with Sunset *magazine since 1971, where she writes, researches, and develops recipes which emphasize the food bounty of the West. She takes an active part in the annual Berkeley Chile Festival.*

Makes 6 to 8 Servings

- 6 large dried red New Mexican Chiles (page 71)
- ¼ cup olive oil
- ⅔ cup cider vinegar
- 1 garlic clove, peeled and pressed or minced
- 1 tablespoon Worcestershire sauce
- ¾ pound romaine lettuce, washed, crisped, and torn into bite-sized pieces
- 1 small red onion, thinly sliced
- 1 small cucumber, thinly sliced
- 2 small, ripe tomatoes, cored and cut in 1-inch wedges
- ½ pound tiny, cooked shrimp, shelled
- 1 cup cilantro (fresh coriander) sprigs
- 1 large ripe avocado

Wipe the chiles. With scissors, cut chiles crosswise into thin strips; discard the seeds and stems. In a 10- or 12-inch frying pan, stir the oil and chiles over low heat until chiles are crisp, 2 to 3 minutes (watch closely to avoid burning). Lift chiles from oil; set aside. Whisk together the oil from chiles, the vinegar, garlic, and Worcestershire.

In a large bowl place half of the romaine. Top with half of the onion, cucumber, tomatoes, shrimp, and cilantro. Repeat layers. If made ahead, cover and chill up to 4 hours. To serve, pit, peel, and slice avocados and chiles over the salad. Spoon dressing over salad and mix.

JÍCAMA AND PEPPER SALAD

Crunchy, tasty, and beautiful, the ingredients for this salad can be prepared earlier for last minute assembly.

Makes 8 to 10 Servings

- 1 head Bibb or leaf lettuce, washed and crisped
- 1 orange bell pepper, seeded and carefully cut into 8 thin rings
- 1 red bell pepper, seeded and carefully cut into 8 thin rings
- 1 yellow bell pepper, seeded and carefully cut into 8 thin rings
- 1 green bell pepper, seeded and carefully cut into 8 thin rings
- 1 purple bell pepper, seeded and carefully cut into 8 thin rings
- ¾ pound jícama (page 96), peeled, thinly sliced and cut into ½-inch by 2 to 3-inch strips
- 1 medium-size red onion, thinly sliced and separated into rings
  Creamy Serrano Dressing (see page 183)

Tear the lettuce into bite sized pieces and prepare a bed on each salad plate. Overlap rings of each color pepper on the lettuce bed. Leave space for 4 to 5 jícama slices laced through several onion rings. In the center place a generous spoonful of the dressing. Serve very cold.

ZESTY SPINACH-CHICKEN SALAD

This is a tasty and satisfying luncheon dish or, without the chicken, it is the perfect salad to accompany any type of curry.

Makes 6 Servings

For the Dressing

¾ cup extra virgin olive oil
¼ cup white wine vinegar
¼ pepper jelly (page 220)
2 tablespoons curry powder (page 217)
¼ teaspoon dry mustard
¼ teaspoon Tabasco Pepper Sauce®
Salt and freshly ground black pepper to taste

For the Salad

About 2 bunches fresh spinach, well washed and spun dry; torn into bite-size pieces

2 cups red onions, cut into thin rings, separated
2 red apples, cored and thinly sliced (not 'Delicious')
1 yellow or red bell pepper, seeded and julienned, or ½ cup each
½ cup sunflower seeds, toasted (page 101)
½ cup dried cranberries or golden raisins
1 cup chicken, grilled and cut in bite sizes
Crumbled crisp bacon and sharp cheddar cheese cubes, optional

Mix all the dressing ingredients together well. Cover and refrigerate at least 24 hours. For salad, toss all the ingredients in a large bowl. Add the dressing; toss to coat. Serve immediately.

RUBY RED GRAPEFRUIT AND AVOCADO SALAD

Texas is the home of the 'Ruby Red' grapefruit and we're mighty proud of it—not only delicious, but also beautiful.

Makes 3 Servings

Leaf lettuce
1 grapefruit, peeled and sectioned (Ruby or pink preferred)

1 avocado, peeled (page 95) and sliced
1 small, red bell, seeded and sliced in thin rings
Zesty Poppy Seed Dressing (page 183) or
Creamy Serrano Dressing (page 183)

On each chilled salad plate prepare a bed of lettuce. Alternate overlapping slices of grapefruit, bell pepper, and avocado. Drizzle generously with the dressing and serve.

INDIAN RAITA

The actual mouth-cooling effect of this traditional Indian yogurt dish is proven (page 57). It is a delightful complement to the burning curries or any other peppery foods.

Makes 6 to 8 Servings

2 cucumbers, onions, or ripe tomatoes, or a combination, diced
2 cups plain yogurt
½ teaspoon ground coriander
½ teaspoon cumin (comino) seeds, sautéed in 1 tablespoon vegetable oil until golden brown (reserve oil)
½ to 1 teaspoon ground cayenne pepper
Pinch of turmeric
Pinch of garam masala (page 92)
¼ teaspoon freshly ground black pepper
Salt to taste
Cilantro (fresh coriander) sprigs for garnish

Mix together the vegetables and yogurt. Add salt, cumin seed and the oil it was sautéed in; mix well. Sprinkle all the spices on top, and toss lightly. The spices can be mixed with the yogurt, but reserve a bit to use with the cilantro sprigs for garnish.
NOTE: Although not typically Indian, chopped fresh dill weed goes well when using cucumbers.

LOCRO DE PAPA
ANDEAN POTATO SOUP

This very hearty soup can be a meal in itself when served with hot corn bread or French bread and a light green salad. Pass a bowl of Salsa Ají with it. I learned to make it in Ecuador, but it is traditional throughout the Andes, where potatoes were first domesticated.

Makes about 5 Cups

- 2 tablespoons vegetable oil
- 1 pound potatoes, peeled and finely chopped
- 1 leek or small red onion, finely chopped
- 2 ajís (page 37) or serranos (page 78), seeded and minced
- 1 potato, peeled and cut into 1-inch cubes
- ¾ cup milk
- 1 teaspoon salt
- 1 teaspoon annato paste or turmeric
- 4 to 8 Bibb lettuce leaves, washed
- ⅓ pound white farmer's cheese or Monterey Jack, cut into 1-inch cubes
- 1 ripe avocado, peeled and cut into ½-inch thick slices

In a large saucepan (2¾ quart) heat the oil over medium heat. Add the chopped potatoes, onion, and chillies and cook until onion is golden. Add warm water until the potatoes are just covered and then add 1 cup more water and bring to a boil. Reduce the heat and simmer, stirring, until potatoes are very tender. Stir briskly in one direction to almost pureé the cooked vegetables. Add the cubed potato and cook until it is tender and the chopped potatoes are dissolved, about 30 minutes. Meanwhile, line deep soup bowls with the lettuce leaves and place a cube or two of cheese in the bowl.

Dissolve the annato in the milk and salt and add to the cooked potatoes and stir in one direction until the soup almost boils. Remove from the heat and spoon immediately into bowls so that the cheese melts. Top each bowl of soup with a slice of avocado.

NOTE: This can be done in a blender but the texture of the potatoes becomes somewhat slick. I have been served it made that way and if I had not had it the "old fashioned" way I would have thought that it was good. It is worth the time to make *locro* by the traditional method.

RED ANAHEIM VICHYSSOISE
WITH SCALLOPS

Greg Higgins, Executive Chef and Manager
Higgins is a popular, award winning chef in Portland, Oregon, known for using classical cooking methods to enhance the phenomenal range of food products found in the Pacific Northwest.

Makes 8 to 10 Servings

- ¼ cup olive oil
- 3 tablespoons garlic cloves, peeled and minced
- 1 large sweet yellow onion, diced
- ½ teaspoon ground cumin (comino)
- 1 tablespoon fresh thyme leaves
- 6 fresh red New Mexican Chiles (page 71), roasted (page 87), peeled, and diced
- 2½ pounds Russet potatoes, peeled and diced
- 2 red bell peppers, roasted (page 87), peeled, and diced
- 6 cups chicken stock
  Salt and freshly ground black pepper to taste
  Cilantro (fresh coriander) leaves for garnish
  Red bell pepper cut into thin strips for garnish
- 1 pound fresh scallops, stirred in 1 tablespoon olive oil in a skillet over medium heat until opaque all the way through

Heat the olive oil over medium heat in a large saucepan or Dutch oven (2¾ quart). Add the garlic, onions, cumin, thyme, and peppers and cook, stirring, until the onions become translucent, then add the potatoes. Continue cooking for 10 minutes, stirring often. Add the chicken stock and bring to a simmer. Cook until potatoes are quite tender, 20 to 30 minutes, then remove from the heat and allow to cool. Purée the soup in a food processor or blender until smooth (several batches will be needed). Thin with more chicken stock if needed and adjust the seasoning with salt and pepper. Serve the soup chilled in shallow bowls garnished with the scallops, cilantro, and red bell peppers.

CARIBBEAN STYLE BEAN SOUP
Junie Hostetler, Native Seeds/SEARCH

A staff member at Native Seeds/SEARCH in Tucson, Arizona, Junie Hostetler's hobby is recipe development using regional produce. The combination of beans and rice is typical of the Caribbean and Central America. In Nicaragua rice and beans are 'Christianos y Moros.' If there are more beans than rice it is 'Moros y Christianos.'

Makes 8 Servings

- 2 cups dried pinto or black beans, rinsed and picked over, or three 14-ounce cans cooked beans, undrained (do not use kidney beans)
- ½ cup onion, chopped
- 1 garlic clove, minced
- 2 teaspoons salt
- ¾ teaspoon dried oregano
- ½ teaspoon ground cumin (comino)
- ¼ teaspoon freshly ground black pepper
- 6 cups water (only one cup if using canned beans)
- 1 4-ounce can green New Mexican Chiles (page 71)
- 3 cups yellow winter squash (Hubbard, acorn), peeled and chopped
- 1 8-ounce can stewed tomatoes
- 2 cups or more steamed rice
- 1 to 2 cups Monterey Jack cheese, cut into small chunks

Soak beans overnight or several hours in the water; drain. Pour into a stock pot (5 quart) and add the onion, garlic, salt, oregano, cumin, and pepper and enough water to cover and cook until the beans are tender (pintos require less time than black beans). Add the chiles, squash, and tomatoes and cook 25 to 30 minutes more over low heat. Serve over hot rice and cheese.

THAI CHICKEN COCONUT MILK SOUP
Joyce Jue, Asian Food Specialist/Author

Joyce Jue is an Asian Food Specialist and author of Wok and Stir-Fry Cooking *who was one of the founders of the Thai cooking school at the Oriental Hotel in Bangkok. This is my absolute favorite Thai dish!*

Makes 6 to 8 Servings

- 4 cups thin coconut milk (page 96)
- 1½ cups chicken stock
- 3 pieces dried galanga (page 96), or 2 teaspoons ground galanga, or peeled and minced fresh ginger
- 3 stalks fresh lemon grass (page 96), cut in half lengthwise, then into 2 inch lengths and crushed
- 3 fresh serranos (page 78), halved and seeded
- 1 large whole chicken breast, skinned, boned and cut into ½ inch chunks
- 5 fresh or dried citrus or lime leaves (page 96), if available
- ½ cup canned straw mushrooms, (optional)
- 4 tablespoons fish sauce (*nam prik*), (page 92)
  Juice of 2 limes
- 1 red serrano (page 78) or jalapeño (page 70), cut into rounds for garnish
- 2 tablespoons fresh cilantro leaves, (fresh coriander) for garnish

Bring coconut milk, chicken stock, galanga, lemon grass and serranos to a boil in a large saucepan (2¾ quart). Reduce the heat to medium and simmer, uncovered, for 15 minutes. Strain and discard the galanga and lemon grass. Add the chicken chunks and citrus leaves; simmer until the chicken is tender (about 3 minutes). Stir in straw mushrooms and the fish sauce and simmer 1 minute longer. Pour into a soup tureen, stir in the lime juice and adjust seasoning. Garnish with the red chilli peppers and cilantro leaves. Serve hot.

GRILLED CORN SOUP
WITH SOUTHWESTERN CREAMS
Stephan Pyles, Chef/Owner/Author

This outstanding Dallas chef, author of New Texas
Cuisine, *and restaurant owner, who has been credited with
single-handedly changing Texas's cooking scene, leads the
food field in his native Texas. You'll love this savory corn
soup which not only pleases the palette, but also the eye.*

Makes 4 to 6 Servings

4	ears fresh corn, partially husked
3	cups chicken stock
½	cup carrots, chopped
¼	cup celery, chopped
½	cup onion, chopped
2	garlic cloves, roasted, squeezed from skins
1	serrano (page 78), seeded and chopped
1	cup half and half cream
	Salt to taste
	Southwestern creams (recipes follow)

The Soup

Over low charcoal fire, grill corn for 5 minutes on each
side. Remove from the fire and when cool, remove
husks. Place chicken stock, carrots, celery, onion,
garlic, and serrano in a large saucepan. Bring to a boil
and let simmer for 5 minutes. Remove kernels from
corn with knife. Add the corn kernels to stock and let
simmer 10 minutes longer. Place all the ingredients
from saucepan into a blender and purée completely,
about 2 minutes (may require several batches). Pass
the mixture though a strainer and return to saucepan.
Add the cream and place pan over low heat. Simmer
for 5 minutes. Keep warm while making the Southwestern creams. Pour soup into individual bowls and
drizzle the red and green creams in a decorative
pattern over the soup's surface.
NOTE: Squeeze bottles can be used to apply the
creams.

The Cilantro Cream

Makes ½ Cup

3	cups water
6 to 12	spinach leaves, well washed and stemmed
1½	cup fresh cilantro (fresh coriander) leaves, loosely packed
4½	tablespoons milk or half and half
3	tablespoons sour cream or plain yogurt

Bring the water to a boil. Add the spinach leaves and
cook for 1 minute. Drain off the liquid and place in ice
water for 1 minute. (This step is optional but ensures a
deep green color.) Place the cilantro, milk and spinach
leaves in a blender and process until smooth. Pass the
mixture through fine strainer into a mixing bowl.
Whisk in the sour cream or plain yogurt. Set aside.

The Ancho Chile Cream

Makes ½ Cup

1½	small anchos (page 74), cut in half and seeded
3	tablespoons milk or half and half
2	tablespoons sour cream or plain yogurt

Place the ancho in a preheated 400°F oven for 45
seconds. Remove from the oven and place in mixing
bowl. Add warm water to cover and let stand for 10
minutes. When the ancho has softened, remove from
water and place in blender with the milk. Process until
smooth. Pass mixture through fine a strainer into
mixing bowl. Whisk in sour cream. Set aside.

HOT AND SOUR SOUP
WITH POBLANOS AND TOMATILLOS
Jimmy Schmidt, Chef/Owner/Author

Author of Cooking for All Seasons, *frequent contributor to* Bon Appetit, *master chef and restaurant owner, that's Jimmy Schmidt, who has created a most unusual soup your guests will love.*

Makes 4 Servings

    3   cups chicken stock, clarified
    3   cups duck stock, clarified
1 ¼   teaspoons green jalapeños (page 70), roasted, peeled, seeded and minced
    3   tablespoons balsamic vinegar
    1   tablespoon rice vinegar
        Juice of ½ lime
    1   teaspoon salt
    ¼   cup poblanos (page 74), roasted (page 87), peeled, and diced
    ¼   cup red bell peppers, roasted, peeled and diced
    ¼   cup yellow bell peppers, roasted, peeled, and diced
    ½   cup tomatillos (page 99), husked and diced
    ½   cup raw duck breast, diced
  12   ½-inch thick slices blue corn tamales (see note below)
    2   tablespoons cilantro (fresh coriander), chopped

In a large saucepan (3¾ quart), combine the stocks and bring to a gentle simmer over medium heat. Add the jalapeño, vinegars, lime juice and salt. Add bell peppers, poblanos, tomatillos, and duck, cook until tender, about 5 minutes. Add the tamales, cooking until warm. Ladle into serving bowls. Sprinkle with cilantro and serve.

NOTE: If blue corn tamales are not available, substitute regular tamales, fresh or frozen, but not canned.

FRIJOL SOUP
Serve with a salad and hot cornbread or tortillas and you have a meal!

Makes 8 Servings

    1   pound dried *frijoles*, pinto, black, or red beans, rinsed and picked over (for the correct flavor, do not use kidney beans)
    2   quarts water
    1   large onion, chopped
    1   medium-size ripe tomato, chopped
    3   fresh serranos or jalapeños, or 6 to 8 fresh or dried chiltepínes, or 3 dried small red chillies (de árbol, japonés, Thai—don't use the large dried peppers; if habaneros are available, substitute 1 or 2 for a distinctive flavor; see index)
        Salt to taste
    1   ham bone (optional; in true Mexican style beans, no meat is added)
    2   garlic cloves, peeled and chopped
8 to 10   sprigs cilantro (fresh coriander)
        Sour cream or plain yogurt, if desired for garnish
        Additional 8 to 10 sprigs cilantro for garnish

Place the beans in a large, deep, heavy stockpot or Dutch oven, cover with water and allow to sit overnight. Drain. Add the 2 quarts of water, onion, tomato, peppers, salt, and ham bone (if desired). Cover and bring to a boil over high heat. Reduce the heat and simmer, covered, for 4 to 5 hours or until beans are very soft. Be careful not to let the beans cook dry and burn. Add *boiling* water as needed, *never cold water or the beans won't be tender.* Once the beans are cooked, add the garlic and cilantro, then purée the soup in a blender, adding water until desired consistency is reached (this will have to be done in batches). This soup may be served thick and eaten as the main dish or thinner if served before the meal. Put soup in warmed bowls and add a dollop of sour cream or yogurt and a sprig of fresh cilantro to each. Serve immediately with toasted tortilla chips, warm tortillas, or cornbread.

EASY TORTILLA SOUP

Tortilla soup is so good, but it need not be a searing experience. I have been served tortilla soup with a whole chipotle swimming on the surface, but I don't recommend it for the novice.

Makes 8 Cups

I	small onion, finely chopped
2 to 4	cloves of garlic, peeled and minced
I	tablespoon vegetable oil
6	cups chicken broth (homemade from chicken cooked with herbs, onions, celery, and carrots is best, but canned will do)
2	10¾-ounce cans chopped tomatoes and green chiles (ex. Rotel)
3	tablespoons fresh coriander (cilantro), chopped
I	teaspoon ground cumin (comino)
	Salt and freshly ground black pepper to taste
I	teaspoon sugar
	Juice of 2 limes
½ to I	cup shredded cooked chicken (optional)
½ to I	cup shredded Monterey Jack cheese
	Lightly salted, tortilla chips, broken
	Sprigs of fresh coriander (cilantro)

In a small skillet wilt the onion and garlic in the oil over a low heat, or omit the oil and wilt them in a microwave. Place the onion mixture in a large stock pot and add all of the ingredients except the cheese, tortillas, and cilantro sprigs. Stir the mixture well, then cover and simmer the soup over low heat for about I hour. If it cooks down too much add hot water to bring it back to 8 cups.

When ready to serve, warm the bowls and bring the soup to a boil, but don't boil. Put a heaping table-spoonful of the cheese and a few of tortilla chips in each bowl. Fill the bowls with very hot soup and top each with several sprigs of cilantro. Serve immediately. This soup, served with Mamie's Jalapeño Cornbread (page 189) or Jalapeño Cornbread (page 190), can make a meal. Serve smaller amounts if it is to be eaten before a meal.

ANDALUCIAN-STYLE GAZPACHO

This recipe is the result of visiting kitchens and eating gazpacho every day for a month in Andalusia, Spain. That area became renowned for gazpacho after its introduction by the Moors long before Columbus discovered America, the home of the tomato.

Makes 6 to 8 Servings

6	cups peeled and chopped ripe tomatoes or canned plum tomatoes
I	small onion, coarsely chopped
½	cup seeded green bell pepper chunks
I	serrano (see page 78), seeded
½	cup cucumber chunks
4 to 5	fresh basil leaves
½	cup stale French bread crumbs, or similar type of bread
2	cups tomato juice
I	garlic clove, peeled and minced
	Freshly ground black pepper
¼	cup extra virgin olive oil
¼	cup white wine vinegar

For the Garnish

½	cup finely chopped onion
½	cup finely chopped ripe tomato
½	cup finely chopped cucumber
½	cup finely chopped and seeded green bell pepper
	Garlic croutons

In a blender, purée the tomatoes, onion, peppers, cucumbers, basil and bread crumbs. Add the tomato juice, garlic, and pepper. Stir in the oil and vinegar. Cover and chill. Serve this smooth, creamy soup in chilled bowls. Pass side dishes of chopped onion, bell pepper, cucumber, and tomato. Garnish with crou-tons.

NOTE: In Andalucia the soup is served icy cold in bowls which have been chilled until frosty, like beer mugs.

MEXICAN SQUASH SOUP
Linda Parker, Native Seeds/SEARCH
Both horticulturist and avid gardener, Linda Parker is also curator of collections at Native Seeds/SEARCH in Tucson, Arizona. She likes to cook what she grows and this tasty squash soup is her specialty.

Makes 4 to 6 Servings

  2 tablespoons butter or margarine
  1 small onion, chopped
  ¼ cup celery, sliced
  4 cups chicken or vegetable stock
  1 dried whole red New Mexican Chile (page 71)
  1½ cups winter squash (Hubbard, acorn), peeled and diced
  1 cup frozen whole-kernel corn
    Grated cheddar or Monterey Jack cheese for garnish
    Pepitas, toasted squash seeds (page 98)

Melt the butter in a saucepan over medium heat and cook the onion and celery, stirring, until soft. Add the stock and red chile and bring to a boil. Add the squash and cook until tender. Add the corn and cook 5 minutes. Remove the chile before serving. Serve sprinkled with grated cheese and/or pepitas. Great with cornbread (page 189, 190).

SOPA DE AJO (GARLIC SOUP)
Donald Counts, MD and
Kathryn O'Connor Counts, Authors
A nutrition-centered Texas medical doctor and his wife, Donald and Kathryn O'Connor Counts (page 184), recommend their savory garlic soup as a way to have your garlic and enjoy it too.

Makes 6 Servings

  10 garlic cloves, peeled
  3 fresh or canned green New Mexican Chile (page 71) peppers, roasted (page 87), skinned, seeded, and mashed
  1 teaspoon tamari soy sauce
  ¼ cup water
  8 cups chicken stock
  1 cup cilantro (fresh coriander) leaves, chopped
  ⅓ cup green onions with greens, chopped
  3 large egg whites
  3 tablespoons cornstarch or arrowroot
  ¼ cup dry sherry
    Cilantro sprigs for garnish

Crush 7 of the 10 cloves of garlic. Combine green chiles, garlic, tamari soy sauce and water in blender and blend until smooth. Mix with the chicken stock in a soup pan and bring to simmer. Slice the remaining three garlic cloves. Add chopped green onions and cilantro to simmering stock and simmer uncovered 30 minutes.

Slightly whip the egg whites and set aside. Mix the cornstarch or arrowroot with sherry. Add to the stock slowly, then stir constantly with whisk for 5 to 10 minutes, until it reaches desired consistency. Pour the egg whites into stock and mix with a circular motion. Turn off heat, cover, and let stand 5 minutes. Serve garnished with sprigs of fresh cilantro.

Meat, Fowl, Seafood

MUSSAMUM (MUSLIM) CURRY

Charlie Amatyakul, Executive Chef

Amatyakul, a suave native Thai, is director of the Thai Cooking School operated by the Oriental Hotel in Bangkok, and before that he was food and beverage director of the hotel. His creative food events caught the eye of Queen Sirikit, and he continues to cater state functions.

Makes 6 to 8 Servings

For the Sauce

Vegetable oil for frying

13 dried, red chillies, (de árbol, guajillo, Thai, New Mexican Chile; see index)

½ cup shallots, finely chopped

½ cup garlic cloves, peeled and finely chopped

1 tablespoon galanga (page 96), sliced or fresh ginger

1 tablespoon cilantro (fresh coriander) root, finely chopped

1 tablespoon lemon grass, finely chopped

1 teaspoon kaffir lime (page 96) peel, chopped or regular lime peel

1 teaspoon black peppercorns

1 tablespoon salt

1 tablespoon coriander seeds

½ teaspoon ground mace

½ teaspoon ground nutmeg

½ teaspoon ground cinnamon bark

½ teaspoon ground cloves

1 tablespoon shrimp paste

4 cups coconut milk (page 96), medium-thickness

¼ cup thick tamarind (page 99) water, (combine 1 cup pulp with ½ cup water)

2 to 3 tablespoons palm sugar (page 98) or white sugar

2 tablespoons fish sauce (page 92)

5 shallots, peeled

½ cup peanuts, roasted

5 bay leaves

5 cardamon pods

To Finish the Dish

1½ lean, boneless beef cut into 1-inch cubes (¼ pound per serving)

3 to 4 cups coconut milk (½ cup per serving; page 96)

In a wok or skillet, simmer cubed beef in coconut milk until tender. Add to curried sauce.

In a large sauce pan heat a small amount of oil over medium heat. Add the chillies, shallots, garlic, galanga, coriander root, lemon grass, kaffir and spices; cook, stirring, until fragrant and the shallots are soft. Remove from pan and pound together to make a paste. Add the shrimp paste. Pound until well blended. Heat 1 cup of coconut milk and cook the paste in it until fragrant. Season with the tamarind, sugar, and fish sauce. Add the remaining coconut milk and simmer until reduced and thick. Add the whole shallots, peanuts, bay leaves, cardamon, and cook for 5 to 10 more minutes.

In a wok or skillet, simmer the beef in the coconut milk until tender. Add to the sauce and mix well. Serve with rice on the side; accompanied by chutneys (207–09).

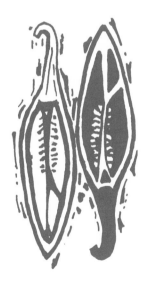

FAJITAS WITH TOMATILLO SAUCE

Kurt Koessel, Chef

Folk in California say that Kurt Koessel (page 112), "is one of the most creative and capable all-around talents ever encountered in the restaurant world." What he has done with Texas fajitas proves the claim.

Makes 4 Servings

For the Meat

- 6 tablespoons New Mexican Chile powder (page 91)
- 4 tablespoons ancho chile powder (page 91)
- 1 tablespoon ground cumin (comino)
- 1 tablespoon kosher salt
- 2 teaspoons dried orange peel
- 2 teaspoons ground cayenne pepper
- 1½ teaspoons dried thyme
- 4 bay leaves, crumbled
- 2 garlic cloves, peeled and crushed
- 1½ cups dark beer
- ⅜ cup fresh orange juice
- 1 pound flank steak, trimmed of fat

For the Tomatillo Sauce

- 10 tomatillos (page 99), husked, rinsed, and finely chopped
- 3 tablespoons cilantro (fresh coriander), finely chopped
- 2 tablespoons finely minced fresh jalapeños (page 70) or serranos (page 78)
- 2 tablespoons fresh lime juice
- Kosher salt to taste
- Corn tortillas

In a non-reactive container, mix together the chile powders, cumin, salt, orange peel, cayenne pepper, thyme, bay leaves, garlic, beer, and orange juice. Put in the meat, coating it entirely with the marinade. Cover the container with plastic wrap and marinate overnight in the refrigerator.

To assemble the tomatillo sauce, mix together the tomatillos, cilantro (fresh coriander), minced jalapeños or serranos and lime juice in a non-reactive bowl. Season with salt to taste. Make at least an hour before serving to allow flavors to blend.

To make the fajitas, let the meat come to room temperature. Meanwhile, build an intense charcoal fire. When the coals begin to turn gray, the fire is ready. Scrape off excess marinade from the meat. On a well-oiled grill, sear the meat on both sides to desired doneness (about 4 minutes on each side for medium rare). Slice thinly and wrap in fresh corn tortillas. Garnish with tomatillo sauce and more fresh cilantro (fresh coriander), if desired.

MEDALLIONS OF BEEF WITH ANCHO SAUCE AND JICAMA-BLACK BEAN GARNISH

Dean Fearing, Executive Chef/Author

Here is a recipe from one of our fabled Texas chefs, Dean Fearing, who has made dining at the Mansion on Turtle Creek in Dallas, Texas, an unforgettable experience. Not only has he achieved national acclaim for his development of southwestern cuisine, but he has also written Mansion on Turtle Creek Cookbook *and* Dean Fearing's Southwest Cuisine.

Makes 4 Servings

- 8 3-ounce beef tenderloin fillets, trimmed of fat and any silver skin
  Salt to taste
  Mansion on Turtle Creek Pepper Mixture, see below
- 3 tablespoons peanut oil
  Ancho Chilli Sauce, see below
  Jícama-Black Bean Garnish, see below
- ¼ bunch fresh cilantro (fresh coriander) leaves, washed and dried

Season the fillets with salt and the pepper mixture. Heat the oil in a large sauté pan over medium-high heat. Place several fillets in hot pan. Do not crowd (cook in batches if necessary). Brown one side, turn, and brown other side. Cook to desired degree of doneness, about 3 minutes on each side for medium-rare. Remove from heat and keep warm.

Ladle Ancho Chilli Sauce over the bottom of each

of four warm dinner plates. Place 2 beef medallions on each plate. Sprinkle jícama black-bean garnish evenly around meat. Sprinkle with cilantro leaves.

Ancho Chilli Sauce
Makes 4 Cups

- 4 anchos (page 74), stemmed and seeded (if peppers are small, use 1 more)
- 1 tablespoon peanut oil
- 1 yellow onion, cut into medium dice
- 2 shallots, chopped
- 2 garlic cloves, peeled and chopped
- 1 fresh jalapeño (page 70), seeded and chopped
- 3 sprigs fresh cilantro (fresh coriander)
- 1 cup chicken stock
- 1 medium ripe tomato, chopped
- ½ cup brown veal demi-glace (page 100)
- ½ cup heavy cream
- ½ tablespoon honey or to taste
  Salt to taste
  Juice of ½ lime or to taste

Place the anchos in a bowl and cover with hot water. Soak for 30 minutes, then drain. Place the anchos in a blender, adding some of the water in which they were soaked, and process until smooth. Set the mixture aside.

Heat the oil in a medium-size saucepan over medium heat. Add the onion and cook 2 minutes. Add the shallots, garlic, and jalapeño and cook, stirring, for 2 minutes longer. Add cilantro, chicken stock, ancho purée, and tomato; simmer for 12 minutes. Add demi-glace, increase heat slightly, and cook until the liquid is reduced by half. Add the cream and heat just to boiling. Pour the hot mixture into a blender or food processor and process until smooth. Add the honey, increasing amount slightly if sweeter sauce is desired. Season with salt and lime juice. Keep warm.

Jícama-Black Bean Garnish
Makes 1½ Cups

- 1 tablespoon peanut oil
- 1 cup jícama, cut into medium dice
- 1 red bell pepper, seeded, membranes removed, and cut into medium dice
- ½ cup cooked black beans (page 109) or use canned
  Salt to taste

Heat the oil in a medium-size sauté pan over medium-high heat. Sauté jícama, pepper, and black beans, stirring, just until heated through, about 2 minutes. Season with salt. The sauce may be made several hours ahead and kept warm. Reheat gently, if necessary.

Mansion on Turtle Creek Pepper Mixture

- 1 cup freshly ground black pepper
- ⅓ cup freshly ground white pepper
- 1½ tablespoons ground cayenne pepper

Combine all ingredients. Cover tightly and store in cool place. Use to season red meats and game before cooking.

TABASCO STEAK
George O. Jackson, Bon Vivant

Jackson, better known as Georg-O, was born in Houston of a Texan father and Mexican mother. As a result of his maternal family background he has spent much of his life in Mexico. He was the originator of several restaurants in Houston and Austin, Texas, but is best known for his photography, hospitality, and love of peppers. This recipe sounds crazy, but it isn't. The pepper sauce acts as a tenderizer and when heated over the coals, it seals the juices in the meat. Advance planning necessary.

Makes 10 to 15 Servings

- 5 pounds of 3½ inch thick sirloin butt beef steak, the best you can buy
- 2 small bottles of Tabasco Pepper Sauce®, depending on amount of meat
- 1 zip-lock bag, large
- 1 stick of soft butter
- 2 to 4 garlic cloves, peeled and crushed

Place the piece of beef in a plastic zip-lock bag with the contents of 2 bottles of sauce. Soak the beef in the sauce in the refrigerator for 3 days; turn often.

Remove the beef from sauce and cook over mesquite wood coals. When the coals are at the hottest point put the steak on a grill 2 inches above the fire. Care must be taken to prevent flame-ups during cooking. Cook for 10 minutes; turn and cook on the other side for 10 minutes; repeat for 2 more 10-minute periods. While the meat is cooking, blend the garlic into the softened butter and slightly melt.

After the meat has cooked for 40 minutes, remove from the fire and place on a cutting board; allow to rest for 10 minutes before carving. After carving, brush the slices with the garlic butter. The meat will have a tangy crust but is not pungent in spite of the sauce.
NOTE: If the meat is room temperature at time of cooking, the final product will be medium rare; if it has just come from the refrigerator, it will be rare. After cutting, if a serving is too rare for some tastes, return the meat slices to the grill for a bit more cooking.

CHIPOTLE RIBS
Jerry Di Vecchio, Food Journalist

Di Vecchio, food and entertaining editor of Sunset magazine, is one of the most significant forces in shaping the cuisine of the West. For these ribs she tells us to buy the so-called English-cut beef short ribs, which are on the leaner end of the rib. Have the butcher saw through the bones at several intervals so you can bend the ribs to fit into the pan more readily. The ribs take several hours to bake, but you don't have to pay any attention to them. And the aromas that develop certainly give promise of good tastes to come. The chipotle flavor permeates and colors the drippings of the beef, and a few tablespoons of the resulting orange-red oil are used to season and tint the rice to serve with the ribs. The rice is lightly toasted in the drippings, so the grains remain separate and plump as they cook in stock. The fat-skimmed juices from the ribs then become a lean and flavorful sauce to anoint both ribs and rice.

Makes 4 to 5 Servings

For the Ribs

- 4 to 5 English-cut beef short ribs (about 4 pounds total), bones cracked and trimmed of fat
- 1 large onion, chopped
- 1 tablespoon mustard seeds
- 1 teaspoon cumin (comino) seeds
- 2 canned chipotles *adobado* or 2 dried chipotles (page 70)
- 2½ cups regular-strength beef or chicken stock, homemade or low-sodium canned
- 1 cup cilantro (fresh coriander), coarsely chopped
- 1 to 2 limes, cut in wedges
- Salt to taste

Arrange ribs in a 3-inch or 4-inch deep 4- to 5-quart metal pan. Sprinkle with onion, mustard seeds, and cumin seeds, then push peppers down between pieces of meat. Add 1 cup of the stock, then cover the pan tightly. Bake in a 400°F oven until ribs are tender enough to pull easily from the bones, about 3 hours. Check once or twice as meat cooks to be sure there is moisture in the pan, adding a little of the remaining 1½ cups stock if meat begins to brown. Uncover meat and skim off and reserve 2 tablespoons of the fat from pan juices. Then bake meat uncovered until it browns on top, 15 to 20 minutes. Lift meat from pan onto a platter and keep warm. Add the remaining stock to pan; skim off the floating fat and discard. Bring to a boil over high heat, stirring to free browned bits and mash the chipotles. Pour stock into a small pitcher. Spoon chipotle rice around ribs and sprinkle with cilantro (fresh coriander). Serve meat and rice with stock, lime juice, and salt, added to taste.

For the Rice
Makes 4 to 5 Servings

- 2 tablespoons drippings reserved from Chipotle Ribs (above)
- 1 cup long-grain white rice
- 2 cups or chicken stock, homemade or low-sodium

In a 2- to 3-quart pan combine drippings and rice. Stir over medium-high heat until grains look opaque, about 5 minutes. Add the stock and bring to a boil on high heat. Cover and simmer over very low heat until rice is tender to bite and liquid is absorbed, 15 to 20 minutes.

PRE-COLUMBIAN CARNE MACHACA CON CHILES y VERDURAS, RECONSTRUCTED SONORAN STYLE
Gary Nabhan, Botanist/Author

Gary Nabhan, of Lebanese descent, has taken to the deserts of the American Southwest and northern Mexico as his ancestors took to those of the Middle East. Gary can make poetry of everything he sees and best of all he can convey that poetry to others. Peppers are his love, especially the tiny chiltepín. He tells us: "Native Americans of the desert Southwest and Sonora have long used the chiltepín. Given the fact that meat was often scarce, but a variety of wild greens, cacti, and herbs were seasonally abundant, I have tried to reconstruct what a pre-Columbian chili-con-carne dish—'Carne Machaca con Verduras y Chiltepíns'—might have been like for native peoples living in what is now southern Arizona or northern Sonora. I have excluded post-Columbian ingredients to the extent I could. In this recipe, wild chillies are but one of several native plants in the matrix, rather than being the primary ingredient of the sauce. Nevertheless, I guess that something akin to this dish served as the precursor to 'carne con chile colorado.'"

Makes about 6 to 8 Servings

- 1½ cups of dried carne machaca (usually beef jerky today, but prehistorically it was dried venison, javalina, or antelope meat)
- 2 cups hot water
- 18 dried red chiltepínes, crushed
- 3 tablespoons or ½ handful dried wild oregano leaves
- 2 to 3 cups freshly-picked wild amaranth (careless weed) greens, washed and coarsely chopped
- 1 cup tender, young prickly pear pads, dethorned, washed and cut into 1-inch long strips
- 1 cup tomatillos (page 99) husked and chopped
- 12 green chiltepínes (page 64), chopped finely
- ¼ cup oil from venison fat, or sunflower seed oil

Rehydrate the meat by soaking it in the water with chiltepínes and oregano for 1 hour; drain off excess water. Heat a small amount of oil in a skillet over medium-high heat and cook, stirring, until browned. Add the remaining ingredients, mix well, and cook, stirring, for another 5 minutes. Serve with tortillas.

JERKED PORK WITH HABANERO

Jon Jividen, Executive Chef

As executive chef of the prestigious Ridgewell's Caterers in Bethesda, Maryland, Jividen is responsible for many big functions in our capital city. With a degree in food service and restaurant management, he went on to the Culinary Institute of America before becoming a leader in the food world in the Washington-Philadelphia area.
NOTE: *The English jerky and the Spanish* charqui, *meaning "dried meat," are derived from a pre-Colombian Andean Indian word* charqui *or the Quechuan,* cusharqui—*which was a freeze-dried meat. In the seventeenth century, Jamaica fugitive slaves or Maroons used the term "jerk" or "jerked" for a method of preserving wild boar meat by seasoning it heavily with chilli peppers (C. chinense) and other local spices for several hours or overnight, then slowly pit-cooking it. However, the current usage of "jerked" does not allude to dried pork jerky but has evolved to refer to a technique for slow smoke grilling highly seasoned or marinated meat, usually pork.*

Makes 6 to 8 Servings

- 5 pounds pork (lean shoulder, leg, or roast), trimmed of excess fat
- 1 large, ripe tomato, finely diced
- 2 green New Mexican Chiles, roasted (page 87), peeled, seeded, and finely chopped
- 1 habanero pepper, seeded and finely chopped (or Scotch bonnet, dátil, or 3 serranos or 3 jalapeños (see index for chillies)
- 1 large onion, finely chopped
- 1 bunch fresh thyme leaves, finely chopped
- 1 bunch green onions (scallions), finely chopped
- 2 to 3 garlic cloves, peeled and minced
- ½ cup soy souce
- ¼ teaspoon ground cayenne pepper
- ¼ cup fresh lime or lemon juice
- 1 cup water
  Salt and freshly ground black pepper to taste

Place meat on cutting board and with a sharp knife punch holes or "jerk" all over [Jividen's words]. Finely chop scallion, garlic, habanero, thyme and set aside. Finely dice onions, New Mexican Chiles, and tomato. Add to chopped vegetables and mix thoroughly. Using your fingers, stuff vegetable mixture into the "jerks" or holes in pork. Place the pork roast in a bowl and pour remaining vegetables and soy sauce over. Cover and marinate overnight in refrigerator.

Place roast in suitable roasting pan with water and lime juice. Season with salt and pepper. Cook roast in 450° oven for 1½ to 2 hours. When fork tender, remove cover and allow to brown. While browning, keep roast moist by basting with juices from pan (see note below). Serve with rice or potatoes (Vinita's, page 159).

NOTE: If gravy is desired, remove the roast from the pan, pour off all but 1 to 2 tablespoons of juices and place the pan on a burner over high heat. Brown the juices, then deglaze (page 100) the pan with a little boiling water. Return the juice to the pan and add enough hot water to make about 1½ cups of gravy. If a thicker gravy is desired, a slurry of 1 tablespoon of cornstarch to ½ cup of water can be added gradually while stirring until desired thickness is reached.

FOURTH STREET GRILL'S
CHILLI STUFFED PORK LOIN
Susan H. Nelson, Chef/Owner
Susan Nelson, educated as an artist and art historian, is the owner of the trend-setting Ginger Island restaurant in Berkeley, California. After her beginnings at Alice Water's Chez Panisse, she and Mark Miller opened the innovative Fourth Street Grill, now Ginger Island. She was the founder of the annual Berkeley Chile Festival.

Makes 6 Servings

	Olive oil for sautéing
15	pasillas (page 72) or anchos (page 74), seeded and minced
10	serranos (page 78), seeded and minced
10	shallots, minced
	Salt to taste
1½	cups pistachios, toasted (page 101) and ground
4	bunches of cilantro (fresh coriander), minced
1	pork loin, boned and trimmed of excess fat
	Fourth Street Grill's Chipotle Mole Sauce (page 181)
	Kitchen string for tying meat

Preheat the oven to 325°F. Heat a little oil in a small saucepan over low heat. Add the chillies and shallots and cook, stirring. They should remain slightly crunchy. Season with salt. Transfer the mixture to a bowl and let cool. Stir in the nuts and cilantro.

Cut the pork loin lengthwise around the loin to "unroll" it into a single flat piece and salt lightly. Spread the chilli-nut mixture over the entire surface. Beginning at the side closest to you, roll the coated meat like a jelly roll. Tie with the string several times along the roll so it won't unroll while roasting.

Place a large sauté pan over a high flame. When the pan is very hot, add the pork loin, turning the meat until it is seared on all sides. Then put the loin, uncovered, in the oven. Roast until the meat thermometer reaches 135°F, approximately 50 minutes. Remove the meat and let it rest for 5 minutes before removing string and slicing into 1-inch slices. Serve with Chipotle Mole Sauce, rice and warm tortillas.

PORTUGUESE STYLE PORK CHOPS
OR CHICKEN BREASTS
Start this the day before you plan to serve it so that the pepper paste can really work; that is, if you don't eat all of the paste before you put it on the meat.

Makes 6 Servings

6	1-inch pork chops or boneless chicken breasts
6	tablespoons mild red pepper paste (page 179)
½	teaspoon freshly ground black pepper
2	cups dry white wine
2	tablespoons olive oil
	Parsley, chopped for garnish

Rub the meat on both sides with the pepper paste; place in a shallow bowl, pour on the wine, cover, and refrigerate overnight, turning the meat once or twice. Make a basting sauce by placing the marinade and olive oil in a saucepan; simmer until the consistency of gravy; adjust seasoning with salt and pepper. Cook meat on a charcoal grill, baste with the sauce. To cook in a skillet, heat a little olive oil until almost smoking; add the meat and brown both sides; add the basting sauce to the meat; reduce heat to low; cover, and cook until well done. Sprinkle with chopped parsley, and serve with rice or pasta.

ROCOTO RELLENO PERUVIAN STUFFED PEPPERS

Arequipa, Peru, is the world capital of the rocoto pepper and its most famous culinary achievement, the Rocoto Relleno. I never dreamed that I would be able to eat anything made from the fiery rocoto, but the way it is done there made it well worth the trip to experience it at its finest. Actually, I think the poblano or the red bell pepper work almost as well.

Makes 12 Small Servings or 8 Large

- 12 rocotos (page 76) or small red bell peppers or poblanos (page 74), see note below
- 3 tablespoons vegetable oil
- 12 baking potatoes, washed, boiled until almost tender and peeled
- 2½ pounds lean pork, beef, or turkey cut into fine cubes or ground as for chili
- 2 tablespoons vegetable oil
- 1 small red onion, chopped finely
- 4 red ajís (page 37) or red jalapeños (page 70) or serranos (page 78), seeded and finely chopped
- 1 tablespoon ground cumin (comino)
- 2 large eggs, hard boiled, and chopped
- ½ cup raisins, soaked in hot water and drained
- ¾ pound Farmer's cheese or Monterey Jack, grated
- 3 tablespoons butter, melted
   Salt to taste
   Paprika
   Fresh cilantro sprigs

For the Peppers

If using rocotos, wear gloves. Cut the tops off the peppers carefully and set aside for lids. Remove the seeds and veins. Place the peppers and their tops in water to cover with 1 teaspoon of salt in a large covered saucepan over high heat; bring to a boil. Reduce the heat to low and simmer for 3 minutes; with the rocotos, repeat with fresh water as often as necessary if still too pungent. Remove from pan, drain, and pat dry with paper toweling.

In a skillet, heat the oil over medium heat, add the onion and cook until translucent. Add the meat and spices, then increase the heat; cook until done but not browned and most of the juice is cooked down. Remove from the heat and add the egg and raisins, season with salt and mix well. Fill each pepper with the meat mixture and cover with its pepper lid.

Peel the almost tender potatoes and cut lengthwise into quarters. In as many flat greased baking dishes as are necessary, arrange the potatoes and peppers in equal groups (ex. 2 slices of potato with each pepper). Brush the potatoes with the butter. Bake in a preheated 350°F oven until the potatoes are tender and slightly browned. Pour some sauce over each pepper and its potato, then sprinkle with the cheese and continue baking until the cheese is melted. Place portions of potatoes with each pepper on a plate with any sauce in the pan. Garnish with paprika and cilantro sprigs and serve immediately.

NOTE: If you have individual oven-proof dishes, place a serving of the pepper and potatoes in each dish, add the sauce, sprinkle with cheese and heat until the cheese is melted. Garnish with paprika and cilantro sprigs.

For the Sauce

- 1 large egg, beaten
- 1 tablespoon vegetable oil
- 1 cup milk
- ¾ pound white cheese, Farmer's or Monterey Jack, grated
   Salt and freshly ground black pepper to taste

In a small saucepan, beat the egg and oil together until well blended. Place over low heat and gradually add the milk while stirring continuously; cook until thickened without boiling. Gradually add one-half of the cheese, setting the remainder aside to sprinkle on the top. If the sauce separates or curdles, pour it into a blender and process until smooth.

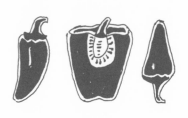

GREEN CHILE CON CARNE

Paul Prudhomme, Chef/Owner/Author

*Chef Paul Prudhomme was born and reared in the
Louisiana Acadian country, and that style of cooking is his
genre. He and his wife (she is the K in K-Paul's) opened
their famous restaurant in 1979 and they now have a
second in New York. His cookbooks, television appearances,
and magazine articles have made Prudhomme a true
homegrown American celebrity. Today his "Magic Seasoning Blends®" can be found almost everywhere; if not, call
1-800-457-2857.*

Makes 6 Servings

3	tablespoons plus 2 teaspoons Chef Paul Prudhomme's Meat Magic®
1	tablespoon ground cumin (comino)
3/8	teaspoon ground nutmeg
1 1/2	pounds boneless pork, ground
1/2	cup pork lard or chicken fat (preferred) or vegetable oil
1 1/2	corn tortillas (6-inch diameter)
1	teaspoon dried oregano leaves
2 1/2	cups chopped onions
2	cups chopped green bell peppers
1 1/4	cups canned diced green New Mexican Chiles (page 71) and their juice
1/4	cups fresh jalapeños (page 70), seeded and minced
1 1/2	teaspoons garlic cloves, peeled and minced
1/3	cup all-purpose flour
5	cups Basic Pork or Chicken Stock (recipe follows)

In a small bowl combine 1 tablespoon plus 1 teaspoon
of the Meat Magic® with 1/2 teaspoon of the cumin
and 1/8 teaspoon of the nutmeg; mix well. Sprinkle the
pork evenly with the seasoning mixture; mix by hand
until thoroughly combined.

In a thick-bottomed, 4-quart saucepan, melt the
vegetable oil over high heat until hot (about 300°F).
Brown the meat in the hot oil, then with a slotted
spoon remove the meat to a plate and set aside.
(Remove as many of the tiny pieces of meat from the
oil as possible). In the same oil fry the tortillas over
high heat until brown and very crisp; drain on paper
towels. Remove pan from heat.

In a small bowl combine the remaining 2 tablespoons plus 1 teaspoon Meat Magic®, 2 1/2 teaspoons
cumin and 1/2 teaspoon nutmeg and the oregano,
mixing well. Add this seasoning mixture to the hot oil
and cook over high heat until seasonings roast, about
10 to 15 seconds, stirring constantly. Add 1 1/2 cups of the
onions; cook about 10 to 15 seconds, stirring constantly and scraping the pan bottom well. Stir in 1 cup
of the bell peppers, 1/2 cup of the green chiles and 2
tablespoons of the jalapeños; cook about 8 minutes,
stirring fairly often (constantly toward the end of
cooking time) and scraping the pan bottom well each
time. Stir in the garlic and cook and stir a few seconds.
Add the flour, stirring until well blended and scraping
the pan bottom clean; cook 2 to 3 minutes, stirring
and scraping almost constantly to make sure mixture
doesn't scorch. (Soups containing ground meat and
flour stick more than other types of soup). Add 1 cup
of the stock, scraping the pan bottom until all
browned matter is dissolved. Then add the remaining
4 cups stock; stir until well blended, being sure to
scrape pan bottom clean again. Continue cooking
over high heat, stirring occasionally.

Meanwhile, remove 1 cup of the stock from this
mixture and place in a food processor. Crumble the
fried tortillas into the processor. Process until the
tortillas are finely chopped, about 30 to 45 seconds.
Stir the tortilla mixture into the cooking stock mixture.

Stir in the remaining 1 cup onions and 1 cup bell
peppers. Add the meat, stirring well. Bring mixture to
a boil, stirring occasionally, then reduce heat and
simmer 50 minutes, stirring and scraping fairly often
(be careful not to let mixture scorch). Stir in the
remaining 3/4 cup green chiles and 2 tablespoons
jalapeños; simmer and stir 10 minutes. Adjust the
seasoning if desired with additional Meat Magic®;
simmer and stir 5 minutes more. Skim any oil from
surface and serve immediately.

Basic Pork or Chicken Stock
Makes 5 cups

10 cups cold water (always start with cold water —enough to cover the stock ingredients)
1½ to 2 pounds pork neck bones (preferred) or other pork bones and/or chicken backs, necks, giblets (excluding liver) and/or bones
1 medium-size onion, peeled and quartered
1 celery stalk
1 large garlic clove, peeled and quartered

Place all the ingredients in a large saucepan; bring to a boil over high heat, then gently simmer at least 4 hours, preferably 8, replenishing the water as needed to keep about 5 cups of liquid in the pan. Strain, cool and refrigerate until ready to use.

NOTE: If you are short on time, using a stock simmered 20 or 30 minutes is far better than using just water in any recipe.

CARNITAS WITH POBLANOS AND FRUIT
Jerry Di Vecchio, Food Journalist

Jerry Di Vecchio instructs that "the cut for this dish is from the shoulder of the pig; curiously, this part is also called butt in some parts of the country. It is usually an inexpensive cut, readily available boned, and because it is laced with fat and connective tissue, it cooks to melting succulence. Here it is roasted to render out excess fat, and the savory brown morsels are served with mildly hot roasted chillies, warm bananas, cool orange slices, and a piquant peanut sauce reminiscent of Indonesia. Dark, relatively mild green poblanos are the first choice, but slender light green New Mexican Chiles also work well."

Makes 6 to 8 Servings

3 to 4 fresh poblanos, about 4 inches long (or green New Mexican Chiles, about 6 inches long)
3½ pounds boned pork butt or shoulder
3 large oranges
3 firm, ripe bananas
Piquant Peanut Sauce
Salt

Rinse chillies and wipe dry. Cut in half lengthwise. Lay cut-side down in a 10-inch by 15-inch baking pan; broil 3 inches or 4 inches from heat until chillies are blistered and blackened, about 15 minutes. Transfer chillies to a bowl, drape with a sheet of plastic wrap and set aside to cool. Rinse and dry pan. Trim excess fat from meat and discard. Cut meat in 1-inch to 2-inch cubes. Put meat in the baking pan, spreading pieces apart. Bake in a 325°F oven, turning pieces several times, until pork is well browned and very tender when pierced, 1½ to 2 hours. Meanwhile, pull charred skin, seeds, and stems from chiles. Also, with a knife, cut peel and membrane from oranges and slice crosswise. Lift meat from platter with a slotted spoon and put on a platter; keep warm. Peel bananas and slice in half lengthwise. Turn in drippings in pan and return to oven until warm, 2 or 3 minutes. Arrange hot bananas, chillies, and sliced oranges around meat. Accompany portions with peanut sauce, adding salt to taste.

Piquant Peanut Sauce
Makes 1 Cup

Mix together ½ cup each of chunky peanut butter and plum jam. Add fresh, seeded, minced jalapeños or serranos and fish sauce (*musc mam* or *nam pla* or salt) to taste. Serve. Can be made ahead; cover and chill up to 1 week.

CHIPOTLE MARINATED LAMB CHOPS WITH MINT CREAM
Bruce J. Auden, Chef/Owner

Englishman Bruce Auden is now a San Antonio, Texas, chef and restaurant owner who has gained wide recognition for his elegant simplicity and innovative dishes. He has developed recipes that require more time marinating and seasoning with fresh herbs than actual cooking time.

Makes 4 Servings

- 1 7-ounce can chipotles *adobado* (page 70)
- ¾ cup balsamic vinegar
- 6 garlic cloves, peeled
- 6 sprigs of fresh oregano
- 2 bunches of cilantro (fresh coriander)
- 16 lamb chops cut from the rack
- 2 tablespoons olive oil
- 4 carrots, cut into 2-inch-long julienne
- 4 leeks, well washed and cut into 2-inch-long julienne
- 2 cups chicken stock
- 12 small red ripe tomatoes, seeded and chopped

Combine chipotles, the ¾ cup balsamic vinegar, garlic, oregano, and ½ cilantro (fresh coriander) into a blender. Process until smooth. Dip each lamb chop into marinade while holding chops by bone. Try to keep the bone dry. Cover and marinate overnight in refrigerator or for 3 hours at room temperature.

In large, heavy skillet, heat oil over medium high heat. Place the chops in the hot pan and cook for 4 minutes per side, then transfer to preheated 350°F oven in same pan. Continue to cook for 5 minutes. Remove pan from oven and chops from pan. Hold chops on serving dish until sauce is finished.

To make sauce, pour 1 tablespoon of balsamic vinegar into pan over medium heat and reduce while scraping lamb juices and marinade from bottom of pan. At this time you may add more marinade; the amount will depend on how pungent you want the sauce (1 tablespoon should be enough). Also add carrots and leeks. Try to keep them on one side, as you will be removing them later. Next, add the remaining cilantro (reserving a few leaves for garnish), chicken stock and tomatoes. Reduce heat until it starts to thicken.

Remove the carrots and leeks to the serving plate. Pour sauce into blender and process until smooth with some chunks. Place the lamb chops on top of the carrots and leeks and pour the sauce over. Garnish with mint cream and watercress salad.

Mint Cream

- 1 cup sour cream
- ½ cup packed fresh mint leaves
- 1 teaspoon balsamic vinegar

Combine all ingredients in a blender and process until smooth. Push through sieve to remove excess leaves. Pour into a squeeze bottle and garnish chops and sauce by squeezing the cream over the plate decoratively.

Watercress Salad

- 1 bunch watercress
- 1 jícama (page 96), cut into 2-inch julienne
- 1 orange, cut into segments
- 2 tablespoons chilli oil (page 91)

Toss ingredients together and arrange on platter.

RABBIT COOKED TWO WAYS WITH HILL COUNTRY PEACH AND TEQUILA SAUCE

Norbert Brandt, Chef/Owner

Brandt is a native of Germany who worked throughout the world before settling in Texas, where he owns and operates seven outstanding restaurants. In 1983 he created and prepared a state dinner in honor of Queen Elizabeth, which President Reagan hosted in San Francisco. This rabbit dish reflects his chosen Texas roots.

Makes 2 Servings

For the Marinade

- 1 medium-size onion, cubed
- 8 sprigs fresh parsley, crushed
- 4 garlic cloves, peeled and crushed
- 1 branch fresh rosemary
- 1 teaspoon crushed black peppercorns
- ½ teaspoon ground cayenne pepper
- 2 bay leaves
- 2 cups white Riesling wine

For the Stock

- 1 tablespoon tomato paste
- 5 cups unsalted chicken stock
- 2 tablespoons oil

For the Sauce

- 2 tablespoons butter or margarine
- 1 cup onions, cubed
- 4 peeled and seedless peaches (very ripe)
- 1 teaspoon fresh green jalapeños, seeded, chopped
- 3 cups of rabbit stock
- 1 pinch sugar
- 1 tablespoon flavored rice vinegar
- 1 cup Riesling wine
- 3 ounces tequila
  Salt and freshly ground black pepper to taste
- 1 teaspoon arrowroot

To prepare the rabbit (or have your butcher do it)

Remove the hind and front legs from the carcass and set aside to marinate. Remove the back loin from the carcass and trim off all excess fat, skin and silver skin (the translucent skin that encloses groups of muscles). Wrap loin well and set aside. Keep carcass, all bones and trimmings for sauce.

Mix all the marinade ingredients well in a large bowl. Set aside. When meat is ready, place the rabbit legs into marinade. Cover and let marinate for 24 hours, moving the pieces every 6 to 8 hours. Remove the meat from the marinade and pat dry. Strain the marinade and set the separated vegetables and liquid aside.

To Prepare the Stock

Place the bones and trimmings in a large pan in a preheated 400°F oven. Then add the vegetables from the marinade. Add 1 spoon of tomato paste, mix well, and continue to roast for 15 more minutes. Add the liquid from the marinade plus the chicken stock. Let simmer for 1 hour then strain the stock.

To Cook the Rabbit

In a heated brazing skillet, add 2 tablespoons of oil and then brown the marinated rabbit legs from all sides; loin will be grilled later. Remove the legs and fat from skillet but keep the same skillet to make the sauce.

To Prepare the Sauce

Melt the butter in the skillet used to cook rabbit legs. Add the onions, peaches, and jalapeños. Cook 2 to 3 minutes over medium heat, stirring continuously. Add the legs, stock, sugar, vinegar, wine, tequila and salt to taste; cover and braise in preheated 400°F oven for about 45 minutes. Then remove the front legs and cook hind legs for 15 minutes more. Remove all legs from the sauce, set aside. Pour the liquid into a blender and mix well. Bring the liquid to boil in a small saucepan and thicken it with the arrowroot.

Place the legs on a serving plate and pour sauce over the legs. Take the loins, season with salt and pepper and grill over medium heat; slice. Garnish the legs with the loin pieces. Serve with wild rice, creamy mashed potatoes, or a favorite starch dish.

CHILE CON QUESO WITH SWEETBREADS

John Sedlar, Chef/Owner/Author

This native New Mexican has created a cooking style founded on the tantalizing flavors and forms of that colorful region. He has melded his European training in French cooking and his background in the Southwest into a unique cuisine which can be found in his book, Modern Southwest Cuisine. *He tells us that "chile con queso in its most basic Southwestern form is a dip of melted cheese, usually Monterey Jack or a processed Cheddar, spices and chillies, served with corn chips. In this recipe, I've transformed the concept into a more delicate sauce to accompany veal sweetbreads. I like to use a good quality Parmesan cheese as the queso, along with an Argentine variety, Reggianito. To give the dish some spice without overpowering the other ingredients, I avoid the green jalapeños usually associated with chile con queso, and use red jalapeños or New Mexican Chiles instead."*

Makes 6 Servings

- 2 quarts water
- ½ teaspoon salt
- 1½ pounds veal sweetbreads

For the Chile con Queso

- 5 ounces Parmesan or other mild grating cheese, finely grated
- 3 cups heavy cream
- 2 medium garlic cloves, peeled and coarsely chopped
- 1 teaspoon freshly ground white pepper
- 1 teaspoon salt
- 6 small fresh red jalapeños (page 70), or 3 fresh green New Mexican Chiles (page 71), roasted (page 87), peeled, seeded, and left whole
- ½ teaspoon freshly ground black pepper

Bring the water and salt to a boil in a large saucepan. Reduce the heat, carefully stir in the sweetbreads and cook them for 30 minutes. When the sweetbreads are almost done, prepare a bowl of ice water. Drain the sweetbreads and plunge them quickly into the ice water to stop the cooking. Carefully pull off any clear membrane from the sweetbreads and cut them into 1½-inch pieces. Set them aside.

While the sweetbreads are cooking, put the cheese, cream, garlic, pepper and ½ teaspoon of the salt in a medium-size saucepan and bring to a boil over moderate to high heat. Boil briskly until the sauce has reduced to 1½ cups, 15 to 20 minutes. Sieve the sauce and keep it warm.

Season the sweetbreads and the peppers with the remaining ½ teaspoon of salt, and sprinkle the sweetbreads with the black pepper. Bring water to a boil in a steamer or a large pot with a steaming rack. Steam the sweetbreads and peppers until warmed through, about 4 minutes.

Spoon the sauce into the middle of each large warmed serving plate. Pat the sweetbread pieces dry with paper towels and place a cluster of them in the center of each plate. Drape the peppers over the sweetbreads.

ROAST CHICKEN WITH WILD MUSHROOMS AND PASILLA SAUCE

Robert Del Grande, Chef/Owner/Author

This Californian, with a Ph.D. in biochemistry, has become an award-winning chef by applying his scholarship to the study of good food. Robert Del Grande, the owner of Cafe Annie in Houston, Texas, also writes about food for major food magazines. Del Grande does it again! This chicken creation is a show stopper at Cafe Annie.

Makes 6 Servings

    1   3- to 4-pound roasting chicken

To roast the chicken, lightly salt and pepper it, then roast in a preheated 300°F oven until the juices at the joints run clear, 45 to 60 minutes. Heat a dry skillet over medium heat.

Wild Mushroom and Pasilla Sauce:

    4   pasillas (page 72)
    2   tablespoons butter or margarine
    2   corn tortillas
    ½   cup shelled pumpkin seeds, toasted
    ½   yellow onion, chopped
    4   garlic cloves, peeled and chopped
    8   ounces wild mushrooms (shiitake), roughly chopped
    4   cups chicken stock
    2   teaspoons maple syrup
    1   teaspoon fresh lime juice
        Salt and freshly ground black pepper to taste

Heat a dry skillet over medium heat, add the pasillas and heat until lightly toasted on both sides, then stem and seed them. Set aside. In the same skillet, lightly toast the corn tortillas and break into pieces. Set aside. Then toast the pumpkin seeds in the skillet until they are puffed and crunchy. Set aside.

Melt the butter in the skillet over medium heat. Add the onion and garlic and cook, stirring, until lightly browned. Add the mushrooms and cook, stirring, until their liquid has evaporated. Transfer the mixture to a blender. Over medium-high heat, pour the stock into the skillet, scraping the bottom to loosen any browned deposits; pour into the blender. Add the pasillas, tortilla pieces, and pumpkin seeds. Process for 10 to 15 seconds. Do not over-purée; the sauce should not be too smooth. Transfer the purée to a sauce pot. Bring the sauce to a boil, then lower the heat and simmer the sauce for 30 minutes. Add the maple syrup and lime juice and season with salt and pepper. Serve over sliced chicken.

VARIATION: Instead of roasting the chicken, quarter it, then brown the pieces in a large deep pan in a little oil over medium-high heat. When the pieces are well browned, add 2 cups of chicken stock and the sauce and bring to a simmer. Cook the chicken in the sauce until cooked through, 30 to 45 minutes. Remove the chicken pieces from the sauce and serve

LEMON AND CHILLI ROAST CHICKEN

Tim Coltman-Rogers, Bon Vivant

Tim Coltman-Rogers was an engaging young Englishman with a contagious joy for living and love of peppers, which he collected on his worldwide travels and grew in special greenhouses at his estate in Northumberland. Peppers brought Tim into my life, and for ten years, Tim brought joy into mine. I never see a Chiltepín without remembering him.

Makes 6 or More Servings

    1   large roasting chicken; figure ½ pound per serving
    ½   pound (2 sticks) butter or margarine, clarified (page 100)
    2   large lemons
6 to 8   chiltepínes, to taste (fresh or dry); substitute Thai, de árbol or serrano
2 to 6   garlic cloves, peeled and minced
    2   tablespoons honey
        Freshly ground black pepper; to taste

Wash the chicken and dry thoroughly. Peel the lemons, being careful not to include any bitter white pith. Chop rind finely and put in boiling water for 1 minute;

drain. Squeeze the lemons; reserve the juice. Mash the chiltepínes and add to the butter, lemon rind, garlic, and black pepper in a saucepan. Heat for 2 to 3 minutes over medium heat.

Gently lift the skin from the chicken's breast meat and fill the space between the skin and the breast meat with the lemon-pepper mixture. Use any surplus sauce to cover the chicken inside and out. Place the uncovered bird on a roasting rack in a pan. Bake in a preheated 400°F oven, basting from time to time. Allow 15 minutes per pound, plus another 15 minutes. The chicken is done when the juices run clear at a joint. Transfer the chicken to platter. Deglaze (page 100) the roasting pan with a little boiling water, lemon juice, and honey (about 1½ to 2 cups).
Serve the chicken and its gravy separately.

STUFFED PEPPERS NOGADA
If stuffed peppers could be thought of as decadent, these Mexican ones would be the ones referred to. Use turkey to cut down on the fat and calories a little.

Makes 8 Servings

 2 tablespoons vegetable oil
 1 medium-size onion, chopped
 1 16-ounce can tomatoes, drained and chopped
 2 tablespoons fresh parsley leaves, chopped
 ½ teaspoon ground cinnamon
 ½ teaspoon ground cayenne pepper
 2 pounds ground meat—beef, pork, or fowl
 ¼ cup raisins, soaked in hot water to cover, and drained
 ½ cup pecans, roughly chopped, or blanched almonds, slivered; or a mixture
 2 large eggs, lightly beaten
 Salt and freshly ground black pepper to taste
 4 large red or green bell peppers, cleaned, halved and parboiled 3 minutes and patted dry
 Nogada Sauce (recipe follows)
 Parsley sprigs for garnish

Heat the oil in a large saucepan over medium high heat. Add the onion and cook until soft. Add the tomatoes, parsley, cinnamon and cayenne; then add the meat, raisins, and nuts. Cook, stirring for 20

minutes or until browned and done. Allow to cool, then stir in the eggs. Season with salt and pepper.

Stuff the bell pepper halves with the meat mixture. Bake in a preheated 325°F oven 30 minutes until thoroughly heated, or microwave until heated. Pour the nogada sauce on top of stuffed peppers and garnish with parsley. This may be served hot or at room temperature as it is done traditionally.

The Nogada Sauce

 3 slices whole grain bread, no crust
 ½ cup cold milk
 2 cups milk
 1 cup pecans or almonds
 Salt to taste

Soak the bread in the cold milk. Purée in blender with the 2 cups of milk, nuts, salt, and milk-soaked bread. The sauce should be fairly thick; adjust with milk. You may warm it slightly before serving on the hot stuffed peppers, but do not cook it.
VARIATION: Instead of the rich nogada sauce, try tomato sauce on page 175 or the following:

Whipped Nogada Sauce

Makes 3 Cups

 2 cups whipping cream
 ½ cup walnuts or pecans, ground in a blender
 ½ cup blanched almonds, ground in a blender
 2 tablespoons fresh parsley, finely chopped
 ½ teaspoon ground cinnamon
 Salt to taste
 12 red bell pepper or pimento strips, 2 inches long and ¼ inch wide

Whip the cream with a whisk or electric beater until it forms soft peaks. Fold in the ground nuts, parsley, cinnamon and salt. Serve at room temperature on top of stuffed pepper halves.

KUNG PAO CHICKEN OR SHRIMP

Pat Teepatiganond, Oriental Cooking Instructor

Pat (short for Patatamatip), is a certified public accountant in Thailand who followed her husband to Texas in 1974, where they opened an Oriental food store. From that base she began teaching various types of Oriental cooking through the University of Texas at Austin. She grows the Thai peppers for her cooking classes.

Makes 4 Servings

For the Marinade

- 1 tablespoon dark soy sauce
- 1 tablespoon rice wine
- ½ tablespoon sugar
- 1 tablespoon sesame oil
- 1 teaspoon tapioca starch

For the Stir-Fry

- 1 cup chicken breast (½ pound), diced, or peeled shrimp, diced
- 3 tablespoons peanut oil
- 3 ounces peanuts, raw or roasted, unsalted
- ½ teaspoon fresh ginger root, peeled and minced
- 4 garlic cloves, peeled and minced
- ½ cup celery, diced
- ½ can bamboo shoots, drained and diced
- 6 dried red chillies (Thai, de árbol or japonés, see index)
- ½ can water chestnuts, diced
- ½ cup carrots, diced
- 2 tablespoons light soy
- ½ tablespoon sugar
- 1 tablespoon chilli paste (page 179)

In a small bowl, mix together the marinade ingredients. Add the chicken, stir to coat, and set aside. In a wok over medium heat, heat 1 tablespoon oil, then stir-fry the peanuts until golden brown. Remove to a paper towel to let cool. Heat the remaining oil in the wok, stir-fry the ginger and garlic until fragrant, then add the chillies and stir. Add the chicken and stir well. If the mixture is too dry, add some hot water, a little at a time, then add the vegetables and stir. Again, if too dry, add some hot water and stir well. Add the soy sauce, sugar and chilli paste, then turn off the heat, add peanuts, and stir well. Serve with steamed rice.

CHICKEN TIKKA

"Tikka" is a Persian word used in Iran, Pakistan, and India, for meat threaded on a skewer. Start this the day before you plan to cook it. It is so good you won't believe how easy it is.

Makes 4 to 6 Servings

- 1 2-ounce boneless chicken breast per serving, cubed if to be cooked on skewer

The Marinade

- 2 tablespoons white wine vinegar
- ¼ cup fresh lime juice
- ½ to 1 teaspoon ground cayenne pepper
- ½ teaspoon ground cumin (comino)
- 1 teaspoon turmeric
- ¼ cup cilantro leaves (fresh coriander), chopped
- 1½ teaspoons paprika
- ¼ cup fresh parsley, chopped
- 1 tablespoon ginger root, peeled and minced
- 1 cup low-fat plain yogurt
  Indian Mint Chutney (page 209) or any chutney

Place all the ingredients, except the chicken, in a blender and purée. Put chicken in a non-reactive bowl, pour blended ingredients over it and mix well. Cover and let marinate overnight.

Scrape off excess marinade, then cook the chicken on a charcoal grill 4 inches to 6 inches above coals but not directly over them. It can be threaded on a skewer. Cover and cook until tender. Serve with Indian Mint Chutney or any chutney. If available at an Indian market, Tikka Masala can be substituted for the dry spices.

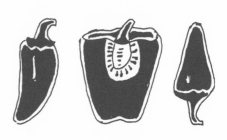

CHILAQUILES WITH POLLO (CHICKEN CHILAQUILES)

Chilaquiles originated in Mexico as a way to use stale tortillas. If you don't have stale tortillas, use packaged tostadas. There are many variations. Some like it soupy, others lean toward the dryer side. Suit yourself.

Makes 6 to 8 Servings

For the Sauce

6	guajillos (page 68)
2	anchos (page 74)
1	cup boiling water
1 to 2	fresh jalapeños (page 70)
½	cup chicken stock
½	medium-size onion, chopped
2	garlic cloves, minced
¼	teaspoon cumin (comino) seed
	Salt to taste
2	tablespoons olive oil

To Finish the Dish

About 2 dozen tortillas or 1 pound dry tortilla quarters or 1 pound packaged natural tostado triangles

2 to 3	cups cooked chicken, shredded
1½	cups Monterey Jack cheese, grated
3 to 4	cups chicken stock
1	cup sour cream or low-fat yogurt
1	medium red onion, sliced into thin rings
1	lime, cut into 6 to 8 wedges

Soak the dried chillies in hot water for 1 hour. Remove, drain, devein, and seed. Place them, the jalapeño, and the stock in a blender with the onion, garlic, cumin seed, and salt; purée. Heat the oil in a skillet and cook the purée over low to medium heat, stirring until it is darkened.

Layer the bottom of a large flameproof dish or casserole with a third of the tortilla pieces. Cover with a third of the chicken, a third of the sauce, and a third of the cheese. Repeat the layers twice. Add the stock and bring to a boil. Simmer until the stock is cooked down. This can also be done in a 350°F oven, but it takes longer.

When the desired consistency is reached, cover the top with sour cream or yogurt and garnish with onion rings and lime wedges just before serving. Do not assemble this until you are ready to start cooking so that the tortillas will not disintegrate. Use your judgment when cooking the stock down. Some like this dish soupier than others.

SICHUAN HOT PEPPER CHICKEN
Cecilia Chiang, Chef/Owner

Cecilia Chiang, a native of Beijing, China, came to America in the early 1960s. Mandarin food was not available so she opened the award-winning restaurant, The Mandarin, in San Francisco, featuring the cuisines of northern China. This dish, however, is from the pepper-growing center of Sichuan.

Makes 4 to 6 Servings

½	3-pound chicken, diced
½	cup bamboo shoots, diced
¾	cup green bell peppers, cut into 1-inch chunks
6 to 8	dried red japonés, de árbol or Thai chillies (see index)
1 to 1½	tablespoons vegetable oil
5½	tablespoons chicken stock
1	tablespoon soy sauce
1	tablespoon cornstarch

Using very little oil (1 to 1½ tablespoons) over high heat, toss and stir diced chicken for about two minutes. Sprinkle with sherry and ½ teaspoon salt. Add bell pepper, bamboo shoots, and chillies. Add chicken stock, soy sauce, and cornstarch solution. (Cornstarch is optional in this dish.) Quick-stir for a minute or so and serve with rice and other dishes.

BREAST OF CHICKEN AND NEW MEXICAN CHILES IN PHYLLO WITH CHIPOTLE SAUCE

This looks more complicated than it is but can be made well before hand. Your guests will be impressed!

Makes 8 Servings

  8 boneless breasts of chicken, skinned
  2 tablespoons olive oil
  4 tablespoons shallots, chopped
  ½ pound mushrooms, chopped
  1½ cups canned green New Mexican Chiles, chopped
  ¼ teaspoon dried thyme
  ¼ teaspoon dried marjoram
  ½ cup sherry
  ½ cup yogurt
    Dash nutmeg, grated
  3 egg whites
  3 tablespoons Parmesan, grated
    Salt and pepper to taste
  16 sheets phyllo pastry
  ¾ cup butter or margarine, melted

Sauté the shallots in the oil in a large skillet until they are soft. Add the mushrooms and sauté for 4 to 5 minutes. Add the green chiles, thyme and marjoram. Sauté 3 to 4 minutes. Add the sherry and sauté until the moisture evaporates. Stir in the yogurt and Parmesan; stir until well mixed. Season with nutmeg, salt and pepper. Allow to cool.

Beat the egg whites in a large bowl until stiff and fairly dry. Gently fold the egg whites into the cooled mushroom mixture.

Use 2 sheets of phyllo for each breast. Put one on top of the other, brushing each with melted butter. Fold in half. Keep unused phyllo well covered with a dampened cup towel. Place 1 generous tablespoon of the mushroom mixture in the middle of the folded phyllo; then place a chicken breast on top. Put another tablespoon of the mushroom mixture on top of the chicken breast. Fold both sides of the phyllo over to the center. Fold each end toward the center and brush that side with butter. Place the folded side down in a shallow baking pan; brush top with butter. Repeat until all 8 breasts are wrapped.

Bake in a preheated 350°F oven for 30 to 40 minutes. Spoon chipotle sauce on top of phyllo envelope or spoon sauce on plate and place the baked phyllo envelope on top of the sauce. Garnish with parsley.

Chipotle Sauce

  3 tablespoons butter or margarine
  3 tablespoons flour
  1½ cups milk
  ½ cup sherry
  1 chipotle, *adobado*
    Salt and pepper to taste

Make a light white sauce by melting the butter in a saucepan, stirring in the flour until creamy, gradually adding the milk so as to prevent lumps, and cooking over a low fire or in the microwave; stir frequently. Add the sherry and mix. Mash the chipotle with a little of the white sauce, then press through a strainer into the pan of sauce; mix well. Salt and pepper to taste.

Serve this sauce either under or over the phyllo envelopes.

CHICKEN BREAST IN PEPPER-APRICOT-LIME GLAZE WITH DIPPING SAUCE

W. C. Longacre, Chef/Owner

Chef Longacre opened his first restaurant in Albuquerque so he could raise enough money to put himself through chiropractic school, and in so doing fell in love with peppers. Now he is only taking the kinks out of cayennes. He is known for his peppery curries and creative culinary style.

Makes 4 Servings

- 4 boneless, skinless chicken (or turkey) breasts, 6 to 8 ounces
  Juice of 2 fresh lemons
- 3 tablespoons extra virgin olive oil
- 2 tablespoons garlic, pressed
  Juice of 2 limes
  Grated zest of 1 lime
- 2 tablespoons honey
- ¾ cup water
- 12 dried apricot halves, roughly chopped
- 1 teaspoon salt
- 2 tablespoons jalapeño (page 70), seeded and minced (more if desired)
- 3 tablespoons pine nuts
- 1 teaspoon ground cinnamon
- 2 tablespoons dark brown sugar, firmly packed
- 3 tablespoons cornstarch
- ½ cup fresh orange juice

Coat the chicken breasts with the lemon juice. Set aside in a nonreactive dish for 5 minutes. Mix together the olive oil, 1 tablespoon of the garlic, the lime juice, lime zest, honey, ½ cup water, apricots, salt, jalapeño, pine nuts, and cinnamon in a small nonreactive saucepan, and bring to a rolling boil. Dissolve the cornstarch in remaining water and pour into mixture, stirring constantly until clear. Broil the chicken for 10 minutes; remove and add a generous portion of glaze to each breast; broil 2 minutes more.

Prepare the dipping sauce by mixing remaining glaze with an equal amount of orange juice. Spanish rice and guacamole (page 113) with cucumber slices accompany this dish.

ZINFANDELI'S WHITE CHILE

David James, Chef

This white chili-con-carne is named for a restaurant once owned and operated by David James and his wife Jane Dunnewold in San Antonio, Texas. David is really involved with the art of "cooking with peppers."

Makes 6 to 8 Servings

- 4 garlic cloves, peeled and minced
- 1 pound large white Great Northern beans, picked over
- 6 cups vegetable or chicken stock
- 3 medium-size onions, diced
- 1 tablespoon vegetable oil
- 4 serranos (page 78), seeded and finely chopped
- 2 teaspoons ground cumin (comino)
- ¼ teaspoon ground cloves
- ½ teaspoon ground cayenne pepper
- 1½ teaspoons fresh *epazote*, chopped
- 4 cups cooked chicken, diced
  Salt to taste
- 3 cups sharp white cheddar, shredded
  Fresh parsley, chopped for garnish, optional

Combine first 3 ingredients and half the onion in a large pot. Bring to a boil. Reduce the heat to medium and simmer until the beans are soft, adding more heated stock if necessary. Heat the oil in a medium-size saucepan over medium heat. Add the remaining onion and cook until translucent. Add serranos and cook another minute. Add cumin, cayenne pepper, *epazote*, and simmer for 5 more minutes. Pour into ovenproof bowls and sprinkle with the cheddar cheese and finish under a broiler until golden. Garnish with chopped parsley if you like.

SOUTH TEXAS TURKEY
WITH TAMALE DRESSING

Once upon a time a national magazine asked me to write a story on a Southwestern Christmas dinner. I told them I could write about a South Texas Christmas dinner but I was a Texan and knew little about what folks who lived in the Southwest did at Christmas. This turkey was the centerpiece of my story. It is really an easy way to make an outstanding dressing.

Yield depends on size of bird

   1   10- to 12-pound unbasted or butterbasted turkey, with neck and giblets (allow ½ pound per person)
6 to 8 fresh red chiltepínes (dry, if you must)
  2½ dozen tamales with shucks removed (allow at least 3 for each guest)
3 to 4 tablespoons vegetable oil (more if necessary)

For the Gravy

      Giblets and neck from turkey
   1 large onion, peeled and quartered
8 to 10 fresh basil leaves or 1 tablespoon dried basil
   1 serrano or jalapeño, chopped
   2 celery stems with leaves, chopped
      Salt and freshly ground black pepper to taste
      Water to cover
  ½ cup all-purpose flour (add more for a thicker gravy)

Thaw the turkey thoroughly if frozen, then remove the giblets and neck and put them aside. Wash the turkey well, making certain the cavity is clean, then dry it with a clean cloth or paper toweling. Place the turkey breast-up on a cooking rack in a pan. Do not put any water in the pan. Preheat the oven to 300°F. With a larding needle or ice pick, make 6 to 8 evenly distributed deep holes in the breast. Push 1 whole chiltepín into each hole as far as possible, as if you were larding the meat.

Remove the shucks from the tamales and break each into about 3 pieces, being careful not to crumble them. Lightly fill both the stomach and neck cavities with the tamale pieces. Close the cavities securely by sewing with cord and large needle (ex. tapestry needle). Rub the entire bird with some of the oil. Cut 4 pieces of aluminum foil large enough to wrap around each wing and drumstick to prevent them from overcooking and drying out. Mold a sheet or two of paper towel over the turkey breast (note below), then saturate the paper with the remaining oil, using more if necessary. Next, mold a 12-inch square of foil over the oil-saturated towel. This keeps the skin from becoming hard and too brown.

Cook the turkey in a preheated oven at 300°F for 20 minutes per pound unstuffed or 25 minutes stuffed. Remove both the toweling and the foil during the last hour of cooking so the turkey can become a golden brown. If you want to speed up the cooking you can start with the microwave, putting the turkey on a large Pyrex dish. Five minutes in the microwave at full power will equal 20 minutes in the oven at 300°F. Every 5 minutes give the turkey a quarter turn. After 4- to 5-minute cooking periods, place the bird on the rack of your roasting pan, cover the breast, legs, and wings with foil and cook it for the remaining time in the oven as directed above. A meat thermometer should register 180°F. When almost done, remove foil to allow browning.

When the turkey is done, place it on a serving platter. Remove any stitching. Cover it with the turkey baker lid or clean dish towels. The bird will slice better if it's allowed to sit covered while you prepare the gravy and get the meal on the table.

NOTE: If you have the tropical herb *hoja santa* available, use large, fresh leaves from the plant (*Piper auritan*) instead of paper toweling to cover the breast.

For Additional Dressing

If the number of tamales required for the guests exceeds the space in the bird's cavity, or if extra dressing is desired, layer those extra broken tamales in a square Pyrex dish and place the dish on the cooking rack directly under the uncooked turkey (the bird will be sitting on the tamales). In this position some of the turkey drippings will go into the tamales, infusing them with the turkey flavor. Check the tamales from time to time; you may want to remove them before the bird is done so the dressing doesn't become dry or overcooked.

For the Gravy

Place giblets, neck, onion, basil, chillies, celery, salt and black pepper in a 1-quart saucepan; cover with water. Bring to a boil. Reduce heat and allow to simmer until you have a rich stock, adding more water as necessary to maintain a quart of liquid. (This may take an hour.) Remove the meat when done and set it aside.

Next, strain the stock and put 1 cup of it in a blender with the flour; whir until smooth. Mix this with the stock in the saucepan. When the turkey is done, remove as much of the melted fat in the pan as possible, saving all the browned juices (caramelized drippings). Then add a cup of hot water to the pan and use a spoon to loosen the browned juices; stir until they're dissolved. Add the brown juices to the flour and stock mixture in the saucepan; they'll give the gravy a rich color and delicious flavor. Place mixture over a high heat until it boils; reduce heat and stir constantly until the gravy reaches the desired thickness. Season with salt.

ANCHO ROASTED TURKEY BREAST, CORN AND TOMATO SALSA
Elmar Prambs, Executive Chef

When I was a young girl, a hotel restaurant was the only place outside the home to "dine." My mother thought it was important that we learn to eat properly in such nice places. To ensure that we would, she drove us 150 miles from our little South Texas town to San Antonio several times a year so that we would have that experience in the Menger, Gunter, and St. Anthony hotels during the 1930s. Today, hotel dining rooms have made a comeback as a result of such creative chefs as Elmar Prambs of the Four Seasons in Austin, Texas. His food is worth driving for.

Makes 6 Servings

For the Chilli Paste

- 3 anchos (page 74)
- ½ cup boiling water
- 1 garlic clove, peeled
- ½ medium-size onion, quartered

- ½ tablespoon fresh lime juice
- ½ tablespoon corn oil
  Salt to taste
- ½ turkey breast (skin on), about 3 pounds
  Corn and Tomato Salsa (recipe follows)

Preheat oven to 350°F and turn to 500°F. Arrange anchos on baking sheet and heat in oven until softened, about 2 minutes. Cut open the anchos, discard the stems, seeds, and ribs, then rinse the anchos and place into a small bowl. Cover with boiling water and let soak for 30 minutes. In a food processor, combine the anchos with some of the soaking liquid, garlic, onion, lime juice, oil, and salt. Process until smooth, about 2 minutes. The ancho purée can be made up to 3 days ahead and refrigerated in a covered container.

Score the turkey skin at 1-inch intervals; rub the ancho purée over the turkey breast. Let marinate at room temperature, for about 1 hour. Cook turkey breast in a preheated 400°F oven for about 30 to 40 minutes; dribble oil out. The internal temperature should register 160°F. Slice and serve with the salsa.

Corn and Tomato Salsa

Makes 3 Cups

- 1 medium-size ear of fresh corn
- 1 large ripe tomato, peeled, seeded, and minced
- 1 small cucumber, peeled, seeded and minced
- 1 small celery stalk, minced
- 1 small onion, minced
- 1 large garlic clove, peeled and minced
- 1 jalapeño (page 70), seeded and diced
- 3 tablespoons fresh lime juice
- ½ teaspoon ground cumin (comino)
- ½ teaspoon salt
- 4 tablespoons chopped fresh cilantro (fresh coriander)

Cook the corn in salted water until tender, about 2 to 4 minutes. Drain and rinse under cold water; scrape the kernels from the cob. In a medium-size bowl, stir together the remaining ingredients until well blended. Cover and refrigerate until ready to serve.

ANATOLIAN STEW

I named this hearty stew Anatolian because the flavors remind me of the superb foods of Turkey. With a salad it is really a one-dish meal, which is best prepared several days before eating.

Makes 8 Servings

- 2 tablespoons olive oil
- 1 medium-size red bell pepper, seeded and chopped
- 1 to 2 jalapeños (page 70) or serranos (page 78), seeded and chopped
- 1 pound ground beef or turkey
- 1 medium-size red onion, chopped
- 1 28-ounce can Italian-style tomatoes, chopped, with liquid
- 1 medium-size eggplant, peeled and cut into large dice
- ½ cup diced carrots
- ½ cup chopped celery
- 3½ cups beef, chicken, or turkey broth
- 1 tablespoon chopped fresh basil
- 1 teaspoon salt
- 1 teaspoon sugar
- ½ teaspoon ground nutmeg
- ½ cup uncooked pasta (small shells)
- 2 tablespoons fresh parsley, chopped
- 1 to 2 garlic cloves, peeled and minced
  Grated Parmesan cheese for garnish

Heat the oil in a large stockpot over medium-high heat. Add the onion, bell peppers, and jalapeño and cook, stirring, until soft. Add the meat and brown; drain off any fat. Add the tomatoes, eggplant, carrots, celery, broth, basil, salt, sugar, and nutmeg. Bring to a boil and cover. Reduce the heat to medium-low and simmer 1 to 1½ hours. Add the pasta, parsley, and garlic, cover, and simmer until the pasta is tender.

This is a thick stew. Add hot water for desired consistency. Ladle into bowls and sprinkle with Parmesan. Serve with hot garlic toast and a green salad.

NOTE: Standing improves flavor.

CHIPOTLE PECAN DUCK SALAD WITH BASIL

David Garrido, Executive Chef/Owner/Author

This unique entrée was created by David Garrido, who was born in Mexico but moved to Texas, where he not only became a Texan, but also a pioneer in the world of New Texas cuisine. David is currently executive chef at Jeffrey's, co-owner of Fresh Planet Cafe in Austin, Texas, and co-author with Robb Walsh of Nuevo Tex-Mex, *an innovative cookbook for pepper aficionados.*

Serves 4

For the Salad

- 2 boneless duck breasts or chicken breasts, grilled and diced
- 1 teaspoon olive oil
- ¼ medium onion, diced small
- ½ carrot, diced small
- ½ celery rib, diced small
- ½ cup pecans, toasted and chopped
  Sour dough toast squares

Heat the oil in a medium-size sauté pan over medium heat; add the onion, carrot, and celery and cook until the vegetables are tender but still crunchy, stirring often; about 5 minutes. Set aside.

For the Salad Dressing

- 1 tomato, grilled and quartered
- 1 chipotle (page 70), soaked in hot water for 10 minutes
- 1 ancho (page 74), soaked in hot water for 10 minutes
- 2 fresh basil leaves
- 2 tablespoons brown sugar
- 2 tablespoons water
- 1 cup mayonnaise, lite if desired
- ½ teaspoon Sea Salt

Place the tomato, chipotle, ancho, sugar, basil and water in a blender and pureé. Strain the pureé into a small saucepan and simmer until reduced to ½ cup, 4 to 6 minutes. Set aside.

In a non-reactive bowl combine the duck, the pureé, vegetables, pecans, and mayonnaise; season with salt and mix well. Divide into 4 portions, place each on a plate. Serve with toast squares.

SEAFOOD

HOT ACAPULCO SHRIMP

From 1944 until 1966 I spent a lot of time in Mexico, much of it on the beach in "old Acapulco" (it's hard to find today) where local vendors sold all sorts of foods from little thatched huts on the beach. My favorite were these succulent shrimp. So easy to prepare!

Makes 4 to 6 Servings

- 2 pounds raw jumbo shrimp with tails, shells left on
- 2 garlic cloves, peeled and crushed
- 1 teaspoon ground cayenne pepper, or more to taste
- ¼ cup fresh lime juice, preferably from Mexican *limones*
- ½ cup (1 stick) butter or margarine, melted

Split the unpeeled, raw shrimp down the belly, being careful not to cut through the back. Butterfly each shrimp by spreading it open; remove the vein. Mix the remaining ingredients with the melted butter in a small bowl; hold each shrimp by the tail and dip in the mixture until coated. Spread the opened shrimp on a cooking rack shell-side down. Cook until just pink on a charcoal grill or under the broiler.

Make a dip of the same ingredients used on the shrimp before cooking and serve in individual ramekins. Jean's Own Chutney (page 207) is nice with these shrimp, as is Creamy Serrano Dressing (page 183).

CHILE ANCHO CHEESE & SHRIMP PIZZA

Paula Lambert, Owner/Cheese Master

Paula Lambert, the "Cheese Lady of Texas" is co-owner and president of the Mozzarella Company in Dallas, Texas, which she founded in 1982. She lived in Italy for a number of years while studying cheese making. Upon her return to Texas, she began producing her own cheeses, incorporating southwestern and Texas ingredients. She ships her tasty cheeses anywhere.

Makes 2 Servings

- pizza dough for 10- to 12-inch pizza
- ½ cup Fresh Tomato Sauce (recipe follows)
- ½ pound Chile Ancho Caciotta cheese, grated (Mozzarella Company)
- 8 to 10 grilled shrimp
- fresh cilantro (fresh coriander) leaves for garnish

Roll out the pizza dough on a floured surface with a floured rolling pin, then cook on a pizza stone or in pizza pan in a preheated 450°F oven for approximately 5 minutes (or use a pre-baked pizza crust). Remove the crust from the oven. Spread the tomato sauce on crust and then top with the grated cheese. Arrange the shrimp on top of cheese. Return to the oven and continue baking until the cheese has melted and the pizza is golden brown. Garnish with fresh cilantro leaves.

NOTE: You can order Chile Ancho Caciotta cheese from the Mozzarella Company (800-798-2954), or substitute mild Monterrey Jack cheese and red chillies.

Tomato Sauce

- 2 tablespoons olive oil
- 1 garlic clove, minced
- 1 cup canned tomatoes, drained and coarsely chopped
- 10 fresh basil leaves, torn into pieces

Sauté garlic in olive oil; add tomatoes and heat to simmer. Cook 2 minutes. Add fresh basil leaves.

SHRIMP PIPIÁN

From Fray Bernadino de Sahagún, the ancient Spanish chronicler, we learn that "the Aztec lords ate many kinds of casseroles; . . . one made of fowl with red chile and tomatoes, and ground squash seeds," a dish which is now called pipián. My Spanish dictionary calls pipián an "Indian fricassee." My English dictionary says a fricassee is "meat cut small, stewed, and served with gravy." It is pre-Columbian Mesoamerican in origin, but whatever it is, it is good. This one is done with shrimp, pepitas and tomatoes.

Makes 6 Servings

For the Shrimp

- 2 pounds raw shrimp in their shells (about 25 to 30 to a pound)
- 1½ cups cold water

Shell and devein the raw shrimp, then wash them under cold running water, pat dry with paper toweling, and set aside. Place the shrimp shells in a 2- to 3-quart saucepan, add the water, and bring to a boil over high heat. Reduce the heat to low, and simmer, uncovered, for about 15 minutes, or until the liquid is reduced to 1 cup. Strain the stock through a sieve into a bowl and set aside. Discard the shells.

For the Sauce

- ½ cup pepitas (page 98), toasted
- 3 medium-size tomatoes, peeled, seeded and coarsely chopped or 1 cup canned Italian plum tomatoes, drained
- ½ cup red onions, coarsely chopped
- ½ cup red bell pepper, seeded and coarsely chopped)
- 6 dried chiltepínes (page 64) crushed or 3 serranos (page 78) or jalapeños (page 70) seeded and chopped, or to taste
- 2 tablespoons cilantro (fresh coriander), chopped
- 1½ teaspoons ground coriander seeds
- 1 garlic clove, peeled and minced
- ½ teaspoon sugar
  Salt and freshly ground black pepper to taste
- 3 tablespoons olive oil
- 2 tablespoons fresh lime juice
- 1 cup long-grain rice cooked (3 cups)
  Pepitas, whole, and fresh cilantro sprigs for garnish

Place the pepitas in a blender and process until completely ground. Add the tomatoes, onions, all peppers, cilantro, coriander seeds, garlic, sugar, salt, pepper and blend at high speed until the mixture becomes a smooth purée.

Heat the oil in a heavy 10- to 12-inch skillet over medium heat, add the shrimp and stir them in the oil until they are pink and firm, about 2 to 3 minutes. Transfer the shrimp to a plate. Add the remaining oil to the skillet and pour in the sauce and cook, uncovered, over moderate heat, stirring frequently, for 5 minutes. Add the cup of shrimp stock and lime juice and cook, stirring, over low heat until heated through. Serve over the cooked rice and garnish with pepitas and cilantro sprigs.

NOTE: Also great on chicken. Cook boneless chicken breasts on the grill or by your favorite method. In the sauce substitute chicken broth or one cup of hot water to which a teaspoon of chicken base has been added for the shrimp stock. Meat base is a prepared, moist meat concentrate—better than cubes—very handy to have a jar in your kitchen.

SHRIMP AMAL

Amal Naj, Journalist/Author

Amal Naj, a native of Calcutta, India, is on the staff of The Wall Street Journal *and is the author of a delightful book called* Peppers *in which he writes about the pepper people he found in my first pepper book. We have had fun cooking together and these succulent shrimp are one of the results. Prepare more than you'd planned because your guests will want seconds.*

Makes 4 Servings

- 4 tablespoons mustard oil or a vegetable oil
- 6 dried red chillies, Thai, japonés, de árbol (see index)
- 4 cinnamon sticks, broken
- 6 cardamon pods, crushed
- 6 whole cloves
- 1 teaspoon fresh ginger, peeled and chopped
- 3 bay leaves
- 1 pound large shrimp, shells left on
- 2 to 4 fresh green chillies; Thai (page 82), serrano (page 78)
- 2 teaspoons cumin (comino), ground
- 1 teaspoon turmeric
- 1 teaspoon salt
- ½ cup white wine

Heat the oil in a large, heavy skillet over medium heat. When the oil starts to give off pungent vapor, toss in the dried chillies, cinnamon, cardamon, and cloves. Stir until peppers begin to darken, add ginger and bay leaves. Stir with wooden spoon for 2 minutes. Raise heat to high; add the shrimp, and stir for two minutes. Add the chopped green chillies, cumin, turmeric, and salt and stir for two minutes. Add the wine; cover, and cook over medium heat for 3 to 4 minutes. Serve the shrimp immediately with shells on. These go well as an appetizer or as an accompaniment to another entrée served with steamed rice.

SHRIMP CREOLE

Most cooks tend to overcook this dish. Shrimp Creole is really just tenderly cooked shrimp in lightly stewed tomatoes with Creole seasoning. You do not want it to be like a marinara sauce for pasta.

Makes 8 Servings

For the Shrimp Boil

- 1 small bunch celery with tops, chopped
- 1 large onion, quartered
- 12 bay leaves
- 4 cloves garlic, peeled and crushed
- 4 lemons, quartered
- 1 teaspoon ground cayenne pepper
- 4 tablespoons salt
  1½ to 2 pounds medium-size shrimp, shells left on

For the Sauce

- 1 tablespoon olive oil
- 1 large onion, chopped
- 1 16-ounce can tomatoes or 12 large, ripe tomatoes; finely chopped
- 4 celery stalks, chopped
- 1 to 2 garlic cloves, peeled and minced
- 1 sprig fresh thyme or a pinch of dried
- 2 bay leaves
- 6 fresh basil leaves, chopped
- ½ to 1 teaspoon ground cayenne pepper or to taste

Put the first seven ingredients into a 5-quart stock pot; cover with water. Boil for 10 minutes. Add the shrimp (shells on) and boil 10 minutes more, until the shrimp are pink. Drain and peel the shrimp, leaving them whole; set aside.

In a deep skillet or Dutch oven heat the oil over medium heat. Cook the onion in the oil until translucent. Add the rest of the ingredients. Cook 20 minutes, stirring frequently. Add the peeled shrimp. Cook 10 minutes more. Caution: never pour water into stewed shrimp as the tomato juice makes gravy enough. Remove the bay leaves. Serve over steamed rice.

OVER-STUFFED PEPPERS WITH SHRIMP, CAJUN STYLE
Justin Wilson, Humorist/Author

Justin Wilson the "Old Cajun" has created stuffed peppers which are as good as his television shows, records, and books—"I garóntee." "Cajuns" are descendants of deported French Acadians who came from Nova Scotia down the Mississippi River to settle a parish they named Acadia in Louisiana.

Makes 8 Servings

  8 large bell peppers
  ¼ cup olive oil or bacon drippings
  1 cup onion, finely chopped
  ½ cup green onion (scallions), finely chopped
  ¼ cup pimento, canned or fresh, chopped
  1 8-ounce can tomato sauce
  4 garlic cloves, peeled and minced
  ½ cup dry white wine
  1½ teaspoons salt
  1 teaspoon ground cayenne pepper
  1½ pounds shrimp, peeled, deveined, and coarsely chopped
  2½ cups cooked rice
  8 bacon strips, cut in half
1 to 2 cups chicken stock

Slice the tops from the bell peppers, remove the seeds, rinse out, and drain. Heat the oil in a large saucepan and sauté the onions and green onions, stirring, over medium heat until the onions are clear. Stir in the pimentos, tomato sauce, and garlic, then add the wine, salt, and pepper and stir. Stir in the shrimp, and remove from the heat. Stir in the rice and make certain everything is mixed together well. Fill each pepper with the rice mixture and place them side by side in a shallow pan large enough to hold all the peppers. Cross the bacon strips over the top. Fill the pan half full with stock, and bake for 1 hour in a preheated 350°F oven. Serve with one of the table salsas in the sauce section (page 169) with the peppers.

GRILLED SALMON WITH SOY AND GINGER
Michael Foley, Chef/Owner

Chef Michael Foley is co-owner of Printer's Row restaurant in Chicago, Illinois. When he isn't cooking at either of his two Chicago restaurants, he's making road trips to search out unique Midwestern ingredients. He is well known for his dedication to quality, innovation, and regional foods.

Makes 4 Servings

For the Marinade

  6 tablespoons soy sauce
  ¼ cup sesame seed oil
  3 tablespoons sherry vinegar
  1 teaspoon ground cayenne pepper
  1 teaspoon chopped red banana pepper (page 59) or red bell pepper
  3 garlic cloves, peeled and crushed
  5 tablespoons fresh ginger, peeled and minced

To Finish the Dish

  4 7-ounce salmon fillets

Place all of the marinade ingredients in a blender and process. Pour the marinade into a bowl and add the fillets; turn over to thoroughly coat. Marinate for 30 minutes.

Drain and squeeze the marinade from the fish. Wipe the grill with an oiled cloth, then grill the fish until cooked to desired degree of doneness.

SALMON WITH ROASTED RED PEPPER SAUCE AND CILANTRO CREAM
Randall E. Cronwell, Independent Chef de Cuisine

Randall E. Cronwell in Portland, Oregon, is one of those well-trained—Culinary Institute of America—chefs, who work independently, giving the harassed professional needed help in order to be able to entertain at home. Bless them!

Makes 4 Servings

  2 pounds salmon fillets, cut into 8 equal pieces
     Salt and freshly ground black pepper to taste
  ½ cup olive oil

For the Red Pepper Sauce

4 large red bell peppers, roasted (page 60), peeled, and seeded
½ cup cream (whole)
Ground cayenne pepper to taste
Fresh lemon juice to taste
Salt and freshly ground black pepper to taste

For the Cilantro Cream

½ bunch cilantro (fresh coriander), stemmed and coarsely chopped
1½ cups sour cream
Fresh lemon juice to taste
Milk, if needed
Cilantro (fresh coriander) sprigs for garnish

Season the fillets with salt and pepper and coat lightly with some of the olive oil. Set aside.

Purée the peppers in a blender and set aside. In a saucepan, blend the cream with the purée and cayenne pepper. Add a little lemon juice and salt. Cook until smooth over low heat, stirring, about 5 minutes.

For the cilantro cream, combine the cilantro, sour cream, and lemon juice. Pour into a blender and process until you have a smooth green sauce. Thin with milk if too thick—you want to be able to drizzle the sauce over the salmon. Set aside.

Heat the remaining oil in a large stainless steel skillet over high heat. Add the salmon fillets, brown one side, and flip over to finish cooking; place on paper towels. Put red pepper sauce on warmed plate first, then the salmon. To finish, drizzle the cilantro cream over salmon. Garnish with cilantro sprigs.

GRILLED SWORDFISH ANCHO
Lewis Aldridge, Chef/Owner
Lewis Aldridge, a native of South Texas, developed a taste for chillies and spicy Mexican food as he grew up. Today he uses those flavors in his tree-shaded Austin restaurant, the City Grill, but he also has a special way with fish.

Makes 4 Servings

6 anchos (page 74), seeded
6 garlic cloves, peeled
1 cup vegetable oil
2 teaspoons dried oregano
½ cup fresh lime juice
Salt and freshly ground black pepper to taste
1 cup sour cream
Milk, if needed
12 green onions (scallions), trimmed to 6"
4 swordfish steaks (6 to 8 ounces each) or mahi-mahi, tuna, marlin, shark, or boneless chicken breasts
1 dozen corn tortillas
Lime wedges

Basting Sauce

Toss the anchos and whole garlic cloves in a little oil. Place them under the broiler until they soften and begin to brown. Be careful not to get them too brown or the sauce will be bitter. Remove from broiler and process in a blender with the remaining oil and lime juice. Add oregano; season with salt and pepper.

Sour Cream Sauce

Mix ⅓ of the basting sauce with the sour cream. Thin with milk if too thick. Refrigerate.

Prepare a charcoal fire. When the fire is very hot, dip the whole onions and the swordfish steaks in the basting sauce. Cook the onions until they are browned on the outside but still crisp in the center. The fish is usually done when both sides are lightly browned. If you have any doubts just cut the center and check it. When done, place the fish in a warm oven.

Warm the tortillas, two at a time, in a lightly oiled teflon or cast iron skillet. Place an onion and a table-spoon of the sour cream sauce on each tortilla then roll. Arrange the onion rolls on the platter with the swordfish, and spoon the remainder of the sour cream sauce over the fish. For even more informality, let your guests roll the tortillas at the table. Garnish with large wedges of lime, and encourage everyone to use the lime, as it is the perfect finishing flavor for the spicy fish.

GRILLED RED SNAPPER WITH SHRIMP AND TOMATILLO SAUCE
Lewis Aldridge, Chef/Owner
Prepare this red snapper dish and you'll agree that Aldridge (page 151) has a special way with fish.

Makes 6 Servings

- 1 pound tomatillos (page 99), husked
- 3 serranos (page 78), seeded
- 6 garlic cloves, peeled
- ½ bunch cilantro (fresh coriander), chopped
  Salt to taste (optional)
  Olive oil for grilling
- 6 portions red snapper fillets, 6 to 8 ounces each
- 24 medium-size shrimp, peeled
  Lime wedges for garnish
  Cilantro (fresh coriander) leaves for garnish

The Sauce

Roast the tomatillos, serranos, and garlic cloves under a broiler until very browned, almost burned. Transfer to food processor and process until smooth. Season with salt. This can be done ahead and reheated over very low fire. If sauce thickens too much, thin with water.

To Cook Fish and Shrimp

Oil the red snapper and place on grill over very hot wood or charcoal fire. Brown lightly on one side, turn and brown other side. Ten minutes per 1 inch of thickness is a good rule of thumb for cooking time, but the best way to tell is to cut 1 fillet open and see if it is done in the middle. Just before fish is ready, put oiled shrimp on grill. The shrimp take only a few minutes to cook.

To assemble, place the fish on a warm platter. Top each fillet with four shrimp and drizzle the sauce in a line down the center. Garnish with the lime and remaining fresh cilantro leaves.

CHILLE CRAB CAKES
Kurt Koessel, Chef
This Koessel (page 112) specialty is good for a light supper or luncheon or as a starter.

Makes 4 to 5 Servings

Crab Mayonnaise

- 2 tablespoons mayonnaise, preferably homemade (page 184)
- 1 teaspoon serranos, seeded and chopped
  Pinch chopped fresh ginger, peeled and minced
  Pinch garlic clove, peeled and minced
  Pinch dry mustard
  Salt and freshly ground black pepper to taste

Mix all of the ingredients for the crab mayonnaise together. Set aside.

Crab Cakes

- 1 egg
- 2 tablespoons chopped cilantro (fresh coriander)
- 1 teaspoon chopped green New Mexican Chile (page 71)
- ½ teaspoon soy sauce
- ½ teaspoon bottled hot pepper sauce, or to taste
- ½ teaspoon freshly ground black pepper
  Pinch "Old Bay" seasoning, optional
- 1 pound crab meat
- 2 to 4 tablespoons dry bread crumbs
  Vegetable oil for frying

In a bowl, stir the egg; add the cilantro, chillies, soy sauce, pepper sauce, and black pepper. To this add all the remaining crab cake ingredients and mix well. Using a scoop of the mixture make a small round "cake" about 2 inches in diameter and ½-inch thick. Sauté the cakes in a little hot oil until brown, approximately 2 minutes on each side. Drain. Serve with Crab Mayonnaise on top.

FRESH MUSSELS WITH SERRANOS AND FRESH MOZZARELLA

John Ash, Chef/Food Journalist

John Ash has a degree in fine arts. After pursuing food at the corporate level with Del Monte Foods in R and D, he began cooking professionally in the early 1970s. Now his artistry is expressed with the foods and wines of Sonoma County, California, at his restaurant, John Ash & Company in Santa Rosa. Here he has produced an entrée which expresses the elegant simplicity he has become known for. There are mussels along the west coast but inlanders could substitute the more available oysters.

Makes 6 Servings

36	large mussels, poached on the half shell, liquor reserved
¼	pound bacon
2	tablespoons extra virgin olive oil
3	large garlic cloves, peeled and minced
¼	cup green onion (scallions) or shallot, finely chopped
1	teaspoon fresh serrano (page 78), seeded and finely chopped
2	tablespoons parsley, finely chopped
4	ounces fresh mozzarella cheese
4	tablespoons dry white bread crumbs
1	large bunch spinach, stems removed

Scrub the mussels with a stiff brush, then wash in a colander in running water. Cook, covered, in a deep, heavy skillet over high heat about 6 to 8 minutes, agitating the pan to cook them evenly. Remove them from the heat the moment the shells open. Leave the mussels in their shells. Drain, reserving the liquid.

Cook the bacon until crisp. Drain well and chop finely. In a separate pan, heat 1 tablespoon of the oil over medium heat, then add the garlic and serrano, and cook, stirring, until just soft. Do not brown. Combine the bacon-garlic mixture and parsley in a bowl. In a separate bowl add drops of olive oil to bread crumbs to lightly coat.

Divide the bacon mixture and place some on top of each mussel. Moisten with a few drops of the reserved poaching liquor. Cover each mussel with a thin slice of fresh mozzarella cheese. Sprinkle with the oiled bread crumbs. If not serving immediately, cover and refrigerate.

To serve, place the mussels on a bed of rock salt or crumpled foil to keep them level. Place them into a preheated 400°F oven or under a broiler until cheese just begins to melt. While the mussels are cooking, quickly wilt the spinach leaves in the remaining olive oil in a saucepan over medium heat and place on six warm plates. Place six mussels on each and serve immediately.

Vegetarian

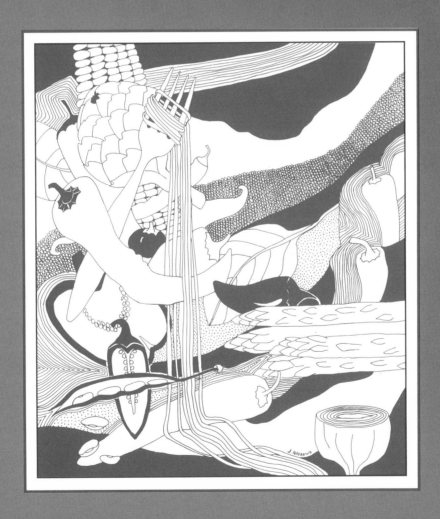

MY GARDEN RATATOUILLE

If you are a gardener you'll love this way to use your produce. It freezes beautifully. In one of my travels in Indonesia I had a delicious ratatouille that used those cucumbers that get yellow and too big—try it.

Makes 4 to 6 Servings

- 1 large eggplant, peeled and cut into 1-inch cubes
- 1 6-inch-long zucchini, cut into 1-inch cubes
- ¼ cup olive oil
- 2 medium-size onions, finely chopped
- 6 ripe tomatoes, peeled and cut up
- 1 bell pepper (page 59), seeded and chopped
- 1 jalapeño or serrano (page 78), seeded and chopped
- 1 garlic clove, peeled and minced
- 1 tablespoon chopped fresh parsley
- 1 bay leaf
- 1 tablespoon Worcestershire sauce
  Salt and freshly ground black pepper to taste

In a large saucepan over medium heat, boil in water to cover or microwave the eggplant and zucchini until just tender. Drain. Heat the oil in a large saucepan over medium heat. Add the onions and cook, stirring, until browned. Stir in the rest of the ingredients and simmer until juices are cooked down and mixture is semi-dry. Allow to cool. Serve the next day either hot or at room temperature.
NOTE: This freezes well when sealed in freezer containers and is a good way to put up hard-to-freeze squash.

CAPONATA

A tasty appetizer or side dish of Italian origin which is even better when made several days ahead. It freezes well, so make a double recipe to save time.

Makes 8 Cups

- 1 cup olive oil
- 2 eggplants, peeled and diced in 1-inch cubes, sprinkled with salt, let stand for 1 hour
- 3 medium onions, halved and sliced very thin
- 1½ cups celery, minced; parboil 2 minutes, drain & measure 1 cup
- 1 red bell pepper, seeded and diced
- ¾ cup tomato sauce or purée
- 2 tablespoons Italian capers, rinsed and drained
- 1 dozen black olives, pitted and sliced
- 1 tablespoon pine nuts or sunflower seeds, or to taste
- ¼ cup red wine vinegar
- 2 tablespoons sugar
- ¼ teaspoon salt
- ½ teaspoon cayenne pepper
- ¼ teaspoon freshly ground black pepper

Rinse and dry eggplant. In a large saucepan heat the olive oil over medium-high heat. When hot, add the eggplant and cook, stirring, until browned. Remove with slotted spoon and let drain on paper toweling. Sauté onions, stirring, in the oil until soft but not brown. Add ½ cup of celery, bell pepper, and the tomato sauce and simmer over medium heat for 15 minutes. Add the capers, olives, pine nuts or sunflower seeds, vinegar, sugar, salt, cayenne pepper, black pepper, and the eggplant. Simmer until thick and condensed, about 20 minutes, stirring often. Add one cup of cooked celery and mix well. Add more tomato sauce if too dry. Adjust seasonings to taste. Serve at room temperature with crusty Italian bread, pita bread, or crackers. This freezes very well.
VARIATION: For a zippy caponata, sauté a minced fresh seeded jalapeño or more (page 70) along with the celery and bell peppers.

STUFFED EGGPLANT JAIPUR

I have tried to duplicate a delectable dish I was served at the beautiful Rambagh Palace in Jaipur, India. I think you will like the results.

Makes 8 Servings

    1 cup uncooked rice
    3 cups chicken stock
    1 small purple/red onion, finely chopped
    2 serranos (page 78) or jalapeños (page 70), 1 red and 1 green, minced
    1 large ripe tomato, chopped finely
    8 small, individual-sized Oriental eggplants or 4 small eggplants cut in halves
      Tomato Sauce (recipe follows)

Place all ingredients, except the eggplants, in a 2-quart saucepan, cover and cook on low heat until tender and fluffy. Bake unpeeled eggplant at 325°F until tender, but not mushy. Hollow 1 side of the Oriental eggplant and fill generously with the rice mixture, pressing it into the cavity. If halves of the larger type are used, hollow out a cavity for the rice mixture and fill. Place stuffed eggplant in a baking dish in the oven until thoroughly warmed before serving with the tomato sauce.

Tomato Sauce

Makes 2 Cups

    2 cups ripe tomatoes, canned or fresh, chopped, with juice
    1 small onion, finely chopped
    1 garlic clove, minced
    1 tablespoon fresh basil leaves, chopped
    1 tablespoon Worcestershire sauce
    ½ to 1 teaspoon ground cayenne pepper
      Salt and freshly ground black pepper to taste
    2 tablespoons olive oil

Place all of ingredients, except the oil, into a blender and purée. Heat the oil in a skillet, add the tomato mixture, bring to a boil. Reduce heat and cook until slightly reduced. Serve hot on the stuffed eggplant. Extra sauce can be served in a small bowl.

ROASTED RED BELL PEPPER MOUSSE

Jamie Morningstar, Chef

After graduating from San Francisco's Culinary Academy, becoming resident chef at Inglenook Napa was like coming home to this Seattle native, for Morningstar is a descendant of the winery's founder.

Makes 4 to 6 Servings

    2 tablespoons vegetable oil
    2 shallots, diced
5 to 6 red bell peppers, roasted (page 87) and peeled
    ½ cup good chicken stock
    2 teaspoons unflavored gelatin
    ¼ cup water, very hot
    ¾ cup whipped cream
      Salt and freshly ground black pepper to taste

Heat the oil in a medium-size saucepan over medium heat. Add the shallots and cook until limp. Add the peppers and cook, stirring, 5 minutes. Drain off excess oil. Add the chicken stock and cook until soft. Pour the mixture into a blender and process until smooth. Dissolve the gelatin in the hot water and add to purée. Strain through a fine sieve. Cool down over an ice bath (bowl of ice water with the mousse in separate bowl on top). When mousse is cool to the touch, fold in the whipped cream and season with salt and pepper.

Fill individual molds with the mousse. For an added touch place a cut-out star of roasted pepper on the mold bottom (which will be the top when unmolded). Tap the mold firmly to remove the air bubbles and refrigerate 4 to 6 hours, overnight if possible. To unmold place in hot water for a few seconds and turn over onto a plate with sauce underneath.

Fennel Salsa

    1 cup fennel bulb finely diced
    1 cup fresh, ripe tomato purée, no skins or seeds
    ½ cup red onion, finely diced
    2 tablespoons jalapeño (page 70), minced
      Salt and freshly ground black pepper to taste

Combine all ingredients and allow to stand at least an hour to let the flavors meld. Serve as garnishing sauce on the plate for the mousse. Use fennel sprigs for additional garnish.

GRILLED STUFFED POBLANOS WITH AVOCADO SALSA
Cindy Pawlcyn, Chef/Co-Owner
Cindy Pawlcyn, executive chef and co-owner of five popular California restaurants, has been working in professional kitchens since she was thirteen years old. She has studied the culinary arts all over the world.

Makes 8 Servings

- 8 poblanos (page 74), Note: in southern and Baja California, these are often mistakenly called Pasilla peppers
- 8 tablespoons Fontina cheese, grated
- 8 tablespoons Monterey Jack cheese, grated
- 8 tablespoons Jarlsburg cheese, grated
- 8 tablespoons white cheddar cheese, grated
- 8 tablespoons Assiago cheese, grated
  Cilantro (fresh coriander) sprigs for garnish
  Avocado Salsa (recipe follows)

Carefully slice off the shoulder of each poblano, leaving the stem, to form a lid. Remove seeds and membranes. Blanch the lids and pods for 2 minutes in boiling, lightly salted water. Refresh in an ice bath and drain.

In a medium-size bowl, mix together all the cheeses. Stuff the peppers with the mixture and replace the top. Grill over medium wood or charcoal fire until cheeses are melted and you have nice grill marks on both sides of the poblanos. To serve, divide the Avocado Salsa among 8 plates and place a poblano on top. Garnish with cilantro sprigs.
NOTE: You can substitute your choice of cheeses for the Fontina and Assiago.

Avocado Salsa

- 4 firm, ripe avocados, peeled (page 95), seeded, and diced
- 1 fresh jalapeño (page 70), roasted (page 87), peeled, and minced
- ½ large red onion, peeled and minced
- 1 cup cilantro (fresh coriander) leaves, minced
- 1 cup green onions (scallions), minced
- ¼ cup rice vinegar (page 98)
- ¾ cup olive oil
  Salt and freshly ground black pepper to taste

In a large nonreactive bowl, mix all ingredients together carefully so as not to mash the avocados. Serve 2 tablespoonsful with each stuffed pepper.

VINITA PARTHASARATHY'S NEW POTATOES WITH POPPY SEED
Vinita, who was a graduate student at the University of Texas at Austin from Madras, India, is one of the people I have studied Indian cookery with. You'll never settle for plain "hash browns" again!

Makes 6 Servings

- 1 to 2 tablespoons vegetable oil
- 6 medium new potatoes, unpeeled, cubed
- 2 to 3 dried red chillies, crumbled (de árbol, japonés, Thai: see index)
- 1½ tablespoons white poppy seed (available in Indian food market)
- ½ teaspoon turmeric powder
- ½ teaspoon ground cayenne pepper
- 1 to 2 serranos (page 78) or jalapeños (page 70), minced
- 1 cup hot water

Heat the oil in a large saucepan over medium heat. Add the potatoes and cook, stirring, until golden. Remove from the oil and set aside. To the same oil, add dry chillies and poppy seed. When lightly browned, return the potatoes to the pan. Add the turmeric, cayenne, salt, green chillies, and water. Simmer over medium heat until potatoes are tender and most of the water is absorbed. This is quite hot, so use fewer chillies if desired.

ANAHEIM STUFFED WITH APRICOTS, GOAT CHEESE AND ALMONDS

Stephen Pyles, Chef/Owner/Author

This is a meatless dish by the unbeatable Stephen Pyles (page 119); not fatless, just meatless.

Makes 4 Servings

- 8 green New Mexican Chiles/Anaheims (page 71), roasted (page 87) and peeled, but left whole
- 2 garlic cloves, roasted, skinned, and puréed
- 8 ounces goat cheese, crumbled
- 4 ounces Caciotta or Monterey Jack, grated
- 1 tablespoon shallots, chopped
- 1 tablespoon fresh cilantro (fresh coriander), chopped
- 1 tablespoon fresh basil, chopped
- 1 tablespoon fresh marjoram, chopped
- ½ cup dried apricots, diced
- 2 tablespoons almonds, sliced, toasted and chopped

  Salt and freshly ground black pepper to taste
- 2 large eggs
- 2 tablespoons heavy cream

  Oil for deep frying

  Yellow cornmeal for dredging

  Apricot Sauce (recipe follows)

  Pico de Gallo (page 174)

Carefully slice the peppers down one side and remove the seeds and ribs, leaving the stem attached. Set aside. In a bowl, combine the garlic, goat cheese, Caciotta, shallots, cilantro, basil, marjoram, apricots, and almonds. Season with salt and pepper to taste. Mix well and carefully stuff the peppers with the mixture. Do not overfill. Close the peppers and refrigerate until needed.

In a small bowl beat the eggs into the cream in a heavy, high-walled saucepan or deep fat fryer, heat enough oil to cover the peppers to 325°F. Dip the stuffed peppers into the egg mixture, then dredge in the cornmeal. Slip the peppers, a few at a time, into the oil and fry until they are lightly browned. Remove and drain well on paper towels. Serve on top of Apricot Sauce and garnish with Pico de Gallo (page 174, Salsa Cruda).

Apricot Sauce

Makes 2 cups

- 1 cup chicken stock
- ¾ cup dried apricots, diced
- 2 tablespoons sugar
- 2 tablespoons white wine vinegar
- ½ cup dry white wine
- 1 shallot, minced
- 1 garlic clove, peeled and minced
- ½ cup (1 stick) butter or margarine, softened and cut into pieces

  Salt to taste

In a small saucepan bring the chicken stock to a boil. Add the apricots and sugar, reduce the heat to medium and cook until soft, about 15 minutes. Place apricots and stock in blender and purée. Return to the saucepan and keep warm over low heat. Combine the wine and shallot in medium-size saucepan over high heat and reduce the liquid to 2 tablespoons. Lower the heat to medium, begin whisking in butter, piece by piece, until all butter or margarine is incorporated. Remove from heat. Stir in the apricot purée, season with salt, and strain. Keep warm over low heat.

PEPPERONATA

Tired of plain old potatoes—try this for a change.

Makes 4 Servings

- ¼ cup olive oil
- 1 large onion, coarsely chopped
- 1 garlic clove, peeled and minced
- 2 large potatoes, peeled and cubed
- 2 large, ripe tomatoes, peeled, seeded, and cut into large chunks
- 3 large bell peppers of several colors, seeded and julienned
- 1 jalapeño (page 70), seeded and chopped
- ¼ teaspoon dried thyme, crumbled
- ½ teaspoon dried basil
- ½ teaspoon ground cayenne pepper, or to taste

In a large skillet, heat the oil over medium heat. Add the onion and garlic and cook, stirring, until the onion is limp. Stir in the potatoes, cover, cook 10 minutes, stirring occasionally. Stir in the remaining ingredients, cover, and cook 10 minutes longer, until the potatoes and peppers are crisp-tender.

CHEF GREWAL'S KHATTA ALOO (POTATOES)

Chef Grewal was my cookery teacher in Aurangabad, India. Indians have a special way with potatoes.

Makes 4 Servings

2 tablespoons vegetable oil
$\frac{1}{8}$ teaspoon cumin (comino) seeds
$\frac{1}{8}$ teaspoon caraway seed
$\frac{1}{2}$ teaspoon ground cumin (comino) seed
$\frac{1}{8}$ teaspoon ground coriander seed
1 teaspoon turmeric
$\frac{1}{2}$ to 1 teaspoon ground cayenne pepper
1 small purple/red onion, chopped finely
1 serrano or jalapeño, chopped finely
1 garlic clove, minced
1 teaspoon ginger root, peeled and minced
$1\frac{1}{2}$ cups diced new potatoes, boiled until tender
2 tablespoons cilantro (fresh coriander) leaves, chopped
2 tablespoons mint leaves, chopped
Juice of 1 lime
Salt and freshly ground black pepper to taste

Heat the oil in a heavy skillet over medium-high heat. Add the cumin, caraway, comino, and coriander. Stir until fragrant. Add onion, garlic, serrano, and ginger; sauté until soft. Add turmeric, coriander, and cayenne. Mix well. Add potatoes, cilantro, and mint; stir to mix. Season with salt and black pepper. Heat thoroughly. Serve with grilled meats or as you would hash browned potatoes.
ALTERNATE: Cauliflower, cooked *al dente*, is exciting prepared this way.

TEX-MEX ENCHILADAS

Don't be afraid. There is no mystery to making an enchilada!

Makes 18 Enchiladas; Allow 2 or 3 Per Serving

Vegetable oil for heating tortillas
18 fresh corn tortillas
Enchilada sauce (page 179)
2 pounds longhorn cheese, shredded
1 large onion, finely chopped

Heat enough oil to cover a tortilla in a skillet over high heat. Dip each tortilla in the oil until pliable and heated or 4 to 5 seconds (do not allow to get crisp). Drain the tortillas on paper toweling and stack them until all are dipped in the oil.

Place the sauce in a saucepan and warm it over low heat. Dip a tortilla in the sauce and place it on a large plate. Place 2 tablespoons of the cheese and $\frac{1}{2}$ tablespoon of onion across the center of the tortilla and roll it up. Place it with the rolled edge down in a 9 x 13-inch baking dish making two rows of eight enchiladas.

Pour the remaining sauce over the enchiladas, taking care not to drown them, and sprinkle with the cheese. Bake in a preheated 400°F oven until the sauce and cheese are bubbling. Sprinkle with onion and serve on a heated plate. Warm and pass extra sauce at the table.
VARIATIONS: The enchiladas may be filled with shredded cooked chicken or pork and strips of Monterey Jack cheese (no onion), small boiled shrimps, mashed *frijoles*, chopped portobello mushrooms, or whatever you dare to try along with a harmonizing shredded cheese and some onion if you like.

For Green Enchiladas (Enchiladas Verdes), which are filled with chicken, Monterey Jack cheese, and a green sauce, use the tomatillo and green chile sauce on page 178 or one of the other green sauces and top each with a dollop of sour cream instead of shredded cheese.

POLENTA WITH BABY VEGETABLES AND CHAYOTE SAUCE

David Garrido, Chef/Owner/Author

Here is another of Chef Garrido's (page 146) inventive recipes—this one is for the vegetarian in your life.

Serves 6

The Polenta

- 3 cups water
- 2 ears of corn, cut off cob; or 1 cup frozen corn kernels
- ¾ cup white cornmeal
- ¼ cup goat cheese
- 1 tablespoon chives, chopped

In a 2-quart saucepan over high heat, bring the water to a boil. Reduce the heat and add the cornmeal and corn and cook until thickened and very smooth, stirring every 2 to 3 minutes; about 40 minutes.

The Vegetables

- 2 cups mixed baby vegetables, cut in quarters; carrots, zucchini, cherry tomatoes, etc.
- 1 ancho (page 74), stemmed, seeded and cut into strips
- 1 pinch saffron
- 2 tablespoons fresh lemon juice
  Sea salt to taste

Place all of the ingredients in a nonreactive bowl and allow to marinate for 1 hour.

For the Sauce

- 1 tablespoon vegetable oil
- 2 shallots, peeled and sliced
- 1 chayote (page 95), peeled and quartered
- 1 serrano, seeded and chopped
- ½ cup dry white wine
- 1 to 3 tablespoons marjoram, chopped
- 3 tablespoons fresh lemon juice
- 1 red bell pepper, diced
  Sea Salt to taste

Heat the oil in a small saucepan over medium heat; add the shallots, chayote, serrano and bell pepper and cook for about 3 minutes. Place the vegetables in a blender, then add the wine and lemon juice and process until smooth. Return the mixture to the saucepan and simmer for 3 minutes; strain. Add the marjoram and season with salt. Keep warm.

Finish the polenta by adding the cheese and ½ of the chives; season with salt. Place the polenta on a serving plate and surround with the vegetables. Spoon the sauce over the vegetables and garnish with the remaining chives. Serve immediately.

CHEESE GRITS WITH NEW MEXICAN CHILES

A jazzed up version of an old Southern favorite.

Makes 12 Servings

- 6 cups water or chicken stock
- 1½ cups instant grits
- 2 teaspoons salt
- 1 teaspoon paprika
- 1 teaspoon cayenne pepper
- 3 large eggs
- 1 pound sharp cheddar cheese, grated (try a mixture with Jack or chèvre)
- 1 4-ounce can green New Mexican Chiles, chopped

Bring the water to a boil in a large saucepan; stir in the grits gradually. Cover and cook until thickened. Stir occasionally to prevent sticking. Add salt, paprika, and pepper sauce.

In a large mixing bowl, beat the eggs lightly. Add a small amount of hot grits to the eggs, stirring constantly so that the eggs do not cook. Gradually stir in the remaining grits. Add the grated cheese and chiles. Pour into a buttered 2-quart casserole and bake in a preheated 325°F. oven for 45 minutes. Serve immediately.

CORN AND GREEN CHILE "PUDDING"

In the days before sweet corn (yes, there were such days) we all looked forward to the first tender field or "Dent" corn every year to stuff ourselves before it got too hard. My favorite summer treat was what my Texas grandmother called corn "pudding," but she didn't know about New Mexican Chiles.

Makes 8 to 10 Servings

- 4 cups corn kernels (thaw if frozen)
- 3 tablespoons butter/margarine
- 4 large eggs
- 2 tablespoons cornstarch (with sweet corn)
- 2 cups milk
- 1 teaspoon salt
- 1 teaspoon freshly ground black pepper
- ½ cup chopped, canned green New Mexican Chiles; if using fresh, peel them first (page 87)

Put 3 cups corn in a blender with butter, eggs, cornstarch, ½ cup of the milk, salt and pepper; process, being careful not to make too smooth a purée (the mixture should resemble scraped corn). Stir this mixture into the remaining corn, milk, and the chiles in a 2-quart greased baking dish. Set baking dish in a larger pan filled with hot water that comes 1 inch up the sides of the dish. Bake in a preheated 325°F oven until a knife blade comes out clean or the pudding is firm (about 1 hour). Sprinkle with paprika if desired. **VARIATION:** If using a microwave, cook for 10 minutes on high, then give the dish a quarter turn and stir the mixture. Repeat, without stirring, until pudding is set (times will vary). Brown the pudding in the oven if desired.

PEPPER AND SPAGHETTI FRITTATA

Vegetarians, this is for you! A mouth-warming experience.

Makes 6 to 8 Servings

- 6 tablespoons olive oil
- 2 medium-size onions, chopped
- 5 medium-size garlic cloves, minced
- 6 to 8 red, orange, and green bell peppers, chopped (about 4 cups)
- ¼ cup sun-dried tomatoes, chopped (page 216)
- 1 jalapeño (page 70) seeded and minced
- ½ teaspoon dried oregano
- 1 teaspoon salt
- ¼ teaspoon freshly ground black pepper
- 6 ounces thin spaghetti, cooked according to package instructions and drained
- 8 large eggs
- ½ cup freshly grated Parmesan cheese
- ¼ cup fresh parsley, minced
- 1 tablespoon fresh basil leaves, minced
- 1 tablespoon minced fresh basil

In a large ovenproof skillet, heat the olive oil over medium-high heat. Add the onions, garlic, jalapeño and bell peppers, and cook over moderately high heat, stirring frequently, until the vegetables begin to brown, taking care not to burn. Season with the sugar, oregano, half of the salt and black pepper. Preheat oven to 350°F. Add the cooked spaghetti to the skillet and toss well. Cook, stirring occasionally, until the pasta is lightly browned, about 10 minutes. In a medium bowl, beat the eggs with ¼ cup of water and the remaining salt and black pepper. Stir in ¼ cup of the cheese and 2 tablespoons of the fresh parsley and the fresh basil. Pour the egg mixture over the pasta and stir with a fork to distribute evenly. Cook without stirring until the eggs are set around the edges. Place in the oven and bake until the eggs are set, about 10 minutes. Slide the frittata onto a platter and cut into wedges. Toss together the remaining ¼ cup cheese and 2 tablespoons parsley and pass separately. Serve with a tasty sauce such as Salsa Cruda (page 174), Pepita Salsa Verde (page 178), Chipotle Sauce (page 180) or your choice.

GREEN-CORN TAMALES

These mouth-watering tamales are made with fresh corn and wrapped in the green, undried shucks. You have to eat them to believe how good they are.

Makes About 28 2½- to 3-Inch Tamales

- Green shucks from a dozen large ears of corn
- 5 cups fresh corn kernels (7 to 8 ears); dent or flint corn, if possible
- ½ cup margarine
- ¾ cup Monterey Jack cheese, cubed
- ¾ cup mild Cheddar cheese, cubed
- 1¼ cup Masa Harina
- 1½ teaspoon salt
- 6 large green New Mexican Chiles, roasted, seeded, peeled and chopped, or 24-ounce can chopped New Mexican Chiles
- ¾ cup chicken stock (this may not be needed)

In the field, when the milk in the corn sets it is called "green-corn." It is the first edible corn-on-the-cob stage of soft Indian corn, dent corn, or flint corn. It is never a sweet corn such as 'Golden Bantam.' Buy a few extra ears of corn in order to have enough good shucks. If you must use sweet corn, add 1 teaspoonful of corn starch for each ear of corn because field corn has much more starch than sweet corn. With a cleaver, chop off the stem end, remove the ugly outer shucks. Carefully remove the others to keep them whole. Using kitchen scissors, trim the pointed ends of each shuck. To make the shucks more pliable, some tamale makers bring a pot of water to a boil, drop the shucks in and turn the heat off, leaving them in the hot water until they are ready to be filled. At that time, the shucks are removed and drained. The shucks should not dry out before being filled. Unlike regular tamales that use dry shucks, the masa is not spread on the fresh shucks. Leave the last several husks on the extra corn to keep it from drying out before you use it.

Hold each ear in a deep bowl and cut the kernels from 7 to 8 ears, enough to have 5 cups. Cream the margarine in a food processor, taking care to scrape the sides of the bowl several times. Add 4 cups of the corn, the cheese, masa, salt, and a little of the stock if the mixture is too thick (it must not be runny; the type of corn used will determine the consistency). Blend until smooth. Coarse chop reserved cup of cut corn; mix it and the chiles into the smooth mixture but do not process again.

To fill the shucks, spread a husk out so that it will curl over the filling. Place about 2½ tablespoons of the filling in the center of the shuck lengthwise. Fold the sides in over the filling and then fold the ends up. Stand the tamales in a steamer or colander, folded ends down. Place the steamer or colander in a pot with enough water to come just below the bottom of the steamer. The tamales should not be standing in water. Cover and place over high heat. When the water comes to a boil, lower the heat to a simmer, and steam the tamales for about 1½ hours. Take care not to let the steamer run out of water. Using tongs, transfer the tamales from the steamer to a serving platter and serve hot. Serve with a table sauce such as: Green Chile (page 178), Salsa Cruda (page 174), or Chipotle (page 180).

Tamales freeze well if wrapped properly. Put cool tamales in a plastic bag, close tightly. Wrap in freezer paper and seal. Label and date the package.

RED CHILE PASTA

Bryan Broadfoot, Bon Vivant

Brian Broadfoot, a native Texan, is a retired Sperry Rand executive who spends time between homes in Austin and San Miguel de Allende, Mexico, taking classes in gourmet cooking and delighting his guests with his skills. Pasta making is his specialty. You'll need a pasta machine for this.

Makes 4 Servings

- 1 teaspoon olive oil
- 1½ cups all-purpose flour, or more as needed
- ½ teaspoon salt
- 2 large eggs
- 1 tablespoon water, or more as needed
- ½ cup Gebhardt's Chili Powder or an available chili powder

Combine all the ingredients in a large mixing bowl and mix until it has the consistency of fine meal. Adjust the water or flour as necessary to make the mixture stick together when kneaded. Knead the dough by hand for 5 minutes; cover and let rest for 30 minutes.

Set the pasta machine to the thickest setting. Work

a quarter of the dough through the pasta machine at one time, taking care to cover remainder with a damp cloth. Repeat 8 times, then gradually reduce the thickness. Hang the processed pasta to let it rest and air dry for 20 minutes before cooking.

Place the pasta in a large pot of rapidly boiling water. Cover and boil until *al dente (*tender but still firm); this cooks very quickly. Serve with your favorite sauce in a contrasting shade of red. Experiment with colors and flavors for desired effect. See the sauce section beginning on page 169.

GREEN CHILE PASTA
Bryan Broadfoot, Bon Vivant
Here is another of Broadfoot's special pastas.

Makes 4 Servings

- 1 7-ounce can Herdez Salsa Verde or Salsa Verde with Tomatillos (page 99)
- ¼ cup fresh spinach, finely chopped; tightly packed
- 2 large eggs
- 1½ teaspoons olive oil
- 2½ cups all-purpose flour
- 1 teaspoon salt

Strain the salsa through cheesecloth to remove all the seeds. Place it in a small saucepan over medium-high heat and reduce it to 2 tablespoons. Place the spinach and eggs in a blender and pureé. Combine the salsa and pureé with all the other ingredients in a large mixing bowl. Mix until it has the consistency of fine meal. Adjust the water or flour as necessary to make the mixture stick together when kneaded. Knead the dough by hand for 5 minutes; cover and let rest and air dry for 30 minutes. Set the pasta machine to the thickest setting. Work a quarter of the dough through the pasta machine at one time, taking care to cover remainder with a damp cloth. Repeat 8 times, then gradually reduce the thickness. Hang the processed pasta and let rest for 20 minutes. Place the pasta in a large pot of rapidly boiling water. Cover and boil until tender but still firm (this cooks very quickly).

Serve with your favorite sauce or a pesto in a contrasting shade of green. Experiment with colors and flavors for desired effect. See the sauce section beginning on page 169.

ROASTED PEPPER AND GOAT CHEESE PASTA
Paula Lambert, Owner/Cheese Master
Paula Lambert (page 147) is one of the leading cheese authorities in America and the co-owner of the Mozzarella Company in Dallas, Texas, which produces traditional cheeses along with Paula's innovative creations.

Makes 4 Servings

- 3 to 5 bell peppers, preferably 2 green, 2 red and 1 yellow, roasted (page 87), peeled, seeded, and cut into long strips
- 1 garlic clove, peeled and minced
- 10 fresh basil leaves, cut in very thin strips
- ¼ cup extra virgin olive oil
- 1 pound spaghetti or bucatini
- 5 to 6 ounces fresh Dallas goat cheese (Mozzarella Company)

Toss the peppers with olive oil, garlic, and basil. Cook pasta in boiling water until tender but still firm, *al dente*. Drain and toss with the goat cheese. Add the pepper mixture and toss gently. May be served warm or at room temperature.

PASTA FROM HELL
Chris Schlesinger, Chef/Owner/Author
Schlesinger has been the Chef/Owner of the East Coast Grill in Cambridge, Massachusetts since 1985. In the 1980s he discovered chillies in Barbados and has been challenged by them ever since. He is co-author of The Thrill of the Grill.

Makes 4 Servings

2 tablespoons olive oil
1 red bell pepper, small dice
1 yellow onion, small dice
3 bananas, small dice
1 cup pineapple juice
  Juice of 3 oranges
  Juice of 2 limes
1 tablespoon habanero or Scotch bonnet peppers or 2 to 3 tablespoons fresh jalapeños, seeded and finely chopped
8 ounces fettucini
  Salt and freshly ground black pepper to taste
¼ cup chopped fresh cilantro
¼ cup grated Parmesan

Heat the oil in a large nonreactive saucepan over medium heat. Add the bell pepper and onion and cook, stirring, for four minutes. Add bananas and juices and cook until soft, 4 to 6 minutes. Remove from the heat and add cilantro and chillies. Cook the fettucini in boiling salt water until *al dente*, and add to mix. Season and garnish with the cheese and serve.
NOTE: It takes at least 2 jalapeños to equal 1 habanero; adjust to taste. The amount of chillies given here is but one-fourth of that used in the original recipe.

PENNE PASTA WITH CHILLIES AND SUN-DRIED TOMATOES
Nancy Gerlach and Dave DeWitt, Food Journalists/Authors
The Chile Pepper Magazine *just could not have been without Nancy and Dave. They went on to write several cookbooks and numerous articles on hot and spicy cooking. No cooking is required to make this tasty pasta sauce.*

Makes 6 Servings

¼ cup crushed red New Mexican Chile (page 92) flakes
½ cup sun-dried tomatoes, cut in slivers (page 216) and soaked in 2 tablespoons olive oil
1 cup black olives, cured in oil, pitted and halved
½ cup fresh basil leaves, chopped
½ cup fresh parsley, chopped
1 teaspoon dried marjoram
3 garlic cloves, peeled and minced
½ cup olive oil
2 teaspoons freshly ground black pepper
¾ pound Parmesan cheese, grated
1 pound penne pasta

Combine all the ingredients, except the cheese and pasta, and let sit at room temperature for a couple of hours or overnight to blend the flavors. Cook the pasta in 4 quarts of salted water until tender but still firm *al dente*. Drain. Toss the pasta with the sauce and cheese until well coated and serve.

SOUTHWESTERN PEPPER TART
Rollie Blackwell, Chef/Owner
Tired of pizza? Prepare one of Blackwell's (page 108) innovative gourmet tarts—this one with peppers.

Makes 12 to 14 Servings

3 tablespoons unsalted butter or margarine
1 small poblano, finely chopped
1 small red bell pepper, finely chopped
1 small purple bell pepper, finely chopped
5 green onions (scallions), finely chopped
3 large eggs, beaten
2 cups heavy cream or 1 cup each lowfat milk and yogurt
   Salt and freshly ground black pepper to taste
8 ounces Chile Ancho cheese (see note page 147), grated, or substitute Monterey Jack, grated with 2 teaspoons of chopped anchos (page 74)
1 ear fresh corn, kernels cut off
2 ripe Roma tomatoes, sliced thinly
2 tomatillos, husked and sliced thinly
2 tablespoons cilantro (fresh coriander) or parsley, chopped

Melt the butter in a medium-size saucepan over medium heat. Add the poblano, bell peppers, and onions; cook, stirring, until softened. In a large bowl, combine the eggs, the cream, salt, pepper, and grated cheese. Pour the egg mixture into a 9 x 13 x 2-inch baking dish, or into 2 glass pie plates. Top them with the sautéed peppers, corn kernels, slices of tomatillo, tomatoes and cilantro. Bake in a preheated 375°F oven for approximately 30 minutes, or until set. Cut into squares or triangles to serve. You can sprinkle cayenne pepper on if you so desire.

GREEN NEW MEXICAN CHILE QUICHE
Real men will like this quiche!

Makes 6 to 8 Servings

3 tablespoons butter or margarine
1 tablespoon vegetable oil
½ cup leeks, including the green top, minced
1 tablespoon flour
4 large mushrooms
1 canned jalapeño, seeded and minced (optional)
4 large eggs
1 cup half-and-half cream
6 ounces Monterey Jack cheese, chilled
¼ teaspoon freshly ground black pepper
½ teaspoon salt
1 teaspoon dry mustard
1 pre-baked, 10-inch deep-dish pastry shell
3 to 4 fresh green New Mexican Chiles, peeled (page 71), seeded, and opened flat, or 1 small can whole green New Mexican Chiles, seeded
2 tablespoons fresh parsley leaves, minced
1 teaspoon dried oregano
½ red bell pepper, seed and sliced into rings

Heat the butter and oil in a skillet and wilt the leek over medium-high heat. Stir in the flour and warm it, but do not let it cook. Remove the skillet from the heat. Stir the mushrooms and jalapeño into the leek mixture. With a fork, mix the eggs and half-and-half together in a large bowl and blend in the leek mixture, cheese, pepper, salt, and mustard.

Cover the bottom of the baked pastry shell with the opened and flattened chiles. Pour the egg mixture over the chiles only to ¼ inch from the top. Sprinkle the top with the oregano and parsley. Place red pepper rings decoratively on top. Bake in a preheated oven at 375°F for 40 minutes, or until the top is well colored. Transfer the quiche to a rack and let it stand 15 minutes before serving. Can also be served at room temperature.
VARIATION: Minced cooked ham can be spread on the baked pastry shell before layering the chiles. The quiche filling can be baked without a crust in a well-greased shallow 4-cup baking dish. Sprinkle the bottom of the dish with ¼ cup of the shredded cheese. Ladle the filling over the cheese and bake as described in the master recipe.

Sauces

S auces are any kind of liquid or semi-liquid seasoning for food. They may or may not use spices. The ancient Latin word for broths or soups (sauces) was "juices" or *ius* in singular form. The French *sauce* and the Spanish and Italian *salsa* succeeded *ius*. Sauce is derived from the Latin for salted, *saltus*. Humans first seasoned their food with salt, then sauces. During the evolution of sauces, only the more-or-less liquid consistency has remained relatively constant, with taste being the unlimited element. Obviously there are many categories of sauces to accommodate myriads of concoctions, and their variations which have been incorporated into virtually every cuisine. In medieval European households, sauces were mainly served with foods preserved by brining and pickling to make them more palatable in a period without refrigeration and with slow transportation. In most of the rest of the world they were used as a vehicle for legumes, vegetables, and/or meat, which were served with the local starch—rice, maize, manioc, potatoes, pasta.

When one thinks of French cuisine, sauces are probably the first thing to come to mind. However, the art of sauces came to France when Catherine de Médicis (1485–1536) married the French king Henry II in 1533 and brought her Italian cooks with her as part of her entourage. The French do not have a monopoly on sauces, only a greater variety of them—perhaps. Some French sauces and techniques have migrated to Latin America, where you can be certain peppers have been added. Capsicums are no longer strangers to French-type sauces found in nouvelle, Southwestern, Nuevo Tex-Mex, and Cajun cuisines.

Gravies are sauces made just before serving to accompany meat. They utilize the fat and browned drippings of cooked meat along with a thickening agent and a liquid—stock, vegetable juices, milk, water. The English-type gravy uses flour for the thickener, but cookery in other cultures may use vegetable purée, cornstarch, or root starches such as potato or arrowroot. Gravies serve as the basis for many Indian dishes which use different combinations of chillies and spices according to the desired outcome. Although no longer commonly used in France, in the fourteenth century French cooks served birds and other meats with a *grané* made with cooked juices or drippings. Today we call it gravy because a medieval English transcriber copied the *n* in the French *grané* as *v*. The addition of chillies does wonders for your everyday gravy (McGee, 1984:328).

Sauces can be cooked or uncooked, hot or cold, sweet or sour, spicy or mild, thick or thin, smooth or lumpy, emulsified or thickened with a starch or gelatin—almost anything goes. Sauce is incorporated into many dishes in Latin America, China, India, Africa, and the Far East. Each of those areas has some form of chilli sauce served as a table sauce to be consumed at the discretion of the user. In Latin America these uncooked table sauces or salsas are traditionally added to food after it is cooked, or served as a condiment instead of being incorporated in the dish as are other sauces such as *adobo*—a chilli-vinegar marinade; *recado*—a simple to elaborate ground herb and spice mixture similar to garam masala; *mole*—elaborate, richly flavored sauces flavored and thickened with chillies; and *pipián*—sumptuous sauces thickened with ground seeds and/or nuts.

Elisabeth Lambert Ortiz is probably the leading authority on table sauces throughout the world—certainly on those using peppers. She sent me pepper seed and sauce recipes from her travels so that I could grow the correct peppers to test sauces collected on her travels. I also collected regional sauce recipes during my own travels and have adapted them to American kitchens so that you can have a wide range to choose from and compare.

Sauce in Spanish is *salsa*. It now refers to almost any chunky, pungent sauce you put on your food or dip into; however, in the beginning of its usage in the United States it referred to a chunky sauce made with tomatoes, onions, and chilli peppers—serranos or jalapeños. At home it can be uncooked or cooked, but bottled or canned salsas must be cooked. Today there are sour and sweet salsas made of fruits, vegetables, beans, or combinations of them, but all contain chilli peppers of one or more types.

In the U.S.A. the manufacture of salsa began in 1947 when the Pace family started bottling a salsa picante in the back of their store in San Antonio, Texas. Pace Salsa Picante became the top selling salsa in the U.S. Since then the use of salsa has exploded, and by 1992 it had become the number one condiment in dollar sales in the U.S.A. There are almost as many books telling you how to make salsas as there are types of salsas, and the uses of them have become unlimited.

The sponsor of a salsa-making contest called me for a list of the types of sauces to include in the competition so that in fairness to the sauce's creator the jury would not judge one type against another. It is not easy to codify pepper sauces. In her authoritative work on Latin American cookery, Ortiz surmises that if codification could be done, it would probably complicate rather than simplify matters (Ortiz, 1979:310). The sauce recipes that follow are divided into two major categories—table sauces and incorporated sauces. Within those two groups are cooked and uncooked sauces. By the way, I did not accept the sponsor's invitation to judge the contest, because I remembered the tears and fits of coughing, gagging, and often pain that accompanied my testing all the peppers I grew during the years I worked on *Peppers: The Domesticated Capsicums*. It did not promise to be a "fun" afternoon.

A word about uncooked sauces. Hand chopping of all uncooked, fresh ingredients is recommended. If a blender or food processor is used, it is very easy to overprocess the ingredients, thereby destroying the desired texture. Some of the vegetables, especially tomatoes, will become frothy and pale. Well-drained canned tomatoes can be chopped in the food processor because cooking has taken place during the canning process.

Sauces are extremely important to capsicum cookery. That old saying, "Sauce for the goose is sauce for the gander" ain't necessarily so. Most of these sauces are more specialized than that. To remove the fear of making sauces, refer to: Harold McGee's *On Food and Cooking*, Sallie Williams's *Complete Book of Sauces*, Lady Maclean's *Sauces and Surprises*, Montagné's *Larousse Gastronomique*.

I wish I had said what Kathy Gunst did about pepper sauces in her book *Condiments*: "A really good hot sauce takes you by the shoulders, gives you a good shake, and slaps your mouth to say HELLO."

BRAZILIAN CHILLI SAUCE
Elisabeth Lambert Ortiz, Author

Elisabeth Lambert Ortiz is a widely traveled Englishwoman whose husband was an official of the United Nations. Extended stays in each country allowed her to make in-depth studies of its cuisine. Their first duty station in Mexico resulted in The Complete Book of Mexican Cooking. *That was followed by books on the cooking of Japan, Latin America, the Caribbean, and the Iberian peninsula. Her intense and continuing interest is in the effects of New World foods on Old World kitchens. One of the principal unifying ingredients of the cuisines examined in those works is peppers—she is probably the paramount authority on their usage in foods of the world. The peppers used in Brazil are the small, very, very hot Malaguetas (probably Capsicum frutescens) not usually available here. Any small chilli can be substituted. I have found pickled Caribbean peppers, usually from Jamaica or Trinidad, to be a good substitute, but you can use chiltepínes.*

Makes ½ Cup

6 to 8 chiltepínes (page 64) or 3 to 4 hot red or green
    chillies, stemmed
  1 medium-size onion, chopped
  1 garlic clove, peeled and minced
      Salt to taste
  ½ cup fresh lime or lemon juice

Crush the peppers, onion, and garlic with the salt using a mortar and pestle, adding the lime juice little by little, or pureé in a blender or food processor. Serve in a bowl to accompany meat, poultry and fish, and dried bean dishes. Use with caution.

CHILEAN PEBRE

Elisabeth Lambert Ortiz, Author

Each Latin American country has a basic pepper table sauce that varies from country to country.

Makes about 1 Cup

- 1 medium-size onion, quartered
- 1 garlic clove
- 2 tablespoons fresh cilantro
- 1 tablespoon fresh parsley
- 1 or more fresh green chillies, seeded (serranos, jalapeños)
- 3 tablespoons olive oil
- 1 tablespoon lemon juice
  Salt to taste

Combine all the ingredients in a food processor. Mince but do not pureé. Let stand for about 1 hour before serving for the flavor to develop. Serve with any meat.

BOLIVIAN LOCOTO SALSA, LLAJWA

Llajwa is the ubiquitous, pungent table sauce of Bolivia where the Rocoto, called Locoto there, is king of all peppers. I went into several kitchens in both homes and hotels where this salsa is made fresh daily to see just how it was made. In most homes it is still made with the batan, *or grinding stones. In more modern kitchens a blender is used but this is always recognizable because the sauce is smoother and somewhat frothy.*

Makes about 1 Cup

- 3 Roma tomatoes, seeded and quartered
- 1 small red onion, or leek, chopped
- 2 rocotos (page 76), seeded and chopped or 4 serranos (page 78) or jalapeños (page 70), seeded and chopped
  Juice of 1 fresh lime
  Several cilantro (fresh coriander) sprigs
  Salt to taste

Place all the ingredients in a food processor and pulse several times until it is almost a pureé but still has some texture. Take care not to over-process and make the sauce frothy.

NOTE: Sauces made with fresh tomatoes in a blender or food processor become quite frothy or foamy, which is not a desirable texture.

A *batan* is similar to a metate but is made of a larger, smoother stone and the grinding stone is much larger and heavier. Most are too large to be moved about.

IXNI-PEC
YUCATECAN HABANERO SAUCE

Elisabeth Lambert Ortiz, Author

This table sauce from Yucatan, Mexico, is not only extremely hot but is flavorful as well, unlike piri-piri which is just concentrated fire. The sauce, pronounced schnee-peck, is served separately from the dishes it accompanies, appearing on tables in small bowls to be used at the diner's discretion. The pepper used is the golden habanero. The Jamaican Scotch bonnet and the dátil have a similar flavor as well as a comparable degree of heat. Use freshly made.

Makes about 1 Cup

- $\frac{1}{4}$ cup onion, chopped
- $\frac{1}{4}$ ripe tomato, peeled, seeded, and chopped
- $\frac{1}{4}$ habanero (page 69), seeded and chopped
- $\frac{1}{4}$ cup Seville (bitter) orange juice or substitute a mixture of 1 part orange juice to 2 parts fresh lime juice
  Salt to taste

In a bowl combine all the ingredients, seasoning with salt. Serve whenever a chilli sauce is called for.

ECUADORIAN CHILLI SAUCE

Elisabeth Lambert Ortiz, Author

This table sauce is also used in Costa Rican homes, even though historically they do not use peppers in their food.

Makes ½ Cup or More

> Fresh red or green chillies (serranos, jalapeños, ají, Thai; see index), seeded and slit
> Red onion, finely chopped or cut into small, thin strips
> Fresh lime or fresh lemon juice
> Salt to taste

Seed the peppers and cut them into fine strips. Combine the peppers with an equal amount of onion in a glass container. Add lime juice to cover. Season with salt and let the stand for 3 to 4 hours before using. Dilute with hot water if desired.

SALSA CRUDA

This is the most commonly used condiment/table sauce in Mexico and it goes by many names—Salsa Picante, Ranchero Salsa, Pico de Gallo—but it is mighty good no matter what it is called.

Makes 1 to 1½ Cups

> 1 medium-size ripe tomato, finely chopped
> ½ medium-size onion or 2 to 3 green onions (scallions or leeks), finely chopped
> 6 sprigs fresh cilantro (fresh coriander), stemmed and minced
> 1 garlic clove, peeled and minced
> 3 serranos (page 78), finely chopped (or jalapeños, Fresnos; see index)
> ½ teaspoon salt
> ¼ teaspoon sugar, a pinch
> ⅓ cup fresh lime juice or half vinegar and half water

Mix together in a bowl. Make fresh daily for the desired fresh crunchy taste. If any is left over it can be simmered with a little oil in a saucepan over medium heat for a few minutes and used over eggs. If you keep the uncooked sauce in the refrigerator longer than the day that is made it is no longer "salsa cruda." You can eat it, but it is not the same. Please call it something else.

IBERIAN PIRI PIRI

Elisabeth Lambert Ortiz remarks that "the pepper family has naturalized itself so ingratiatingly into the Old World that the hottest pepper sauce I have ever encountered comes from Portugal, Molho de piri-piri. Piri-piri sauce is made from a pepper with wanderlust, an immigrant from Brazil that became naturalized in Angola and finally migrated to Portugal to become that nation's favorite." The dried red piri-piri pepper is called jindugo in former Portuguese Africa. It is sold in Portugal in two sizes, the tiny 1-inch long type that is like the Brazilian malagueta pepper (probably Capsicum frutescens, not to be confused with melegueta pepper or Grains of Paradise from Africa's west coast) and a larger variety, about 3 inches long. Both are extremely hot. Many households simply put the whole, stemmed, dried red peppers in a glass jar, filling it about a third full of peppers, then topping it off with olive oil. The sauce is left to mature for a week or so.

Makes about 1½ Cups

> 6 3-inch piri-piri peppers (page 93), stems removed (*chiltepíns* or any tiny chilli)
> 1 cup olive oil
> ¼ cup mild vinegar such as distilled white or cider vinegar
> ½ teaspoon coarse salt

Chop the peppers coarsely and pack them into a glass jar. Add the oil, vinegar and salt and shake or stir to mix. Cover tightly and store for about 2 weeks before using. Shake before each use. As well as the homemade piri-piri sauce there is a commercial bottled sauce.

SPANISH ROMESCO SAUCE

Elisabeth Lambert Ortiz, Food Writer

This cold sauce is used primarily with fish and shellfish but is also good with vegetables and grilled meats. It comes from Tarragona, south of Barcelona, and is Catalonia's most famous sauce. In Spain, the peppers used are either the romesco, a long thin, smooth-skinned pepper, or the round, smooth-skinned ñora (nyora in Catalan); both are dark red and closely resemble the Mexican guajillo, which gives a most beautiful red color to any food cooked with it, but you can substitute the dried red New Mexican Chile. The sauce should not be fiery, but should be slightly hot. Dried hot red chillies, such as chiltepínes or japonés, seeded, are added to the sauce to add piquancy. There are many versions of romesco sauce. This is a fairly standard one.

Makes about 2 Cups

- ½ cup red wine vinegar
- 2 dried *ñoras* or *romescos* or red New Mexican Chiles (page 71), seeded
- 1 to 2 hot dried red chillies, seeded (japonés, de árbol, Thai, Chiltepín; see index)
- 1 cup extra virgin olive oil
- 2 slices French-type bread, cut ½-inch thick
- 2 medium-size ripe tomatoes, peeled, seeded and chopped
- 4 garlic cloves, peeled and minced
- ½ cup almonds, blanched, toasted, and ground
- 1 ounce hazelnuts, toasted and ground
  Salt to taste

Soak all seeded peppers in warm water until they are soft, about 30 minutes. Drain, pat dry on paper towels and chop coarsely. Set aside. Heat ¼ cup of the oil in a small skillet and fry the bread until it is golden on both sides. Lift out to drain on paper towels and chop coarsely. Set aside. Add the ripe tomato and garlic to the oil remaining in the pan and sauté 3 to 4 minutes. Remove from heat and allow to cool. Place the tomatoes, parsley, chillies, garlic, almonds, and hazelnuts in a blender with the remainder of the oil and the vinegar and process until well-mixed. Tear the bread into pieces and add to the blender and pureé into a smooth, thick sauce. The sauce should have some texture. Season with salt and pepper. If desired, thin with tomato juice or water as more vinegar will make it too sour and more oil separates out. Let the sauce sit for at least 2 hours before serving then stir or beat lightly before using.

Keep tightly covered in the refrigerator for several weeks. No need to limit this thick, red sauce to fish—try it on chicken, veal, pork, or as a spread for bread.

AFRICAN HOT SAUCE

African countries, like Latin American countries, each have a blistering chilli sauce for the table which will vary from country to country. African chillies are especially pungent.

Makes 2½ Cups

- 1 12-ounce can tomato sauce
- ¼ cup chopped onion
- 1 garlic clove, peeled and minced
  Juice of 1 lemon
- 2 to 8 small fresh red chillies (Thai, chiltepín, cayenne, or jalapeño; see index)
- 1½ teaspoons grated fresh horseradish

Put all the ingredients in a blender or food processor and pureé. Store in a tightly covered jar in the refrigerator. Serve with meats, poultry, or fish.

VARIATION: Add 1 tablespoon to 1 cup of mayonnaise and use as a dressing for seafood or poultry salads.

JAVANESE SAMBAL

Sambals are pungent chilli sauces indigenous to Indonesia but varying from island to island.

Makes ½ Cup or More

- ¼ whole coconut, peeled
- 3 fresh green chillies (Thai, serrano)
- ½ teaspoon shrimp paste or mashed anchovy
- 1 garlic clove
- ¼ teaspoon palm sugar (or brown sugar)
- 1 tablespoon tamarind or fresh lime juice
  Salt to taste

Pound all ingredients together into a paste or mix in a blender.

BORNEO SAMBAL

In Kalimantan (Borneo) this sambal is made fresh daily. Serve as a table sauce with everything.

Makes ½ Cup

- 5 green chillies (Thai, serrano)
- 1 shallot or green onion
- 1 garlic clove
- ¼ teaspoon shrimp paste or anchovy
- ½ teaspoon brown sugar
- 1 small lime, juiced
- ¼ teaspoon salt

Boil the whole peppers for 6 minutes; drain. Pound all the ingredients together in a *molcajete* (mortar) to make a creamy paste or pureé in the blender.

MAGHREB HARISSA

In the Maghreb—a collective term for Morocco, Tunisia, and Algeria—this indispensable sauce may be called Harissa, Tchermila, or Charmoula. It is used in cooking as a seasoning for stews (tagines) and couscous, as a table sauce, or as a marinade for fish.

For the Paste

Makes ½ Cup

- 1 ancho, soaked, seeded and chopped
- 4 tablespoons dried cayennes, japonés, de árbol or any red chilli (see index)
- 6 garlic cloves, peeled
- 1 teaspoon caraway seed
- 1 teaspoon coriander seed
- 1 ground cumin (comino)
  Salt to taste
- ¼ cup olive oil, more if necessary to make a smooth paste

Soak the chillies in hot water to cover for 1 hour; drain and chop. Place in blender or spice mill with the garlic and spices and purée. Season with salt. Place in a tightly covered jar. It will keep in the refrigerator for several weeks.

For the Sauce

Makes 1 Cup

- 1 cup olive oil
- ½ cup wine vinegar
- 1 teaspoon Harissa Paste, or more if desired
- 1 tablespoon sweet paprika
- 1 tablespoon fresh lemon juice
- 1 tablespoon fresh parsley, minced
- 1 tablespoon cilantro (fresh coriander), minced

Place all ingredients in a small saucepan over high heat and stir until warmed through but do not boil. Remove from the heat and beat well; pour into small sauce dish. Serve immediately with grilled chicken or meat.
NOTE: In Morocco the sauce is primarily used as an overnight marinade for small white fish, which are then drained and dredged in flour before frying in oil or baking.

BANANA PEPPER SAUCE

This sauce is not pungent and can be served cold with fish, tongue, or veal. When your garden is full of Banana Peppers, try this sauce.

Makes about 2 Cups

- 1 medium-size onion, chunks
- 1 cup cooked English peas
- 3 small ripe tomatoes, cut into chunks
- ½ teaspoon dried oregano
- ¼ teaspoon dried thyme
- 3 fresh or pickled yellow Banana Peppers (yellow bell pepper, 'Cubanelle' or any sweet ethnic type)
- 1 tablespoon vegetable oil
- 3 tablespoons vinegar
- 1 tablespoon capers, rinsed and drained
- 12 green olives, pitted and sliced

Combine all the ingredients except the capers and olives in a blender. Process until creamy. Stir in the capers and olive slices. Store tightly covered in the refrigerator, but use within the week.

JAMES T'S FLAME SAUCE

W. C. Longacre, Chef/Owner

Longacre (page 143) did not reveal who James T. is, but that does not affect the taste of this delicious sauce, which is a great condiment on eggs, grilled meats, or as a dip for chips.

Makes 3 Cups

- ¾ cups water
- 12 habaneros (page 69) or dátils (page 66), seeded and chopped
- 2 cups fresh papaya, seeded, skinned, and medium-chopped
- 1 teaspoon dry mustard
- 3 fresh jalapeños (page 70), seeded and minced
- 1 large red onion, finely chopped
- 2 large ripe tomatoes, medium-chopped
- 1 teaspoon ground cayenne pepper
- 1 teaspoon freshly ground white pepper
- 2 tablespoons fresh oregano, minced
- 1 tablespoon fresh parsley, minced
- 1 tablespoon fresh cilantro (fresh coriander) leaves, minced
- 1 tablespoon fresh basil leaves, minced
- 2 tablespoons balsamic vinegar
- 1 tablespoon salt
- 2 tablespoons dark brown sugar, firmly packed
- 2 tablespoons garlic cloves, peeled and minced

Place all the ingredients in a saucepan and bring to a boil. Reduce the heat to medium and simmer for 3 to 4 minutes. Allow to cool, covered, overnight in the refrigerator before using. This sauce should last several weeks if kept refrigerated in a tightly closed container.

ROASTED SERRANO SALSA

Mark Miller, Chef/Owner/Author

This table sauce is one of the salsas which made Mark (page 105) famous.

Makes 3 Cups

- 6 serranos (page 78)
- 1 pound ripe roma tomatoes, finely diced
- 2 tablespoons sweet red onion, minced
- ¼ cup fresh orange juice
- 2 tablespoons yellow bell pepper, seeded and very finely diced
- 2 tablespoons cilantro (fresh coriander), finely chopped
- 1 tablespoon rice vinegar (page 98)
- ½ teaspoon salt
- ½ teaspoon sugar

Cook the serranos in a black iron skillet over medium-high heat cook until blackened. Remove about half of the blackened skin, and then chop finely. Mix together with all the remaining ingredients. Let stand for 1 hour. Cover, and refrigerate until ready to serve.

NEW MEXICAN CHILE SALSA VERDE

This is a green table sauce to be spooned onto eggs, meat, or what-have-you.

Makes 1 Generous Cup

6 to 8 canned or fresh green New Mexican Chiles
　　(page 71), roasted (page 87), peeled and seeded
　1 teaspoon jalapeños, fresh or canned, seeded and
　　chopped
　1 garlic clove, peeled and crushed
　½ teaspoon salt
　1 tablespoon cilantro (fresh coriander) leaves,
　　chopped
　2 tablespoons onion, chopped
½ to 1 teaspoon olive oil
　¼ teaspoon sugar

Place the chiles and garlic in the bowl of a food processor and pulse for a few seconds until the mixture is puréed but still has texture. Add the other ingredients and pulse the processor several times. Season with salt. Serve at room temperature. This salsa keeps well for several days covered in refrigerator.

VARIATION: Jalapeño Salsa Verde; substitute canned pickled jalapeños (*en escabeche*) for the green chiles or use fresh jalapeños with 2 tablespoons vinegar or lime juice.

PEPITA SALSA VERDE

Another wonderful sauce for chicken enchiladas (page 161) but without the acidity of tomatoes or tomatillos.

Makes about 4 Cups

2 to 4 tablespoons pumpkin seeds (*pepitas*)
　1 cup green New Mexican Chiles (page 71)
　2 fresh serranos (page 78), seeded (optional)
　¾ cup fresh parsley, roughly chopped
　1 garlic clove, peeled
　　All-purpose flour, if needed
　3 cups chicken stock
　¼ cup vegetable oil
　　Salt and freshly ground black pepper to taste

Toast pumpkin seeds (page 101) until browned or use toasted pumpkin seeds (*pepitas*). Pureé the *pepitas*, chiles, garlic, and parsley together in a blender. Add a little flour if a thicker sauce is desired. Add a little of the chicken stock and process, then strain through a sieve. Heat the oil in a medium-size saucepan over medium heat. Add the strained mixture and remaining stock to the hot oil, heat thoroughly and serve.

SALSA VERDE WITH GREEN CHILES AND TOMATILLOS

This versatile sauce is excellent for chicken enchiladas, or to use as a table or a dipping sauce.

Makes 2 Cups

　1 13-ounce can tomatillos (page 99) or 8 large
　　fresh, husked and washed
　½ cup fresh green New Mexican Chiles (page 71),
　　peeled and seeded and chopped, or 1 4-ounce
　　can; measure after chopping
1 to 2 serranos, (page 78) seeded (optional)
1 to 2 garlic cloves, peeled and crushed
　1 tablespoon cilantro (fresh coriander) leaves,
　　chopped
　½ teaspoon salt
　¼ teaspoon sugar

If using fresh tomatillos, steam until just tender. Pureé the tomatillos with the chiles, garlic, cilantro and salt in a blender. This can be used as is or it may be simmered with a tablespoon of olive or vegetable oil for a few minutes and served hot.

NOTE: When using this sauce for chicken enchiladas (page 161), use Monterey Jack cheese instead of cheddar and top with a dollop of sour cream. Garnish with *pepitas*.

VARIATION: when using as a dipping sauce add 1 or 2 avocados, peeled, seeded, and mashed. Stir in well.

BASIC RED CHILLI PASTE

This is a paste to keep in the refrigerator to use as a base in many different recipes. It really saves time to have it on hand.

Makes 2 to 3 Cups

    2   cups water for soaking peppers, reserve
    4   anchos (page 74)
    2   guajillos (page 68)
    2   chipotles (page 70)
    1   large onion
    4   garlic cloves, peeled
    2   teaspoons ground cumin (comino)
    2   teaspoons ground oregano
    1   teaspoon salt

Soak the chillies in hot water to cover about 1 hour. Remove from the water and remove the seeds, stems, and veins. Reserve 2 cups of the soaking water. Place all the ingredients in a blender and process until it is a smooth, thick paste. Use the soaking water as needed. Store in a tightly covered jar in refrigerator for several weeks or freeze. Use to flavor sauces for chilaquiles (page 141), enchiladas (page 161), and other dishes.

RED NEW MEXICAN CHILE SAUCE

To be used over enchiladas (page 161), or anything.

Makes 4 Cups or More

    2   tablespoons vegetable oil
    1   tablespoon margarine
    2   tablespoons all-purpose flour
    ¼   teaspoon ground cumin (comino)
    ½   cup fresh ground red New Mexican Chile (see page 71)
    1   cup cold water
2 to 3 cups chicken stock
    1   garlic clove, peeled and minced
        Salt to taste

Heat the oil and margarine; add the flour, stirring constantly until it reaches a deep golden color—almost scorched but not quite. Remove from heat. Add the cumin. Mix the ground chile with the cold water until there are no lumps. Whisk it into the flour paste off the heat. Return to heat and slowly add stock.

Simmer for 15 to 20 minutes, stirring frequently. Add the garlic and season with salt to taste. Simmer 5 minutes longer. If lumpy, run in blender for a few seconds.

This sauce will keep well for a week in the refrigerator. Use over enchiladas, chiles rellenos, burritos, or anything.

TEX-MEX ENCHILADA SAUCE

The browned flour is a tasty Texas twist.

Makes 3 to 4 Cups

    8   anchos, guajillos, or dried New Mexican Chiles (see index) or some of each
    2   tablespoons ground cumin (comino)
    2   teaspoons dried oregano
    1   medium-size onion, chopped
    2   garlic cloves, peeled and minced
    3   tablespoons vegetable oil
    2   tablespoons all-purpose flour, browned
    1   6-ounce can tomato paste
    2   cups water or beef or chicken stock
        Salt and freshly ground black pepper to taste

Wash the peppers. Cover with boiling water and let stand at least an hour but no longer. Drain and reserve water. Remove stems, seeds, and veins. In a blender purée the peppers, spices, garlic, and onion with a cup (more if needed for desired consistency) of strained soaking water.

In a skillet, heat the oil over medium heat, add flour and stir until smooth and golden brown. Add pepper paste, tomato sauce, and remaining water. Simmer about 30 minutes or until thickened. Season with salt and pepper.

NOTE: If you have a jar of Basic Red Pepper Paste (page 179) use ½ cup or more, if desired, instead of going through the steps, using the first 5 ingredients, to make a paste.

NOTE: I like to use already browned flour which I keep on hand in a tightly covered jar in the refrigerator. The real Tex-Mex flavor comes from flour that has been browned almost to the scorching point. It is a rather tedious process of constant stirring and watching, so brown at least a cup each time.

CHIPOTLE BARBEQUE SAUCE

This sauce differs from the Count's Chipotle Sauce (page 184). It is to be served hot over grilled or barbequed meats.

Makes 4 Cups

- 2 tablespoons vegetable oil
- 1 medium-size onion, chopped
- 2 garlic cloves, peeled and crushed or pressed
- 1 16-ounce can solid-pack tomatoes, chopped
- 1 12-ounce can tomato sauce
- 1 chipotle (page 70), chopped, or to taste
  Salt to taste

In a medium-size saucepan over medium heat, heat the oil. Add the onion and cook, stirring, until clear. Add the remaining ingredients and cook 15 to 20 minutes.

HOMEMADE 'TABASCO' SALSA

For authentic flavor grow your own true Tabasco peppers; however other small, fresh, ripe, red chillies may be substituted. The true Tabasco pepper seed is not commercially available but several seed houses sell 'Greenleaf Tabasco'. This is not a fermented sauce as is the original McIlhenney product.

Makes 1 Cup

- 3 dozen fresh, large Tabasco (page 78) or small, red chillies
- 5 garlic cloves, peeled
- 1 cup Herbed Chilli Vinegar (page 215), or cider vinegar
- 1 teaspoon salt
- 1 teaspoon sugar

In a small nonreactive saucepan, cook the peppers and garlic in the vinegar until tender. Place in a blender with the salt and sugar and purée. Run through a sieve if necessary. Dilute this paste with spiced vinegar until it is the consistency of rich cream. Pour into a nonreactive saucepan, bring to a boil, then pour into hot, sterilized (page 206) bottles to within ½ inch of the rim, wipe the rim clean and seal with a scalded top. Store in the refrigerator once opened.

VARIATION: Substitute any ripe, red chilli for the tabascos, such as serrano, jalapeño, or cayenne, and use dry sherry instead of the vinegar for a mellow sauce. Proceed as directed.

CASCABEL CHILE AIOLI

Stephen Pyles, Chef/Owner/Author
Aioli is garlic mayonnaise. Pyles (page 119) makes this thick sauce something special.

Makes 1 Cup

- 2 large egg yolks
- 1 tablespoon red wine vinegar
- ½ cup corn oil
- ¼ cup olive oil
- ¼ teaspoon ground cascabel (page 61)
- ¼ teaspoon ground sweet paprika
- ¼ teaspoon ground New Mexican Chile (page 71)
- ¼ teaspoon ground cayenne pepper
- ½ teaspoon salt
- ½ shallot, minced
- 1 small garlic clove, peeled and minced
- 1 teaspoon fresh lime juice

In mixing bowl, whisk together the egg yolks and vinegar. Combine the two oils. Continue to whisk and drizzle the oils into the yolks. Add remaining ingredients and whisk just long enough to combine thoroughly. This can be prepared in a blender as you do mayonnaise. Aioli combines well with fish.

CHILE ANCHO AND HAZELNUT MOLE
Greg Higgins, Executive Chef and Manager
The traditional Mexican mole sauce is a very long drawn out affair. Higgins's (page 117) simplified version is hard to beat.

Makes 3 to 4 Cups

8 anchos (page 74)
2 red jalapeños (page 70), roasted (page 87), peeled and seeded
4 ripe roma tomatoes, peeled and seeded
1 cup hazelnuts, toasted
4 garlic cloves, peeled and browned in a little hot oil
2 cups chicken stock
½ teaspoon ground cinnamon
1 teaspoon ground cumin (comino)
1 tablespoon dark unsweetened cocoa powder
Salt and freshly ground black pepper to taste

Wash the anchos in cold water, then remove stems and as many of the seeds as possible. Soak in warm water until soft. Purée the anchos, jalapeños, tomatoes, hazelnuts, and garlic in a food processor. Add stock as needed to facilitate the purée. Add the cinnamon, cumin, and cocoa powder and continue processing. Add more chicken stock to thin to a sauce consistency. Season with salt and pepper.

Serve the mole with enchiladas of chicken or pork, or as a condiment with grilled poultry or pork dishes. Thinned with oil, it makes an excellent marinade for grilled items.

FOURTH STREET GRILL'S CHIPOTLE MOLE SAUCE
Susan Nelson, Chef/Owner
Although this rich Chipotle Mole Sauce was designed to go over Susan's pork loin (page 131), it is splendid on any grilled meat or chicken dish.

Makes 2 Quarts

5 pasillas (page 72)
5 mulatos (page 74)
3 anchos (page 74)
3 dried New Mexican Chiles (page 71)
1 can chipotles *adobado* (page 70)
4 tablespoons garlic cloves, peeled and minced
3 tablespoons ground cinnamon
2 teaspoons ground clove
4 ounces Mexican sweetened chocolate
1 cup golden raisins
1 cup whole almonds
1½ cups fresh orange juice, or to cover
Chicken stock as needed
Salt to taste

Briefly rinse and remove the stems of the first four chiles listed. Put all the ingredients except for the orange juice, chicken stock, and salt into a large non-reactive saucepan. Pour the orange juice over the other ingredients to cover and bring to a boil. Turn off the heat and let the mixture sit until all the dried chiles are softened, about 20 minutes.

Purée the contents of the pot in a blender (in batches if necessary) and strain through a sieve into a heavy-bottomed saucepan. Thin the sauce with a little chicken stock, until the consistency of heavy cream. Place the sauce over low heat and simmer for no less than 1 hour, thinning as needed. Season with salt.

This sauce can be easily kept in the refrigerator for weeks in a covered container. Serve with chile stuffed pork loin or grilled meats.

PORTUGUESE STYLE RED PEPPER PASTE FOR MEATS

Allow extra sauce so the cook won't eat it all up before the dish is prepared.

Makes 1¼ Cups

    8   large red bell peppers, roasted, seeded, and peeled
    2   jalapeños or serranos (page 70, 78), roasted and seeded
2 to 3 large garlic cloves, peeled
    6   tablespoons olive oil
    1   teaspoon salt, or to taste

Place the peppers, salt, garlic, and half the oil in a blender jar and process until smooth. Slowly add remaining oil and blend until the consistency of whipped cream. Place in a jar; seal tightly; store in refrigerator.

When ready to use as a dry marinade for poultry, pork, or lamb, allow paste to return to room temperature before rubbing on all sides of the meat. Allow the rubbed meat to sit several hours or overnight. Scrape off excess before cooking.

PONTCHARTRAIN SAUCE

Tony Beckwith, Chef/Manager

This tasty Cajun sauce is a favorite of Tony Beckwith, a native of Argentina, who has been with Green Pastures for more than fifteen of its forty-five years. That widely acclaimed restaurant founded by Mary Faulk Koock, a great cook, food writer and friend, in the historic 1894 Faulk house, is still owned and operated by a member of the Koock clan.

Makes 8 Cups

    4   cups chicken stock
    4   cups beef stock
    ½   cup (1 stick) butter or margarine
    ½   cup all-purpose flour
    2   large green bell peppers, seeded and chopped
    2   large red bell peppers, seeded and chopped
    2   white onions, chopped
    1   bunch green onions (scallions), chopped
    4   garlic cloves, peeled and minced

    1   pound shrimp, blanched until just pink, shelled, and chopped into bite-size pieces
    1   pound uncooked crab meat, picked over for crab shell
        Salt and freshly ground black pepper to taste
    1   teaspoon thyme
    1   teaspoon red chilli flakes
    ½   cup sherry
    1   tablespoon fresh parsley, minced

As Cajun cooks always say, first make a roux. Heat the stocks together in a medium-size saucepan. In a large saucepan melt the butter over medium heat. Add the flour to the butter and stir constantly. When the roux is an aromatic, nutty brown, gradually add the heated stocks. Stir until the consistency of a heavy gravy. Allow to simmer on low heat, stirring as needed, and strain before use.

In a large heavy skillet or Dutch oven, sauté the peppers, garlic and onions in a little butter over medium heat until soft and translucent. Add the shrimp and season with salt, pepper, thyme, and hot red pepper flakes. Add the strained roux. Simmer 10 minutes. Add the crab and sherry. Continue to simmer for 5 minutes. Garnish with parsley and serve over grilled or sautéed fillets of red snapper or redfish.

GREEN NEW MEXICAN CHILE PESTO

A Southwestern answer to Italian pesto. Use in any recipe calling for pesto or serve as an appetizer on French bread or crackers.

Makes 1 to 1½ Cups

    6   fresh green New Mexican Chiles (page 71), peeled (page 87), seeded, and chopped
    ½   cup olive oil
    2   cups packed well-washed fresh spinach, chopped
    ½   cup chopped fresh parsley
    2   garlic cloves, peeled
    2   teaspoons chopped fresh or dried basil
    2   tablespoons pine nuts or sunflower seeds
        Salt to taste

In a blender, purée all the ingredients to make a smooth sauce. Thin with water if necessary.

RACY PESTO SAUCE

A South Texas answer to Italian pesto. Use in any recipe calling for pesto. Make it when your garden's basil is rampant.

Makes 6 Servings

 2   cups fresh basil leaves, washed
 2   garlic cloves, peeled and minced
 ½   cup olive oil
 ½   cup Parmesan cheese, freshly grated
 ¼   cup sunflower seed or pumpkin seeds (*pepitas*), toasted
 1   serrano (page 78), seeded, or to taste
 ½   cup water
 ¼   cup heavy cream
     Salt and freshly ground black pepper to taste

Blanch the basil leaves and garlic in boiling water for a few seconds. Roll in a towel to remove water. Place the basil, olive oil, Parmesan, serrano, sunflower seed, garlic, and the olive oil in a blender. Purée until very smooth. Season with salt and pepper to taste. Pour the sauce into a saucepan; stir in the cream. Heat without boiling. Serve the sauce over freshly cooked pasta. Toss to mix and serve with grated Parmesan.
NOTE: Omit the cream and serve as a dip with raw vegetables, on sliced tomatoes, or on crusty Italian bread. It will keep in a tightly sealed container in the refrigerator for a couple of weeks.

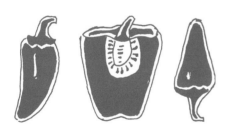

ZESTY POPPY SEED DRESSING

This is delicious on fruit salads of any kind, but has a special affinity for grapefruit and in combinations where grapefruit is present.

Makes 3½ Cups

 1½   cups sugar
  2   teaspoons dry mustard
  1   teaspoon salt
  ¼   cup white or cider vinegar
  1   thick slice of onion
  1   serrano (page 78), seeded or 1 teaspoon ground cayenne pepper
  2   cups vegetable oil (do not use olive oil)
  3   tablespoons poppy seeds

Mix the sugar, mustard, salt, and vinegar in a blender. Add the onion and serrano and purée thoroughly. Add the oil slowly, processing constantly at medium speed, and continue to beat until thick. Add the poppy seeds and process for a few minutes. Store in the refrigerator. Stir before using.

CREAMY SERRANO DRESSING

This is a fairly thick dressing. Not only is it great for salads but it is also delicious with boiled shrimp or as a dip.

Makes ¾ Cup

   1   teaspoon Dijon mustard
   ¼   teaspoon dried tarragon
   1   garlic clove, peeled
   ¼   teaspoon sugar
 1 to 2   serranos or 3 to 4 green chiltepínes or jalapeños (see index)
   3   tablespoons fresh lime juice (never bottled)
   1   egg yolk, uncooked
 2 to 3   parsley sprigs
   ½   cup olive oil

In a blender, combine the mustard, tarragon, garlic, sugar, chillies, salt, and black pepper. Process. Blend in the egg yolk, parsley, and lime juice. Pour the oil in very slowly. Keep well covered in the refrigerator. Use within a week.

CHIPOTLE MAYONNAISE

Donald Counts, MD and Kathryn O'Connor Counts, Authors

Donald and Kathryn Counts (page 122), have written A Texas Family's Cookbook, *which is based on her family's culinary heritage as one of the oldest of the legendary South Texas ranching families.*

Mayonnaise

Makes 4½ Cups

- 1 large egg
- 1 large egg yolk
- 1 teaspoon dry mustard
- 1 tablespoon fructose (page 99), (honey or corn syrup) to taste
- 1 teaspoon freshly ground white pepper, or to taste
- 1 teaspoon ground cayenne pepper
- 4 teaspoons white wine vinegar or fresh lemon juice
- 4 cups vegetable oil, or as needed

Place all the ingredients except the oil into a blender and blend at high speed for 2 minutes. Slowly dribble in oil until desired consistency is reached (the machine will begin to slow down). Add extra pepper or fructose to taste.

NOTE: The key to success in making this cold sauce in a blender is using fresh eggs and adding oil in a slow, steady stream. If it should separate, remove it from the blender and wash and dry the blender, then add another egg yolk and a teaspoon of paprika or parsley flakes to the blender and process for a second or two, then slowly dribble in the separated mayonnaise.

ALTERNATIVE: The harried cook can cheat by adding the Salsa Chipotle to "store-bought" mayonnaise.

Salsa Chipotle

Makes about 4 Cups

- 4 chipotles (page 81) *adobado*, canned, to taste
- 1 28-ounce can whole tomatoes
- 6 to 8 fresh basil leaves
- 1 small white onion, quartered
- 1 tablespoon vinegar, optional

Place all the ingredients in a blender, including some liquid from peppers, and purée well. Keeps well in refrigerator if tightly closed.

To Finish Mayonnaise Sauce

- ½ cup Salsa Chipotle, or to taste Mayonnaise

Fold salsa into mayonnaise and serve as a dip for boiled shrimp or other seafood or as a spread for sandwiches.

BETTER'N ANYTHING

Can't eat vegetables unless they are wallowing in cheese sauce or hollandaise? Now you can! This sauce is not only flavorful but also healthy, beautiful—full of vitamins and color—and easy. Use it instead of mayonnaise on salads and sandwiches. Pick the color of peppers to compliment the vegetable's color. Try it on baked potatoes; your kids and guests will love it. Also a wonderful dip for vegetables at your next party.

Makes 2 Cups

- 6 medium bell peppers, all the same color; roasted, skinned, and seeded
- ½ cup olive oil
- 1 cup plain yogurt, "lite" or no-fat
- 2 serranos (page 78) or jalapeños (page 70), seeded and chopped
  Salt and freshly ground black pepper to taste

Place all of the peppers and oil in a blender and process until smooth. Add the yogurt and process until just blended. Season with salt and pepper. Serve on hot or cold vegetables or pour sauce on a plate; arrange the vegetables on top. Garnish with fresh greens and/or paprika. Tightly cover and store in the refrigerator for up to a week.

NOTE: The roasting not only imparts flavor but provides the neccessary cooking. Don't skip the process. This mixture can be thinned down to the consistency of soup with milk, water, or broth, and served chilled as a refreshing appetizer.

SMOKY APPLE CHILLI SALSA

Want to impress your friends? Here is an easy way to make them think you had to work hard to make something that tasted so good. Great on creamed cheese with Ritz® type crackers.

Makes 6 to 8 Cups

- 5 large green jalapeños (page 70), roasted (page 87), peeled, and seeded
- 2 large green bell peppers (page 60), roasted, peeled, and seeded
- 3 Chiltepínes, crushed or 1 teaspoon ground cayenne pepper
- 1 cup cider vinegar
- 4 garlic cloves, peeled and crushed
- 1 tablespoon liquid smoke extract
- 1 teaspoon salt
- 2 tablespoons corn starch
- 1 50-ounce jar of prepared applesauce
- 1 cup apple juice or water

Place all the peppers and the next 5 ingredients in a blender and purée. In a large, 2- to 3-quart saucepan place the applesauce and add the juice or water, and contents of the blender, and mix well. Bring to a boil over high heat, stirring. Reduce heat to medium low and simmer until desired consistency. Store in the refrigerator in tightly closed containers for up to three weeks.

For longer keeping, put the boiling salsa into clean jars and seal with scalded lids. Process in a boiling water bath for 15 minutes according to directions on page 206. Remove from water bath, tighten lids, and cool on racks out of a draft.

GREEN NEW MEXICAN CHILE BUTTER

Jamie Morningstar, Chef

Morningstar's (page 158) pretty butter is a guest pleaser and nice to keep on hand.

Makes ½ Pound

- 1 4-ounce can of diced green New Mexican Chiles (page 71) (drain off excess liquid)
- ½ pound (2 sticks) unsalted butter or margarine at room temperature (see note below)
  Salt and freshly ground black pepper to taste

Combine all the ingredients in a food processor and pulse a few times to get mixture going. Then let the machine run until all ingredients are well mixed. Butter will be a light green color.

NOTE: If using margarine, make sure it is well chilled.

RED NEW MEXICAN CHILE BUTTER

Jamie Morningstar, Chef

This reddish colored butter makes a good partner to serve with Morningstar's (page 185) Green New Mexican Chile Butter.

Makes ½ Pound

- 1 teaspoon dried New Mexican Chile (page 71), crushed
- 1 tablespoon garlic, peeled and chopped
- ½ pound sweet butter or margarine at room temperature
  Salt and freshly ground black pepper to taste

Combine all the ingredients in a food processor and pulse a few times to get mixture going. Then let the machine run until all ingredients are well mixed.

NOTE: If using margarine, make sure it is well chilled. Serve this butter with grilled New York steak, salmon, chicken, or anything else that you may want to try.

PANCETTA CHILI BUTTER

Patricia Windisch, Chef
Patricia Windisch is the executive chef at the Beringer Vineyards in St. Helena, California, and has been a cooking instructor in Tokyo, Japan, and in California. This butter is wonderful on grilled steak, salmon, chicken, or anything else you may want to try.

Makes ½ to 1 Cup

- ½ cup (1 stick) unsalted butter or margarine, softened
- 1 slice pancetta, ½ inch thick, diced (see below)
- 2 shallots, minced
- 3 garlic cloves, blanched for 3 minutes, peeled and mashed
- 1 fresh red New Mexican Chile (page 71), peeled, seeded, and diced
- ½ red bell pepper, seeded and diced
- 2 teaspoons Tabasco Pepper Sauce®
- ¼ teaspoon freshly ground black pepper
- 1 tablespoon fresh chives, minced
- 1 tablespoon fresh lemon juice
  Salt to taste

Sauté the pancetta in a small skillet until browned. Remove from the skillet to paper towel and cool. In the same skillet, sauté the shallots until translucent. Cool, then combine with the rest of the ingredients. Place on a sheet of plastic wrap and shape into 1-inch cylinder. Refrigerate.

Remove from refrigerator 30 minutes before serving and slice into ¼-inch rounds.

NOTE: Pancetta is a very peppery Italian bacon. Substitute any good bacon, but increase the black pepper to ½ teaspoon.

SPICY BEER BATTER

This batter is a delightful light, puffy coating for fish, chilli rellenos, shrimp, or anything that needs to be batter-fried. I like it better than tempura batter.

Makes 8 to 10 Servings

- 1 cup all-purpose flour
- 1 teaspoon baking powder
- ½ to 1 teaspoon ground cayenne pepper
- 1 teaspoon paprika
- ½ teaspoon salt
- 1 8-ounce can of light beer
  Vegetable oil

Sift all of the dry ingredients together in a large mixing bowl. Just before you are ready to fry the food, add the beer and mix well but do not beat. Dip the pieces of food to be fried into the batter one at a time. Heat enough vegetable oil to cover the food pieces in a deep skillet over high heat until a little sample of the batter sizzles. Lower the food into the oil a few pieces at a time—too many at one time will lower the temperature below the optimum for frying—and cook until golden on all sides turning as necessary. Remove the food from the fat with a slotted spoon or pancake turner and drain on paper toweling. Serve at once.

Breads

SERRANO AND BLUE CORN MUFFINS

Stephen Pyles, Chef/Owner/Author

Texas own super-chef, Stephen Pyles (page 119), created this variation of the American pioneer's standby—cornbread.

Makes 12 Muffins

- $\frac{1}{2}$ cup (1 stick) butter or margarine
- 6 tablespoons vegetable shortening, oil, butter, or margarine for sautéing
- 3 serranos (page 78), stemmed, seeded, and diced
- 1 green bell pepper, seeded and diced
- 4 tablespoons red onion, diced
- 3 garlic cloves, peeled and minced
- 1 cup all-purpose flour
- 1$\frac{1}{2}$ cups blue cornmeal (page 95) or yellow corn meal, if necessary
- 2 tablespoons sugar
- 1 teaspoon salt
- 1 tablespoon baking powder
- 2 large eggs
- 1 cup buttermilk, at room temperature, mixed with a pinch of baking soda
- $\frac{1}{2}$ cup heavy cream
- 3 tablespoons cilantro (fresh coriander), chopped

Lightly butter and flour 2 muffin tins. In a saucepan, melt the butter or margarine and shortening. Set aside to cool. Heat a little butter in a small saucepan over medium heat. Add the peppers, onion, and garlic and sauté, stirring, until the onion is clear. Set aside. In a large mixing bowl, sift together the dry ingredients and set aside. In a separate bowl, beat the eggs lightly and add melted butter or margarine and shortening. Stir in the buttermilk, cream, cilantro, peppers, and onion. Add the liquid mixture to dry ingredients and beat just until smooth; do not overmix. Pour the batter into the muffin tins and bake in a preheated 375°F oven for 12 to 15 minutes.

MAMIE'S JALAPEÑO CORNBREAD

Mary "Pud" Lauderdale Kearns, Specialty Food Business/Author

Mary Kearns is probably the only person ever named after a fruit cake. She grew up in her parents' multimillion-dollar mail-order food business "Mary of Puddin Hill, Inc." in Greenville, Texas, where she is vice-president of marketing and director of new product development. Her book, The Puddin Hill Cookbook *is a delightful compilation of her family's recipes and stories. The 500°F cooking temperature in this recipe is no mistake. A meal by itself!*

Makes 8 Servings

- 1 cup grated American or cheddar cheese
- 2 tablespoons pickled jalapeño peppers, drained and chopped
- 1$\frac{1}{2}$ cups yellow cornmeal
- 2 tablespoons baking powder
- $\frac{1}{2}$ teaspoon salt
- 2 large eggs, beaten
- 1 cup buttermilk
- 3 tablespoons shortening, melted, or vegetable oil
- 1 17-ounce can cream-style corn
- 1 4-ounce can chopped green New Mexican Chiles (page 71), hot or mild

Combine the cheese and jalapeños; set aside. In a large bowl, blend cornmeal, baking powder and salt. Combine eggs, buttermilk and shortening or oil in a small bowl and mix thoroughly. Add to dry ingredients, stirring until just blended. Stir in corn and green chiles. Generously grease a 10-inch iron skillet with shortening and place in preheated 500°F oven for 5 minutes. Pour the batter into the hot skillet. Sprinkle the reserved cheese and jalapeño mixture over the batter. Bake for 15 minutes. Remove and let stand 5 minutes before cutting. The cornbread should be very soft in the center and it does not have the texture of regular cornbread. You may substitute more green New Mexican Chiles for the jalapeños if your system is not up to the heat!

EASY JALAPEÑO CORN BREAD

This should not be a sweet cornbread. My family loved it topped with stewed tomatoes and lots of butter—real country style. Another country favorite is cold, left-over cornbread crumbled into a glass of sweet milk and eaten with a spoon—called "crumble-in" or "crumblin."

4 to 8 Servings (depending on appetite)

   3 canned or pickled jalapeños (page 70), drained and chopped
1½ cups yellow stone-ground cornmeal
  ½ cup all-purpose flour
  1 teaspoon granulated sugar, or up to 1 table-spoon depending on taste
  ½ teaspoon baking soda
  1 teaspoon salt
  2 teaspoons baking powder
  2 large eggs, at room temperature
  1 cup buttermilk
  1 tablespoon vegetable oil
    Vegetable oil to grease pan

In a mixing bowl, combine the cornmeal, baking soda, sugar, flour, salt, and baking powder; set aside. In a separate bowl, mix the eggs, buttermilk, and oil; stir until smooth and creamy. Add the jalapeños and mix. Stir liquid into cornmeal-flour mixture. Blend with spoon to form smooth batter but do not overstir. Grease 9" pan (preferably cast iron) with oil and preheat the pan in 400°F oven. Remove from the oven and pour batter into hot pan. Return to oven and bake for 20 to 30 minutes or until a wooden toothpick inserted in the corn bread comes out clean. Cut and serve immediately.

FRENCH TOAST CALIENTE
International Connoisseurs of Green and Red Chile

This New Mexican group used to put out a newsletter that had recipes in it. Try this one for Sunday brunch.

Makes 4 to 6 Servings

  2 large eggs
  ½ teaspoon salt
  1 cup milk
  ½ teaspoon pure vanilla extract
  1 tablespoon mashed canned jalapeños (page 70)
6 to 8 slices bread (try French or sourdough)
    Vegetable oil, optional

Beat the eggs lightly, then add salt, milk, vanilla, and jalapeño; mix well. Dip the bread into the mixture and brown on both sides in heated vegetable oil in a skillet or on a grill over medium heat. Serve with your favorite syrup, honey, Chilli Pepper Jelly (page 220) or Capsicum Marmalade (page 219).

CHILE AND CHEESE SCONES
Susan Deaver, Chef

Susan Deaver is pastry chef for Cody's Café in Berkeley, California.

Makes 12 Scones

2½ cups white flour
  1 cup whole wheat flour
  2 tablespoons brown sugar, firmly packed
  2 tablespoons baking powder
  1 teaspoon baking soda
  1 teaspoon salt
  ¼ cup bran
  ¾ cup (1½ sticks) cold butter or margarine, cut in small pieces
  1 fresh green jalapeño (page 70), seeded and chopped, or substitute Santa Fe Grande (page 76)
  1 red 'Fresno' chilli (page 67), seeded and chopped
1½ cups dried currants or cranberries

6 ounces Asiago, Parmesan or Romano cheese, cut in small cubes

2 large eggs

1 cup plain yogurt

1 large egg, beaten

Into a large mixing bowl, sift together the flours, sugar, baking powder, baking soda and salt. Stir in the bran. Rub the butter in with your fingertips, until mixture resembles coarse crumbs. Add the chillies, currants, and cheese. In a separate small bowl, whisk the eggs and yogurt together and stir into dry mixture. If necessary, add more yogurt to make a soft dough. Drop by large spoonfuls onto greased baking sheet. Brush with beaten egg. Bake in a preheated 350°F oven 10 to 12 minutes.

EASY CUBAN CONFETTI BREAD
This colorful bread can be made in a food processor—great for the novice bread maker.

Makes 2 Loaves

1 package dry yeast

2 cups lukewarm water

2 teaspoons salt

1 tablespoon sugar

½ teaspoon ground cayenne pepper

6 to 7 cups all-purpose white flour

3 tablespoons dehydrated green New Mexican Chile or green bell pepper flakes

2 tablespoons crushed red pepper flakes

2 tablespoons white corn meal

Dissolve the yeast in the water. Add the sugar and salt. Put flour and cayenne in food processor and pulse 2 to 3 times (can be mixed in a mixer with dough hook). Pour liquid down funnel gradually. Process until it forms a ball. After dough is formed but no sooner (adding too soon will pulverize flakes), add pepper flakes; pulse only until well-distributed throughout dough ball, taking care not to pulverize the pepper flakes. Put in greased bowl and cover with a clean cloth. Turn oven to 110°F and place dough in oven and let rise until doubled (temperatures above 120°F

will kill the yeast), about 1 hour. Turn the oven off.

Remove the dough from the bowl. Cut the dough in half and shape in two long loaves. Slash the tops. Place on a shallow baking pan that has been dusted lightly with corn meal. Place a bowl of boiling water in cold oven. Place bread in cold oven then set at 400°F. Bake until done (about 40 to 45 minutes). Cool on rack.

CHEESE BITES
Keep a well-wrapped roll of this dough in the freezer for emergencies.

Makes 24 or More

2 pounds sharp Cheddar cheese, grated, at room temperature

½ pound butter (2 sticks) or margarine, at room temperature

3 cups all-purpose flour

½ teaspoon freshly ground black pepper

4 teaspoon salt

5 teaspoons ground cayenne pepper

In a processor or mixer, process the ingredients until they are creamed. Roll in long roll and wrap in wax paper. Chill thoroughly. Slice or use a cookie press. Arrange, with space between each, on an ungreased cookie sheet. Bake in a preheated 400°F for over 7 minutes or until just barely brown. Take care not to overbrown. Serve as an appetizer or with soups and salads.

VARIATION: A half a cup of finely chopped nuts or Post Grapenuts Cereal can be worked into the dough after it is creamed.

Desserts

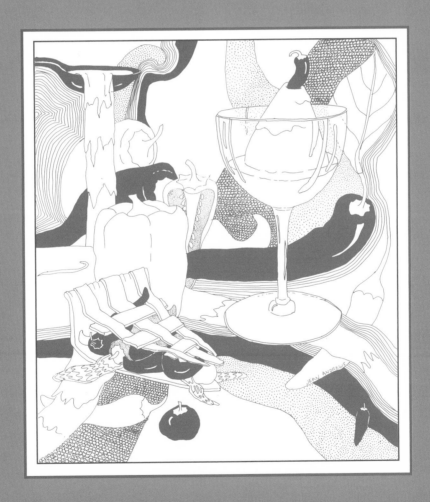

HONEYDEW COMPOTE WITH LIME, GINGER, AND A HINT OF SERRANO
John Ash, Chef/Owner/Food Journalist
John Ash's (page 153) refreshing dessert is easy and great after a heavy meal.

Makes 6 Servings

- ½ cup fresh lime juice
- 2 teaspoons grated lime peel
- ½ cup water
- ⅓ cup sugar
- 1 tablespoon fresh ginger, peeled and minced
- ½ teaspoon serrano, seeded and finely slivered
- 1 teaspoon fresh mint, finely slivered
- 1 large honeydew melon (3 pounds or so), seeded and cut from the rind in uniform shapes
  Fresh figs and mint sprigs for garnish

Combine the fresh lime juice, peel, water, sugar, ginger and serrano slivers in a small saucepan. Bring to a boil, reduce heat and simmer for 5 minutes until sugar is dissolved. Cool. Strain before using. To serve pour syrup over melon and, if possible, allow to marinate refrigerated for at least 1 hour. Garnish with slices of fresh fig and the fresh mint.

Also very nice garnished with a slice or two of good proscuitto or Bayonne ham.

ANCHO FUDGE SAUCE
This "to die for" dessert sauce is homage to Helen Corbitt, my mentor.

Makes 3 cups
- ½ cup butter or margarine, but not lite
- 2¼ cups confectioner's sugar
- ⅔ cup evaporated milk
- 6 ounces (squares) bitter-sweet chocolate
- ½ teaspoon salt
- 1 tablespoon ancho powder, more to taste (page 90)
- 1 cup pecans, walnuts, or almonds; toasted and chopped (optional)

Mix butter and sugar in top of a double boiler or a microwave proof bowl; add the milk, chocolate, salt, and ancho. Cook over hot water for 30 minutes or in microwave for 10 to 15 minutes. Do not stir while cooking. Remove from the heat and beat. Store well-covered in the refrigerator and reheat as needed. For a thinner sauce add cream, never water. Serve over ice cream (try mocha or peppermint) or cake and sprinkle with nuts.

TOASTED CHILE CUSTARD
Kurt Koessel, Chef
Koessel (page 112) does special, very pleasing things with peppers in desserts.

Makes 4 Servings

- 2 large eggs
- 2 large egg yolks
- ⅓ cup brown sugar plus 2 tablespoons, firmly packed
- 2 teaspoons toasted and ground de Árbol (page 63) or japonés (page 81) chilli or ground cayenne pepper
- ¼ teaspoon salt
- 2 cups cream
- ¼ teaspoon pure vanilla extract

In a bowl, whisk together the eggs and egg yolks with the ⅓ cup brown sugar and the salt until just mixed. In a saucepan, scald the cream with the vanilla. Add half the scalded cream to the egg mixture, stirring constantly. Add 1¾ teaspoons of the chilli and combine with the rest of the cream in the pan; cook over low heat, stirring constantly, until the custard coats the spoon. Pour the custard into four 4-ounce ramekins, place in a larger pan filled with water that comes halfway up the sides of the ramekins and bake in a preheated oven at 300°F for 35 minutes or until a knife inserted in the center comes out clean. Cool 3 hours in the refrigerator. When ready to serve, sprinkle approximately ¼ teaspoon of the ground chillies over the top of each custard. Top with a thin layer of sifted brown sugar. Place under the broiler, watching constantly, until sugar is melted but not burned. Serve immediately.

FOURTH STREET GRILL'S CHILE FESTIVAL BROWNIE
Kurt Koessel, Chef

Koessel (page 112) uses the ancient combination of chillies and chocolate, two New World gifts to the Old World, going back to the pre-Colombian period. At that time the Amerindians did not have sugar to combine with their chocolate and chilli. In brownies and other rich chocolate sweets you will find that the addition of a little ground ancho or pasilla will cut the cloying sweetness without adding noticeable pungency.

Makes 10 to 12 Servings

- ¾ cup butter (1½ sticks) or margarine
- 6 ounces semi-sweet chocolate, broken into small pieces
- 3 ounces unsweetened chocolate, broken into small pieces
- 3 large eggs
- ¾ cup sugar
- ½ cup dark brown sugar or ground *piloncillo* (Mexican brown cone sugar), firmly packed
- 2 teaspoons vanilla
- 1 tablespoon commercial chili powder, or a combination of ground ancho (page 74) and dried New Mexican Chile (page 71)
- ½ teaspoon ground cayenne pepper or to taste
- ½ teaspoon ground coriander seed, optional
- ⅛ teaspoon ground cloves
- 1 cup all-purpose flour
- ½ cup raisins, soaked overnight in 1 cup dark Mexican beer and drained
- ½ cup pecans, toasted and coarsely chopped

Preheat oven to 350°F. Combine chocolate and butter in heavy-bottomed pan and cook over low heat just until the chocolate melts. Cool. Beat the eggs in a mixing bowl until they start to thicken. Add the sugars and continue beating until mixture is light and fluffy. Stir in vanilla and chocolate mixture.

Lightly toast the spices in a skillet over low heat, stirring often to be careful spices don't burn. Combine the flour and spices in a bowl with a whisk. Gently stir the dry ingredients into wet ingredients. Drain any excess liquid from raisins. Gently add raisins and nuts, stirring just until combined. Don't overmix.

Pour mixture into a greased and floured, 9-inch round cake pan. Bake just until set, 25 to 30 minutes. Cool in the pan. Turn out and cut into wedges. If desired, dust with confectioner's sugar and serve with vanilla ice cream.

MONTEZUMA'S BROWNIES
Carol Kilgore, Herbalist

My erudite Texas friend, Carol Kilgore, is a wonderful editor who helped me with my books. She is not only an expert herbalist and gardener who allowed me to grow peppers on her farm, but also a respected cook who created this recipe just for this book.

Makes 12 to 16 Servings

- 2 anchos, dried
- 8 ounces (squares) unsweetened baking chocolate, chopped
- 1½ cups pecans, toasted
- ½ cup butter
- ½ cup (1 stick) margarine, unsalted
- 5 eggs
- 2¾ cups sugar
- 1½ teaspoons vanilla
- 1½ cups flour

Select pliable anchos; do not wash. With scissors, stem, seed, and cut lengthwise. Microwave the cut anchos for 2 minutes on high; stir. Continue cooking and stirring at 1-minute intervals until the peppers are crisp, about 5 minutes. Crumble them gradually into an electric spice grinder or blender and reduce to a fine powder. Use 2 tablespoons of the powder in the recipe.

Microwave the pecans on high power for 8 to 10 minutes or until they are crisp but not browned; stir occasionally. Chop toasted pecans coarsely.

In a large bowl, microwave the chocolate, butter, and margarine at 1-minute intervals until just melted; stir occasionally. Remove and continue stirring until chocolate mixture is well blended. Stir in the 2 tablespoons of powdered ancho.

In a large mixer bowl, beat the eggs until light. Add the sugar gradually. Add the vanilla. Stir in the chocolate mixture. Add the flour, beating just to blend. Stir in the pecans. Pour the batter into a 9-inch by 13-inch pan sprayed with non-stick cooking spray. Bake at 375°F for about 35 to 40 minutes until a toothpick inserted into the cake center will come out with moist crumbs. Take care not to overbake. Cool in pan, then cut in rectangles. Serve warm.

NEW WORLD PIE: CHILLIES TO CHOCOLATE PLUS PECANS

The pecans, chocolate, and chillies which make this dessert fit for the gods are all products of the New World. How the Old World must have suffered without them.

Makes 8 Servings

- 1 cup semi-sweet chocolate chips
- 6 tablespoons (¾ stick) butter or margarine cut into pieces
- 2 large eggs, slightly beaten
- ¼ cup plus 1½ teaspoons granulated sugar
- ¼ cup all-purpose flour
- 1 tablespoon of freshly ground ancho, mulato, or pasilla (see note on page 72)
- ¼ teaspoon salt
- 1 teaspoon instant coffee granules
- ½ cup milk-chocolate chips
- 1 cup pecans, coarsely chopped
- 1 9-inch, deep pie crust, lightly baked and cooled
- ½ cup sour cream
  Paprika

Melt the cup of semi-sweet chocolate chips and butter in a heavy medium saucepan over boiling water or in a microwave oven, stirring until smooth, then cool to room temperature. In a mixing bowl, whisk the eggs and sugar until well blended. Whisk in the melted chocolate-butter mixture, then gently fold in the flour, chilli, salt, and coffee until well mixed. Add half of the milk-chocolate chips along with the pecans and stir until evenly distributed. Spread the batter over the cooled crust and bake in a preheated 325°F oven for about 25 minutes until a toothpick inserted in the center comes out clean, taking care not to overcook the pie.

The pie is best served while still warm. Sprinkle the remainder of the milk-chocolate chips on top of the warm pie and cover it tightly with foil. Allow to stand on a rack until ready to serve. Remove the foil and cut into wedges. Serve the slightly warm pie with a dollop of sour cream and garnish with paprika.

NOTE: If the pie is baked ahead of time don't put the remaining chocolate chips on until it is rewarmed. Put it in a preheated 200°F oven until just warm, then sprinkle with the chocolate chips, wrap, and serve as directed above. Leftovers should be heated before serving.

APPLE PIE WITH NEW MEXICAN CHILES

International Connoisseurs of Green and Red Chile

Another great New Mexican recipe to surprise your family and guests with.

Makes One 9-inch Pie

- 5 cups apples, peeled and sliced (not 'Delicious')
- ¾ cup sugar
- 2 tablespoons butter or margarine
- 1 teaspoon ground cinnamon
- ½ teaspoon ground nutmeg
- 2 teaspoons pure red New Mexican Chile, ground (page 71)
- 1 cup water
  Salt to taste
- 1 9-inch, deep pie crust

Combine all ingredients except the crust in a large saucepan and cook over medium heat (this can be done in microwave) until apples are slightly tender and juice is thick, 20 to 25 minutes. Pour into the unbaked pie shell, dot with additional butter or margarine, cover with top crust and cut vents into it (or cover the top with lattice strips of crust) and sprinkle with additional sugar. Bake 30 to 40 minutes in 375°F oven.

ARIZONA CHILTEPÍN ICE CREAM

Gary Nabhan, Botanist/Author, and Muffin Burgess, Native Seeds/SEARCH

Botanist, arid land expert, award winning author, poet, MacArthur Fellow, are but a few of Gary Nabhan's accomplishments. He and Burgess, an expert in tree-ring dating, are among the founders of Native Seeds/SEARCH and the annual Chile Festival in Tucson, Arizona. Both are interested in anything to do with chillies—from growing to eating. This recipe was created for two big Arizona chilli events. When first made, the chilli fumes put a couple of chilli-ignorant kitchen workers in the hospital. The creators warn that "it's so hot that you immediately have to eat more ice cream to cool down your mouth!"

Makes a Bunch

- 1 gallon vanilla ice cream
- ¼ to ½ cup green chiltepínes (page 64) pickled in brine; thoroughly rinsed and puréed

In small batches, blend the ice cream and chiltepines together in an electric blender until green flecks are thoroughly mixed into the ice cream. Firm in the freezer if necessary. Serve small portions.

FROZEN FRUIT DESSERT

For your sweet tooth, a dessert that will not put you completely over the top on calories if you can eat just one small (half-cup) serving.

12 or More Small Servings

- 1 8-ounce package cream cheese or lite no-fat yogurt, dripped (page 101)
- ½ cup sugar or use artificial sweetner to taste
- 3 ½ cups fruit; canned or fresh mango, fresh peaches or nectarines, puréed in blender
- 2 serranos (page 78), seeded and chopped
- 1 teaspoon red pepper flakes, seedless type
- 1 8-ounce carton frozen lite whipped topping, thawed

Place the cream cheese and sugar in the bowl of a food processor with the plastic blade and process until smooth. Gradually add the fruit purée and peppers and pulse until blended. Add heaping spoonfuls of the whipped topping, beating with a spoon, or whip after each addition to combine. Pour the mixture into a 10 x 15-inch pan. Freeze until firm, about 3 hours or overnight. To serve, cut into rectangles and remove with a spatula. Garnish with fresh fruit or edible flowers.

ALTERNATE: Spoon the mixture into individual ½-cup size paper cups and freeze until firm. Run under warm water to remove and serve on a plate with puréed fruit over or under each serving. Garnish with a sprig of mint. Cover unused frozen cups with plastic wrap and keep frozen until needed.

CITRUS-GÜERO SORBET

This refreshing sorbet is a real crowd pleaser.

Makes 8 Servings

- 4 Hungarian Wax or any *güero* (yellow) chilli, seeded and chopped (for flavor with less heat use Banana peppers, yellow bell, or half sweet and half pungent peppers; see index)
- 2½ cups sugar
- 5½ cups hot water
- 8 large oranges, peeled and chopped
- ¼ cup tequila, cointreau, or mixed
- ½ cup fresh lemon or fresh lime juice to taste
- 6 tablespoons light corn syrup

Combine 4 cups of water with the sugar in a saucepan and heat until the sugar dissolves, then bring to a boil. Cool to room temperature, then refrigerate for 2 hours.

Purée the remaining ingredients with 1½ cups water and refrigerate until well chilled, at least 2 hours. Stir the sugar mixture into the fruit. Pour the mixture into an ice cream maker and follow the directions for making ice cream.

Serve the sorbet as a dessert or as a refresher between courses of a large meal.

VARIATION: Use 4 white grapefruit and a drop or two of green food coloring instead of the oranges, and jalapeños (page 70) instead of *guerös*. Jalapeños have a flavor very different from the yellow chillies.

NEW WORLD TRUFFLES

These rich morsels evolved from my New World Pie. Don't eat if calorie counting.

Makes 24 Truffles

1½ cups milk chocolate chips
¼ cup (½ stick) butter or margarine
1 tablespoon finely ground ancho (page 74)
½ teaspoon finely ground cayenne pepper
½ cup no-cholesterol egg product
2 tablespoons Kahlùa liqueur or brandy
  Ground pecans or other nuts

Place the chocolate and butter in the top of a double boiler over barely simmering water. Cover, and let stand until it is partially melted; remove the cover and stir until completely melted. Remove the top pan of the double boiler, keeping the water in the bottom heated. Add the ground chillies and mix well. Stir the egg product into the chocolate mixture and return it to the pan of fully simmering water. Stir the mixture continuously until it is quite hot but not boiling. Continue cooking and stirring for 3 minutes. Remove the boiler top from the heat and add the liqueur gradually while stirring. Set the pan in a large bowl of iced water. Add ice as necessary to keep the water very cold. Stir constantly until the entire mixture forms a fairly firm, nonsticky ball.

Place slightly rounded teaspoonfuls of the candy on a sheet of wax paper and let them dry for 1 to 2 hours, or until firm enough to handle. Put the ground nuts on a sheet of wax paper and roll each truffle in the nuts. Allow the truffles to dry for 30 minutes to 1 hour, then shake off the excess nuts. These truffles will keep for 2 to 3 days at room temperature, but they are best fresh. To keep them up to a week, they may be refrigerated in a tightly closed container but they should be allowed to return to room temperature before serving.

SUNSET JALAPEÑO TRUFFLES

Jerry Di Vecchio, Food Journalist

Upon graduating with a degree in Home Economics and Journalism, Jerry went to work for Sunset magazine and has been there for more than forty years. Now the food and entertaining editor, she has been responsible for all the Sunset food publications. She has been a significant force in shaping the fresh, innovative, and multicultural cuisine of the West that has captured the attention of the nation. These truffles are a spicy surprise!

Makes 25

6 fresh jalapeños (page 70), seeded and minced (not canned or pickled)
¼ cup white vinegar
½ to 1 teaspoon ground cayenne pepper, or more
½ cup granulated sugar
¼ cup (½ stick) butter/margarine, softened
2 tablespoons orange peel, grated
3 cups confectioners' sugar (more or less)
¼ cup unsweetened cocoa powder

In a 1- to 2-quart saucepan, combine jalapeños, vinegar, cayenne, and granulated sugar. Stir until dissolved. Boil without stirring until 220°F on a candy thermometer, 6 to 7 minutes. Remove from heat and let cool for 15 minutes.

In a bowl, beat butter with electric mixer until fluffy. While still beating, add jalapeño syrup and orange zest. Stir in the confectioner's sugar and beat until mixture holds shape when patted into a ball. Add more confectioner's sugar if necessary. Divide into 1-tablespoon portions. Shape into truffles and roll in the cocoa. Place on plate and chill until firm.

ALTERNATES: Instead of rolling in the cocoa, dip the truffle into a dipping chocolate according to directions on the package.

Finely chopped nuts can be worked into the sugar mixture.

ANCHO FUDGE

This is my adaptation of a smooth, rich fudge recipe from the innovative kitchens of Sunset *magazine.*

Makes 3 Pounds

 2 tablespoons butter or margarine, softened
 2 cups half-and-half cream
 4 cups sugar
 ½ cup light corn syrup
 1 teaspoon salt
 ½ to 1 tablespoon ground ancho (page 74), depending on tolerance
 8 ounces semisweet chocolate, chopped (do not use morsels)
 4 ounces unsweetened chocolate, chopped
 1 tablespoon vanilla or rum extract
 2 tablespoons butter
 1½ cup pecan halves, broken

Line a 9-inch square pan with foil. Butter the foil lightly. In a 3- to 4-quart saucepan, mix cream, sugar, corn syrup, salt, and ancho. Place over high heat and boil about 3 minutes, stirring occasionally. Reduce the heat to medium and add the chocolates, stirring gently until melted and mixture begins to simmer. Insert a candy thermometer. Bring the mixture to a boil and stir occasionally until the mixture reaches 235°F or a drop of candy spooned into cold water forms a soft ball, about 30 to 40 minutes. Remove from the heat and add the butter and vanilla, then place the pan with the candy in another pan containing cold water to aid cooling. Let the mixture stand undisturbed until it is cool enough to touch. Using a strong, flat-ended spoon, stir and beat until the candy becomes smooth and glossy and begins to thicken and mound but is still soft and workable. Add the nuts and mix. Scrape the fudge into the foil-lined pan. Let stand until firm. Remove from the pan and remove the foil. Cut the fudge into 1-inch squares and serve. The uncut fudge can be wrapped in airtight plastic or foil and stored at room temperature up to 1 week.

CANDIED CHILLIES

Try these in a drink instead of a cherry.

Yield is Variable

 ½ pound whole small fresh red serranos (page 78), jalapeños (page 70), cascabellas (page 63) or cherry peppers with stems
 1 quart water
 4 cups granulated sugar
   Red food coloring, optional

Place the whole chillies and the water in a saucepan and bring to a boil over medium heat. Reduce the heat immediately and simmer uncovered over low heat for 15 minutes. Add 1 cup of the sugar and continue cooking uncovered over low-medium heat for 15 minutes. Add a second cup of granulated sugar and continue cooking for 30 minutes. Add the third cup of granulated sugar and cook for 30 minutes. Add the food coloring and the final cup of granulated sugar a little at a time while stirring. Put the lid back on and cook for 30 minutes more. Care must be taken not to caramelize the sugar.

Place an oiled rack on a sheet of waxed paper. Remove the chillies with a slotted spoon, and place on the rack, allowing the excess syrup to drip onto the paper. If any stems come off, reattach them. Allow the chillies to sit at room temperature overnight. Store in an airtight container lined with waxed paper.
NOTE: If these are too hot, try to find some ripe, red TAM-mild jalapeños or sweet cherry peppers.

Preserves
& Condiments

We can thank the Arabs for preserves, marmalades, jellies, jams, and those sweet condiments that grace our tables and rot our teeth. The Arabs took over the Greco-Roman practice of conserving fruits in honey, and extended or improved the process with the addition of sugar. Sugar had come to Arabia from India, where the technology of making "raw" sugar originated around 500 B.C., following the introduction of sugarcane (*Saccharum officinarum*), probably from tropical New Guinea (Simpson, 1986:249; Wilson, 1983:1; McGee, 1984:385; Aykroyd, 1967:10). As early as 325 B.C. the Greek geographer Strabo reported that sugarcane was present in India. Sugar was carried westward by the Persians in the sixth century A.D. The Arabs got it from them and introduced the cane to Syria, north Africa, and Spain. The English words "sugar" and "candy" are derived from the Arabic version of the Sanskrit *Sharkar* and *Khandh*, both of which mean "sugar."

The Crusaders were introduced to the new sweet when they took their religious crusade to the lands of the infidels in the Levant. When they returned to their medieval European homelands they took a craving for the new sweetener with them. Nonetheless, only a small amount made its way to Europe via the Middle East and Venice before 1500. Throughout that early period in Europe, honey was the primary sweetener, while the costly imported sugar was reserved for medicinal purposes.

In 1773, only seventy-five years after settlement, Portugal's island of Madeira had become the world's largest producer of sugar (Duncan, 1972:11). That same year the Portuguese introduced sugarcane to their other Atlantic islands to the south where the climate was more suitable for sugarcane culture.

In attempts to meet the demand and bring the price down, sugar cultivation was carried farther and farther west as settlers followed the early explorers to the New World, where highly desired tropical and subtropical crops could grow. The sweltering American sugar plantations were established in order to satisfy the European yearning for sweets, and millions of Amerindians and Africans were enslaved to appease that craving. With all of the new production, the price of that luxury item became somewhat lower, making it possible for people other than the wealthy to enjoy sugar. The amount and the range of sugar usage increased as worldwide sugar production increased. Now it was possible to afford that sweetener for other than medicinal purposes, and sugar-preserved fruits began appearing as a final dessert course.

Not only did sugar effect a culinary change, but it also produced the fortunes that made the Industrial Revolution possible. A considerable addition to those fortunes came from rum, a by-product of the sugar industry, which became the official liquor of the English navy. For a single plant species, one that offers no special benefaction to the health or well-being of humankind, sugar has had an extraordinarily broad influence on Western history (McGee, 1984:388).

Sugar-preserved fruits and syrups had dual roles, first as healing (or therapeutic) potions and later as table delicacies. The knowledge of the making of these fruit confections migrated from the Middle East to medieval Europe, thence from Europe to America. The arrival of the art of making preserves and sweetmeats was the most outstanding addition to gastronomy in Renaissance Europe. Italians were the basic revolutionaries in the realm of preserves, and a significant book on preserving was *Bastiment de recettes*, an Italian publication that introduced the completely unknown art of making preserves, jams, and jellies into France. To me, the dry sandy desert seems an unlikely place, but during the same period, in sixteenth-century Egypt, there was a minor industry in preserves and sweetmeats. In my travels I have observed that speaking Arabic and eating sweets go hand-in-hand—obviously a very longstanding tradition.

During the sixteenth century the job of sweetmeat cooks—called *confituriers*—was to make not only jellies and preserves but also liqueurs and cordials. The Western world was in its formative stage of preserve-making when the French physician Michel de Nostradamus separated preserved fruit into two categories—dry and liquid—for his *Opuscule* in 1555. His liquid preserves included the fruit-based jellies, jams, and preserves in syrups similar to those we make today. Anything that could be eaten with the fingers—candied fruits, nuts, seeds, and vegetables—comprised dry preserves. His recipes used both sugar and honey as sweeteners for the liquid kind, but only sugar for the dry type (Wheaton, 1983:40).

During the period of European expansion, sugar was still a luxury. Europeans, who took their recipes for preserves and marmalades with them to their colonies in the New World, soon found that cane sugar was exorbitant in the North American colonies, so most early colonial cooks followed the Native American practice of using maple sugar. At the end of the nineteenth century, cane sugar became affordable and plentiful following the Spanish-American War, when the sugar-growing territories of Cuba and the Philippines came under American control. Sugar consumption in Anglo-America soared immediately after that event, and Americans also started adding it to pickled vegetables and fruits such as cucumbers, radish pods, purslane, gherkins, peppers, and peaches. In the United States cooks began treating pickles as more than just a "salad" (served mixed with olive oil, as in the eighteenth century) or as a condiment eaten with meat. Pickles became something to be eaten alone or as a side dish (Weaver: Personal Communication, 1990).

Before you can have pickles you must have vinegar, and before you can have vinegar you must have alcohol, because vinegar is the product of a fungus-implemented fermentation of an alcoholic liquid. This fungus or "mother" is a cloudy, thick layer which forms on the surface in an opened bottle of wine or unpasteurized vinegar. Consequently, humans have had vinegar as long as they have had wine. If the start-up liquid has been pasteurized, or if the percentage of alcohol is high enough, no "mother" will form, hence no vinegar. No one knows for certain when winemaking began, but it is estimated to have been between 8000 B.C. and 3000 B.C. As a condiment, vinegar has long been held in high regard, as testified by a reference to it in the Book of Ruth (2:14). "And Boaz said unto her, at mealtime come thou hither, and eat of the bread, and dip thy morsel in the vinegar [wine]." Pickles were known in Mesopotamia, ancient Egypt, Greek and Roman antiquity, and China, as well as in India (Montagné, 1961:PP?). Pickles, in general, were made by cooks in European cultures as early as vinegars were available to preserve them. The ancient Celts used cider vinegar, and the Romans used wine vinegar—in short, pickles have been around for a very long time.

The British came to favor another type of pickle—pickled stuffed mangoes—after they began trading with the Portuguese along the Malabar coast of India beginning early in the seventeenth century. In the British Isles there were no tropical mangoes; consequently small melons and cucumbers were substituted and stuffed with a mixture of six or seven spices, garlic, and horseradish mixed with olive oil before they were pickled in a crock full of vinegar. In fact, British cooks took to "mangoing" various other substitutes. When the English colonized America, they brought the recipe for "mangoes" with them but had to use small muskmelons and green bell peppers. Pepper mangoes were so popular that bell peppers were and still are called mangoes in several parts of the United States (page 60).

Chutney is a sweet and sour fruit condiment that originated in India and was introduced to Europe by early British or Dutch trading ships and later through the colonization of India by England. The word chutney may come from the Hindi *chatna*, meaning "taste." Making chutney was a means of preserving fruits in a tropical climate. Indian cooks are also big on very hot, spicy pickles, *achaar* (see page 90). Mixed vegetable pickles, also called *achaars,* which we call chow chows, are another Indian specialty. I wondered whether the term chow chow could have come from India along with the relish, as a corruption of *achaar—chaar* or *char*, so I asked food historian William Woys Weaver, whose specialty is relishes and preserves, for an opinion. He deduced that it was entirely possible that Dutch traders and colonists in southern India and Ceylon picked up the term with the relish, because he had learned that early Pennsylvania Dutch used a corrupted form, *jar jar*, as their initial way of writing chow chow. He went on to say that he believes the term can be traced to the U.S. Centennial in 1876, since a great many commercial foods were sold there, among them packaged pickles from India. Also, many Philadelphia hotels and food specialty shops offered India goods—they were quite chic in the 1870s. Today, chutney is having a well-deserved resurgence on our tables.

Not only in the art of making relishes, chutneys, and pickles are peppers a marvelous addition, but I also find their acridity a perfect complement to the sometimes cloying sweetness of preserves, marmalades, and jellies. There is a physiological basis for this. When foods with different taste characteristics are mixed, these characteristics do not meld to produce a new taste but rather suppress or enhance one another: salt added to sweet enhances the latter, while acid and acrid things mitigate sweetness. Don't be afraid to try them in your favorite plum or peach jam. Serranos or chiltepínes will add zest without changing your fruity flavor, while jalapeños impart a distinct flavor that may or may not be desirable.

Putting Peppers By

It was through my hobby of gardening and pickling and preserving my harvest that I met and fell in love with peppers in the early 1970s. At that time, peppers were indispensable to pickles and relishes, and now, I find them equally vital to my preserves. The addition of capsicums to a sweet fruit enhances and compliments the satiating sweetness of the sugar. The pickle and relish book that I had begun, along with the recipes I had developed, went in the closet during my pursuit of peppers. Now, years later, I have rescued those tasty recipes from oblivion by including them in this book.

One hot Texas summer, while I was peeling and preserving a bumper crop, an old-timer dropped by my kitchen and drawled to me, "Honey, you better put up enough for two or three years, cuz you might not make a crop next year." He was right. However, if your colorful, tasty products are to last more than a few weeks, care must be taken to ensure that the homemade condiments and preserves are sterile before they are put in the pantry. There is so much hard work involved in preserving that it is a shame to risk losing all those ingredients and such effort through careless procedures. Unless you have ideal storage—30° to 50°F and dry and dark—giving the product of your labors a boiling water bath according to directions will ensure that you and your friends will enjoy the fruits of your garden. The four things that cause spoilage in preserved food—bacteria, enzymes, molds, and yeast—can be controlled by heat, hence the hot water bath. You will need a six- to seven-quart, nonreactive pot to cook in—too many boilovers in anything smaller—a large preserving kettle with a lid and a jar rack for the water bath, and a pair of tongs designed to lift jars from hot water.

The Choices

Pickling.

Canning relishes and sauces that have been acidified with vinegar can be a very satisfying experience, and family and friends will be provided with taste treats throughout the year. For pickles, the fruit and/or vegetables are left whole or cut to a specific size, while in relishes they are chopped. Only the very freshest, firmest fruits and vegetables, and whole spices (ground spices will cause darkening during storage) should be used and the recipe directions followed exactly. They are sealed and stored as are other canned foods, but they require a wait of at least three or more weeks before eating for the flavors to meld. A boiling-water bath will guarantee a safe relish or pickle that will keep for several years at 50 to 70°F in a dark, dry place, although the contents darken with age. After opening they will keep in a tightly closed container in the refrigerator almost indefinitely.

Preserving.

Preserving is an ancient procedure for safeguarding fruits and vegetables by increasing their sugar content to a concentration in which microbes are dehydrated by osmotic pressure, and are thereby destroyed. Sugar, fruit, pectin, and acid are the common denominator of jelly (made from juice), preserves (whole or large pieces of fruit in syrup), jam (made from ground or crushed fruit), and marmalade (a soft jelly with bits of citrus throughout).

Fruit
Select full-flavored, slightly underripe fruits to overcome the sweetness of the sugar.

Acid
No fruit will thicken or gel without acid. Underripe fruit is higher in acid than fully ripe fruit. Lemon juice is frequently added to low acid fruits.

Pectin
This is what makes jelly gel. Pectin occurs to some extent in all fruits and decreases with maturity. Commercial pectin—liquid or crystalline—takes the guesswork out of jams and jellies. It's not cheating to use one. Capsicums require the addition of such supplemental pectin.

Sugar

This acts as a preservative and aids the formation of gels. Honey or corn syrup can be used for half the sugar in jams and marmalades, but only a quarter in jellies.

In the process of preserving, the fruit to be preserved—whole or cut up—is first simmered for 10 to 20 minutes in a small amount of water to extract pectin. If the fruit is deficient in either pectin or acid, then add commercial pectin or pared lemon slices. Follow the printed directions from the pectin package exactly. Additional or excessive cooking will break down the pectin molecules. The correct amount of sugar is added and the mixture is kept at a rolling boil until the desired consistency is reached. If a sample of the preserves fails to gel when cooled in a spoon, additional lemon juice or pectin can be added to stabilize the ingredients. Measure carefully and NEVER double a recipe because the additional cooking required not only darkens the fruit but also lessens the flavor. Experience is a big help until you get the hang of preserving, or ask an experienced friend, or refer to McGee (1988:170–72) for the science of the thing.

Properly sealed preserves stored in a dark, dry place at 50°F to 70°F should keep indefinitely. Once opened, jars of preserves should be tightly closed and stored in the refrigerator at 32°F to 50°F, where they will keep up to a year. Jellies and preserves which have sugared or turned too dark to be acceptable on the table can be melted with a little water and used in salad dressings, sauces, or to baste and glaze meat while cooking.

NOTE: For insurance I treat them as jellies and pour ¼ inch of melted paraffin on the hot preserves before capping.

Canning

The *Capsicum* is a low-acid fruit/vegetable, which must be canned in a pressure canner for safety. The risk of botulism makes it too risky to can peppers at home.

The How Tos

Jars, lids, and sterilizing them.

Use modern self-sealing jars, unused flat lids, and reusable rings/bands which can be purchased at the supermarket, hardware store, or feed store. If you have saved jars from previous years, be certain the rims are intact and use only new lids (used rings are okay). The jars and lids must be washed thoroughly before each use. If a boiling-water bath is to be used they will not need to be sterilized prior to filling; however, the jars should be hot when they receive the boiling fruit. Before you start cooking, fill the clean jars one quarter full of very hot water and place them in a flat pan in a 225°F oven so they will be the right temperature when the fruit is ready to be poured. Do not boil the self-sealing lids; instead put them in a glass or metal container, scald by covering them with boiling water and let them rest until you are ready for them.

Filling the jars

Fill the hot, clean jars to within ½-inch of the rim. If air bubbles appear, run a sterile knife down the inside of each jar to release the air. Wipe the rims clean with damp paper toweling, and seal with scalded lids. Put the band on, then tighten it completely before the hot jars are placed in the boiling-water bath. Do not tighten the lids after the bath or you will break the seal.

Boiling-water bath

After sealing the hot jars of goodies, place them on a rack in the canning kettle. Add enough steaming hot water—never cold water—to cover the jars an inch or two. Cover the kettle and turn the heat up. When the water reaches a rolling boil, start timing: 20 minutes for quart jars of whole dill or sour pickles, 5 minutes for jars of sweet pickles and relishes such as chutney, piccalilli, relish, peppers, chow chow, pickled jalapeños, and preserves. Be certain the water boils steadily throughout the processing period. If necessary, add boiling water to replace any that evaporated. When the processing time is up, remove the jars from the canner at once. Place on racks to cool out of the breeze. After the jars are cool, check the seal by pressing the lids. If the lid pops back, the jar is not sealed; store in the refrigerator. If the lid stays down, store in cool (50°F to 70°F), dry place.

NOTE: Jellies should not receive a boiling water bath but should be put up in sterilized jars (boiled for 15 minutes at 212°F) to within ½-inch of the rim and sealed immediately with a ¼-inch layer of melted paraffin in order to prevent surface mold. Cover with scalded lids.

To melt paraffin

Place paraffin in a clean can which has been bent at the rim to form a pouring spout. Place the can in a sauce-pan of boiling water to melt. Never place it over the flame, as it catches fire easily. Be very careful when melting paraffin.

JEAN'S OWN CHUTNEY

This is a lot of work, but well worth the trouble. I came up with this recipe after analyzing over 50 chutney recipes. Use any two different firm fruits, which are seasonally available. 'Granny Smith' apples or dried Turkish apricots are a good standby for one, then use others such as green tomatoes, figs, loquats, peaches, etc., for the second. Tamarind is the secret weapon. After learning about chutney in Colonial India, the Brits found they liked the liquid part of the concoction as well as the solids. As a consequence, a famous sauce was born—Worcestershire—the distinctive ingredient of which is tamarind (page 99)

Makes about 9 Pints

- 4 cups brown sugar, firmly packed
- 2 cups granulated sugar
- 1 quart cider vinegar
- 1 pound golden raisins, ground in blender with 1 cup fresh lime juice
- 1 cup tamarind juice and pureé or a pureé of ½ cup dried apricots, soaked in water to make 1 cup, plus 2 tablespoons Worcestershire sauce
- 1 cup red onion, chopped
- 2 garlic cloves, peeled and minced
- 1 teaspoon salt
- 12 'Kieffer' or hard, green canning pears (not 'Bartlett') or 'Granny Smith' apples, pared, diced (8 pounds before peeling)
- 3 tablespoons preserved ginger (page 96)
- 4 tablespoons fresh ginger, peeled and sliced thin
- 4 cups red bell peppers, seeded and 1-inch diced or mixed sweet peppers or mango, slightly underripe; or 4 cups peaches, peeled, seeded, and chopped or sliced; or other such fruit as citron melon; or green tomatoes

- 2 to 4 serranos or jalapeños (page 70), seeded and sliced
- 1 cup fresh lime juice

In Spice Bag:

- 2 cinnamon sticks
- 20 whole cloves
- 2 dried red chillies or ½ teaspoon ground cayenne pepper
- 1 teaspoon ground nutmeg
- 2 teaspoons ground allspice
- 1 teaspoon turmeric
- 1 teaspoon ground mace

Place the sugars, spice bag, and vinegar in large 6- to 7-quart nonreactive pan and cook until clear, stirring to dissolve the sugar. Add the dried fruit pureés, onions, garlic, and salt and cook until thickened over a low-medium heat. Add the sliced fresh fruits, gingers, and peppers; boil gently for 15 minutes, no more, stirring frequently. Cover immediately and let sit overnight. Next day, adjust the seasonings and cook the chutney down by simmering 15 to 20 minutes. This final cooking down may take more or less time but must be watched very carefully to prevent scorching. Remove the spice bag and pour the boiling chutney into hot, clean jars. Seal and process in a boiling water bath according to the directions on page 206. Remove and place on racks out of draft to cool. Allow flavors to meld for 3 weeks before serving.

This fairly dark-colored chutney is great with meats, curries, over cream cheese as an hors d'oeuvre, or in sour cream on fruit salad. Cover tightly and refrigerate once opened. It will keep almost indefinitely in the refrigerator.

FRESH CHILLI PAPAYA CHUTNEY

Stephen Lombardi, Chef

San Antonian Steve Lombardi claims that coming to Texas really expanded his horizons where peppers apply. He especially lilkes to combine fruit and peppers with a Mexican-Oriental flare as demonstrated in this uncooked fruit chutney, which is eaten fresh and not preserved in jars.

Makes 2 Quarts

- 2 tablespoons butter or margarine
- ½ medium-size red onion, diced fine
- 2 medium-size poblanos (page 74), seeded and diced fine
- 1 bunch green onions (scallions), chopped
- 3 celery stalks, finely diced
- ½ large red bell pepper, seeded and diced
- 1 fresh jalapeño (page 70), seeded and minced (optional)
- 3 large papayas (page 98), cut into medium dice
- ½ cup raisins, preferably golden
- 1⅓ cups sugar
- ⅓ cup red wine vinegar
- 2 tablespoons fresh lemon juice
  Pinch of salt

Melt the butter or margarine in 4-quart saucepan over low heat, add vegetables and stir until soft. Add the fruit and remaining ingredients, cover and simmer over low heat for 12 to 15 minutes. Do not allow to boil.

Can be served hot or cold, and works best with fowl, pork, or seafood. Adding some to a blender hollandaise makes for a nice sauce. It can be preserved (page 205) or stored tightly covered in refrigerator safely for up to 2 weeks.

RED PEPPER AND TOMATO CHUTNEY

This is one of the easier cooked chutneys for the novice — but good!

Makes 10 cups

- 6 cups ripe tomatoes, peeled and quartered
- 1 cup red bell pepper or any sweet red pepper, seeded and sliced lengthwise
- 2 red chilli peppers, jalapeños, serranos, Fresno, (see index)

- 2 'Granny Smith' apples, cored and sliced into narrow wedges
- 2 red onions, sliced and separated into rings
- 3 tablespoons mustard seed
- 1 tablespoon salt
- 4 cups cider vinegar

In a Spice Bag

- 1 tablespoon cloves, whole
- 1 tablespoon allspice, whole
- 2 tablespoons fresh ginger, peeled and sliced
- 2 tablespoons celery seed
- ½ teaspoon cumin seeds, bruised
- 3 tamarind pulps, remove pods and seed (page 99; see note 1 below)
- 3 cups brown sugar
- 1 6-ounce pouch liquid pectin (Certo), see note 2 below

Place tomatoes in a 6- to 7-quart nonreactive kettle. Add the peppers, jalapeños, apples, onions, mustard seed, and salt. Simmer over medium-low heat gently for 30 minutes. Put all the other spices and the pulp and seeds of the tamarinds in a spice bag or piece of muslin secured with a rubber band. Place the spice bag and the vinegar in a 2-quart nonreactive pan; bring to a boil, then reduce the heat to medium and simmer for 30 minutes. Remove the spice bag and strain the vinegar into the tomato mixture. Add the sugar and bring to a rolling boil. Reduce heat to medium-low and simmer for 1 hour. Turn the fire off and cover. Let the chutney sit overnight.

The next day bring the chutney to a rolling boil and add the pectin (see note below). When the mixture comes to a rolling boil again, boil for 1 minute. Remove from the heat and pour up into hot, sterilized jars. Wipe the rims with wet paper toweling, seal with a thin layer of melted paraffin and cap. Wait three weeks to allow the chutney to mellow before using.

NOTE 1: If tamarinds are not available, substitute 6 to 8 dried apricot halves and 3 tablespoons Worcestershire sauce.

NOTE 2: Chutney can be made without the commercial pectin by boiling much longer, until it has thickened. This reduces the volume considerably and makes for a darker product.

CRANBERRY CHUTNEY

Although cooked, do not can this chutney; it is better as a fresh accompaniment to meat, especially poultry. A delightful change from the traditional cranberry sauce.

Makes 3 to 4 Cups

- 2 cups fresh cranberries
- ½ cup water
- ½ cup golden raisins
- 1 small onion, thinly sliced and separated into rings
- 1 to 2 serranos (page 78) or fresh jalapeños (page 70), seeded and thinly sliced
- 1 cup sugar
- ¼ teaspoon ground ginger
- ¼ teaspoon ground cinnamon
- ⅛ teaspoon ground allspice
- ⅛ teaspoon salt
- 1 cup fresh pineapple, diced or 8-ounce can pineapple tidbits, drained

Combine all the ingredients except pineapple in a nonreactive Dutch oven or similar deep pan; stir well. Cook over medium heat, uncovered, until reduced and thickened, 10 to 15 minutes or until reduced and thickened. Add the pineapple, bring to a boil, remove from heat, let sit covered, until cool.

Serve with turkey, ham, lamb, or in baked acorn squash halves. Cover and keep refrigerated for 7 to 10 days.

INDIAN STYLE MINT CHUTNEY

It is worth growing a big mint bed to ensure a mint source for this habit-forming uncooked chutney from the sub-continent.

Makes 1 Cup

- 1 cup fresh cilantro (fresh coriander) leaves
- 1 cup fresh mint leaves
- 1 large garlic clove, peeled
- 3 tablespoons red onion, roughly chopped
- 1 small green tomato, cored or 2 tomatillos (page 99), husked
- 4 to 6 fresh green chillies (serrano, Thai, Fresno,

Santa Fe Grande; see index), seeded
- 2 tablespoons fresh lime juice
- 2 tablespoons olive oil
- 1 teaspoon salt

Put all the ingredients in a blender and process until coarsely puréed. Serve with curry dishes or any meats or as a dip with unsalted chips.

VARIATION: The timid may mix several spoonfuls of this in plain yogurt or sour cream, to taste. Use as a dip with chips, cold chicken, lamb, or vegetables.

BOLIVIAN SARZA

Not quite a chutney—but a cooked Bolivian sweet-sour sauce that is a real taste teaser and pleaser. This is from Hacienda Candelario, an old cattle ranch.

Makes 2 Cups

- 2 tablespoons vegetable oil
- 1 cup red onion, finely chopped
- 2 red ajís (page 37) or 3 serranos (page 78) or jalapeños, finely chopped; or to taste
- 1 Roma tomato, chopped
- ¾ cup golden raisins, soaked in hot water to make a cup until softened
- 1 teaspoon ground nutmeg
- 1 teaspoon sugar
  Salt to taste

Heat the oil in a medium-size saucepan over medium heat and cook the onions and chillies until the onion is transparent. Add the tomatoes and cook, stirring until tender. Add the cup of raisins and soaking water, and the nutmeg. Cook until thickened. Season with salt. Pour warm sauce into a bowl and serve as a condiment with meats.

CHOW CHOW

Chow chow, according to the dictionary, is a mixed pickle in mustard. The name comes from achaar *(page 90), which is a Indian condiment flavored with mustard seed. After studying numerous chow chow and mustard pickle recipes I have come to the conclusion that there is little, if any, difference between the two. We always had a jar labeled Crosse and Blackwell Mustard Pickle on our table and my father called it chow chow in spite of its label. The main difference appears to be the size of the vegetable, which is smaller in chow chow. I prefer the smaller bits. The combination of vegetables is variable. A lot of folks call any preserved vegetable relish chow chow.*

Makes 10 to 12 Pints

Use a mixture of the following vegetables to make 4 quarts:
Small (2-inch to 3-inch) green cucumbers, sliced
1 red bell pepper, seeded and chopped
1 green bell pepper, seeded and chopped
Pearl Onions, peeled (canned cocktail onions may be substituted)
1 head cauliflower, cut into florets
Tiny green salad tomatoes, cut in half if too large
Whole tiny snap beans
Lima beans, shelled
Tiny pickled gherkins (buy these bottled)

For the Brine

1 cup salt
4 cups boiling water

For the Sauce

1½ cups all-purpose flour
1 teaspoon ground cayenne pepper
6 tablespoons dry mustard
1½ tablespoons turmeric
2 quarts cider vinegar
2½ cups sugar
3 tablespoons celery seed
1 tablespoon mustard seed

Combine the vegetables in a crock. Stir the brine ingredients together until the salt is dissolved, then pour over the vegetables to cover. Let stand overnight.

In a large nonreactive saucepan bring the vegetables and brine to a boil. Let stand 10 minutes. Rinse thoroughly in cold water. Drain. Combine the vegetables in a large nonreactive kettle.

Make a paste of the flour and ground spices with a small amount of the vinegar. In a nonreactive saucepan, bring the remaining vinegar, sugar, and seeds to a boil. Slowly stir in the flour mixture and cook until smooth and thickened. Combine with the vegetables. Simmer over medium heat until the vegetables are just barely tender. Pour into hot, clean jars according to directions on page 206, and process in a boiling-water bath for 15 minutes as described on page 206.

VARIATION: For a snappier chow chow, add 1 tablespoon or more canned nacho-sliced jalapeños to the vegetables.

HAYDEN'S RELISH

I have never known who Hayden was but when I was a child a neighbor gave this recipe to my mother and it has always been our very favorite relish. We made it every summer. Thank you, Hayden, wherever you are! My non-cooking husband loved this relish so much that in the Texas summers, before air conditioning and electric grinders, he would do all the grinding in that heat to make certain I put up a batch each summer.

Makes 12 to 18 Pints

1 gallon firm, ripe tomatoes, cored and coarse-ground (about 4 pounds)
1 gallon green and red bell peppers, seeded and coarse-ground (about 5 pounds)
1 gallon cabbage, medium-chopped (about 6 pounds)
1 quart red onions, chopped (about 4 pounds)
1 cup non-iodized salt
6 jalapeños (page 70), seeded and chopped
8 cups 5% cider vinegar
6 cups granulated sugar
2 tablespoons mustard seed
2 tablespoons celery seed
2 teaspoons turmeric

2 teaspoons ground cinnamon
1 teaspoon ground clove
1 teaspoon ground ginger

Place the ground vegetables in a large container such as a plastic dishpan and mix with the salt. Let stand for 2 hours. Lift from juice, drain. Put in a large nonreactive pan (6 to 7 quarts or larger) and add the remaining ingredients. Boil the vegetables and spices for 30 minutes, stirring frequently.

Pack into hot, clean jars, seal and process in a boiling water bath for 10 minutes according to the directions on page 206. Refrigerate in a tightly closed jar once opened. The relish will keep for several months.

Delicious with meats, ham, mixed in mayonnaise for salad dressing, in deviled eggs, tuna salad, and on hamburgers.

OLD FASHIONED PEPPER RELISH

Remember the women's sections at the county fair? This bottled relish was always there. It is a gardener's delight. Serve it with grilled meats, barbecue, in tuna or chicken salad, or on sandwiches and hamburgers.

Makes about 10 Pints

8 cups bell peppers of all colors, seeded and coarse ground (or a garden mix of poblano, banana pepper, 'Cubanelle', New Mexican Chile (see index), about 15 large; measure after grinding

4 jalapeños (page 70) or serranos (page 78), or your garden chillies, seeded and coarse ground

8 cups red onions, coarse-ground (about 8 to 10 large)

4 cups 5% white vinegar

1 cup water

3 cups sugar

2 tablespoons salt

3 tablespoons mustard seed

2 tablespoons celery seed

1 teaspoon fresh ginger, peeled and minced

Place the ground peppers, chillies, and onion in a large container (plastic dish pan will do); cover with boiling water and let stand for 10 to 15 minutes. Drain and return to container. Mix 1 cup vinegar and 1 cup

water; heat to boiling, then pour over drained vegetables. Let stand 15 minutes. Drain again.

Place vegetables in a large (6- to 7-quart) non-reactive pot; add the remaining ingredients and place over high heat. Bring to a rolling boil. Pour the mixture into clean, hot jars. Process in hot water bath according to directions on page 206. Remove from the water and place on racks out of draft. Check your seal by tapping the metal cap. It should ring. If the sound is dull, use in the next 6 weeks. Tighten lids. Allow to mellow for a month before using.

MEDITERRANEAN RELISH

This easy eggplant and green New Mexican Chile cooked relish is reminiscent of the Mediterranean flavors, but with peppers alien to that region.

Makes 2 Cups

1 1-pound eggplant

4 mild, green New Mexican Chiles (page 71) or sweet banana peppers (page 59), seeded and finely chopped

1 fresh jalapeño (page 70), seeded and finely chopped

2 garlic cloves, peeled and crushed

2 tablespoons onion, grated

3 tablespoons fresh lemon juice or white wine vinegar

1 tablespoon fresh basil, chopped

6 tablespoons olive oil
   Salt and freshly ground black pepper to taste

Pierce the unpeeled eggplant with a fork in two or three places. For good flavor, bake in a preheated 375°F oven for 20 minutes, turning once. Place the baked eggplant over a gas flame, hot charcoal, or under a broiler and roast until soft and blackened. Remove the blackened skin under cold running water; then press gently to remove any bitter juices. Chop the pulp fine and mix with the peppers. Add the garlic, onion, and lemon juice, then gradually stir in the oil. Season with salt and pepper to taste. Chill before serving. Keep in the refrigerator, covered, for up to a week.

FRESH MANGO CHILLI RELISH
Heidi Insalata Krahling, Executive Chef
A Californian with a maiden name of Insalata and with a gourmet chef for a father, Heidi Krahling's flavorful future with food seemed inevitable. In 1988 she was chosen as one of USA Today's *Best Women Chefs for that year. This is a zesty, tropical relish to be served fresh.*

Makes Approximately 1 Quart

- 2 cups diced mango (avoid the fibrous parts) or papaya, or a mix of both
- ¼ cup green onions (scallions), thinly sliced on the bias
- ¼ cup red onion, diced finely
- 3 red jalapeños (page 70), diced finely; green will do
- 1 poblano (page 74), roasted (page 87), peeled, seeded and diced finely
- 1 bunch cilantro (fresh coriander), stemmed and chopped
- 3 tablespoons rice vinegar (page 98)
- ½ cup olive oil
- 2 teaspoons cumin seed, toasted (page 101) and ground
  Zest and juice of 1 lime
  Zest and juice of 1 orange

Mix all ingredients together in a nonreactive bowl. Adjust with citrus juices and salt. Serve with your favorite fish or fowl.

PENNSYLVANIA DUTCH MANGO RELISH
William Woys Weaver, Food Historian/Author
Pennsylvanian Bill Weaver, a descendant of Colonial Dutch, is one of the foremost American food historians. He collects and grows heirloom seed from the American Dutch colonies. A pioneer in his field, he is not satisfied with writing award winning books such as America Eats, *and lecturing on the history of food, but he also indulges his passions—preserving and pickling and collecting culinary artifacts—and peppers!*

Makes 8 to 8½ Pints

- 14 medium-size onions (2½ pounds)
- 12 large green bell peppers, seeded (2½ pounds)
- 12 large red bell peppers, seeded (2½ pounds)
- 4 small, fresh red chillies, seeded; cayenne, serrano, Thai (see index)
- 3 cups cider vinegar
- 3 cups brown sugar
- 3 tablespoons celery seed
- 3 teaspoons pickling salt

Chop the onions and peppers to a fine, even texture. Put them in a nonreactive preserving kettle and add the vinegar, sugar, celery seed, and salt. Bring this to a gentle boil and cook 15 minutes. Put the relish in sterile canning jars. Seal and give a 5-minute hot water bath. Allow to mature for 1 to 2 weeks before using. ALTERNATIVE: Add 2 or more chilli peppers, serranos or jalapeños for a zippier relish.

PEPPER AND MELON MANGOES
William Woys Weaver, Food Historian/Author
Here's another of Bill's wonderful relishes from the restored kitchen of his historic (1805) twenty-eight-room "Land Tavern" home in Devon, Pennsylvania.

Makes 3 Quarts

- 20 small bell peppers, green or mixed colors
- 3 quarts water
- 7½ tablespoons pickling salt (never table salt)
- ½ pound cabbage, shredded finely
- ¼ cup fresh-grated horseradish
- ¼ cup fresh-grated ginger
- 8 tablespoons mustard seed
- 1 tablespoon ground mace
- 1 tablespoon ground cloves
- 1 tablespoon ground cinnamon
- ½ cup bell peppers of mixed colors, chopped
- 20 garlic cloves, peeled and minced

Pickling Brine

- 1½ quarts water
- 2½ cups sugar
- 1 tablespoon pickling salt

Wash the peppers and carefully slice off the top leaving the stem in place, set aside for lids. Slit each pepper down the sides leaving the bases intact. Remove the seeds and veins. Make a brine of the water and pickling salt and "lay" (submerge in brine) the peppers in this overnight. The next day, drain the peppers and discard the brine.

Mix the shredded cabbage, horseradish, ginger, mustard seed, spices, and chopped peppers. Put a clove of garlic in each pepper and stuff peppers with the vegetable mix. Replace the tops. Use clean toothpicks to hold the tops in place. Put the peppers in hot, sterilized, widemouth jars (3 1-quart jars). While packing the jars, bring the pickling brine to a boil in a large saucepan (2½ quart) and boil 5 minutes, then pour it over the vegetables. Seal the jars and give them a 15-minute water bath (page 206). Not only good, they make a beautiful, edible garnish on a meat platter.

BELL PEPPER MANGOES, HISTORICAL RECIPE

William Woys Weaver, Food Historian/Author

This original recipe (don't try to prepare it) for pickled stuffed mangoes originated in India long before a British army defeated India in 1803. In fact, the pickled mangoes had reached England and its American colonies before the American Revolution or the British colonization of India. Since the British carried on an extensive trade with the Portuguese on the Malabar coast beginning early in seventeenth century, it is believed that the Portuguese introduced this delicacy to the British traders, who carried it to England. In the British Isles there were no tropical mangoes, consequently small melons and cucumbers were substituted. In fact, British cooks took to "mangoing" various other substitutes. "Mango" is a borrowed Portuguese word for the Tamil Indian "mangas." When the English colonized America they brought the recipe with them but substituted small muskmelons for the mangoes. Those early small muskmelons were quite different from the modern cantaloupe that we often call muskmelon. For authenticity you would have to use the Hoagen cantaloupe which has smooth skin and green flesh. By the eighteenth century most American cooks made their stuffed mangoes with green bell peppers, which first arrived in Virginia in 1621. Pepper mangoes were so popular that bell peppers were and still are called mangoes in several parts of the United States.

One of those colonial recipes tells us: "Take large firm green bell peppers. Carefully cut the stem end out in a nice circle; set aside. Core and remove the seed. With thread or string, tie the cut-out piece to each pepper and put them into a brine solution made of 22½ ounces salt to 6 quarts water for 2 days. Remove from the brine, rinse, and drain. Pat them dry. Cover the bottom of a big kettle with several layers of grape or cabbage leaves, add a little alum, and cover the stuffed peppers with more grape or cabbage leaves. Cover the kettle tightly, place over low heat and let the peppers steam. After steaming, stuff the bell pepper/mangoes with the following mixture:" (proportions unknown).

Serves unknown amount

grated horseradish
white mustard seed
mace
ground nutmeg
finely chopped ginger root
black pepper
turmeric
olive oil

Stick a garlic clove into each mango. Replace the stem end and tie the mangoes well with thread; put them in stone crocks. Pour boiling vinegar over them, and cover the crocks carefully; allow to sit several weeks before using. This stuffing was sometimes called "piccalilli," and was the forerunner of piccalilli relishes (Weaver, 1983:168).

HOME CANNED SALSA

In the Fall, when peppers and tomatoes are at their best, put up some salsa to pep up dreary winter meals.

Makes 1 Quart

  2 cups long green New Mexican Chiles, 'Fresnos', jalapeños, or 'Santa Fe Grandes', chopped
  4 pounds (about 8 large) ripe tomatoes, cored and quartered
  1 large onion, quartered
  4 cloves garlic, crushed
  4 cups cider vinegar
  1 cup sugar (reduce to ¼ or ½ cup if desired)
  1 tablespoon salt
  ½ teaspoon coriander seed
  1 teaspoon fresh oregano leaves

In a food processor, purée the chillies, tomatoes, onion, and garlic (a few at a time) until smooth. For a chunkier salsa, pulse the processor until you reach desired "chunkiness" before the vegetables are a purée. Put into a large (6-quart) kettle and mix in the sugar, salt, spices and 2 cups of the vinegar. Without cover, simmer over medium heat until salsa is reduced by half (about 1½ hours); stir frequently.

Add the remaining vinegar and continue simmering and stirring until the salsa is reduced to 1 quart (about 30 to 40 minutes). Remove from heat.

To can, ladle hot salsa into hot, sterilized half-pint preserving jars to within ½ inch of the rim. Run a sterilized knife down inside of jar to release air bubbles. Wipe rims clean. Seal with scalded lids. Process in hot water bath for 15 minutes. Lift out and allow to cool on rack. When cool, press lid to check seal. If lid pops back, jar is not sealed; store in refrigerator. If lid stays down, store in a cool, dry place.

If you have a garden or farmer's market, this recipe can be doubled and made several times to take advantage of the seasonal produce.

This basic Salsa Picante can be varied with the addition of any or all of the following:

  2 red bell peppers
  1 cup banana peppers, chopped
  ½ cup cilantro leaves, chopped
  1 teaspoon cumin
  1 teaspoon freshly ground black pepper

CAYENNE PEPPER CATSUP

This famous Creole preparation is very hot but is excellent with oysters. It makes a great gift.

Makes 4 to 5 Cups

  4 dozen ripe cayenne peppers (page 61)
  4 cups best-quality white or cider vinegar or sherry (very mellow)
  3 tablespoons grated fresh horseradish
  5 onions, sliced
  1 teaspoon sugar
  1 garlic clove, peeled and minced
  1 cup hot water

Place all of the ingredients in a nonreactive stockpot and boil together, uncovered, until the onions become soft. Remove from the heat and place in a blender; purée well. Return the purée and bring to a boil.

Pour into hot, clean jars, seal, and process in a 5-minute boiling water bath as described on page 206. Refrigerate once opened.

NOTE: Ripe red New Mexican Chiles (page 71), 'Santa Fe Grandes', jalapeños, 'Hungarian Wax', or serranos can be used, but the flavor will be a little different with each.

PICKLED JALAPEÑOS OR 'HUNGARIAN WAX' PEPPERS

Peter Piper would love to pick a peck of these pickled peppers.

Makes about 8 Pints

  1 gallon 'Hungarian Wax' peppers, jalapeños, serranos, left whole, or your garden chilli mix; or sweet peppers, if you must (see index)
  1 gallon water, plus 1 cup
  2 cups salt
  5 cups 5% white vinegar
  2 tablespoons sugar
  1 tablespoon pickling spice
  2 small onions, quartered

2 carrots, parboiled and sliced
8 cloves of garlic, unpeeled, parboiled 2 minutes
8 tablespoons olive or vegetable oil

Thoroughly wash peppers. Prick with a fork or make several small slits in each. Bring the gallon of water to a boil and dissolve the salt in it to make a brine solution. Let cool. Put the peppers in the cool brine solution in a crock (do not use a metal container). Place a clean plate on top of the peppers with a quart jar full of water on it to hold them down in the brine. Leave in brine for 12 to 18 hours.

Rinse the peppers thoroughly to remove all salt. Drain. Combine the 1 cup of water, the vinegar, sugar, and pickling spice in a stockpot and bring to a boil. Reduce the heat and simmer 10 minutes. In each hot, clean jar place ¼ onion, 1 tablespoon of the oil, several carrot slices, 1 garlic clove, then pack the peppers into the jars. Pour in the hot liquid. Seal jars. Process in a boiling water bath according to directions on page 206 for 20 minutes. Store 3 weeks before using. Refrigerate in tightly closed jar, once opened. These pickled peppers will keep several months in the refrigerator.

HERBED CHILLI VINEGAR

Herb growers will love this. I make it every year because my non-herb-growing friends have come to look forward to it.

Makes 3 Gallons

1½ gallons fresh herbs: salad burnet, lemon balm, marjoram; lemon thyme, chives, tarragon; or rosemary, thyme, basil, oregano
6 to 8 garlic cloves, peeled and crushed
2 to 3 jalapeños or serranos, slashed (any garden chillies will work)
1 small onion, sliced
3 gallons cider vinegar
    Dried small red chillies
    Sprigs of rosemary or other herbs

Place the herbs and vegetables in a very large pickling crock or nonreactive container (3-gallon); press with a wooden spoon to bruise. Pour container full of vin-

egar. Cover the container with plastic wrap. Mark with the date.

Three to four weeks later, remove the cover and strain the vinegar through muslin, coffee filters, or 2 layers of paper towels. Sterilize enough bottles to hold 3 gallons. Place a dried red chilli and a sprig of rosemary (other herbs will serve) in each bottle. Using a funnel, fill each bottle to within 1 inch of top. Cork, using a wooden mallet to insert cork firmly. Store as you would pickles, etc. (page 205). Use this vinegar in salads, on vegetables, in salad dressings, or to marinate meats.

ZESTY JALAPEÑO VINEGAR

An easily made vinegar to have on hand to pick up vegetables and salads.

Makes 3 Cups

6 or more jalapeños (page 70)
1 cup water
2 cups apple cider or white vinegar
2 tablespoons olive oil
3 garlic cloves, peeled and crushed
½ teaspoon oregano, fresh or dried
1 slice of onion
1 teaspoon peppercorns, crushed

Cut the jalapeños in several places with a knife. Place all ingredients in a saucepan and bring to a boil. Reduce heat and simmer for five minutes. Cool and place in a glass jar or bottle. Store in refrigerator.

Use on vegetables, cooked greens, in salad dressings, or substitute for vinegar or lime juice in sauce recipes.

DRIED RED PEPPERS

Attention gardeners! Try drying your surplus peppers.

Makes about 1 percent of the fresh weight so do as many as your oven will hold

12 unblemished red bell peppers, quartered or cut in ¾-inch strips, cored and ribs removed. Do at least 12 at a time, or as many as your oven permits.

Preheat the oven to 140°F. In a large steam basket, steam the peppers for 10 minutes. Drain, then dry on paper towels. Place the peppers, cut-side down, on cheese cloth-covered racks. Set the racks on baking sheets. Dry the peppers in the oven for 8 to 10 hours, or until just short of being crisp; or to crisp if desired. Turn the pepper pieces once about mid-way in the drying time. Keep the oven door slightly open to allow moisture to escape. Let the peppers cool completely before packing in airtight containers. Try 'Cubanelles', 'Sweet Bananas', or your garden's surplus. Marinated in olive oil with herbs and garlic, the pepper strips make a nice appetizer, or use plain in salads and casseroles.

"SUN DRIED" TOMATOES

Mark Miller showed me how to dry tomatoes this way, which retains more flavor than by long sun drying.

Makes 2 to 3 Cups

4 to 5 pounds ripe Roma tomatoes (no other kind)
Cayenne pepper

Go to a farmer's market or wait for a special on Roma tomatoes. Select tomatoes approximately all the same size, otherwise some will dry quicker than others, causing you to have to watch them closer. Buy enough to do several broiler pans full at a time or whatever your oven will hold. Oil the broiler racks and place racks in broiler pans. Cut the tomatoes in half and place the cut side down on racks. Fill the pan and place it in a 190°F oven. The length of cooking time will depend on the size of the tomatoes. Turn them once about mid-drying time. It will take from 16 to 24

hours or a little more depending on the size of the tomatoes. If some "dry" before the others, remove them and return pan to oven. Don't let them get crisp. When the tomatoes are as "dry" as you desire, remove them from the pan and cool. They can be seasoned with cayenne pepper, salt, or whatever. I put them in a closed container unseasoned but they keep longer packed with olive oil and marjoram. Having them on hand plain, you are free to use them in many ways. They will keep several weeks in the refrigerator or longer if you freeze them.

Try serving them as appetizers with a good bleu-cheese or mozzarella chunks, a side dish of olive oil with crushed parsley and basil, and pieces of fresh, crusty French bread to dip in the oil.

EASY PEPPER SAUCE PICKLES

These will surprise you. These simple, very crisp pickles keep very well and make great hostess gifts.

Makes 8 Pints

1 gallon sliced hamburger dill pickles
5 pounds sugar
1 12-ounce bottle chilli pepper sauce
3 tablespoons pickling spice
Mustard seed

Drain the pickles well. Use the glass gallon pickle jar and return the sliced pickles to it in alternate layers with the sugar and pepper sauce. Screw the lid on tightly. Allow to sit for 1 week. Each day turn the jar of pickles upside down so that one day they sit with the top up and the next day the bottom is up.

After a week, remove the pickles and pack them into sterile jars to which have been added 1 teaspoon of the pickling spice and ½ teaspoon mustard seed. Put the scalded lids on tightly. Refrigerate tightly closed once opened; they keep almost indefinitely.
NOTE: A small, dried or fresh red chilli pepper added to the pickles so that it can be seen through the jar adds a bright touch.

CURRY POWDERS OR MASALAS

A visit to the huge Indian market in Durban, South Africa, and markets of all sizes throughout India made me realize that the spices used to make curries are variable. Almost anything goes, except the commercially prepared standardized stuff called curry powder in American supermarkets. Those colorful, aromatic piles of ground spices might vary in composition but not in freshness. They were all recently ground. If you want to grind your own, try one of the following combinations; however, you can also use them as a base to compose your own. Use whole spices and crush them in a mortar, whirl in a blender, or grind them in an electric spice mill until fine, then sift and return any large particles for further powdering. Experiment! Tightly cover and store in the refrigerator. It will keep a year. Better yet are the plastic containers with the type of rubber stoppers that allow the air to be pumped out like those used on wine bottles.

CURRY POWDER NO. 1

Makes about $\frac{3}{4}$ Cup

- $4\frac{1}{2}$ teaspoons freshly ground black pepper
- $1\frac{1}{2}$ teaspoons cardamom seed
- 2 teaspoons ground cayenne pepper
- $1\frac{1}{2}$ teaspoons ground cinnamon
- $1\frac{1}{2}$ teaspoons cumin (comino) seed
- 2 tablespoons plus $1\frac{1}{2}$ teaspoons ground ginger
- $4\frac{1}{2}$ teaspoons mustard seed
- 1 teaspoon sweet paprika
- $\frac{1}{4}$ cup turmeric
- $\frac{1}{2}$ teaspoon crushed dried red chillies, (de árbol, Thai, japonés, chiltepínes; see index)

CURRY POWDER NO. 2

Makes about 6 Tablespoons

- 2 teaspoons freshly ground black pepper
- $\frac{1}{2}$ teaspoon cardamom seed
- 6 to 8 whole cloves
- 4 teaspoons ground coriander
- 4 teaspoons ground cumin (comino)
- 2 teaspoons ground ginger
- $\frac{1}{2}$ teaspoon ground mace
- $\frac{1}{2}$ teaspoon mustard seed
- 4 teaspoons turmeric
- $\frac{1}{2}$ teaspoon crushed dried red chillies (de árbol, japonés, chiltepínes; see index)

CURRY POWDER NO. 3

Makes about $\frac{1}{4}$ Cup

- 1 teaspoon freshly ground black pepper
- $\frac{1}{2}$ teaspoon cardamom seed
- $\frac{1}{4}$ teaspoon ground cinnamon
- 3 teaspoons coriander seed
- $\frac{1}{2}$ teaspoon ground cumin (comino)
- $\frac{1}{2}$ teaspoon fenugreek seed
- 1 teaspoon ground ginger
- 1 teaspoon mustard seed
- 3 teaspoons turmeric
- $\frac{1}{4}$ teaspoon crushed dried red chillies, (de Árbol, Thai, japonés; see index)

ROASTED PEPPERS IN OLIVE OIL

This goes with most anything. I was told how to do this by a native Italian, Enzo Domani, of Saint Augustine, Florida, the largest eggplant processor in the world, who said every self-respecting Italian cook always kept these peppers on hand for the family to snack on.

Makes about 1 Quart

6 pounds red, green, and yellow bell peppers, 'Cubanelles' or any ethnic type (page 65), roasted (page 87) and peeled

2 sprigs fresh thyme, rosemary, and/or basil

2 garlic cloves, peeled and halved

1 tablespoon red or white wine vinegar

¾ cup extra-virgin olive oil, or to cover

Place the peeled peppers in a large bowl. Quarter them and remove the cores, seeds and ribs over the bowl to catch the juices. Place the peppers in a wide-mouth quart jar with the herbs and garlic. Strain the juices over the peppers. Add the vinegar and enough oil to cover the peppers. Stir to release any air bubbles; cover. These peppers will keep for 2 to 3 weeks in the refrigerator or even longer in a container designed so that the air can be removed with a pump.

Serve as an accompaniment to meat dishes, on crusty, warm French bread, or on sandwiches. Use the oil for seasoning.

ALTERNATE: Core, seed, and remove veins from the raw peppers. Cut into strips. Heat the olive oil in a heavy skillet and fry the peppers until limp. Place the peppers, garlic, and herbs in a wide-mouthed glass jar. Add the vinegar, the oil they were cooked in, plus enough more olive oil to cover. Stir to release any air bubbles; cover. These will keep in the refrigerator for a week or so.

LEMON AJÍ MARMALADE

This delectably different marmalade has received rave notices from those who have tasted it.

Makes 10 cups

6 large, yellow and or orange bell peppers, seeded, peeled, and chopped

12 Lemon Ají peppers or small yellow chillies, minced

8 lemons, peeled and juiced

2 cups water

½ teaspoon baking soda

10 cups of granulated sugar

¼ teaspoon salt

2 6-ounce pouches of liquid fruit pectin (Certo) Paraffin

Score the citrus skin in quarters and remove; cut skinned fruit in half and juice. Set juice aside. Cut excess white from the peel and thinly slice the peel in the food processor. Place the lemon peel and soda, with enough water to cover, in a covered saucepan; bring to a boil and simmer until rinds are tender (20 to 30 minutes). Remove from heat, drain and rinse. Place the lemon pulp in a food processor and purée. Place the fruit, peel, and peppers in a large bowl and mix—there should be 6 cups. Divide the mixture into two 3-cup portions to be cooked separately. Better results are obtained when making preserves by keeping your "batches" small. Never cook a doubled recipe of preserves.

Place 3 cups of the mixture in a 6- to 7-quart nonreactive pot and add 5 cups of sugar. Add 1 cup of water, salt, and the lemon juice to the citrus peel and pepper mixture. Bring to a boil over high heat, then reduce the heat and simmer for 5 to 10 minutes. Raise the heat to high and bring to a rolling boil that won't stir down and continue boiling and stirring for 2 to 3 minutes. Add 6 ounces of the pectin. Let the marmalade return to a boil and boil for exactly 1 minute. Remove from heat. Skim the foam, if necessary. Pour hot marmalade to within ½-inch of the rim of hot sterilized jelly jars. Wipe the rims with damp paper toweling. While still very hot pour on a ¼-inch layer of melted paraffin (page 207). Put scalded lids on the jars and tighten and place on a rack to cool. Repeat the process using the other half of the fruit, sugar, and pectin. Keep tightly closed in the refrigerator once opened. Use it up so that it won't turn to sugar, but if it does, melt the marmalade in a saucepan over low heat or in the microwave and use it for a sauce with meats. Additional chillies can be used for a more pungent marmalade.

CAPSICUM MARMALADE
Phil Colman, Curator

Coleman has been curator of invertebrates at the Australian Museum of Natural History in Sydney since the early 1960s. His pursuit of natural history has carried over to plants and cooking, especially peppers. My interest in mollusks led me to Phil, and his interest in peppers led him to me, and a friendship and sharing of shells and recipes followed.

Makes 5 to 6 Cups

- 4 oranges, thinly sliced
- 2 lemons, thinly sliced
- 6 red capsicums (bell peppers), seeded and thinly sliced
   Sugar
   Paraffin

Combine the citrus fruits in a nonreactive saucepan with enough water to cover. Bring to a boil and cook until the rinds are tender. Drain and add the peppers. Measure the contents. For three parts of fruit, add one part sugar. Place capsicums, citrus and sugar in a large nonreactive kettle and cook over low heat until sugar is dissolved. Increase heat to medium and cook until thick.

Pour into sterilized jars; cover with hot paraffin, and seal with scalded lids (page 206). Refrigerate once opened.

JEAN'S CAPSICUM MARMALADE

Have you ever wondered what to do with all those grapefruit rinds? Wonder no more—use them for this spirited marmalade, and don't think you can just eat it on toast—chicken and ham delight in it.

Makes 10 cups

- 2 lemons, peeled and juiced
- 2 grapefruit, peeled and juiced, see note 1 below
- ½ teaspoon baking soda
- 6 large, red bell peppers, roasted (page 87), peeled, seeded and chopped
- 4 to 6 chiltepínes or small red chillies, minced (additional for a more pungent marmalade) see note 2 below

- 10 cups of sugar
- 2 cups water
- 1 6-ounce can orange juice concentrate
- ¼ teaspoon salt
- 2 pouches liquid fruit pectin (Certo)
   Paraffin

Score the citrus skin in quarters and remove; cut skinned fruit in half and juice. Set juice aside. Cut excess white from skin; then slice thinly in food processor. Place the sliced citrus peel and soda, with enough water to cover, in a covered nonreactive saucepan; bring to a boil and simmer until rinds are tender (20 to 30 minutes). Remove from heat, drain and rinse well.

Grind or process the citrus pulp, reserving the juice. Mix the pulp, tenderized peel, and peppers together in a 6- to 7-quart nonreactive kettle; there should be about six cups of the mixture. Divide it in half and set one half of it aside. Place 3 cups of the fruit mixture in the preserving kettle with 5 cups of the sugar. Add 1 cup of water, ½ can orange juice concentrate, and ½ of the juice to the citrus and pepper mixture. At this point, there should be two equal batches of the fruit mixture. Bring the first batch to a boil over high heat, then reduce the heat and simmer for 5 to 10 minutes. Raise the heat to high and bring to a rolling boil that won't stir down; continue boiling and stirring for 2 to 3 minutes. Add one pouch of the liquid pectin; let return to a boil and boil for 1 minute. Remove from heat. Skim the foam, if necessary.

Pour hot marmalade in hot, sterilized small jelly jars. Wipe the rims with damp paper toweling. While still very hot, pour on a thin layer of melted paraffin (page 207). Put scalded lids on the jars and tighten and place on a rack to cool. Repeat the process using the other half of the fruit, sugar, and pectin.

ADVICE: Better results are obtained when making preserves by keeping your "batches" small. Never cook a doubled recipe of preserves; however when you have all the ingredients and are geared up, go ahead and make two small batches.

Keep tightly closed in the refrigerator once opened. If it turns to sugar, melt the marmalade in a saucepan over low heat or in the microwave and use it for a sauce or a glaze with meats.

NOTE 1: In the winter when citrus fruits are at their best, freeze and save the rinds of your breakfast grapefruit until late summer and fall when the peppers are at their peak and you have more time to make the marmalade.

NOTE 2: When using chiltepínes, don't try to remove the seed. Mash the little peppers in a small amount of hot water in a little dish and let them stand for a couple of minutes, then use just the pungent water so the one who eats the jelly won't get a killer bite.

CHILLI PEPPER JELLY

Tasty, savory, tangy, piquant, appetizing—this jelly is all these things. Once you have introduced it to your repertoire of delectables you'll find you must have it to go with chicken and meats as well as on your hot breads, waffles, and pancakes.

Makes 7 cups

- ¼ cup fresh chillies; chiltepínes, jalapeños, habaneros (see index), seeded and chopped
- ¾ cup bell peppers, use same color as the chillies
- 6½ cups sugar
- 1½ cups white vinegar
- 1 6-ounce pouch liquid pectin (Certo)
  Food coloring (optional)
  Paraffin

Peppers can be chopped in a food processor if care is taken not to get them too fine. Mix the peppers, sugar, and vinegar together in a 6- to 7-quart nonreactive pan; boil for 2 minutes. Let cool 5 minutes. Add the pectin and 1 or 2 drops of food coloring, then bring to a rolling boil and boil for 1 minute (do not exceed manufacturer's recommended time).

Pour into hot, sterilized jelly jars to ½ inch from the rim. Wipe the rims with a clean damp cloth and seal immediately with melted paraffin (page 207). Place scalded lids on the jars and tighten. Place on a rack to cool. Store in the refrigerator once opened. If the jelly turns to sugar, melt it and use it to baste or as a sauce for meats or in salad dressing.

For a clear jelly, strain the mixture after it has boiled for 2 minutes; return to the pan, bring to a boil and continue as directed; however, the flecks of pepper are attractive. The color of the jelly can be enhanced with a drop or two of food coloring, if desired.

Any chilli—jalapeños, habanero, dátil, serrano, chiltepínes—can be used, but don't mix them if you want a distinct flavor typical of that variety.

ALTERNATIVE: Try a chilli pepper jelly that is not from scratch.

- 2 habanero or Scotch bonnet chillies or 4 jalapeños, 4 serranos, or 8 chiltepínes, or to taste; stemmed, seeded, and finely chopped
- 1 cup white vinegar
- 1 cup sugar
- 4 10-ounce jars apple or current jelly

Mix the chillies, vinegar, and sugar in a 4- to 5-quart nonreactive sauce pan. Bring to a boil over high heat and boil, stirring, until the mixture is reduced to about ½ cup, about 7 minutes. Remove the jelly from the jars with a sterile spoon and stir it into the pepper mixture. Boil, stirring, until jelly melts. Ladle the hot jelly back into the unwashed jars to within ½ inch of the rims. Wipe rims clean with damp paper toweling and tighten lids onto the jars. If there is any jelly left over, put it into a covered dish for immediate use.

After 1 to 2 hours, agitate the jars to redistribute the pepper pieces. When jelly is cool, store it in the refrigerator up to 4 months.

Notes

Which Way Did They Go?

1. At the time of the discovery, four or five of the more than twenty different wild capsicums had been domesticated through selection by the skillful agriculturists who inhabited the New World, and no others have had their genetic makeup altered to produce another domesticated species since that time. *Capsicum annuum* var. *annuum* (cayenne, bell pepper), the most common of the group, was domesticated in Mesoamerica (roughly, the area between a line extending from the Gulf of Mexico to the Pacific at the mouth of the Rio Grande River in northern Mexico and another just below present day Belize in Central America to the south); *C. frutescens* ('Tabasco'), then only semidomesticated and now insupportable, could have come from anywhere in the American tropics; *C. chinense* (habanero, Scotch bonnet) originated in Amazonia; *C. baccatum* var. *pendulum* (*ají* amarillo) arose in the highlands of Peru or Bolivia; and *C. pubescens* (rocoto) is an Andean domesticate. See "Look at Me: Cultivar Descriptions" for specifics.

2. In correspondence, botanist W. Hardy Eshbaugh related that there was recent evidence suggesting *Capsicum annum* var. *aviculare/glabrisculum* may have extended north of the Rio Grande River, to southern Arizona, coastal Louisiana and Florida in the pre-Columbian era; however, he offered no documentation and, to date, has found none. Archaeologists at UT-Austin in 1999 assured me that no *Capsicum* seeds dating before the coming of the Spanish have been found north of the Rio Grande River—to their present knowledge.

3. Herbals contain the names and descriptions of herbs or plants in general. Most of the earliest were prepared by medical doctors. Although few pre-Columbian Amerindian manuscripts survived the Conquest, those that did show that some peppers and numerous depictions of capsicums have been found on pre-Columbian artifacts.

4. Fuchs's botanical masterpiece appeared in 1542 as *De historia stirpiuim* in Latin. The following year (1543) an edition in the vernacular German was called *New Kreüterbüch*.

5. Mesoamerica (map 3 p. 11) is an area in North America roughly extending from coast to coast near Tampico, Mexico at the Tropic of Cancer to an angled line running from Cape Gracias a Dios on the Gulf of Honduras south-southeast to the Pacific coast of westernmost Panama.

6. At the dawn of the great explorations in the fifteenth century Europeans were carnivorous while the rest of the world was basically vegetarian, but both craved spices. The vegetarians used spices to perk up their bland starch-legume diets, and the carnivores used spices not only to camouflage the putrid flavor and odor of spoiling meat but to help preserve perishable foods, and to make foods preserved by salting and pickling more palatable. Although there was no refrigeration, several methods for preserving food were known.

    Until the late seventeenth century European agriculturists endured a persistent shortage of winter feed for cattle. The result of this was the need to slaughter a sizable number of cattle each fall and to preserve the meat for winter consumption by the methods commonly practiced at the time—salting, pickling, drying, and powdering with spices. Large quantities of spices from India and the East Indies served to modify the flavor of meats and vegetables preserved by those unpalatable means. Whatever the reason, the demand for these aromatic seasonings resulted in a profitable spice trade. It has been known that spices have germicidal properties but to be effective had to be used in greater concentration than ordinarily used in food (Rosengarten, 1973:20). More recent studies reveal the phenolics in the volatile oils have both antimicrobial effects as well as antioxidative action (Govidarajan, et al, 1987:191). The spice trade led to capsicums but capsicums have been found to have very low volatiles content and their antimicrobial activity is not significant (Ibid:192).

Not all peoples attempt to mask the smell and taste of spoiled food. In fact, some pay extra for "high" meats and cheeses while others prepare sauces from fermented fish.

7. Archeologist William C. Sturtevant, in a paper written in 1961, also states that *Capsicum annuum* and or *C. frutescens* were being grown by the Tainos (Arawaks) at the time of contact. He based his statement on the records of the Columbian chroniclers and a paper written by Heiser and Smith in 1953. That paper was written when only those two species were accepted and before the authors had isolated *C. chinense*. I think Sturtevant's diagnosis would probably have been different if he had seen their 1957 paper which discussed the dominant *Capsicum* species in the West Indies—*C. chinense*. Not that *C. annuum* could not have been there, and I think it was, but evidence other than the outdated research he cited will be needed.

8. Peter Martyr (1493) reported that maize, which along with several varieties of *C. annuum* var. *annuum* was first domesticated in Mexico, was brought to Iberia when Columbus returned from his first voyage in 1493. Carl O. Sauer (1966:54), writing in 1966, also tells us the maize-beans-squash complex, which originated in Mesoamerica, was growing in island *conucos* (mounded gardens).

In addition, by the time of the discovery, the Mexican turkey, immediately noticed and favored by Europeans because it was superior to their domestic fowl, had "passed, along with other Mesoamerican traits and intruders, into Coiba country and was taken from there to Darièn (Panama) and on to Santo Domingo (West Indies), between which places there was [among the Spanish] frequent communication," Sauer continues. People carrying the turkey and some corn to feed it could have carried peppers. I think the Spanish had already picked up annual peppers somewhere in the Spanish Main (West Indies Islands + southern littoral of Caribbean + the intermediate sea) before Cortes's conquest of Mexico in 1521, otherwise Martyr could not have seen and described them, and soon thereafter the Portuguese got them from the Spaniards.

9. Nahuatl, the language of the Aztec overlords of Tenochtitlan, was the official trade language within large stretches of pre-Columbian Mesoamerica, and it is still spoken by a million and a half people in Mexico. The Nahuatl word *chilli,* meaning the *Capsicum* plant, is not found in Emilio Tejera's Dictionary of indigenous words of Santo Domingo where the Spanish first headquartered. All of the early writers— Chanca, Martyr, C. Columbus, F. Columbus, de las Casas—used the South American/Caribbean name *aji* when speaking of peppers. It was not until Cortés opened Mexico in 1521 that the word *chilli* became known. Dr. Francisco Hernández, the king's historian and physician, who lived in Mexico from 1570 to 1577, was the first to use chilli in print.

10. According to anthropologist Sophie D. Coe (1994:69), Montezuma and Moctezuma are Spanish mangling of the name of the Aztec Emperor Motecuhzoma, which means "angry like a lord."

11. The authors determined the pre-Columbian distribution of capsicums by research using methods such as archaeological evidence, comparative genetics, and chromosomal studies, along with Vavilov's method of analyzing the geographic distribution of morphological (shape) variance.

12. This was but one of several reports providing evidence that capsicums were the earliest spice yet known to have been used by humans, even earlier than Middle Eastern saffron which came into use approximately 3,000 years ago.

13. We know he brought the finger-shaped (now cayenne-type) back on his first voyage because it was described by Martyr when he described the plants collected on that journey. How it got to the West Indies from Mesoamerica is a question of great importance but without precise answer. Those described by Martyr are the same as those pictured in Fuchs and are but little different from the more common cultivars in Mexico described by Hernández. More than two hundred years later that finger-shaped pepper acquired the name cayenne—but that is another story.

14. There are several translations of the log of Columbus with minor variations. Those I have looked at have been translated by V. W. Brooks, J. M. Cohen, C. Jane, R. H. Funson, and S. E. Morison.

15. They were all dead when he returned later that year.

16. Varieties of tiny chillies, both *Capsicum annuum* var. *annuum* and *Capsicum frutescens* are commonly called *meleguetas*, especially in Brazil, where the spelling is *malagueta,* after the African spice *Aframomum melequeta,* which is not related to either black or red pepper. According to Fuchs, *melegueta* pepper is named for Melle or Mèlèga in the northern Niger area of Guinea, Africa. This member of the ginger family is a small, aromatic, sorghum-sized seed confusingly called Guinea pepper or grains of paradise, terms also applied to chillies and cardamom. Traveling to Europe across the Sahara desert it was known in Lyons and Venice during the thirteenth century as a less expensive substitute for black pepper. Following the Portuguese establishment of a fort and trading post at Elmina on the Bight of Benin on the West African coast in 1482, Elmina became the center for a

flourishing sea trade in ivory, slaves, gold-dust, and melegueta pepper. During the sixteenth century that littoral was first known as the Melegueta Coast, then as the Grain Coast after Grains of Paradise, another name for that spice. After the discovery, chillies of the finger-type also came to be called "ginnie" pepper. To complicate matters even further a New World tree of the myrtle family, *Pimenta dioica,* which produces allspice, has long been called the Malagueta Pepper tree (Gomez-Ortega, 1780:16). None of the three plants are in any way related to each other or related to black pepper.

17. The unique North American symbiotic maize-beans-squash complex recognized by geographer Carl O. Sauer in 1966, and referred to as the "Three Sisters" by Native Americans, is a concept critical to any study of *Capsicum* diffusion. I suggest that chillies were an adjunct to that triad and were not only grown and eaten with them, but also traveled with them throughout the tropical and subtropical world and from there into more temperate areas. In that case they would be called the "Three Sisters and Little Brother"—no one would ever take a pepper to be female.

18. Columbus's second son Fernando was born in 1488 at Córdoba as a result of a liaison during the six years Christopher waited, unemployed, in the shadows of King Fernando and Queen Isabella's battle tents as they pursued the final destruction and surrender of the Moors at Granada. Fernando Columbus and Bartolomé de Las Casas, a record keeping Dominican friar who traveled in the West Indies, had access to the Columbus papers, and both recorded full narratives of his life and voyages.

19. According to Samuel Elliot Morison, (1963:328), at the time of the European arrival in America, ocean-going canoes such as these were used by the Arawak and Carib Indians only for interisland trade. Ferdinand's description of the canoe and its contents leaves no doubt that it was Honduran/Maya. The Amerindian mariners hugged the coast just as their contemporary Mediterranean mariners did. Although some did venture into the open sea it was only to reach nearby offshore islands from Mesoamerica or interisland within the West Indies (A.P. Andrews, 1991:72). Theoretically the trade between Continental America and the West Indian Islands only went by a roundabout route—south through Central America, east across Tierra Firme (Panama, Columbia, Venezuela), and thence north into the islands (Sauer, 1966:54). It is, however, highly possible that one or more of these Mesoamerican canoes reached the Greater Antilles with its contents without establishing regular communication with the West Indians.

20. During the spring semester of 1991 botanist Dr. Charles B. Heiser, Professor Emeritus Indiana University, held the Jean Andrews Visiting Professorship in Tropical and Economic Botany at The University of Texas at Austin. I was privileged to have conversations with him on this question at that time. The following pertinent correspondence was an outgrowth of those conversations.

In August of 1991, while reexamining Fuchs's herbal at my request, Heiser found something of particular interest to the diffusion of New World plants. He reports: "Fuchs describes four American plants—maize, beans, squash, and peppers (maybe more, but I haven't had time for checking). The cucurbit is *Cucurbita pepo.* This, like *Capsicum annuum,* we thought was found only in Mesoamerica and not in the West Indies at the time of the discovery. (The species most likely to be in the West Indies was probably *Cucurbita moschata.*) Therefore, I think it likely that Columbus got the squash seed the same time as he did *C. annuum.*" These statements are based on place of origin—*C. pepo* in Mesoamerica; *C. moschata* from South America had traveled with the Arawaks to the West Indies—without mentioning the possibility of a pre-Columbian movement from Mesoamerica to the West Indies. Nevertheless it backs up my theory that the Mesoamerican plants were available within the Spanish Main before the discovery and conquest of Mexico. That herbal illustrates both Sauer's (1966:54) corn complex and peppers, thereby adding weight to Stoianovich's (1966:1030) thesis that "there is little chance that corn came from the New World to Europe by itself," and to my theory that peppers traveled as part of that complex.

21. As implausible as it may appear, between 1502 and 1510 we were told by Valentin Fernandes, a German in the employ of Portugal, that during the same year the Spanish made their first American mainland contact (1502), the Portuguese introduced Indian corn/maize to their Island of São Tomé from an earlier introduction to their trading bases in Guinea (now Ghana), Africa (Jeffereys, 1954:193). That corn/maize would have had to come to Africa from a West Indian source via Iberia, the Canaries, the Cape Verdes, or Madiera because at that time the only recognized New World mainland contact the Portuguese had made was in Brazil (1500) and that was too late for them to have established maize in Africa from an unknown Brazilian source, then transported it to São Tomé so soon after the discovery. Also, in 1502 Columbus made his fourth voyage, which took him to the mainland. Mexico was yet to be discovered. Although Brazil was discovered in 1500, at that time and for the next thirty years, the Portuguese had little or no contact with that country,

which was very much in its natural state and without maize. Finally, the first documented Portuguese visit to the West Indies in 1509, was much too late.

22. Writing in 1864, O'Gorman reveals that Las Casas's observations cannot be definitely dated; the best we can do is to say he made them between the time of his first arrival in Española in 1502 and his last visit to that island in 1532. In Seville some twenty-five years after making the first draft, Las Casas separated the *Historia* and the *Apologética* and enriched them with numerous interpolations. Since Las Casas remarked that the peppers he saw were "like those already known in all Spain" it would be very significant to know when he was referring to them growing in Spain—at the time of his first sighting, at the time of his first draft, or when he made his final revision. His first visit to Española coincided with Columbus's discovery of the mainland in 1502. During his second stay in the West Indies (1508 to 1515), Las Casas farmed a grant of land on the river Arimáo in Española between 1513 and 1514 (O'Gorman, 1967:xxxiv). I tend to think he made his agricultural observations during that sojourn, which was well before the discovery of Mexico, thereby strengthening my thesis that there was pre-Columbian Mesoamerican exchange with those islands.

23. Although the Portuguese were the first Europeans to explore and lay claim to Africa, where they were dominant until 1600, it is very precarious to allege that a vast Portuguese province existed in Africa. In the west, Angola, Guinea, the Islands of Cape Verde, São Tomé, and Principe represented the extent of Portuguese dominion—their islands were the most significant. A population promoting miscegenation and Westernization was never established as it was later in Brazil; however, although little beyond the seaboard was under their control, a large coastal zone reveals Portuguese influence (Rodriquez, 1965:14–15).

24. As stated by Charles Boxer, the four principal causes of Portuguese exploration in chronological order were: (1) crusading zeal, (2) desire for Guinea gold, (3) quest for Prester John, a powerful if implausible schismatical Christian priest-king, (4) search for spices. The spices, however, only become a significant objective after the death of Prince Henry in 1460. By that time west African slave trade was going strong (Boxer, 1969a:6).

25. Fernand Braudel relates that coasting, or hugging the shoreline, was prevalent in the Mediterranean and much of India during the fifteenth and sixteenth centuries. Mediterranean sailors were fainthearted when it came to taking their boats across the seas even though yearly voyages to London and Antwerp were not uncommon. Sailing close to shore provided protection against the elements, and having the coastline in sight aided navigation. The small capacity of the boats made necessary almost daily stops to renew water, wood, and supplies. These stops gave ample opportunity for bartering and exchange, and for accidently spreading seed in food scraps. Merchants would voyage with their wares, and every seaman, from captain to cabin-boy, had a packet of merchandise on board. The long trips were a sequence of selling, buying, and exchanging the cargo. The only things resembling our "destination-conscious" modern shipping were the large specialized salt and grain ships. The others were more like floating markets. The practice of seamen carrying merchandise for sale persisted throughout the days of the sailing merchant ships (Braudel, 1976:107).

26. The growing of sugarcane in plantations by the Portuguese is critical to our study of the movement of New World *Capsicum* because it was in these equatorial plantations that tropical red peppers first became cultivated in the Old World and from them it moved around the globe. The slave trade which was an outgrowth of that institution—sugar plantations—was a prominent vehicle for the diffusion of peppers and other food plants in the "Columbian Exchange." For more about sugar see page 99 (Fage, 1959:45).

27. Essentially the trade castle was designed as a self-sufficient community. Each fort maintained a large garden where European vegetables were grown from imported seed. After contact was made with Asia and America, tropical fruit trees were introduced. Support crops like maize, beans and manioc were also introduced. One of the persuasive motives for cultivating new crops and anti-scorbutic fruits was to supply the slave-ships with provisions for the Atlantic crossing; and another was to furnish a base to repair and provide fresh produce for their own ships—especially on the return voyage (Lawrence, 1964:37–39). During four-hundred years of the trade, a total of between twenty to thirty million slaves may have been embarked. Records of Danish ships were better than on British and Dutch vessels. Their records show that fifteen percent of the slaves died on the crossing to America as compared to thirty-five percent of the officers and crew during a round trip.

In 1997 I traveled alone on a pilgrimage to those West African trade castles. Standing at the gateway of the entry bridge spanning the moat surrounding awe-inspiring Elmina (1482) was the most emotional experience of my twenty-year *Capsicum* quest.

28. The most important of the papal bulls was the *Inter coetera*, which granted to Spain and Portugal everything they could discover on their side of the imaginary line. In 1529 the Treaty of Zaragossa attempted to settle the problem which resulted when that first line

went through the then unknown Far East. Spain and Portugal made an agreeable exchange that allowed Spain to retain the Philippines which fell within Portuguese territory by the lines of those treaties. Those treaties unwittingly determined the Old World destination of many New World plants. By 1600 the Protestant powers of Europe chose to ignore those Catholic bulls and sailed their ships into the forbidden area.

29. São Tomé and the Cape Verde Islands off the coast of West Africa were critical Portuguese bases during the late fifteenth century and early sixteenth century. Because the Portuguese introduced New World plants to their working plantations on these islands and Guinea very soon after the discovery, they are significant locations in the movement of these new plants around the world. Little São Tomé, with its greenhouse-like climate in the equatorial Atlantic about 275 miles from shore, an attack deterring distance, became the headquarters of the Portuguese slave trade and an obligatory shipping point on the metropole-Angola-Mozambique sea route (Abshire & Samuels, 1969:23).

30. The Canary Islands, which were the only inhabited islands in the eastern Atlantic before the coming of the Europeans, were known to classical mariners in the fifth century B.C. and then lost until a French or Genoese ship rediscovered them in the fifteenth century. These islands became indispensable to sailing ships. Those ships going to India usually took a trade wind-determined route by way of Madeira, the Canaries, Cape Verde Islands, near to the Brazil bulge, down to and around the Cape of Good Hope, Mozambique, up to Cape Guardafui near the Red Sea, and across the Indian Ocean to Goa. Returning from Goa or Cochin, the returning voyagers dropped down south of Madagascar to the Cape of Good Hope, then to or west of the Cape Verde Islands, on to the Azores, then home to Lisbon. These islands were named for the wild dogs, canis, which inhabited the area when they were discovered. Later, yellow finches, which also lived on the islands, were named canaries for the islands and not vice versa.

31. Boxer has estimated that during the sixteenth century Portugal never had a population of more than a million and a quarter. Of that number approximately twenty-four hundred to four thousand left Portugal yearly for overseas, the majority being able-bodied and unmarried young men, bound for Goa and the Far East, few of whom ever returned (the death rate on the India bound ships was 50 percent). Emigration by women was discouraged.

The largest number of women going in any given year was fifty-four, but something between five and fifteen would have been a more likely annual figure. There were never more than seven thousand persons in the "white" population in Portuguese Asia. One reason for this scarcity of white women and their posterity was the fact that so many Portuguese men, including the soldiers, chose to live with a harem of African slave girls, in preference to Asian women, rather than marry while they were young.

There was no clear racial prejudice, and inevitably those men born in Portugal who spent several years in the east took native wives. In India, Portuguese blood inclined to get more diluted as time went by. The lack of pure blooded Iberians forced the selection of local Indian and half-caste recruits to man ships and forts. At the same time a similar all-male situation existed among the Spanish in the West Indies. It was 1502 before the first European women arrived in the New World. Unlike the Portuguese, the Spanish later encouraged the immigration of marriageable women, with some success, and attempted to teach European ways to the native population (Boxer, 1975:66; Hart, 1950:250).

32. Cabral determined the practical course for sailing ships from Europe to the Cape of Good Hope, which is still followed, and he also discovered Madagascar. He initiated the system for fortified factories where goods could be stored, thereby eliminating the delay of the fleets until purchases could be made (Greenlee, 1937:xxxiii).

33. At the time of its discovery, Brazil, unlike Mexico and India, was in its original state, undeveloped by its stone-age inhabitants.

34. In 1509 the West Indies was inhabited by eight to ten thousand Europeans. Between the time ninety men in the initial Columbus band set foot on the islands in 1492 until then, three million Native Americans died—three hundred Arawaks and Caribs for each Spaniard (Means, 1935:31).

35. In the highlands of Mexico the Spanish encountered a climate and landscape more comparable to their Extremadura and Andalucia than the tropical West Indies. Also, the people they found there were practicing an intensive seed agriculture within a society somewhat similar to their own feudal system instead of the relatively primitive inhabitants of the islands (Means, 1935:31).

36. By 1550 the Spanish population in the West Indies had dwindled until it did not exceed fifteen-hundred. Hispaniola had a thousand Spaniards and twelve to thirteen thousand Africans. In fact, Africans were the bulk of the people on the islands. The first Negro slaves were brought to the West Indies in 1502 directly from Spain, where enslavement of Jews, Moors and Negroes was an established institution.

37. According to Sauer (1969:152), "Columbus brought some maize to Spain, but only here and there, as in remote Galicia adjoining Portugal, did maize become

a common food." Here is another possible place for the Portuguese to have acquired maize seed.

38. Personal correspondence with Professors Murdo MacLeod, historian University of Florida, and Samuel M. Wilson, anthropologist, University of Texas at Austin, has assured me that the Portuguese were not present or active in any way in the Caribbean before the introduction of slaves from Africa around 1509. This would reaffirm my suggestion that the New world seed that went to West Africa and the Atlantic Islands within the first ten years following the discovery was not acquired directly from the West Indies by the Portuguese.

39. Jeffreys accepts the American origin of maize but he contends that it was in Africa and other parts of the Old World before Columbus as a consequence of trans-Atlantic contact in the centuries immediately preceding European Discovery. He insists there were Arab-Negro contacts with the Americas beginning about A.D. 900. Carl Sauer also puts forth some argument for that belief (Sauer, 1969:155-57). There are several things one should know about maize and its propagation. At that time maize had been domesticated so long that it had become incapable of self-propagation. It originated in the tropics and will grow under very adverse conditions and in wet lands. It produces a crop within sixty days—at least two and often three or four a year. The seed does not keep well compared to other crops. Edgar Anderson (1947:4) reports that "even under ideal conditions, it cannot be kept alive more than a few decades," therefore seed would have to be carried by humans and not by drift. When humans recognize the value of such a plant, it could be multiplied rapidly under difficult conditions—there were nine years from the time Columbus brought it to Spain and the time it was introduced to São Tomé. They could have propagated it immediately; you didn't have to clear a field, but only drop a seed in a little hole in the ground. If it had already been so well known in Spain and West Africa as those authors contend, why did Columbus bring it back from Hispaniola with the other curious new plants? Let's just call it "Speedy Gonzales" and be thankful that it took beans, squash, and peppers with it.

40. Climate is but one of the limiting factors in our environment. Besides temperature there are day length, water, nutrients, space, soil characteristics, and damaging interactions. Tropical and subtropical plants originated near the equator where season and distance from that line dictate the amount of natural sunlight on any given date. Plants are categorized as short-day, long-day, or day-neutral types. Tropical plants like capsicums are short-day plants because at the equator nights and days are the same length. Days lengthen as

you move away from the equator in either direction, affecting the flowering period. In recent years scientists discovered how to control photoperiodism and thus to modify the flowering process to suit the needs of the grower. In the past growers did this, consciously or unconsciously, by selecting seed from those short-day tropicals which survived and bloomed beyond tropical areas.

41. Duarte Barbosa was a Portuguese official in India from 1500 to 1517 who wrote an account of the countries bordering the Indian Ocean. After completion of that valuable work detailing his on site observations, he returned to Europe and went with Ferdinand Magellan on his voyage across the Pacific to the Philippines in 1519. Magellan's wife was Barbosa's sister.

42. The Flemish botanist Matthias de Lobel (1538 to 1616) observed that capsicums had been brought to Antwerp from Goa and Calicut at a very early date. From that we may assume the Portuguese very certainly began exporting them in competition with black pepper soon after they had introduced New World capsicums following their arrival in 1510 and before 1538.

43. Coffee first came to the notice of Europeans traveling in the Levant in the sixteenth century. In 1615 Venetian traders shipped coffee beans to Europe. The Dutch had introduced tea five years previous to that, and the Spaniards had initiated cocoa (made with water) drinking eighty years before that (Roden, 1983:76). These beverages accompanying dessert were quite revolutionary at the end of the seventeenth century.

44. I think that disbelief in the rapidity with which New World food plants spread has bred a school of thought that insists there is evidence that maize, for example, was grown in Guinea, Turkey, and Granada, Spain before Columbus; however, none of the evidence is botanical. Until biological evidence is found to support the claims, we should not doubt that the Old World and the New World each had unique flora and fauna up to the point of the Columbian exchange.

45. The banana is an example of this rapidity. The Moslems introduced it to Spain where it was cultivated in the twelfth century. From there it went to the Spanish Canary Islands and in 1516 it was brought to Hispaniola. Bananas became very abundant in the islands and on the mainland by 1526, and universal in the Americas wherever there were Christians, according to Oviedo's account in his 1535 edition (Wiener, 1920:129). In 1526 he also tells of the eggplants that were brought from Spain having become "as natural to America as Guinea was to Negroes, and far better than those that grew in Spain."

1. The Swahili coast of East Africa from Somalia to Sofala (near present Beria, Mozambique), was linked with Arabia and India. The culture there was essentially Arab and Persian although highly Africanized. The trade with the Persian Gulf, the Red Sea, and India was of long standing (Boxer 1969b:39).

2. Most early inventions having to do with the technology of guns were Muslim/Moorish discoveries. Their early firearms used flint stone to spark the gun powder. At the time of the European conquest of America, gunflints from Albania were preferred. Gunflints are tangible evidence of international commerce and technical excellence. Archaeologists working in Mesoamerica and South America have found that the Spaniards used Albanian gunflints in their Miquelet locks to slaughter and conquer the Amerindians. It made no difference where the flints came from, just so they were the best; consequently, rival armies often used flints from the same source. Huge numbers of guns of the Spanish and Turkish types were produced during that period. All of the early gunflints of Spain actually came from Albania, and were but one small item in a prosperous commerce reported by Witthoft (1966:40). The mariners on the trading ships which stopped for supplies at frequent intervals could have noticed new foods and carried them with them. This historic gunflint commerce might shed some light on Edgar Anderson's Anatolian mystery (see footnote 10), except Anatolia is so near Aleppo and on the route to Istanbul.

3. Peppers, like maize, could have been introduced to Abyssinia (Ethiopia) and Egypt from the Portuguese in India or by coasting Muslim traders from any of the Portuguese garrisons established to refit the Indian fleet along the Swahili Coast of eastern Africa— Mozambique, Mombassa, Malindi, Sofala. The supplies for these garrisons came from India or possibly the Portuguese Atlantic Islands, not from Mother Portugal. The Portuguese had an embassy at Massawa, the main port of Ethiopia, from 1520 (Wright, 1949:68). The Turks centered their activities at Harar, Ethiopia.

   Once the plants were being cultivated in that area, pilgrims from all over the Muslim world—India, Persia, Turkey, Syria, Gujarat—could have encountered seed on their journey to Mecca via the Red Sea port of Jedda (Jidda, Juddah, Juda). At this early period, 1520–1542, maize and possibly the other members of the complex —beans, squash, peppers—were more readily available for transfer to Europe from the Moslem regions of the Mediterranean than from the West Indies via the Iberian peninsula, hence in Europe they were known as "Turkish corn" and "Turkish peppers" (Ibid:64). At that time Turkey included Arabia and Syria.

4. Depending on which Indian seaport they sailed from, the vast convoys of ships reached the Red Sea in May or November every year. At Jedda they were met by congregations of caravans that could contain as many as 20,000 people and 300,000 animals at one time (Braudel, 1976:550). Jedda was also the port that served the pilgrims journeying to nearby Mecca.

5. Stoianovich recounts that in Hungary corn/maize is known as "maritime millet or grain" in reference to its arrival there by way of the Black Sea or the Adriatic. He asserts that there is little chance that corn came alone from the New World to Eastern Europe; but rather it arrived as part of Sauer's whole beans-maize-squash complex. In the New World, peppers were closely associated with that complex.

6. Hormuz was an island port open to every type of immigrant, every form of trade, and every kind of smuggling, whether by Venetians, Armenians, the Turks themselves, or the Portuguese adventurers who departed in astounding numbers for Turkey, where their knowledge of the East Indies was an important asset in the underground trade. Through Hormuz the best of India went to Venice. Hormuz was captured by the Portuguese in 1515 and held until 1662 (Braudel, 1976).

7. Until 1900 most of the cultivation of capsicums in India was carried on in the Goa area, and they became known in Bombay as *Gowaí mirchi,* Goa pepper (Watt, 1889:135).

8. After their capture of Hormuz and Muscat, the Portuguese dominated seaborne trade in the Persian Gulf but they could not completely close this route to Muslim traders because they needed to maintain good relations with Persia as a buffer to the marauding Turks (Boxer, 1969b:59).

9. Matthioli (1544) was the first of the great herbalists to recognize the New World origins of maize and other plants. Even if this does mean they did not originate in India as earlier herbalists had proposed, it does not negate the possibility that they were first introduced to most of the Old World from India after having been carried from their American place of origin by the Portuguese and Spanish at the beginning of the sixteenth century.

10. In a fascinating paper the ethno-botanist Edgar Anderson (1958:15) relates the "Anatolian Mystery" surrounding the fact that Anatolia, Turkey, is an important center of diversity (according to Vavilov) for many American domesticated food plants. He asks, "How did the tomato, along with chili peppers, tobacco, big-headed sunflowers, squashes, and of all things, pop-corn, get so thoroughly established in the eastern end of the Mediterranean?—One thing I do know: this tomato center does not extend to India."

    Because Anderson's observation of the early concentration of New World food plants in Turkey is critical to their European diffusion, I looked for any possible linkage. One possibility I noted was that the majority of the Sephardic Jews who were expelled from Spain at the same time Columbus sailed for America, went to Turkey, followed by Holland and Morocco (Singer, 1905:501; Browne, 1935:269). Since they may have left without knowledge of the New World plants and since Jews have never played much part in things agricultural this may not be significant. However, in view of writings by Rabbi Lewis Brown in which he remarked that the Muslims were "strangely tolerant" of Jews and the Arabs depended on them to show them the way in "the vast world beyond the desert," I include the suggestion. At that time Jewish traders traveled everywhere from England to India, from Bohemia to Egypt; however, their most common merchandise was slaves (Browne, 1935:196).

11. Ferdinand and Isabella of Spain were Manuel's in-laws.

12. The fifteenth-century Portuguese caravels were adapted from the Arabic or Mediterranean vessels into a handy lanteen-rigged craft of 100–150 tons or more. Galleons were longer and narrower than carracks, with less superstructure and more guns. At the height of its maritime power, little Portugal never had more than three hundred ocean-going ships at any one time (Boxer, 1969b:16). In the eighty-three years following da Gama's first voyage to India and the uniting of the Spanish and Portuguese crowns, six hundred and twenty ships left Portugal for India, and of these, two hundred and fifty-six remained in the East (Parry, 1953:95). There were never more than ten carracks in Indian waters at any one time (Moreland, 1920:204). Most of the Portuguese ships used in that area were built with European plans in Gujarat or Goa, using the superior Indian teak wood (Melink-Roelofsz, 1962:60). The small wooden plank Gujarat and Goan boats, designed for coasting with the monsoon winds, employed no nails, but were sewn together with coconut fiber cord *(coir)*. While in Goa and Cochin on the Malabar coast of India, I was able to examine and photograph boats of the same construction which are still used by fishermen along both the Arabian Sea and the Bay of Bengal.

13. The term Southwestern China includes Guizhou, Yunnan, Sichuan, Hunan, and Hubei on the authority of Laufer (1919), Chang (1977), and Ho (1955).

14. The Turkish standing army was usually made up of twelve to fourteen thousand *Janissaries* (unmarried infantry); ten to twelve thousand cavalry, each with four horsemen; plus irregulars. Two-hundred thousand took part in the invasion of Hungary (Scheville, 1922:230). It would take a lot to feed all those mouths on a daily basis.

15. The Levant is the non-European coast of the eastern Mediterranean extending from Greece to Egypt.

16. The existence of Venice as a great mercantile center can be explained in terms of the sea and the great waterways: the Brenta, the Po, and the Adige, converging on its lagoons. Small boats were constantly coming and going along these rivers and canals. Venice was the meeting point of sea routes and the continental routes that in spite of the Alps linked Central Europe with the Adriatic and the Levant. Waterways were critical to sixteenth-century travel (Braudel, 1976:127).

17. Venice closed her mainland frontiers in mid-1530 to all products coming by overland mule trains from Genoa or any foreign place. She forced the merchants of western Italy to come by sea to Venetian markets.

18. This was related to me by T. P. Ramamoorthy, Ph.D., a Tamil botanist with The University of Texas at Austin, whose family is of Cochin, India. Calicut, Cochin, and Goa (in that order) were the ports first reached and dominated by the Portuguese in the late fifteenth and early sixteenth centuries.

19. Another personal observation: today the great spice market in Istanbul, Turkey, is still called the Egyptian Market.

20. The American gallinaceous bird, the turkey, received unsuitable common and scientific names following its introduction into Spain early in the sixteenth century. It may or may not have been introduced to eastern Europe by the Turks but because of its spreading tail it was called by the same name given to a much earlier Turkish introduction (Schorger, 1966:3). It was the most popular and rapidly assimilated of any of the New World food introductions.

21. In French, India is *l'Inde,* while Indies is *les Indes.*

22. After this study I can no longer dismiss such names as "Turkish pepper," "Indian Pepper," "Calicut Pepper," *poivre d'Inde,* etc. as being, in Sauer's words, "casually convenient names for an alien and unknown source," as many authorities on foodways and New World plants have done. The herbalists and others who tagged them by such names were much closer to the scene, both in time and place, than are the debunkers. It is easier to dismiss the terms than it is to try to find out why they may have been applied. My investigation is but a start and an invitation to those who have the linguistic skills and patience to investigate old Turkish, Indian, German, Balkan, Venetian, Portuguese, and Spanish documents to do so. I regret I am not capable of doing so.

23. Parry probably referred to "grain" because "corn" was the English name applied to ALL grains for human consumption at time of the discovery of America and much of the Colonial period—wheat, rye, oats, barley,

millet, etc. To the English colonists, maize (*Zea maiz*), the new American grain crop, was a new type of corn and the colonials called it by its West Indian name—maize or Indian corn. By the middle of the eighteenth century the Americans had dropped the "Indian" and used only the word "corn" for maize. After the first livestock was brought from Europe to America it became necessary to return to Europe to obtain grain to feed the domesticated animals until sufficient grain crops could be cultivated in the American colonies. With the grain was seed from other plants that grew in the "corn field" such as corn poppies, corn flowers, corn daisies, and they soon became American "wild flowers." It is very confusing to read the old literature concerning corn because, for the most part, the corn referred to was not Indian corn, but wheat or one of the other grains. The inhabitants of the Old World accepted maize as both food and feed readily and rapidly but they wouldn't call it maize.

24. In 4(3):31 of *The Journal of Gastronomy,* the date which I attributed to Oviedo's report of the introduction of chillies to Italy should be 1535, the date of his *La Historia de las Indias,* and not 1526, the date of his *Sumario de la Natural Historia de las Indias.* Those nine years could make a considerable difference.

25. Days spent poring over books containing hundreds of Italian still-life paintings covering three centuries revealed little, if any, interest or acquaintance with New World fruits and vegetables. The Caravaggio-like painting had a squash, one tomato and two pepperoncini type peppers—one red and one yellow. A couple more had tomatoes. Obviously, the plants were not widely known in Italy.

26. Edgar Anderson (1958:14) reports that the Italians learned about the use of tomatoes from the Turks. Their original name for tomato is *pomo di moro,* the "apple of the Moors," later corrupted to *pomo d'oro,* and even more corrupted as *pomo d'amor* or love apple.

27. At the end of the sixteenth century the English herbalist John Gerard assumed peppers came to Spain and Italy from Guinea and India.

28. English privateers first ventured into the Spanish Main after 1560, but trade was not their objective. Their early activities were carried on without establishing bases.

29. I like to think that Catalina de Aragon (Katharine), the fifth and last child of Fernando and Isabella, the sponsors of the discovery of peppers by Christóbal Colón, was responsible for the introduction of the *Capsicum* to England and thence to Anglo-America. A wonderful, wish-filled scenario, yet—a possibility!

Hot Spots Today

1. In her book *Ethnic Cuisine*, food writer Elizabeth Rozin states that a flavor principle is a distinct combination of seasoning ingredients used consistently by an ethnic group (Rozin, 1992:xiv).

2. The account of the use of war dogs by the conquistadors is a fascinating, but little know facet of the conquest of America (Varner & Varner, 1983). The origin of the barkless, native Indian dog, which was small, fat, and used primarily for food, has not been determined. One theory is that these dogs may have emigrated from Asia with their masters (Weidensaul, 1999:52).

3. *Pili-pili*, *berbere*, *beri-beri*, and *piri-piri* are sound-alikes that could be different spellings of a local name for the same sauce.

4. The east coast of Africa is a different culture from that of West Africa, Sub-Saharan Africa, and North Africa. Although the foreign influences have been Africanized, the Arab, Persian and East Indian are still discernable. Boxer includes that area from Somaliland to Sofala, known by the Portuguese as *Estado da India*, in Asia. The coasts of the Indian Ocean, Persian Gulf and Red Sea were closely connected economically, politically, and culturally through trade. Goa, India, was the headquarters for the area from which the Portuguese dominated the trade (Boxer, 1969b:40). (Footnote 3, page 227)

5. In 1990, after my second trip to Turkey, I became "addicted" to a particular ground red chilli I found in the market at Urfa, and since then I have carried a small container of it in my purse. It is a challenge to stay supplied because it is not commercially available in Texas and *very* few seeds are left in the product with which to grow my own. Friends have brought it to me from Turkey. However, I did find it again in Aleppo, Syria, and restocked. After my talk about my Aleppo pepper at a presentation at Rutgers University, a member of my audience sent me a little bagful of "Aleppo Pepper." From that gift I located a Syrian market in Boston which has it. The merchant says he will not ship it, but Boston is closer than Urfa or Aleppo. In the meantime my crop gets a little larger each summer.

6. One way that intermixing occurred was through the Ottoman system of army recruitment. The entire standing army was continually replenished either by capture or a levy on the children of the Christian population. Every four years they selected a number of the most promising fourteen- to eighteen-year-old boys, whom they educated as Turks and Muslims. They became the sultan's slave family, and the best went on to be entrusted with the affairs of govern-

ment. Other than the sultan, there was hardly a born Muslim wielding a sword or scepter.

7. Leavened wheat bread is believed to have originated in ancient Egypt.

8. Some of the more common Middle Eastern/Mediterranean seasonings that were available before the "Columbian Connection" were onions, leeks, garlic, mint, dill, parsley, fennel, anise, coriander, and lemon.

9. An example of how difficult it is to change food habits: my son, who is a ship captain, was engaged in transporting supplies back to the United States that had been shipped to the Persian Gulf area for the Desert Storm operation. He told me about his experience with the unused, hermetically sealed meals-in-a-bag (MREs) that were prepared at great expense to feed our military forces. Tons of those carefully balanced, bagged meals were not consumed. Since it was going to be so costly to ship that food back to the United States, our government offered them to the local authorities to feed their starving people. Evidently it takes more than starvation to make Middle Easterners eat American food, in its scientifically designed package, because they turned it down. They just couldn't eat something so different.

  The *Austin American Statesman* of November 10, 1991, ran a story on those MREs which reported that in response to comments from American GIs after the Gulf War, future MREs will contain more packets of candy, non-melting chocolate bars, and *hot sauce*. We had the Astropod in space, now we'll have chili-peppers in the front lines. How can we lose?

10. It was a very exciting experience for me to stand at the sites of the ancient Portuguese quays below the majestic cathedrals in Old Goa (now Panaji) and picture just such a scene. The cities on the Malabar coast, where there are large numbers of Catholic Christians with Portuguese names, are quite distinct from other Indian towns. Not only is the architecture different, but the Catholics wear simple Western-style clothing instead of the typical woman's sari or man's sarong.

11. The Moghuls (Mughul in Persian) were Central Asian Turks who invaded India from Afghanistan and ruled from 1527 to 1707. Do not confuse them with the Mongols of Chinese Mongolia, although at an early date there was a mixture of Turkish and Mongolian blood, long since diluted to little more than a memory.

12. The Indian method of putting spices in hot oil to release the flavor is a practice of critical importance to the story of the movement of peppers because that same method is used in Turkey and the Balkans, though not in Italy and the western Mediterranean. The method of preparation probably came from India along with the foods being prepared.

13. During my second two-month "food trip" to India I discovered why my curries had never tasted quite right. I had been using our common dried white or yellow onions in their preparations while only the much sweeter purple/red onion or the mild shallot are available to cooks in India. For authenticity, use purple onions or shallots in all Indian recipes calling for onions.

14. Yogurt is the Turkish name for a dairy product (curds) which originated with the original nomadic Turks, who depended on animal food. It and other Turkish foodways traveled with the conquering Moghuls throughout the Middle East and India (Lewis, 1981:117).

15. In 1989 I attended the Oriental Hotel Cooking School under Charlie Amatayakul in Bangkok, Thailand.

16. The ancient monsoon seafarers left their wives and families at home. During long separations caused by waiting for favorable monsoons, they cohabited with native women. The children of these "marriages" were schooled in the religion of the father and when they grew up they, in turn, helped to spread their father's faith among their mother's people, hence the large Moslem population in Indonesia today (Boxer, 1969b:45).

17. The voyage of Magellan's *Victoria* is probably the single most exceptional voyage in the history of navigation. Magellan, who had previous experience sailing in Malayan waters, was searching for the Moluccas in an attempt to break the Portuguese spice monopoly, when he overshot his mark and hit the Philippines instead (Boxer, 1969a:17).

18. The famous "Spanish shawls" were originally embroidered on Chinese silk by Chinese hands in the Philippines, from whence they voyaged aboard the Manila galleon to Acapulco, Mexico, then by mule train to Vera Cruz and on across the Atlantic to Sevilla, where they are known as *Mantones de Manila*. Today there are shawl "factories" in Seville where local women embroider the same type of Manila shawl.

19. Restaurants originated in China during the T'ang dynasty (A.D. 618–907). In the Sung dynasty which followed, sex was added to the menu of those sociable meeting places. Even though that delicacy is no longer offered, the Chinese probably eat out more than any other culture.

20. Since 1949 there have been many changes in Chinese life; naturally, they would affect food habits. I'm certain regional differences have become less obvious as a result of the commune system combined with increased food importation, better transportation, and improved communications, as well as advances in storage, irrigation, and agricultural technology. There has been little systematic inquiry to determine the extent of change in culinary practices. What the Western

tourist eats is not the daily fare of the people but is redolent of pre-1949 cookery. For an excellent "case study" in which scholars of food-in-culture have presented a descriptive history of food habits in China, read *Food in Chinese Culture* edited by K. C. Chang.

21. I am indebted to and envious of Maria Johnson, whose linguistic skills made it possible for her to examine documents from Hungary and Turkey that are not decipherable to the average scholar.

22. In 1989 I spent a pleasurable and informative week attending the Eighth International Conference on Ethnological Food Research in Philadelphia, during which time Halasz and I held many interesting paprika palavers.

23. As further evidence of contact between Venice and the Ottomans, polenta originated in Macedonia, where it was originally made from coarse wheat. New World corn went from Turkey to Macedonia, and then it, along with the recipe, probably journeyed to northern Italy together. Spaghetti was a souvenir Marco Polo brought back to Italy from his oriental journeys.

What is a Pepper?

1. Both the *Capsicum* and the bean pod are fruits, but the chilli is not a pod despite that traditional designation. A pod is a dry, dehiscent fruit that splits open along two sutures to release the seed, as in a legume.

2. Domestication is an evolutionary process operating under the influence of human activity. In plants there is genetic modification from their wild state through selection, or by using modern biotechnology. According to Heiser (1973), domestication is completed when man controls the breeding of the organism. A domesticated type is usually incapable of survival without the care of humans, although some domesticates—horses, pigs, and a few domesticated plants—can revert to a wild-type existence. According to Heiser (1973:163), once humans began to select for particular qualities in a plant species, whether consciously or not, they had begun the workings of domestication (ex. sugarcane, maize). It is complete when humans control the breeding of the organism. Selection continued to be the main method of improving plants and animals for thousands of years. Modern genetics has speeded up the process.

3. To cultivate means to conduct activities involving the care of a plant; it is concerned with human activities. A plant can be cultivated both before and after it is domesticated. Domesticated and cultivated are often used synonymously, but in fact, they have quite different significance.

4. The diffusion of capsicums to Africa and Asia took place in such a short time that many years later Europeans thought they had originated in the Orient. Evidence of that is the name *chinense* given to a species by Nicholas Jacquin in 1776 when he stated that he had named it for its home.

5. Those interested in more information than is given in this chapter may want to go to *Peppers: The Domesticated Capsicums*, or some of the material listed in its bibliography.

6. A cultivar is a population variant or hybrid that has originated and persisted under cultivation. The word is formed from "cultivated variety" and is abbreviated as "cv." There are hundreds of bell pepper cultivars, for example, each with a name in conformity with the *International Code of Nomenclature of Cultivated Plants*, and that name must be markedly different in the way it is written from the scientific name, which is regulated by the *International Code of Botanical Nomenclature*. Examples of cultivar names: *Capsicum annuum* var. *annuum* cv. 'Caloro'; *Capsicum frutescens* cv. 'Tabasco'.

    A cultigen is a plant that has been modified to the point it can only survive with human assistance. It is only known in cultivation.

7. By definition a variety is a group or type within a species or subspecies which differs in some significant respect from other members of the species such as pod shape. The name given to the group/type is actually the common or generic name for its qualified members. It was first used to classify commercially significant cultivars in the U.S. by P. G. Smith, et al., in *Hortscience* 1987, 22[1]:11–13. That form of classification is being expanded, but now includes mostly those of *Capsicum annum* var. *annum*, because other species are only recently becoming commercially important in North America.

8. In 1997 Dr. Richard Willis (nutritionist at UT-Austin) and I attempted a modified version of the Brit's metabolism study using whole Chiltepín fruits without the mustard. We found that the entire fruit had absolutely no effect on human metabolism, evidently acting like any encapsulated source of capsaicin—passing from the stomach unchanged. However, we did find that crushed Chiltepínes without the mustard did elevate the metabolism for a few hours, but not to the scale as that of the pepper sauce and mustard in the Henry & Emery study.

9. Vanillyl amide compounds or capsaicinoids in *Capsicum* are predominantly capsaicin (CAP sixty-nine percent), dihydrodcapsaicin (DHC twenty-two percent), nordihydrocapsaicin (NDHC seven percent); homocapsaicin (HC 1 percent), homodihydrocapsaicin (HDHC one percent). Several more analogues of these in trace amounts bring the number to ten. CAP

and DHC are the primary heat contributors, but the delayed action of HDHC is the most irritating and difficult to quell.

10. While other guests were sitting lethargically at the table following a long, sumptuous dinner party, I emptied a sackful of peppers I had brought to my hosts into the middle of the table. Even as the bright pods, representing nearly all species, were falling into a vivid pile, the sated guests jumped up, began touching the peppers, talking animatedly all at one time, and dashing for cameras—completely revitalized. I am continually amazed at the way chillies excite people as no other food does.

Look at Me

1. It was during my visit to the ancient Portuguese trade castles of Elmina (1482) and Quidah (Juda) on the Gold Coast of West Africa that I received the inspiration to track down the origin of the word cayenne. There I purchased a little book in French and English which introduced me to another book written early in the eighteenth century titled *The Knight of Marchais' Travel in Guinea, the Neighboring Isles and to Cayenne.* My curiosity was aroused. Upon my return to Austin, Texas, I went immediately to the splendid libraries at the University of Texas and found a copy of that book in the rare book section of the Latin American Collection. I knew that necessary rules operant in that library would restrict my usage of the four volumes, but with pencil and notepad (the only tools permitted) in hand, my search was on. Besides the help of the skilled librarians who oversee that remarkable collection, it took quite a while before I found a translator of French who was skilled in Old French, then a Brazilian who was familiar with Tupi, but fourteen months after returning from my solo trip to West Africa, I came up with the solution. Noted geographer and holder of the Webb Chair at UT-Austin, Terry Jordan, concurs.

2. In the eighteenth century reports of the voyage of the Chevalier des Marchais in 1722, 1726, and 1727 by R. Pere Labat (1731:[3] 62), we learn that an island off the coast of French Guiana (1643) was already known as Cayenne Island.

3. An African spice, *Afromomum melegueta,* or grains of paradise, is the original "ginnie pepper"; however, after the Portuguese introduction of the American cayenne-type pepper to Africa, that type was also called "Ginnie pepper."

4. New Mexicans do not like to credit Oñate with introducing peppers to New Mexico because he was a Spanish creole. Perhaps they are not aware that his wife was the mestizo granddaughter of the conquistador Cortés and the great granddaughter of the Indian chieftain Moctezuma, a renowned lineage (Cornish, 1917:453).

Cooking with Peppers

1. At our local farmer's market I was admiring one of the pepper displays when a basketful of habaneros reminded me of how I discovered my chlorine bleach cure for capsaicin burn. After telling the grower, a retired professor, about the process she exclaimed, "That's it! My partner and I always thought we were immune to capsaicin burn when our employees' hands always got burned and ours never did, but now I know why. We have always kept a bowl of water with chlorine bleach in it on the counter so that we could keep our cleaning rags sterile. Every time we do something we use a rag from the bowl to wipe up with. All this time it has been neutralizing the capsaicin while we thought we were immune."

2. In recent years breeders have not only developed yellow and orange bell peppers but also variously colored cayennes, jalapeños and others. There are even new bell peppers with a green color at maturity such as 'Monster Brand Bell Pepper'. The mature color depends on the cultivar chosen. Except in those few new mature green cultivars, the green color is indicative of immaturity.

3. Most vacuum sealers are too bulky and expensive for the ordinary kitchen, but kitchen stores sell other types, such as Vacu Products, in several sizes. These plastic containers have stoppers and a pump to remove air like those used to preserve opened champagne. In lieu of those, displace air with paper towels and/or suck air out with a straw or tube before completely sealing. Repeat this each time you open the container. Oxygen is the culprit you want to get rid of.

4. Freezing breaks all plant cells, thus on thawing exposes the compounds to the destructive effects of oxidation through oxidases. Boiling before freezing inactivates the oxidases, thus reducing capsaicin loss (Tom Mabry, personal communication, 1999). For further information on freezing food refer to McGee, 1984:168.

Bibliography

ABSHIRE, D. M. and M. A. SAMUELS

1969. *Portuguese Africa: A handbook.* New York: Praeger Publishers.

AJAYI, J. F. A. and M. CROWDER

1972. *History of West Africa.* Vol. I. New York: Columbia University Press.

AMERICAN DIETETIC ASSOCIATION

1985. Pepper research "heats up." *Jour. Amer. Dietetic Assn.* 85(July):798.

ANDERSON, E.

1947. "Corn before Columbus." Des Moines, IA: Pioneer Hi-Bred Corn Co.

1958. Anatolian mystery. *Landscape.* Pp.14–16, Berkeley: Turtle Island Foundation. Calif.

1967. The bearings of botanical evidence on African cultural history. In *Reconstructing African cultural history.* Ed. by C. Gabel and N. R. Bennett. Pp.167–80, Boston: Boston University Press.

1967. *Plants, man and life.* Berkeley: University of California Press.

ANDERSON, E. N., J. R., and M. L. ANDERSON

1977. Modern China: South. In *Food in Chinese culture.* Ed. by K. C. Chang, Pp. 317–82, New Haven: Yale University Press.

ANDREWS, A. P.

1991. America's ancient mariners. *Natural History.* October. Pp. 72–75.

ANDREWS, J.

1984. *Peppers: The domesticated Capsicums.* Austin: University of Texas Press.

1988. Around the world with chili pepper: The post-Colombian distribution of domesticated *Capsicums. The Journal of Gastronomy.* 4(3):21–35.

1991. A newly recognized variety of chili-pepper (*Capsicum* Solanaceae) developed in the United States. *Phytologia.* 69(6):413–15.

1993. Towards solving the "Anatolian mystery": Diffusion of the Mesoamerican food complex to southeastern Europe. *Geographical Review.* 83(2):194–204.

1993. *Red hot peppers.* New York: Macmillan Publishing Co.

1995a. *Peppers: The Domesticated Capsicums.* Revised. Austin: University of Texas Press.

1995b. A botanical mystery: The elusive trail of the datil pepper to St. Augustine. *Florida Historical Quarterly.* Fall. Pp. 132–47.

In press.*Capsicums.* In *Cambridge history and culture of food and nutrition project.* Edited by K. F. Keple, New York: Cambridge University Press.

ANGHIERA, P. M. d'.

1964.*Decadas del Nuevo Mundo, por Pedro Martir de Angleria, primer cronista de Indias.* Mexico, D. F.: Jose Porrua y Hijos, Sucs.

ARBER, AGNES

1953. *Herbals: Their origin and evolution, a chapter in the history of botany.* Cambridge: Cambridge University Press.

ARBERRY, A. J.

1939. A Baghdad cookery book. In *Islamic culture.* Hyderabad, India, Pp. 13–47, 189–214.

ARNOTT, MARGARET L.

1975. *Gastronomy: The anthropology of food and food habits.* The Hague: Mouton Publishers.

AYKROYD, W. R.

1967. *Sweet malefactor: Sugar, slavery and human society.* London: Heineman.

BAILEY, L. H.

1923. *Capsicum. Gentes herbarum.* 1:128–29.

BAKER, H. G.

1970.*Plants and civilization.* Belmont, Calif.: Wadsworth.

BALABAA, S. I., M. S. KARAWYA & A. N. GIRGIS

1968. The capsaicin content of *Capsicum* fruits at different stages of maturity. *Lloydia.* 31(3):272–74.

BARBOSA, D.

1918. *The book of Duarte Barbosa: An account of countries bordering on the Indian Ocean and their inhabitants.* Trans. by M. L. Dames, Vol. 1, London: London: Hakluyt Society.

BARRACLOUGH, G.

1982. *The Times concise atlas of world history.* Maplewood, N. J.: Hammond.

BENÍTEZ, ANA M. de

1974. *Pre-Hispanic cooking.* Mexico: Ediciones Euroamericanas.

BENNETT, D. J., and G. W. KIRBY

1968. Constitution and biosynthesis of capsaicin. *J. Chem. Soc.,* no. 442.

BLAKE, J. W.

1937. *European beginnings in West Africa: 1454–1578.* London: Longmans, Green and Co.

BONIFACE, B. R.

1971. *A historical geography of Spanish Florida circa 1700.* Unpubl. master's thesis; University of Georgia.

BOXER, C. R.

1952. Maize names. *Uganda Journal.* 16(2):178–79.

1953. *South China in the sixteenth century.* London: Hakluyt Society. 2d. ser., vol. 106.

1963. *The great ship from Amacon: Annals of Macao and the old Japan trade 1555–1640.* Lisboa: Centro de Estudios Historicos Ultramarinos.

1967. Spaniards and Portuguese in the Iberian colonial world: Aspects of an ambivalent relationship 1580–1640. In *Salvador de Madariaga.* Bruges: Liber Amicorum.

1969a. *Four centuries of Portuguese expansion: 1415–1825.* Berkeley: University of California Press.

1969b. *The Portuguese seaborne empire, 1415–1825.* London: Hutchinson.

1975. *Mary and Misogyny: Women in Iberian expansion overseas; some facts and personalities.* London: Duckworth.

1980. *Portuguese India in mid-seventeenth century.* Delhi: Oxford University Press.

1984. *From Lisbon to Goa 1500–1750. Studies in Portuguese maritime enterprise.* London: Variorum Reprints.

1985. *Portuguese conquest and commerce in southern Asia 1500–1750.* London: Variorum Reprints.

BRADFORD, E.

1971. *The Mediterranean: Portrait of a sea.* New York: Harcourt Brace Jovanovich.

BRAND, D. D.

1967. Geographical exploration by the Spaniards. Pp. 109–44.

Geographical exploration by the Portuguese. Pp. 145–50. In *The Pacific Basin.* Ed. by D. R. Friis, New York: American Geographical Society.

BRAUDEL, F.

1976. *The Mediterranean and the world in the age of Philip II.* Vols. I and II. New York: Harper and Row.

1979. *The wheels of commerce.* Vol. II. New York: Harper and Row.

1982. *The structures of everyday life: The limits of the possible.* New York: Harper and Row.

BROOKS, V. W. (Translator)

1924. *Journal of first voyage to America by Christopher Columbus.* New York: Albert and Charles Boni.

BROWNE, L.

1935. *Stranger than fiction.* New York: Macmillan.

BULLARD, R.

1961. *The Middle East, a political and economic survey.* London: Oxford University Press.

CANDOLLE, A. P. de

1852. *Prodromous.* 13:411–29. Paris: Masson.

CASAS, B. de las

1699. *An account of the first voyages and discoveries made by Spaniards in America.* London.

1967. *Apologética historia sumaria, 1520–1561.* Ed. by E. O'Gorman. Vol. I. Mexico: Universidad Nacional Autónoma de México.

CHANCA, D. A.

1497. Letter to the municipal council of the city of Seville, Spain. In *The letters of Christopher Columbus.* Ed. R. H. Major. Pp. 19–71. 2d ed. London: Hakluyt Society, 1870.

CHANG, K. C. (Ed.)

1977. *Food in Chinese culture: Anthropological and historical perspectives.* New Haven: Yale University Press.

CIKOVSKY, N.

1988. *Raphaele Peale still-lifes.* New York: Harry N. Abrams.

COE, S. D.

1994. *America's first cuisines.* Austin: University of Texas Press.

COETZEE, R.

1892. *Funa food from Africa: Roots of traditional African food culture.* Durban/Pretoria: Butterworth.

COHEN, J. M. (Ed.)

1969. *The four voyages of Christopher Columbus.* Baltimore: Penguin Books.

COLES, P.

1968. *The Ottoman impact on Europe.* London: Thames and Hudson.

COLUMBUS, C.

1971. *Journal of first voyage to America by Christopher Columbus.* Freeport: Books for Libraries Press.

COLUMBUS, F.

1947. *Vida del Almirante don Cristobal Colon.* México: Fondo de Cultura Economica. [1571].

COVINGTON, J. W.

1959. Trade relations between southwest Florida and Cuba 1600–1840. *Florida Historical Quarterly.* 38:114–28.

CROSBY, A. W., JR.

1972. *The Colombian exchange: Biological and cultural consequences of 1492.* Westport, Conn.: Greenwood Press.

1986. *Ecological imperialism: The biological expansion of Europe 900–1900.* Cambridge: Cambridge University Press.

CRUXENT, J. M., and I. ROUSE
1969. Early man in the West Indies. *Scientific American.* 22(5):42–51.

DAMES, M. L. (see Barbosa, D.)

DAVIDSON, B.
1961. *The African slave trade.* New York: Little, Brown.

DIEHL, A. K. and R. L. BAUER
1978. Jaloproctitis. *New England Journal of Medicine.* 229(20): 1137–38.

DOBBY, E. H. G.
1961. *Monsoon Asia.* London: University of London Press.

DRUMMOND, J. C., and A. WILBRAHAM
1969. *The Englishman's food: A history of five centuries of English diet.* London: Jonathan Cape.

DUNCAN, T. B.
1972. *Atlantic islands: Madeira, the Azores, and the Cape Verdes in seventeenth century commerce and navigation.* Chicago: University of Chicago Press.

DUNKLE, J. R.
1955. *St. Augustine, Florida: A study in historical geography.* Unpubl. Ph.D. diss., Worcester, Mass.: Clark University.

DUNLOP, D. M.
1971. *Arab civilization to A.D. 1500.* London: Longman Group.

DUYVENDAK, J. J. L.
1949. *China's discovery of Africa.* London: Arthur Probsthain.

EDWARDS, P. G. (Ed.)
1967. *Equiano's travels.* London: Heinemann.

ELTON, G. R. (Ed.)
1962. *The new Cambridge modern history.* Vol. II. Cambridge: Cambridge University Press.

ESHBAUGH, W. H.
1964. A numerical, taxonomic and cytogenetic study of the genus *Capsicum.* Ph.D. diss., Indiana University.

1968. A nomenclatural note on the genus *Capsicum. Taxon.* 17:51–52.

1980. The taxonomy of the genus *Capsicum* (Solanaceae). *Phytologia.* 47(3):153–66.

1982. The genus *Capsicum* (Solanaceae) in Africa. *Bothalia.* 14(3 & 4):845–48.

1983. Peppers: History and exploitation of a serendipitous new crop. In *Advances in New Crops.* Proceedings Second National Symposium New Crops: Resources, Development, and Economics.

ESHBAUGH, W. H., S. I. GUTTMAN, and M. J. MCLEOD
1983. The origin and evolution of domesticated *Capsicum* species. *J. Ethnobiology.* 3(1):49–54.

FAGE, J. D.
1959. *Ghana: A historical interpretation.* Madison: University of Wisconsin Press.

FAIRBANKS, G. B.
1975. *The history and antiquities of the city of St. Augustine, Florida* [1858]. Gainesville: University Presses of Florida.

FARB, P., and G. ARMELAGOS
1980. *Consuming passions: The anthropology of eating.* Boston: Houghton Mifflin.

FERET, B. L.
1979. *Gastronomical and culinary literature: A survey and analysis of historically-oriented collections in the USA.* Methuen, N. J.: Scarecrow Press.

FERNANDES, VALENTIM
1514. *Roteiro quatrocentista transcrito por Valentim Fernandes.* in: *Os mais antigos roteiros da Guiné.* Ed. Damião Peres. Lisbon: Academia Portuguesa da Historia.

FERNÁNDEZ, M. G.
1971. The life of Las Casas. In *Bartolomé de las Casas in history.* Ed. J. Friede and B. Keen. Pp. 67–125. DeKalb: Northern Illinois University Press.

FINAN, J. J.
1950. *Maize in the great herbals.* Waltham, Mass.: Chronica Botanica Co.

FISHER, W. B.
1978. *The Middle East.* London: Methuen.

FRANKLIN, D.
1984. Heated research of pepper pain. *Science News.* 126 (Sept.):132.

FREYRE, G.
1966. *The masters and the slaves: A study in the development of Brazilian civilization.* New York: Alfred A. Knopf.

FRIIS, H. R.
1967. *The pacific basin: A history of its geographical exploration.* New York: American Geographical Society.

FUCHS, L.
1543. *New Kreuterbuch* (*De historia stirpium* in 1542). Basel: Isingrin.

FUSON, R. H. (Translator)
1987. *The Log of Christopher Columbus.* Camden, Maine: International Marine Publishing House.

GALE, J. S.
1972. *History of the Korean people.* Seoul: Royal Asiatic Society, Korean Branch.

GEERTZ, H.
1967. Indonesian cultures and communities. In *Indonesia.* Ed. R. T. McVey. Pp. 24–96. New Haven: HRAF Press.

GERARD (GERARDE), J.
1597. *The herball or generall historie of plantes.* London: John Norton.

GIBAULT, M. G.
1912. *Histoire des légumes.* Paris: Librairie Horticole.

GODE, P. K.
1960. The history of maize (maká) in India between A.D. 1500–1900. In *Studies in Indian cultural history.* 2(32):283–94.

GOMEZ-ORTEGA, C.

1790. *Historia plantarum Novae Hispaniae*. Matriti, ex typographia Ibarrae heredum.

GOVINDARAJAN, V. S.

1985. *Capsicum*: Production, technology, chemistry and quality. Botany, cultivation and primary processing. *Crit. Rev. Food Sci. Nutr.* 22(2):108–75.

1986a. *Capsicum*: Production, technology, chemistry and quality. Processed products, standards, world production and trade. *Crit. Rev. Food Sci. Nutr.* 23(3):206–88.

1986b. *Capsicum*: Production, technology, chemistry and quality. Chemistry of the color, aroma, and pungency stimuli. *Crit. Rev. Food Sci. Nutr.* 24(3):244–355.

GOVINDARAJAN, V. S., V. S. RAJALAKSHMI and N. CHAND

1987. *Capsicum*: Production, technology, chemistry and quality. Evaluation of quality. *Crit. Rev. Food Sci. Nutr.* 25(4):185–282.

GREENHILL, B.

1956. The Karachi fishing boats. *Mariner's Mirror*. 42(1):54–66.

GREENLEE, W. B.

1937. *The voyage of Pedro Alvares Cabral to Brazil and India*. London: Hakluyt Society.

GREWE, R.

1987. The arrival of the tomato in Spain and Italy: Early recipes. *The Journal of Gastronomy*. 3(2):67–82.

GRIGSON, J. (Ed.)

1974. *The world atlas of food*. New York: Simon and Schuster.

GUNST, K.

1984. *Condiments*. New York: G. P. Putnam's Sons.

HABIB, I.

1982. *An atlas of the Mughal Empire*. Delhi: Oxford University Press.

HALASZ, Z.

1963. *Hungarian paprika through the ages*. Budapest: Corvina Press.

HANCE. H. F., and W. F. MAYERS.

1870. Introduction of maize into China. *Pharmaceutical Jour. Trans.* Dec. 31, Pp. 522–25.

HARDING, C.

1964. *Trade and navigation between Spain and the Indies in the time of the Hapsburgs*. Gloucester, Mass.: Peter Smith.

HARLAN, J. R.

1975. *Crops and man*. Madison, Wisconsin: Amer. Soc. of Agronomy, Crop Soc. of Amer.

HARMAN, J. E.

1969. *Trade and privateering in Spanish Florida 1732–1763*. Jacksonville, Florida: St. Augustine Historical Society.

HARRIS, M.

1974. *Cows, pigs, wars, and witches: The riddles of culture*. New York: Vintage Books.

HART, H. H.

1950. *Sea road to the Indies*. New York: Macmillan.

HEISER, C. B.

1965. Cultivated plants and cultural diffusion in nuclear America. *Amer. Anthropology.* 67:937–49.

1969. *Nightshades: The paradoxical plants*. San Francisco: W. H. Freeman and Co.

1973. *Seed to civilization: The story of man's food*. San Francisco: W. H. Freeman and Co.

1976. Peppers: *Capsicum* (Solanaceae). In *Evolution of crop plants*. Ed. N. W. Simmonds. Pp. 265–68. London: Longman.

1985. *Of plants and man*. Norman: University of Oklahoma Press.

HEISER, C. B., and B. PICKERSGILL

1975. Names for the bird peppers [*Capsicum*—SOLANACEAE]. *Baileya.* 19:151–56.

HELPS, A.

1896. *The life of Las Casas the Apostle of the Indies*. London: George Ball & Sons.

HENDERSON, S. G., B. E. NICHOLSON, G. B. MASEFIELD, and M. WALLIS

1969. *The Oxford book of food plants*. Oxford: Oxford University Press.

HENKIN, R.

1991. Cooling the burn from hot peppers. *JAMA.* 266(19): 2766.

HENRY, C. J. K. & B. EMERY

1985. Effect of spiced food on metabolic rate. *Human nutrition: Clinical nutrition.* 40(4):165–68.

HERNANDEZ, F.

1651. *Nova plantarum, animalium et mineralium Mexicanorum Historia, rerum medicarum novae*. Trans. into Latin from 1628 ed. by A. Reccho. Rome.

1943. *Historia de las plantas de Nueva Espana*. Vol. I. Mexico City: Inst. Biol. University Autonomo.

HILLMAN, H., and D. SHILLING

1979. *The book of world cuisines*. New York: Penguin Books.

HO, P. T.

1955. The introduction of American food plants into China. *American Anthropologist.* 55:191–201.

HOOKER, S. H.

1985. *Herbals and closely related medico-botanical works, 1472–1753*. Lawrence, Kans.: University of Kansas.

HOURANI, G. F.

1951. *Arab seafaring in the Indian Ocean in ancient and early medieval times*. Princeton: Princeton University Press.

HOUSTON, J. M.

1959. Land use and society in the plain of Valencia. In *Geographical Essays in Memory of A. G. Ogilie*. Eds. R. Miller and J. W. Watson. Pp. 166–94. Edinburgh: Nelson.

1949. The social geography of the Huerta of Valencia. Unpublished Ph.D. diss., University of Oxford.

HULTMAN, T. (Ed.)

1985. *The African news cookbook*. New York: Penguin Books.

HUNZIKER, A. T.

1958. *Synopsis of the genus Capsicum*. VIII Congress International de Botanique, Paris, 1954. Proceedings Sec. 4(2):73–74.

HSW, V. Y. N., and F. L. K. HSU

1979. Modern China: North. In *Food in Chinese culture*. Ed. K.C. Chang. Pp. 295–316. New Haven: Yale University Press.

IZZEDDIN, N.

1953. *The Arab world: Past, present, and future*. Chicago: Henry Regnery.

JANE, C.

1988. *The four voyages of Columbus*. New York: Dover Publications.

JEFFREYS, M. D. W.

1953. *Pre-Colombian maize in Africa*. London: Macmillan Journals. 172 (4386):965–66.

1954. Maize names. *Uganda Journal*. 18(2):192–94.

1975. Pre-Colombian maize in the Old World: An examination of Portuguese sources. In *Gastronomy: The anthropology of food and food habits*. Ed. by M. L. Arnott. Pp. 23–66. The Hague: Mouton Publishers.

JOHNSON, M.

1981. North Balkan food, past and present. In *National and regional styles of cookery, Proceedings*. Pp. 122–33. Oxford Symposium 1981. London: Prospect Books.

JUDGE, J.

1986. Where Columbus found the New World. *National Geographic*. 170(5):562–99 (with Supplement of 70 Pp. and a map.)

KALRA, J. I. S., and P. D. GUPTA

1990. *Prashad: Cooking with Indian masters*. New Deli: Allie Publishers.

KARTTUNEN, FRANCES

1983. *An Analytical Dictionary of Nahuatl*. Austin: University of Texas Press.

KRAMARZ, I.

1972. *The Balkan cookbook*. New York: Crown Publishers.

LABAT, R.

1731. *The Travels of Pyrad de Laval*. 4 Volumes. Amsterdam: La Compagnie.

LABORDE CANCINO, J. A., and O. POZO COMPODONICO

1982. *Presente y pasado del chile en Mexico*. Pub. Especial Num. 85. Mexico City: Nac. de Invest. Agri.

LANE, F. C.

1940. Notes and suggestions: The Mediterranean spice trade in *American History Review*. 45:581–91.

LATOURETTE, K. S.

1964. *A short history of the Far East*. New York: Macmillan.

LAUFER, B.

1907. The introduction of maize into eastern Asia. *Proceedings 15th Congress Americanists*. Vol. I. Pp. 224–57.

1919. Sino-Iranica: Chinese contributions to the history of civilization in ancient Iran, with special reference to the history of cultivated plants and products. *Field Museum of Nat. His.* No. 201, 15(3):185–621.

1929. The American plant migration. *The Scientific Monthly*. 28:235–51.

LAWRENCE, A. W.

1964. *Trade castles and forts of West Africa*. Stanford: Stanford University Press.

LEE, T. S.

1954. Physiological gustatory sweating in a warm climate. *Jour. Physiol.* 124:528–42.

L'ÉSCLUSE, C.

1611. *Curae posteriores post mortem*. Antwerp.

Le MAGNEN, J.

1981. Neurophysiological basis for sensory mediated food selection. In *Criteria of food acceptance*. Ed. by J. Solms and R. L. Hall. Zurich: Forster Verlag AG, p. 268.

LEWIS, R.

1981. Turkish cuisine. *National and regional styles of cookery, Proceedings*. Pp. 117–21. Oxford Symposium 1981. London: Prospect Books.

LOBELIUS, M.

1576. *Plantarum sev stirpium historia*. Antverpiae.

LONG-SOLIS, J.

1986. *Capsicum cultura: La historia del chili*. Mexico: Fondo de cultura economica.

MacARTHUR, D.

1964. *Reminiscences*. New York: McGraw-Hill.

MACLEAN, L.

1978. *Sauces and surprises*. Glasgow and London: Collins.

MacLEOD, M.

1973. *Spanish Central America: A socioeconomic history*. Berkeley: University of California Press.

MacNEISH, R. S.

1967. A summary of the subsistence. In *The prehistory of the Tehuacan Valley*. Vol. I, *Environment and subsistence*. Ed. D. S. Byres. Pp. 290–309. Austin: University of Texas Press.

MAGA, J. A.

1975. *Capsicum*. In *Critical revisions in food science and nutrition*. Pp. 177–99. Cleveland: CRC Press.

MAJUPURIA, I.

1980. *Joys of Nepalese cooking*. Gwalior-1, India: Smt. S. Devi Madhoganj.

MANNIX, D. P.

1978. *Black cargoes: A history of the Atlantic slave trade, 1518–1865*. New York: Penguin Books.

MARCHANT, A.

1941. Colonial Brazil as a way station for the Portuguese India fleets. *Geographical Review*. New York: Amer. Geog. Soc. Vol. 31, July. Pp. 454–65.

MARTINEZ, M.

1979. *Catalogo de nombres vulgares y cientificos de plantas Mexicanas.* Mex. DF: Fondo de Cultura Economica, Mex. DF, Amer. de. University 975.

MARTIUS, C. F. P. von

1863. *Glossaria linguarum Brasiliensiium: Glossarios de diversas lingoas e dialectos, ques fallao os indios no imperio do Brazil.* Erlangen: Druck von Junge & Sohn.

MARTYR, P. (see Anghiera, P. M. d')

MASADA, Y., K. HASHIMOTO, T. IMOUE, and M. SUZI

1971. Analysis of the pungent principles of *Capsicum annuum* by combined gas chromatography. *Journal of Food Science.* 36: 858.

MATTHIOLI, P. A.

1544. *Commentarii in sex libros Pedacii Dioscoridis.* Lyon: Anazarbeen de la matit.

McCLURE, S. A.

1982. Parallel usage of medicinal plants by Africans and their Caribbean descendants. *Economic Botany.* 36(3):291–301.

McCUE, G.A.

1932. The history and use of the tomato: An annotated bibliography. *Annals of the Mo. Bot. Gard.* 39:289–348.

McGEE, H.

1984. *On food and cooking: The science and lore of the kitchen.* New York: Collier Books.

1990. *The curious cook: More kitchen science and lore.* San Francisco: North Point Press.

McLEOD, M. J. S, S. I. GUTTMAN, and W. H. ESHBAUGH

1982. Early evolution of chili peppers (*Capsicum*). *Econ. Bot.* 36(4):361–68.

1983. Peppers (*Capsicum*). In *Elsevier plant isozyme monograph.* Ed. by S. D. Tanksley and T. W. Orton. Pp. 361–68. Las Cruces, N. M.: New Mexico State University.

McVEY, R.

1963. *Indonesia.* New Haven: Southeast Asia Studies, Yale University.

MEANS, P. A.

1935. *The Spanish Main: Focus on envy 1492–1700.* New York: Scribner's.

MEILINK-ROELOFSZ, M. A. P., and GODINHO, V. M.

1962. *Asian trade and European influence in the Indonesian Archipelago, 1500–1630.* The Hague: Martinus Nishoff.

MILLER, P.

1768. *The gardener's and botanist's dictionary.* 8th ed. London: Miller.

MINTZ, S. W.

1988. Food origins and syntheses in Caribbean history. *Journal of Gastronomy.* 2(4):35–43.

MIRACLE, M. P.

1967. *Agriculture in the Congo basin. Tradition and change in African rural economics.* Madison: University of Wisconsin Press.

MONARDES, N.

1574. *Joyfull news out of the newe founde worlde.* Trans. by J. Frampton. New York: Alfred A. Knopf. Repr. 1925.

MONOD, T.

1960. Notes botaniques sur les iles de São Tomé et de Principe. *Baulletin de l'I.F.A.N. 22,* Series A: 19–83.

MONTAGNÉ, P.

1968. *Larousse gastronomique.* New York: Crown Publishing, Inc.

MOORE, F. W.

1970. Food habits in non-industrial societies. In *Dimensions of nutrition.* Ed. by J. DuPont. Pp. 181–221, Boulder: Colorado Associated Universities Press.

MORAN, E. F.

1975. Food, development, and man in the tropics. In *Gastronomy.* Ed. by M. L. Arnott. Pp. 169–86. The Hague: Mouton Pub.

MORELAND, W. H.

1920. *India at the death of Akbar: An economic study.* London: Macmillan, Ltd.

1939. The ships of the Arabian Sea about A.D. 1500. *Journal of the Royal Asiatic Society.*

MORISON, S. E.

1942. *Admiral of the ocean sea.* Boston: Little, Brown.

1963. *The journals and other documents of the life of Christopher Columbus.* New York: Heritage Press.

MOTE, F. W.

1979. Yüan and Ming. In *Food in Chinese culture.* Ed. by K. C. Chang. Pp. 193–258. New Haven: Yale University Press.

MULHERIN, J.

1988. *Spices and natural flavorings.* New York: Macmillan.

MURAKAMI, N.

1917. Japan's early attempts to establish commercial relations with Mexico. In *The Pacific ocean in history.* Ed. by H. M. Stephens and H. E. Bolton. Pp. 467–80. New York: Macmillan.

MURATORI, C.

1952. Maize names and history: A further discussion. *Uganda Journal.* 16(1):76–81.

MURDOCK, G. P.

1959. *Africa, its peoples and their cultural history.* New York: McGraw Hill.

MUROGA, N.

1967. Geographical exploration by the Japanese. In *The Pacific basin.* Ed. by D. R. Friis. Pp. 96–108. New York: Amer. Geog. Soc.

NABHAN, G. P.

1985. *Gathering the desert.* Tucson: University of Arizona Press.

NELSON, E. K.

1910. Capsaicin, the pungent principle of *Capsicum*, and the detection of Capsaicin. *J. Ind. Eng. Chem.* 2:419–21.

NEWMAN, B.

1945. *Balkan background*. New York: Macmillan.

NEWMAN, J.

1981. Regional and other differences of Chinese cookery. In *National and regional styles of cookery, Proceedings*. Pp. 33–41, Oxford Symposium 1981. 1981. London: Prospect Books.

NOVO, S.

1967. *Cocina Mexicana: Historia gastronomica de la Ciudad de Mexico*. Mexico D. F.: Editorial Porroua SA.

NUTTALL, Z.

1906. The earliest historical relations between Mexico and Japan. From original documents preserved in Spain and Japan. In *University of Calif. Publications. American Archaeology and Ethnology*. 4(1):1–47.

OGINI, F. G.

1977. *An outline history of West Africa, 1000–1800*. Nigeria: Macmillan.

O'GORMAN, E. (Ed.)

1967. *Apologética historia sumaria*. Vol. 1. Mexico: Universidad Nacional Autónoma de Mexico.

ORTA, G. Da

1563. *Colloquies on the simples and drugs of India*. London: Henry Southern. Repr. 1913.

ORTIZ, E. L.

1979. *The book of Latin American cooking*. New York: Alfred A. Knopf.

1986. *Complete book of Caribbean cooking*. New York: Ballantine.

1988. *The book of Japanese cooking*. New York: M. Evans.

1989. *The food of Spain and Portugal*. New York: Macmillan.

OVIEDO y VALDÉS, G. F. De

1851–1855. *Historia general y natural de las Indias*. Toledo. [1535–1547].

PANAGOPOULOS, E. P.

1966. *New Smyrna: An eighteenth century Greek odyssey*. Gainesville: University of Florida Press.

PARES, C. H.

1995. *Huellas Ka-Tu-Gua*. Vol. I. Ensayos, Caracas: University Central of Venezuela.

PARRY, J. W.

1945. *The history of spices*. New York: Chemical Pub. Co.

1953. *Europe and a wider world: 1415–1715*. London: Hutchinson's University Library.

PARRY, V. J., H. INALCIK, A. N. KURAT, and J. S. BROMLEY

1976. A history of the Ottoman empire to 1730. Chapters from the *Camb. Hist. of Islam and The New Cambridge Modern History*. Ed. by M. A. Cook, Vol. II. Cambridge: Cambridge University Press.

PERRY, C.

1983. Grain foods of the early Turks. In *Food in motion: Migration of foodstuffs and cookery techniques*. Ed. by Alan Davidson. Pp. 11–22, London: Prospect Books.

PICKERING, C.

1879. *Chronological history of plants*. Pp. 560, 976. Boston: Little Brown.

PICKERSGILL, B.

1969. The domestication of chili peppers. In *The domestication and exploitation of plants and animals*. Ed. by P. J. Ucko and G. W. Dimbleby. Pp. 443–50, London: Gerald Duckworth.

1984. Migrations of chili peppers, *Capsicum*. spp. in the Americas. In *Pre-Colombian plant migration*. Ed. by Doris Stone. Pp. 106–23. 14th International Congress of Americanists. Cambridge: Peabody Mus. of Arch. and Ethnology, Harvard University.

PICKERSGILL, B., and C. HEISER, JR.

1976. Cytogenetics and evolutionary change under domestication. *Phil. Trans. Royal Soc. London*. 275:55–69.

PORZIO, F. (Ed.)

1989. *La natura morta in Italia*. Vol. 2. Milan: Electa.

POST, L. C.

1933. The domestic animals and plants of French Louisiana as mentioned in the literature with reference to sources, varieties and uses. *Louisiana Historical Quarterly*. 16:554–86.

POUNDS, N. J. G.

1979. *A historical geography of Europe 1500–1840*. Cambridge: Cambridge University Press.

PRAKASH, O.

1961. *Food and drinks in ancient India*. Delhi: Munshi Ram Manohar Lal.

PROCTOR, V. W.

1968. Long-distance dispersal of seeds by retention in digestive tract of birds. *Science*. 160(3825):321–22.

PURSEGLOVE, J. W.

1963. Some problems of the origin and distribution of tropical crops. *Genetics Agraria*. 17:105–22.

1968. *Tropical crops: Dicotyledons*. New York: Halsted Press.

QUINN, J.

1975. *Minorcans in Florida: Their history and heritage*. St. Augustine: Mission Press.

RAYCHUDHURI, H., and T. RAYCHANDHURI

1981. Not by curry alone: An introductory essay on Indian cuisines for a western audience. *National and regional styles of cookery, Proceedings*. Pp. 45–56. Oxford Symposium 1981. London: Prospect Books.

REVEL, J. H.

1982. *Culture and cuisine*. New York: Doubleday.

RICK, C. M.

1978. The tomato. *Scientific American*. 238:78–87.

RIDLEY, H. N.

1930. *The dispersal of plants through the world*. Ashford, Kent, England: L. Reeve.

ROBELO, C. A.

1904. *Dictionario de Aztequismos*. Mexico: Ediciones Fuente Cutural.

RODEN, C.

1980. Early Arab cooking and cookery manuscripts. *Petis Propos Culinaires*. 6:16–27.

1983. The spread of kabobs and coffee. In *Food in motion: Migration of foodstuffs and cookery techniques*. Ed. by Alan Davidson. Pp. 74–79. London: Prospect Books.

1985. *A book of Middle Eastern food*. New York: Alfred A. Knopf.

RODRIQUES, J. H.

1965. *Brazil and Africa*. Berkeley and Los Angeles: University of California Press. (Photocopy); Diffusion.

ROMANS, B.

1961. *A concise natural history of east and west Florida*. Gainesville: University of Florida Press.

ROOSEVELT, A.

1984. Problems interpreting the diffusion of cultivated plants. In *Pre-Colombian Plant Migration*. Ed. by Doris Stone. Pp. 2–18. Cambridge: Peabody Mus. of Arch. and Ethnology, Harvard University.

ROOT, W.

1971. *The food of Italy*. New York: Atheneum.

ROOT, W., and R. ROCHEMONT

1976. *Eating in America: A history*. New York: Morrow.

ROSELLI, B.

1940. *The Italians in colonial Florida*. Florida: Drew Press.

ROSENGARTEN, F., JR.

1973. *The book of spices*. New York: Pyramid Books.

ROUSE, I.

1953. *Guianas: Indigenous period*. Mexico: Programa de Historia de America.

1966. Mesoamerica and the eastern Caribbean area. In *Handbook of Middle American Indians*. Ed. by R. Wauchope. Vol. 4. Pp. 234–41.

ROUSE, I and L. ALLAIRE

1978. Caribbean chronology. In *Chronologies in New World Archaeology*. New York: Academic Press. Pp. 431–81.

ROZIN, E.

1982. The structure of cuisine. In *The psychobiology of human food selection*. Ed. by L. M. Barker. Pp. 189–203. Westport, Conn.: AVI Publishing.

1983. *Ethnic cuisine: The flavor principle cookbook*. Brattleboro, Vt.: Stephen Green Press.

1992. *Ethnic cuisine: How to create the authentic flavors of 30 international cuisines*. New York: Penguin Books.

ROZIN, E., and P. ROZIN

1981. Culinary themes and variations: Traditional seasoning practices provide both a sense of familiarity and source of variety. *Natural History*. 90(2):6–14.

ROZIN, P.

1982. Human food selection: The interaction of biology, culture, and individual experience. In *The psychobiology of human food selection*. Ed. by L. M. Barker. Pp. 225–52. Westport, Conn.: AVI Publishing Co.

1990. Getting to like the burn of chili pepper. In *Chemical Senses*. Ed. by B. G. Green, J. R. Mason and M. R. Morley. Pp. 231–69. New York: Marcel Dekker, Inc.

ROZIN, P., L. EBERT, and J. SCHULL

1982. Some like it hot: A temporal analysis of hedonic responses to chili pepper. *Appetite: Journal for Intake Research*. 3:13–22.

ROZIN, P., and A. F. FALLON

1981. The acquisition of likes and dislikes for food. In *Criteria of food acceptance*. Ed. by J. Solms and R. L. Hall. P. 35. Zurich: Forster Verlag AG.

RUMPHIUS, G. E.

1741–50. *Herbarium Amboinense*. Ed. by J. Burman. Vol. 5. Amsterdam: F. Chansuion, J. Catuffe, and H. Vywerf.

RUSSEL, R. J., F. B. KNIFFEN, and E. L. PRUITT.

1961. *Culture worlds*. New York: Macmillan.

SANNA, L., and R. J. SWIENTEK

1984. HPLC quantifies heat levels in chili pepper products. *Food Processing*. October: 70.

SASS, L. J.

1981. Religion, medicine, politics and spices. *Appetite: Jour. for Intake Research*. 2:7–13.

SAUER, C. O.

1952. *Agricultural origins and dispersals*. Cambridge: MIT Press.

1966. *The early Spanish Main*. Berkeley: University of California Press.

1969. *Seeds, spades, hearth, herds: The domestication of animals and foodstuffs*. Cambridge: MIT Press.

SAUER, J. D.

1988. *Plant migration: the dynamics of geographic patterning in seed plant migration*. Berkeley: University of California Press.

SCHAFER, E. H.

1977. T'ang. In *Food in Chinese culture*. Ed. by K. C. Chang. Pp. 85–140. New Haven: Yale University Press.

SCHEVILL, F.

1972. *The Balkan Peninsula and the Near East: A History from the earliest times to the present day*. London: C. Bell and Sons.

SCHOPF, J. D.

1911. *Travels in the confederation 1783–1784*. Philadelphia: Wm. J. Campbell.

SCHORGER, A. W.

1966. *The wild turkey: Its history and domestication*. Norman: University of Oklahoma Press.

SCHURZ, W. L.

1939. *The Manila galleon*. New York: E. P. Dutton.

SIMON, A.

1951. *A concise encyclopedia of gastronomy*. New York: Harcourt, Brace.

SIMOONS, F. J.

1961. *Eat not this flesh: Food avoidances in the Old World*. Madison: University of Wisconsin Press.

SIMPSON, B. B., and M. CONNER-OGORZALY.
1986. *Economic botany*. New York: McGraw Hill.
SINGER, I. (Ed.)
1905. *The Jewish encyclopedia*. Vol. XI. P. 485. New York: Funk and Wagnalls.
SMITH, C. D.
1979. *Western Mediterranean Europe: A historical geography of Italy, Spain and Southern France since the neolithic*. London: Academic Press of Harcourt Brace Jovanovich.
SMITH, J. E., JR.
1967. Plant remains. In *The prehistory of the Tehuacan Valley*. Vol. I, *Environment and subsistence*. Ed. by D. S. Byers. Pp. 220–55. Austin: University of Texas Press.
SMITH, P. G., and C. B. HEISER
1951. Taxonomic and genetic studies on the cultivated peppers *C. annuum* L. and *C. frutescens*. *Amer. J. Bot.* 38:367–68.
1957. Taxonomy of *Capsicum sinense* Jacq. and the geographic distribution of the cultivated *Capsicum* species. *Bull. Torrey Bot. Club*. 84(6):413–20.
SMITH, P. G., B. VILLALON AND P. VILLA
1987. Horticultural classification of peppers grown in the United States. *HortScience*. 22(1):11–13.
SOKOLOV, R.
1991. *Why we eat what we eat: How the encounter between the New World and the Old changed the way everyone on the planet eats*. New York: Summit Books.
SOLANKE, T. F.
1973. The effect of red pepper (*Capsicum frutescens*) on gastric acid secretion. *Journal Surgical Research*. 15:385–90.
SORRE, M.
1962. The geography of diet. In *Readings in cultural geography*. Ed. by P. L. Wagner and M. W. Mikesell. Chicago: University of Chicago Press.
SPIKE, J. T.
1983. *Italian still life paintings from 3 centuries*. New York: National Academy of Design.
SPINDEN, H.
1928. Thank the American Indian. *Scientific American*. 138(Apr.):330–32.
STAVRIANOS, L. S.
1958. *The Balkans since 1453*. New York: Holt, Rinehart and Winston.
STOIANOVICH, T.
1966. *Le maïs dans les Balkans*. In *Annales: Économies sociétés civilizations*. 21(2):1026–40.
STURTEVANT, E. L.
1885. Kitchen garden esculents of American origin. *The American Naturalist*. 19(6):542–53.
STURTEVANT, W. C.
1961. Taino agriculture. In *The evolution of horticulture systems in native South America: Causes and consequences*.

Ed. by J. Wilbert. Pp. 69–82. Caracas: Sociedad de Ciencias Naturales La Salle.
SUPER, J. C.
1988. *Food, conquest, and colonization in sixteenth century Spanish America*. Albuquerque: University of New Mexico Press.
TANNAHILL, R.
1981. *Food in History*. New York: Stein and Day.
TEJERA, E.
1951. *Palabras indijenas de la isla de Santa Domingo*. Ciudad Trujillo, R.D.: Editora del Caribe, C. por A.
TODD, P. H., JR., M. C. BENSINGER, and T. BIFTU
1977. Determination of pungency due to *Capsicum* by gas-liquid chromatography. *Jour. of Food Sci.* 42(3):660–65.
TREASE, G. E., and P. W. C. EVANS
1983. Drugs of biological origin. *1983 Pharmacognosy*, 12th Ed. by Bailliere Tindall.
TURNBULL, A.
1788. The refutation of a late account of New Smyrna. *The Colombian Magazine*. Pp. 684–88.
TURNER, W.
1538. *Libellus de re herbaria*. London: Ray Society. Reprinted 1965.
TYLER, S. L.
1988. *Two worlds: The Indian encounter with the European. 1492–1509*. Salt Lake City: University of Utah Press.

UCKO, P. J., and G. W. DIMBLEBY
1969. The domestication and exploitation of plants and animals. London. Papers given at a symposium.
UNKNOWN
1986. Metabolism and toxicity of capsaicin. *Nutrition Reviews*. 44(1):20–22.
VAN HARTEN, A. M.
1970. Melegueta pepper. *Economic Botany*. 24:208–16.
VARNER, J. G., and J. J. VARNER
1983. *Dogs of the conquest*. Norman: University of Oklahoma Press.
VERRILL, A. H.
1937. *Foods America gave the world*. Boston: L. C. Page and Co.
VOGT, J.
1978. *Portuguese rule on the Gold Coast: 1469–1682*. Athens: University of Georgia Press.
WALDO, M.
1967. *Dictionary of international food and cooking terms*. New York: Macmillan.
WALSH, W. T.
1939. *Isabella of Spain*. London: Sheed and Ward.
WATT, G.
1889. *A dictionary of the economic products of India*. Delhi, India: Cosmo Pub., Vol. II. Reprinted, 1972.

WATTS, D.

1987. *The West Indies: Patterns of development, culture and environmental change since 1492*. Cambridge: Cambridge University Press.

WEAVER, W. W.

1989. *America Eats*. New York: Harper and Row.

WEIDENSAUL, S.

1999. Tracking America's first dog. *Smithsonian Magazine*. 29(12):44–57.

WEINER, L.

1920. *Africa and the discovery of America*. Philadelphia: Innes & Sons.

WEST, R. C., and J. P. AUGELLI

1976. *Middle America: Its lands and peoples*. Englewood Cliffs, N. J.: Prentice-Hall.

WESTRIP, J. P.

1981. Some Persian influences on the cooking of India. In *National and regional styles of cookery. Proceedings*. Pp. 67–95. Oxford Symposium 1981. 1981. London: Prospect Books.

WHEATON, B. K.

1983. *Savoring the past: The French kitchen and table from 1300 to 1789*. Philadelphia: University of Pennsylvania Press.

WHEATON, B. K., and P. KELLY

1988. *Bibliography and culinary history*. Boston: G. K. Hall.

WIENER, L.

1920. *Africa and the discovery of America*. Philadelphia: Innes and Sons.

WILLIAMS, S. Y.

1990. *The complete book of sauces*. New York: Macmillan Publishing Co.

WILSON, A. C.

1983. Sugar: The migrations of a plant product during 2000 years. *Proceedings*, Pp. 1–10. Oxford Symposium 1983. *Food in motion: The migration of foodstuffs and cookery techniques*. Ed. by Alan Davidson. London: Prospect Books.

WILSON, S. M.

1990. *Hispaniola: Caribbean chiefdoms in the age of Columbus*. Tuscaloosa: University of Alabama Press.

WINCHESTER, S.

1988. *Korea: A walk through the land of miracles*. London: Grafton Books.

WITTHOFT, J.

1966. A history of gunflints. *Penn. Archaeologist*. 36:1–49.

WOLF, L.

1970. *The cooking of the Caribbean Islands*. New York: Time-Life Books.

WRIGHT, A. C. A.

1949. Maize names as indicators of economic contacts. *Uganda Journal*. 13(1):61–81.

YULE, H., and A. C. BURRELL

1886. *Hobson-Jobson: A glossary of colloquial Anglo-indian words and phrases and of kindred terms, etymological, historical, geographical, and discursive*. Ed. by W. Cooke. New Delhi: Munshiram Manoharlal. 1979.

Subject Index

(Note: Page references in italic type refer to pages that contain illustrations.)

cilantro, 95–96
citrus hystrix, 96
City Grill (Austin, Tex.), 151
clarifying butter, 100
coasting, 12, 224 n25
coban, 61
Cochin (India), 228 n18
Cocina de la familia (Ravago), 108
coco nucifera, 98
cocoa, 226 n43
coconut milk, 96
cocos nucifera, 96
Cody's Cafe (Berkeley, Calif.), 190, 192
Coe, Sophie D., 222 n10
coffee, 16, 226 n43
cola de rata, 64
Colombia, 37
color, of peppers, 57, 232 n2 (Cooking with peppers)
Colorado, 71
Columbian Exchange, 16, 224 n26
Columbus, Christopher, 8; in Central America, 9, 10, 13, 15, 18–19; European foods, dispersal of, 14, 16, 36–37; maize, dispersal of, 14, 226 n39; peppers, discovery of, 3, 5, 9; peppers, dispersal of, 222 n13; pimiento, use of term, 50; voyages of, 13; in West Indies, 9, 10, 37
Columbus, Ferdinand, 5, 9, 223 n18
comino, 96
Complete book of Mexican cooking (Ortiz), 172
Complete book of sauces (Williams), 172
condiments, 90–95, 204
Condiments (Gunst), 172
Congo, 20, 69
congo peppers, 80
Congressional Record, 53, 71
consumption of peppers, frequency of, 27, 34, 46
Cooking for all seasons (Schmidt), 120
cooking terms, 100–101
Cooper, Brian, 77
cora, 78
coriander, 95–96
coriandrum sativum, 95–96
corn. See maize
corn meal, blue, 95
corn syrup, 99
Coronado, 71
Cortés, Hernán, 5, 18, 52, 232 n4 (Look at me)
costeño, 68, 81
Cotaxtla Cónico, 78
Cotaxtla Gordo, 78
Cotaxtla Típico, 78
Counts, Donald: Texas family cookbook, 184
Counts, Kathryn, 184
Covilha, Pero de, 12
Coyote Cafe: Foods from the Southwest (Miller), 105
Coyote Cafe (Santa Fe, N.M.), 105
creme fraiche, 96

Creole cuisine, 49, 62
criollos, 81
Crosby, Alfred W., 16, 26, 36
Crusades, 36, 41, 203
crushed red pepper, 92
cuaresmeño, 70
cuauhchilli, 64
Cuauhtemoc, 78
Cuba, 8, 9, 14, 204
Cubanelle, 65, 65, 80, 87
Cubanelle PS, 65
cucurbita pepo, 98
cuisine, 34–36, 49, 230 n9; in Africa, 38–39; in East Asia, 45–46; in Europe, 4, 46–48, 171; in Latin America, 36–38, 171; in the Middle East, 39–41; in Monsoon Asia, 41–45; in North America, 48–49, 62, 171; role of spices in, 4, 35–36, 58, 221 n6, 222 n12
cultigen, 231 n6
cultivar, 231 n6
cultivation of plants, 51, 231 n3
cumin, 96
cuminum cyminum, 96
curry powder, 92
cymbopogone citratus, 96–97
cyphomandra bettacea, 99

D

Da Caravaggio, Meresi. See Caravaggio, Meresi da
da Gama, Vasco. See Gama, Vasco da
dátils, 66, 66–67, 69, 77
de agua, 70, 81
de Albuquerque, Afonso. See Albuquerque, Afonso de
De Candolle, Alphonse. See Candolle, Alphonse de
de Covilha, Pero. See Covilha, Pero de
De historia stirpium (Fuchs), 4, 221 n4
De La Salle, René. See La Salle, René de
De Las Casas, Bartolomé. See Casas, Bartolomé de las
De Lobel, Matthias. See Lobel, Matthias de
De Medicis, Catherine. See Catherine de Medicis
De Nostradamus, Michel. See Nostradamus, Michel de
De Oñate, Juan. See Oñate, Juan de
de onza, 81
De Oviedo, Gonzalo. See Oviedo, Gonzalo de
Dean Fearing's Southwest Cuisine, 126
déglace, defined, 100
dehydration of peppers, 89–90
del monte, 64
demi-glace, defined, 100
dhow, Arabian, 17
Dias, Bartolomeu, 12
diets, traditional. See cuisine
dogs, 36, 229 n2
domestication of plants, 51, 221 n1, 231 n2
drying of peppers, 88–89

Dunnewold, Jane, 143

E

Early Jalapeño, 70
Early Sweet Banana, 59
Early Sweet Pimento, 79
East Africa, 20, 39, 227 n1, 229 n4
East Asia, 26–27, 45–46
East Coast Grill (Cambridge, Mass.), 166
East Indies, 37
Eat the Heat (Borssén), 46
Eclipse, 71
Ecuador, 19, 37–38
eggplants, 226 n45
Egypt: cuisine in, 40–41, 203, 204; influence in Turkey by, 228 n19; introduction of peppers to, 227 n3
elettaria cardamomum, 95
Elmina Castle, 12, 12, 224 n27
England: cuisine in, 32, 46, 171; influence in North America by, 33, 48; peppers in, 20, 29, 32–33, 229 n29; trade of, 32, 229 n28
environmental influences on plants, 226 n40
epazote, 96
Escluse, Charles L' See L'Escluse, Charles
Eshbaugh, W. Hardy, 4, 5, 51, 221 n2
Esmeralda, 75
Española Improved, 71
Espinalteco, 70
Ethiopia, 21, 39, 227 n3
Ethnic cuisine (Rosin), 229 n1
ethnic peppers, 48, 65, 80
Europe, 27–33. (See also names of specific countries); beans, maize and squash in, 27; cuisine in, 46–48, 203–204; cuisines influenced by, 36–38, 41, 48–49; food habits in, 4, 221 n6; foods introduced to Latin America, 14, 16, 36–37; influence in West Indies by, 225 n34; influence of Turkey in, 30–31; trade routes to, 27–33, 28

F

fagara, 96
Far East, 24–27. (See also names of specific countries); cuisine in, 41–46, 171, 204; cuisines influenced by, 49; influence of Holland in, 45; influence of Portugal in, 10, 12, 13–15, 22, 24–25, 26, 27, 41, 45, 228 n18; influence of Spain in, 44, 45; peppers in, 24–25, 30, 63; trade routes to, 23, 24–25
Fearing, Dean: Dean Fearing's Southwest Cuisine, 126; Mansion on Turtle Creek Cookbook, 126
Ferdinand V, King of Spain, 32, 33, 228 n11
Fernandes, Valentin, 223 n21
finger peppers, 63
firearms trade, 22, 227 n2
fish sauce, 92

five-spice powder, 92
flavor of peppers, 57–58, 85
flavor principle, 35, 229 n1
Flor de Pabellon, 75
Floral Gem, 67, 67
Floral Gem Jumbo, 67
Floral Grande, 67
Florida, 66
Florida Historical Quarterly, 66
food habits. See cuisine
Food in Chinese culture (Chang), 230 n20
food names, Amerindian, 44
food, preservation of, 221 n6
food processor usage, 172
food taboos, 34, 35, 40, 41, 42, 43
food ways. See cuisine
foods, American, 16, 222 n8, 223 n20, 226
    n38, 227 n9–10. (See also beans; maize;
    peppers; squash)
foods, European, in Latin America, 14, 16,
    36–37
Four Seasons (restaurant: Austin, Tex.), 145
Fourth Street Grill (Berkeley, Calif.), 131
Frampton, John, 33
France: cuisine in, 46, 171; cuisines
    influenced by, 38, 48; influence in North
    America by, 33, 62
freezing (food preparation), 86, 88, 232 n4
    (Cooking with peppers)
French-Canadians, 49
Fresh Planet Cafe (Austin, Tex.), 146
Fresno, 67, 67–68, 77, 82
Fresno Grande, 67
Frieda's (produce business: Los Angeles,
    Calif.), 110
fructose, 99
frying peppers, 80
Fuchs, Leonhart, 29, 30, 63, 222 n13, 223
    n20; De historia stirpium, 4, 4, 7, 10,
    221 n4

G

galanga, 96
galleon, 17
Gama, Vasco da, 13, 15
garam masala, 92
Garcia, Fabian, 71
Gardener's Dictionary (Miller), 77
Garrido, David: Nuevo Tex-Mex, 146
Gathering the desert (Nabhan), 65
Genoa (Italy), 29
Georgia Pimento Growers Association, 53,
    74
Gerard, John, 20, 229 n27
Germany, 29–31, 38, 48
Giant Yellow Banana, 59
ginger (food family), 50
Ginger Island (Berkeley, Calif.), 112, 131
Ginger Island restaurant (Berkeley, Calif.),
    131
ginger (spice), 96
ginnie peppers, 15, 50, 222 n16, 232 n3
    (Look at me); in Africa, 20; and cayenne

peppers, 62–63; and chile de árbol, 64;
    in England, 20, 33; and habanero pep-
    pers, 69
glucose, 99
Goa (India), 13, 24, 41, 227 n7, 228 n18, 230
    n10
Goa peppers, 42, 227 n7
Golden Cayenne, 62
Golden Greek, 73
gorda, 70
Gourmet Dallas, 108
gourmet peppers, 79
Govindarajan, V. S., 55
grains of paradise, 20, 39, 50
Grande Gold, 77
Granite Cafe (Austin, Tex.), 109
gravies, 171
Great Britain. See names of specific coun-
    tries
Great chile book (Miller), 105
Greater Antilles, 5
Greece, 40–41, 204
Green Pastures (restaurant), 182
Greenleaf Tabasco, 78
grinding (food preparation), 100
guajillo, 68, 68; and cascabel, 61; and cay-
    enne peppers, 63; and costeño, 81;
    preparation of, 89–90; and pulla, 82
Guatemala, 14
güero, 76, 77, 81
Guinea, 12, 15
Guinea peppers, 50, 69
gunflints, 22, 227 n2
Gunst, Kathy: Condiments, 172
Györgyi, Albert Szent. See Szent-Györgyi,
    Albert

H

habanero peppers, 37, 69, 69, 77
Hacienda Candelario, 209
Hades Hot, 62
Halasz, Zoltan, 29, 47, 231 n22
Hapsburg Empire, 32
hari mirch, 80
harissa, 92
Hatch, 71
hawk's bill, 81
Heiser, Charles B., Jr., 5, 52, 222 n7, 223
    n20, 231 n2
Henry II, of France, 171
Henry, the Navigator, Prince of Portugal, 11
Henry VIII, King of England, 33
Herb garden cookbook (Hutson), 112
herbal, defined, 221 n3
herbs, chopping of, 100
Hernandez, Francisco, 53, 222 n13
high-pressure liquid chromatography, 56
Hispaniola: beans, maize and squash in, 7–
    8; exploration by Columbus, 8, 9, 10;
    influence of Spain in, 14, 15; peppers in,
    5, 7, 9, 10; population of, 225 n36
hoisin sauce, 92
Holland: cuisine in, 46; influence in Japan

by, 45; influence in North America by,
    33, 48; trade of, 31, 62
hominy, 97
Honduras, 9, 223 n19
honey, 99, 203
hontaka, 81
Hormuz (Iran), 22, 28, 227 n6
Hortscience, 231 n7
hot cherry, 63
Hot chili, 67
Hot Portugal, 62
hot sauce, Mexican, 94
huachinango, 70
huarahuao, 64
Huasteco 74, 78
huayca, 53
Hungarian cherry, 63
Hungarian wax peppers, 59, 59
Hungarian Yellow Wax, 59
Hungary, 46–47
Hutson, Lucinda: Herb garden cookbook,
    112; Tequila: Cooking with the spirit of
    Mexico, 112
Hybrid Gold spike, 77
hybrids, 52

I

Ibn-Madjid, Ahmad. See Ahmad-Ibn-
    Madjid
illicium verum, 99
Improved No. 9, 71
indentured laborers, 66
India, 24–25, 230 n10; cuisine in, 41–42, 171,
    203, 204, 230 n13; cuisines influenced
    by, 39, 41, 42, 43, 45; influence of Portu-
    gal in, 10, 12, 13, 22, 24–25, 41, 228 n18;
    influence of Turkey in, 24, 42; maize in,
    15, 25; peppers in, 10, 16, 25, 30, 63, 80,
    226 n42, 227 n7; spice preparation meth-
    ods in, 42, 230 n12; trade of, 13, 20, 23,
    24, 26, 41, 228 n18
Indian Ocean, 12, 23
Indians, American. See Amerindians;
    Mayans; Mezo-Indians; Neo-Indians;
    Paleo-Indians
Indonesia: cuisine in, 43; cuisines
    influenced by, 42, 46; influence of Islam
    in, 43, 230 n16; peppers in, 25, 80–81
Industrial Revolution, 203
Inglenook Napa (Calif.), 158
Inter coetera, 224 n28
International Board for Plant Genetic Re-
    sources, 64
International code of nomenclature of culti-
    vated plants, 231 n6
Iran, 40–41, 42
Iraq, 40–41
Ireland, 48
Isabella I, Queen of Spain, 32, 33, 228 n11
Islam, 12, 25, 32, 40; influence in Indonesia
    by, 43, 230 n16; influence in North Af-
    rica by, 20–21
Islamic world. See Middle East

Sturtevant, William C., 222 n7
Sub-Saharan Africa, 20, 39
sucrose, 99
sugar: as recipe ingredient, 98, 99, 203–206; trade of, 29, 41, 203
sugar, brown, 98
sugar, maple, 204
sugar, palm, 98
sugarcane, cultivation of, 12, 14–15, 36–37, 203, 224 n26
Suleimán, the Magnificent, 27
Sunnybrook, 74, 79
Sunrise, 71
Sunset, 71
Sunset magazine, 115, 128, 199, 200, 201, 202
Super, John C., 16
Super Sweet, 63
Swahili Coast (Africa), 20, 227 n1
sweating (food preparation), 101
Sweden, 46
sweet banana peppers, 59
sweet cherry, 63
sweet green peppers, 60
Syria, 40–41, 203
Szent-Györgyi, Albert, 54

T

Tabasco, 66, 78, 78–79
Tabasco Brand Pepper Sauce®, 78–79, 93
taboos, food, 34, 35, 40, 41, 42, 43
Tainos, 222 n7
TAM Mild Chile, 71
TAM Mild Jalapeño-I, 70
TAM Rio, 77
tamales, 99
tamarillo, 99
tamarind, 99
tamarindus indica, 99
Tamaulipas (Mexico), 5
Tampiqueño, 78
taxonomy of peppers, 51–54
tea, 226 n43
Tequila: Cooking with the spirit of Mexico (Hutson), 112
Texas A&M University, 70
Texas family cookbook (Counts), 184
Tex-Mex cuisine, 171
Thai Cooking School, 118, 125, 230 n15
Thai hot sauce, 92
Thailand, 25, 43, 82
theobroma cacao, 97
Thrill of the grill (Schlesinger), 111, 166
Tierra Firme, 19, 37
típico, 78, 81
TMR 23, 71
toasting (food preparation), 90, 101
Tom Thumb, 63

tomatillos, 99
tomato, 14, 32, 229 n26
Tomato peppers, 79, 79
Tomato Pimento, 79
tomato, roma, 98–99
tomato, tree, 99
Torrido Chili Peppers, 67
tortilla, 99
trade castles, 224 n27
trade routes: to Africa, 12, 20–21, 23; to Asia, 23, 24–27; to Europe, 27–33, 28; to Latin America, 7, 18–20; to the Middle East, 21–24, 23; to North America, 33
traditional diets. See cuisine
Trappey Company, 67
travieso, 68
Treaty of Paris, 62
Treaty of Tordesillas, 13, 16
Treaty of Zaragossa, 224 n28
tree tomato, 99
trompa, 68
trompillo, 61
Truhart, 74
Truhart Perfection, 74
tunas, 97
Tunisia, 39, 40–41
Tupians, 62
Turkey, 21–24. (See also Ottoman Empire); American foods in, 227 n10; cuisine in, 39–40; cuisines influenced by, 40, 42, 47; diversity of population in, 40, 229 n6; influence in Europe by, 27–28, 30–31, 47; influence in India by, 24, 42; influence in the Mediterranean region by, 29, 31, 32, 229 n26; influence of Egypt in, 228 n19; influence of Spain in, 21–22; peppers in, 40, 229 n5; trade of, 12, 23, 24, 28, 29
turkey, 30–31, 222 n8, 228 n20
Turkish pepper. See paprika
Turnbull, Andrew, 66
Turner, William, 29, 33

U

uchu, 53
United States. See names of specific states; North America
Uruguay, 38

V

vacuum sealers, 232 n3 (Cooking with peppers)
vanillyl amide compounds, 55, 231 n9
variety, 231 n7
vegetables, methods for preparing, 100, 101, 172
Venezuela, 37

Venice (Italy), 12, 29, 30, 228 n16–17
Verdeño, 74, 75
vinegar, 204
vinegar, rice, 98
vitamin content of peppers, 54

W

Walsh, Robb, 146
war dogs, 36, 229 n2
Washington, George, 33
water chile, 81
Waters, Alice, 131
Weaver, William Woys, 60, 204; America eats, 212
Weil, Andrew, 58
West Indian Hot peppers, 69, 77, 80
West Indian Scotch bonnet, 69
West Indies. (See also Caribbean region; Cuba; Hispaniola); agriculture in, 7; influence in North America by, 33, 66; influence of Europe in, 225 n34; influence of Portugal in, 15; influence of Spain in, 14, 15, 225 n31; peppers in, 4, 5, 9, 52, 62, 79–80; population of, 225 n36; voyages of Columbus to, 8
Western European cuisine, 47–48
wheat, 36, 48
wheat bread, 230 n7
Williams, Sallie: Complete book of sauces, 172
Willis, Richard, 231 n8
Wilson, Samuel M., 226 n38
wilting of vegetables, 101
wine, rice, 98
Wok and stir-fry cooking (Jue), 118

X

x-cat-ik, 81

Y

Yellow Cheese, 74
Yellow Cheese Pimento, 79
yesil biber, 40
yogurt, 42, 101, 230 n14
Yolo Wonder, 60
yuca, 97
Yucatán (Mexico), 14

Z

zanthoxylum armatum, 96
zanthoxylum piperitum, 99
zanthoxylum planispinum, 96
Zaragossa, Treaty of, 224 n28
zea mays, 95, 97
Zinfandeli's (San Antonio, Tex.), 143
zingiber officinale, 96

Recipe Index